A NEW TRANSLATION

OF THE

HEBREW PROPHETS,

WITH AN INTRODUCTION AND NOTES.

BY

GEORGE R. NOYES, D.D.,

HANCOCK PROFESSOR OF HEBREW, ETC., AND DEXTER LECTURER IN HARVARD UNIVERSITY.

VOLUME I.

CONTAINING

JOEL, AMOS, HOSEA, ISAIAH, MICAH, NAHUM, ZEPHANIAH, HABAKKUK, AND OBADIAH.

FIFTH EDITION.

BOSTON:
AMERICAN UNITARIAN ASSOCIATION.
1874.

UNIVERSITY PRESS: WELCH, BIGELOW, & CO.,
CAMBRIDGE.

CONTENTS

OF THE FIRST VOLUME.

INTRODUCTION.

In order to understand the prophetic writings, it is of the highest importance that one enter upon the study of them with just views of the nature of the prophetic office. An incidental part of the work of the Hebrew prophet, that of predicting the future, has occupied so important a place in Christian theology, that his general office and the main business of his mission have been kept out of view. Within a few hundred years the very terms *prophet* and *prophecy* have acquired a new meaning. When Jeremy Taylor wrote his treatise called "The Liberty of Prophesying," the term *prophesying* was understood in a much wider sense than it is at the present time. In his day prophets denoted public religious teachers, and by the liberty of prophesying, he understood the liberty of giving public religious instruction by speech or writing without annoyance from the civil power, or from any other source.

Undoubtedly this general sense of the terms *prophet* and *prophesying* is the true one. No term by which the Hebrew prophet is denoted in the Old Testament means predicter. He is called inspired speaker, seer, watchman, but never predicter, or foreteller of future events. His office was to proclaim the whole will of Jehovah to the Hebrew people. By public speech, by written history, and by various forms of poetic composition, he aimed to bring the rulers and people of Israel to a right state of feeling and conduct in relation to Jehovah, their supreme national king and moral governor, and to keep them in it. In other words, his office was to make and keep the rulers and people what they ought to be in political, moral, and religious respects. Constituting no legal order in the state, like the priests, having no privilege of birth, making no claim to official respect, feeling no dependence except upon the Divine spirit and their own souls, they were, by virtue of their natural, supernatural, and acquired powers, and by a certain authority naturally conceded to them by the people, at the same time political counsellors, popular orators, and religious teachers, having great influence in the Jewish commonwealth.

The prophetic office had its origin in the theocratic national constitution and theocratic national mind of the Hebrews. As God, their invisible sovereign, did not manifest himself to the multitude in an immediate and sensible manner, it became necessary that there should be a human representative of Jehovah to his people. To this office of representative of Jehovah to his people, those regarded themselves as called, commissioned, and sent, whatever might be their tribe, occupation, or parentage, who felt with irresistible conviction that they possessed in their souls the will of Jehovah; that they were the chosen organs, by which he might make known his will in regard to political, moral, and religious concerns. They felt that their minds were illumined and moved by the holy spirit of God, and that the thoughts which they expressed in speech or writing, under this illumination and influence, were to be regarded as the word of God. נְבִיאִים, *inspired speakers*, is their most common appellation. We have, however, no reason to suppose that the prophets of the Old Testament, any more than St. Paul and the prophets mentioned in the New Testament, connected the idea of absolute infallibility with inspiration. Nor do their writings afford any indications of such infallibility.

The Hebrew prophets conceived of the spirit of God as giving life to all animated beings; intelligence to man, skill to the artist, wisdom to the sovereign, resolution and strength to the warrior, and, above all, a lofty enthusiasm, profound knowledge of the true and the excellent, and a far-reaching insight into the mind of God, to the prophet. Divine communications were not, as in the heathen world, regarded as coming through inanimate objects, through lightning and thunder, the entrails of animals, the flight of birds, or the unconscious mind of man. Everywhere in the Old Testament, those who received the spirit of God, and consequently spoke the word of God, are represented as conscious, voluntary, intelligent agents. Everywhere they speak and act as such. Their thoughts are expressed according to the common laws of the association of ideas. The operation of the holy spirit was to move the feelings, to illuminate the reason, to strengthen the imagination, to command the conscience, but not to furnish the prophet with objective knowledge of contingent events, or to make his intuitions infallible. Hence one prophet differs from another, just as one poet of any nation differs from another. The effect of the Divine influence on any individual varied according to his capacity of receiving it; according to his bodily organization, his intellectual, imaginative, and moral powers, the strength of his natural feelings, his susceptibility of religious fervor, his education, condition, and all the circumstances in which he was placed. The Hebrew prophet was capable of receiving the Divine spirit in larger measure than the rest of his countrymen. He was in a greater or less degree a man of genius. He was filled with a lofty enthusiasm, and an invincible energy. He was moved, excited, rapt into ecstasy. He was endowed with an uncommon capacity for discerning the true and the excellent. His pure reason, illuminated by God, pierced into the character of the Divine government and its issues. His comprehensive and far-reaching understanding, intently employed on the causes, character, and consequences of everything which concerned the well-being of the people of God, foresaw events hidden from common eyes. His exalted imagination presented to him visions of God. His pure and sensitive conscience heard the call of God, and felt a Divine command or commission in relation to all which he felt and saw. He had thus a marked superiority over his contemporaries, and this superiority he attributed to the spirit of God. The influence of the Divine spirit upon his soul is the key for the explanation of all the various language which is used to express the reception of Divine communications; such as hearing the voice of God, seeing visions of God, having the word of God come to him, &c.

If it be asked what was the criterion to the prophet that he was a true messenger of God, or had a Divine commission, the answer is, that no one of them, whose writings have come down to us, has given us information of any criterion by which he knew that he was a prophet, except the possession of his spiritual gifts, and the strength of his own conviction that he was under the influence of the spirit of God. These gifts, and this strong, irresistible conviction, were to him the seal of his mission. Just as in modern times a Christian believes that he is born of the Spirit, when he manifests the fruits of the Spirit, so the ancient prophets believed that they possessed the spirit of God in an extraordinary degree, or were inspired prophets, because they possessed prophetic gifts in an extraordinary degree, and had their convictions borne into their minds with extraordinary power.

Maimonides and several other Jewish writers have come to the same conclusion. "All prophecy makes itself known to the prophet that it is prophecy indeed, by the strength and vigor of the perception, so that his mind is freed from all scruple about it." This he concludes to be the true meaning of Jer. xxiii. 29. "Is not my word like a fire, saith the Lord, and like a hammer that breaketh the rock in pieces?" on which he makes the following comment. "Such a thing is the prophetical spirit by reason of the strength of its impression and the forcibleness of its operation on the heart of the prophet." See John Smith on Prophecy, in Watson's Tracts, Vol. IV. p. 320, &c.

Had, then, the Hebrew prophets no criterion by which they and others might know that they were inspired by God, different from that which was possessed by Savonarola, Luther, Milton, or Fox? If they had, they have not told us what it was. It seems to follow, therefore, that infallibility ought not to be connected with the scriptural idea of inspiration. For mere strength of conviction that one is moved to think, speak, or write by the spirit of God, or, which is the same thing, by Divine inspiration, is not at the present day regarded as evidence that one is infallible.*

I have spoken briefly of the general office and work of the Hebrew prophet, and of his internal qualifications for the discharge of his duties, omitting many topics that might be interesting in a full treatise. I now come to the inquiry, What was the nature of the prophetic predictions? The essential part of the work of the prophet was, as we have seen, to persuade rulers and people to be what they ought to be in political, moral, and religious respects. Their predictions are to be regarded as means

* See Note to the Introduction.

of accomplishing this great end. These constituted the motives by which they hoped to stir up kings and people to a right course, or to deter them from a wrong one; to humble them when elated with a false confidence, or to comfort them when discouraged under overwhelming national calamity.

These predictions consist of representations of the future, having reference partly to the people of God, that is, the kingdoms of Israel and Judah, and partly to foreign nations, which, in the way of interest, friendship, or enmity, &c., had some connection with the people of God. We never find the Hebrew prophets uttering predictions respecting countries unknown to the Hebrews, such as Japan, or America, or India, but only respecting those nations from which at the time of the prediction they had something to hope or to fear, or which they had cause to love or to hate, such as successively the Assyrians, the Babylonians, the Syrians, the Phœnicians, the Philistines, the Egyptians, the Edomites, the Moabites, the Ammonites, the Arabians. Sometimes the prediction relates to an individual who was concerned in the business of the state.

The predictions of the prophets are always presented as motives of conduct to their contemporaries. They are never made as independent truths, without reference to the circumstances of the times. They are not merely apocalyptic, or for the mere gratification of curiosity. They always have a practical relation to the people in the time of the prophet. They are always presented as promises of happiness, or threatenings of distress, and this generally as the fruit of the conduct of the people, and thus as a revelation of the righteousness of God, or of the retribution of which God is the author.

Here we have one principal source of the Hebrew predictions, namely, *the laws of Divine retribution*. It was a fundamental doctrine of Judaism that the future condition of a nation, as well as of an individual, would be so ordered by the Almighty as to constitute the reward or punishment of present conduct. For this reason it was, that the prophets were led to cast their eyes into the future, in order to find motives to urge kings and people to the course which they recommended. In order to make these motives more distinct, vivid, and impressive, they did not deal in general and abstract denunciations of woe, but with piercing sagacity, derived from natural genius, from the assiduous contemplation of the future, and from the influence of the Divine spirit on their minds, they undertook to point out the particular events which would happen in the future; that is, they not merely promised or threatened, but predicted. More or less of the same practice has prevailed among political and religious reformers from that time to this. But it prevailed in a remarkable degree among the Hebrew prophets, so that their writings constitute a distinct and peculiar class. They believed that they had an insight into the future, which the human understanding, without the aid of the Divine spirit, would not have afforded them. The popular faith supported them in their general claims, though their particular messages were often rejected with incredulity, contempt, or persecution.

This I regard as a very important view of the nature of the predictions of the prophets. They belong to the category of *motives* with which the prophets urged upon their contemporaries the great objects of their mission, namely, that of keeping the people in a right political, moral, and religious condition. They are the application of the doctrine of an earthly retribution to the particular condition and circumstances of the community in the time of the prophet. See Is. i. 19, &c.; Jer. vii. 3, &c., xxi. 1–9.

The practical character and aim of the predictions in relation to the contemporaries of the prophet are also seen in those cases in which evil is threatened Israel from foreign nations, with which they were, or wished to be, in alliance. The design was to withdraw or deter Israel from impolitic alliances, dangerous to religion, by threatening evil or destruction from the nation from which the rulers were seeking aid, or the advantages of an alliance.

The same practical character and aim are evident in predictions of prosperity. The design was to keep the people in grateful dependence upon Jehovah; to inspire patient submission under the temporary chastisement or trials which were to end in good; to comfort and encourage them, so that, though humbled, they should never waver or doubt in regard to the benevolent designs of God toward the posterity of Abraham.

So in those predictions in which calamity or destruction is threatened to foreign nations, such as Egypt, Babylon, Tyre, &c., there is in general a practical object in reference to the people of God. It is to encourage them when foreign nations assume a threatening aspect; see Is. x. 5, &c., xxx. 27, &c. xxxi. 1, &c. Hab. ii.; partly to deter them from untheocratic alliances, Is xx. 5, &c., xxx. 3, &c.; partly to console them under the injustice and oppression which they have suffered, Is. xxi. 1, &c. xlvii.; Ezek. xxv. – xxxv.; Jer. l., li.; and partly to make the people feel their dependence on Jehovah by exhibiting his righteous judgments.

From the nature of the case, the prophets could not be guided by the principle of retribution in predictions of prosperity and blessedness, so much as in predictions of woe. It is only in a very qualified sense that any people, much less so perverse a people as the Jewish is represented to have been, can be said to merit blessings from Jehovah. Still there is some regard to this principle, inasmuch as the prophets scarcely ever predict prosperity, unless it is preceded by righteousness. See Is. xliii. 25; Ezek. xxxvi. 25, &c. Sometimes the piety of the fathers, or promises made to the fathers, seem to be the grounds of predictions of prosperity. Is. xxxvii. 35; Mic. vii. 20. Hence it is that denunciations of woe are generally, and sometimes by a very rapid transition, followed by promises of peace, favor, and glory. See Amos ix. 11; Mic. iv. 1 – 10, and very numerous passages of the same kind elsewhere.

Thus it appears that the principle of an earthly retribution lies at the foundation of most of the predictions, but with some qualifications and limitations.

Another important remark is, that the prophets whose genuineness is undoubted, when they make definite predictions, introducing the names of persons, nations, cities, &c., keep within the sphere of human vision, and direct attention to those nations to which the vision of a Hebrew politician would naturally be directed. Their predictions are conformed to the political horizon of their time, and are definite and explicit in the same degree in which the circumstances of the time afford clear indications of coming events. Thus Amos, Hosea, and Isaiah bring chiefly to view the Assyrians. Isaiah mentions the Babylonians also, who were in his day meditating a separation from the Assyrians. Later prophets, as Habakkuk, Jeremiah, and Ezekiel, utter predictions relating to the Chaldeans who destroyed the Assyrian monarchy. Ezekiel even mentions the Scythians, under the names of Gog and Magog.

It is evident, not only that the preceding propositions are true, but also that in this way alone their predictions would be of any value, or have any influence with their contemporaries, the readers or hearers to whom they were addressed. Had the prophets predicted calamity as coming from a monarch of whose name they had never heard, or from nations beyond the sphere of Jewish knowledge or interest, or from nations which had little or no power to inflict injury upon them, it is plain that their predictions would have been disregarded and have been followed by no practical effects. They never predict calamity from very small or very remote nations, from which nothing was to be feared. Such predictions could have no more been expected to influence the Jews, than the prediction of destruction to our country at the present day from India or Japan could be expected to influence us. In order that their predictions might excite any interest, or produce any effect, it was necessary that they should have a certain degree of probability in the minds of the people.

I now come to the question how far the predictions of the prophets were verified by events, or fulfilled; and if fulfilled, whether in such a manner as to afford evidence of miraculous foreknowledge in the prophets.

Before the examination of particular cases, one or two preliminary observations are to be made. The prophets expressly state many of their predictions to be conditional, suspended on the conduct of those whom they addressed. This is implied in the principle on which most of them are founded, namely, the principle of Divine retribution. See Jer. xviii. 7–10; Jer. xxvi. 16–19. It follows, then, that every case of the non-fulfilment of a prediction is not a proof of error on the part of the prophet; because the prediction was conditional, and there may have been a reformation in the people which averted the predicted calamity.

On the other hand, every fulfilment of a prediction is not a proof of infallibility or miraculous foreknowledge Many events may be predicted by human sagacity, meditating on the causes of events, and on the circumstances in which nations are placed. Such men as Edmund Burke, John Adams, and others, men of genius and sagacity, having their patriotic minds continually intent upon all the political signs in their horizon, have made very remarkable predictions. In order to prove miraculous foreknowledge, the event predicted must be clearly beyond the limits of human sagacity and calculation. In order to prove such foreknowledge, the event must also be fulfilled in the way and manner expected by the writer. For instance, if it should be now predicted that London is, at a future day, to be destroyed by the French, it would not be a miraculous fulfilment of the prediction, if, some centuries hence, that city should be destroyed by the Russians, or by the gradual operation of natural causes. It would be safe to predict of many cities that they would come to an end in some way, and some time or other.

How then was it with the predictions of the Hebrew prophets? Were they fulfilled in such a manner as to imply miraculous foreknowledge? The only way to arrive at a correct answer is to examine every particular prediction, and the circumstances under which it was made, in order to perceive what indications of the event might have been present to the mind of the writer, and, secondly, to examine history, to see how far events correspond to his language. Our limits will not allow us to examine all the predictions of the prophets. I will take two or three of the most remarkable, and endeavor to proceed without perverting the meaning of the prophetic writers, or falsifying the facts of history. Rationalistic interpretation, when employed in the interest of apologetic theology, ought to be at least as odious as when employed in the interest of physical or metaphysical philosophy.

A prediction which will at once occur to the reader of the Scriptures is that against Babylon. It is found in Is. xiii., xiv., xxi. 1–10, xl.–lxvi., and in Jer. l., li. In Is. xiii. 17–22 we read: —

> "Behold I stir up against them the Medes,
> Who make no account of silver,
> And as to gold, they do not regard it.
> Their bows shall strike down the young men,
> And on the fruit of the womb they shall have no compassion;

Their eye shall not pity the children.
So shall Babylon, the glory of kingdoms
The proud ornament of the Chaldeans,
Be like Sodom and Gomorrah, which God overthrew
It shall never more be inhabited;
Nor shall it be dwelt in through all generations.
Nor shall the Arabian pitch his tent there,
Nor shall shepherds make their folds there.
But there shall the wild beasts of the desert lodge,
And owls shall fill their houses;
And ostriches shall dwell there,
And satyrs shall dance there.
Wolves shall howl in their palaces,
And jackals in their pleasant edifices.
Her time is near,
And her days shall not be prolonged."

In ch. xlv. 1, Cyrus is mentioned by name as the leader of the Medes and Persians against Babylon.

Now if this prediction, contained in what is called the Book of Isaiah, really proceeded from the prophet Isaiah, the son of Amos, it would present a somewhat difficult problem. For in that case it would have been written about two hundred years before the capture of Babylon by Cyrus, and at a time when the Medes could not have been regarded as dangerous to the Babylonian monarchy. At any rate, it could not have been foreseen by any human intelligence that Cyrus the Persian should lead the Medes against Babylon. If, therefore, it could be proved to satisfaction that this prediction was written about two hundred years before the capture of Babylon by Cyrus, it would be impossible to explain, on the ground of mere human intelligence, how Isaiah could have foreseen so much as he did respecting Cyrus and the Medes. But if miraculous knowledge be supposed, it would be equally difficult to explain how it was, that, in the most important particulars relating to this event, he was in error. The writer of the prediction, after the utmost allowance is made for figurative language, plainly supposed that Babylon would be *totally* destroyed by the Medes under Cyrus. Now the destruction of that great city has taken place. So far the prediction was fulfilled in some degree, as every one knows. But this destruction was not effected at the time, nor by the instruments, which the writer had in mind.

Cyrus took the city without trouble, but he neither battered down the walls,* nor put the inhabitants to the sword. He did not even injure it; but made it his winter residence during his reign, as the third city in the Persian empire, the next after Susa and Ecbatana. It was not till fifty years after the time of Cyrus that the walls of Babylon were beaten down in consequence of a rebellion against Darius Hystaspis.† Xerxes afterwards plundered the temple of Belus. But the city still continued to flourish, so that Alexander the Great, when he took the city about two hundred years after the time of Cyrus, and four hundred after that of Isaiah, found it full of the riches of the East. After his time it seems to have gradually declined, and to have been brought to ruin not so much by sudden destruction as by the building of other cities, especially the city of Seleucia by Seleucus. About one hundred and thirty years before Christ it was taken possession of by the Parthians. According to Quintus Curtius, about one fourth part of it was inhabited in his time. Now this gradual ruin of Babylon many hundred years after the time of the prediction above quoted is not what was in the mind of the writer when he made it. His prediction is of the utter destruction of the city by the Medes under Cyrus; of the putting most of the inhabitants to the sword, and of the captivity of others. So that, supposing the prediction to have come from Isaiah, one part of it implies miraculous prescience, and the other contradicts such a supposition.

But the truth is, that there is no sufficient evidence that the predictions concerning the destruction of Babylon came from the prophet Isaiah. On the contrary it appears to me susceptible of demonstration that Is. xl.–lxvi. was written by a genuine prophet, the most eminent of all the prophets in religious insight, only a short time before the return of the Jews from the exile in Babylon. And though the arguments which make it appear that ch. xiii., xiv., and xxi. were written at about the same time are not so strong as in the case of ch. xl.–lxvi., they are such as have left no doubt in the minds of the most impartial and learned inquirers.‡ The predictions, then, were written when it could have been learned by a careful observer of what was going on, that the Medes

* Herodotus, III. 159. † Ibid.

‡ See the Commentaries of Gesenius, Rosenmueller, Knobel, Ewald, Hitzig, &c.

were about to invade Babylon, and when it was probable that so fierce a people would take the city, and would not take it without destroying it. In this last particular, the unknown prophet and Jeremiah were in error, as also in regard to the general way in which Babylon was to come to an end.

Another remarkable prediction, which occurs in several of the prophets, is that against Edom. Her complete destruction is predicted in the most emphatic terms, and with a great variety of images of desolation. Is. xxxiv., lxiii.; Ezek. xxxv.; Amos i. 11, 12; Obadiah. It is said,

> "Her streams shall be changed into pitch,
> And her dust into brimstone,
> And her whole land shall become burning pitch.
> Day and night it shall not be quenched;
> Her smoke shall ascend forever."— Is. xxxiv. 9, 10.

From a comparison of the passages in which this prediction occurs, it is evident that the prophets expected it to be fulfilled about the time of the return of the Israelites from the captivity, when they should be in the highest degree of prosperity. Now the destruction of Edom as a nation has taken place, as has that of many other nations, including the Jewish. But when the prophets made the prediction of such a sudden, entire, and perpetual desolation, they could not have foreseen that the Edomites would retain their courage and enterprise in the time of the prophet Malachi (see ch. i. 4), several hundred years after the predictions, or that the Edomites would one day be united to the Jews as a nation (Jos. Ant. xiii. 9. 1), or that Herod, an Edomite, would become king of the holy people. So great are the difficulties in regard to the prediction concerning Edom, that some interpreters, such as J. D. Michaelis, suppose it is yet to be fulfilled. Some also suppose Edom to denote Rome, even Christian Rome.

Another interesting prediction in the Old Testament is that concerning Tyre by Ezekiel, in ch. xxvi. It is very explicit. The devastation and plunder of the city were to be complete, and were to be effected by a particular king, Nebuchadnezzar. The siege, the taking of the city, the quantity of plunder, &c., are all described. "For thus saith the Lord Jehovah: Behold, I will bring against Tyre Nebuchadnezzar, king of Babylon, a king of kings from the North, with horses, and with chariots, and with horsemen, and a vast multitude of people. Thy daughters upon the land shall he slay with the sword; and he shall set a tower against thee, and cast up a mount against thee, and lift up the buckler against thee; and his battering rams shall be set against thy walls, and thy towers shall he break down with axes. By reason of the great number of his horses, their dust shall cover thee; thy walls shall shake at the noise of the horsemen, and of the wheels, and of the chariots, when he entereth into thy gates, as men enter into a city that is broken through. With the hoofs of his horses shall he tread down all thy streets; thy people he shall slay with the sword; and the idols of thy strength shall fall to the ground. And they shall make a spoil of thy riches, and make a prey of thy merchandise; and they shall break down thy walls, and destroy thy beautiful houses; and thy stones and thy timber and thine earth shall they lay in the midst of the waters. And I will cause the noise of thy songs to cease, and the sound of thy harps shall be no more heard. And I will make thee like a naked rock; thou shalt be a place to spread nets upon; thou shalt be built no more; for I, Jehovah, have spoken it, saith the Lord Jehovah." There is no question here as to the authorship of the passage, or the time when the prediction was made. Here, too, there was a fulfilment of one point in it. Tyre has been destroyed at some time, and in some way. But there is no evidence that it was destroyed at the time, in the way, and by the person indicated in the prediction. There is no evidence that Nebuchadnezzar took the city, but rather much reason to believe the reverse. Heeren, in his Researches into the Politics, &c. of the Asiatic Nations, says that "Tyre had to defend itself against Nebuchadnezzar during a siege of thirteen years; but that in reality he ever took it or destroyed it, as is commonly asserted, there is no historical proof." And in a note he says: "The capture of Tyre by Nebuchadnezzar is confirmed by no Phœnician or Greek writer. It rests on the prediction of Ezekiel alone. But a later oracle of the same prophet, xxix. 18, shows that the attempt to subdue it failed." (Heeren, Vol. II. p. 11.) The subsequent prediction in Ezekiel to which Heeren refers is found in ch. xxix. 18 – 20, the plain meaning of which is, that Nebuchadnezzar did not succeed in taking Tyre and getting plunder from it, and that therefore he should get his wages from the plunder of Egypt. Ezekiel must then have been in error in his prediction concerning Tyre. What he predicted was a very probable event, considering the power of Nebuchadnezzar. That the Tyrians should be able to sustain a siege of more than thirteen years was not to have been expected. But when the prophet undertook to predict a contingent event with precision and confidence, he went beyond his depth, and was disappointed.

Similar results would follow an examination of the prediction of the return of the Israelites from the captivity at Babylon and the subsequent glory of the nation, Is. xl.–lxvi., Jer. xxxi. 4–15, when compared with Jewish history. The same remark also applies to Ezekiel's prediction concerning Egypt, ch. xxix., xxx., xxxii., and to others which might be adduced.

From a view of all the cases which have been examined, and I think the same result would follow an examination of all the predictions in the writings of the prophets except those *post eventum* in the ungenuine Book of Daniel, it is clear, — 1. That they were not written after the event predicted; for, in this case, they would have been made to correspond more nearly with the facts of history. 2. The sincerity and good faith of the prophets are apparent in all their predictions. They were guided by the doctrine of an earthly retribution in human affairs, and by the indications which their political horizon afforded in regard to coming changes. They often manifest a high degree of penetration into futurity as men of genius and sagacity, having their patriotic minds continually strained to discern all the political changes which might affect the people of Jehovah, and inspired by that holy spirit which God gives to all who seek it aright. That some of their predictions failed of fulfilment, resulted from their having made declarations too circumstantial and particular in regard to the special designs of the Deity. They were right in their general principles, that under the government of God righteousness exalteth a nation, and that sin brings ruin on a people and on individuals. But when they undertook to tell the time when, and the manner how, the retributions of Heaven would be accomplished in regard to a particular nation, or individual, they erred, as all must err when they undertake to predict particular contingent future events. Their faculty was the faculty of foreboding, not of objective sight, and it was fallible. The predictions are clear. History is also clear and inexorable. The prophets are as instructive and valuable as God meant they should be. And why should we undertake to be wiser than Omniscience? Why try to make history conform more nearly to the predictions of the Jewish prophets than the providence of God has made it? Surely He knows how to make his truth prevail in the world, and establish his empire in the hearts of men, without the aid of human artifices and inventions, such as may be found in abundance in elaborate Biblical commentaries, and in books of travels.

> "Will ye speak falsehood for God?
> Will ye utter deceit for him?
> Will ye be partial to his person?
> Will ye contend earnestly for God?
> Will it be well for you, if he search you thoroughly?
> Can ye deceive him, as one may deceive a man?
> Surely he will rebuke you,
> If ye secretly have respect to persons." — Job xiii. 7–10.

One class of predictions remains to be considered, distinguished from those which have been thus far discussed both by the nature of the subject and by their influence upon the theology of the Christian Church, namely, the Messianic predictions. I hardly know how to speak of this subject with sufficient brevity for this Introduction. And yet I cannot pass over it without trying to give the intelligent reader the means of arriving at correct views. It will be well to consider the origin, nature, and fulfilment of the Messianic predictions.

I. Their origin. In a large sense such predictions may be said to arise out of the nature of man, and to be peculiar to no particular nation. What may be called the Messianic idea arises out of the dissatisfaction which in every age has been experienced with the present condition of society in connection with faith in the government of a benevolent Deity. In all ages men have felt that society was not what it ought to be, and what it might be, if men had the right spirit, and would do and be what they ought to do and be. Now with faith in a God of infinite benevolence, how natural is it for the imagination to picture such a state of society in the future; to look to Divine Providence for such a regeneration of humanity as shall lay the foundation of a kingdom of God upon earth, — the restoration of all things to the true condition designed by the Creator. Such a golden age has been anticipated by several of the ancient classical writers, and in various religious systems. Such an age is longed for and predicted by various classes of reformers at the present day. The feeling on which such anticipations are founded is alluded to by the Apostle Paul, when he says (Rom. viii. 19, &c.), that "the creation is earnestly expecting the manifestation of the sons of God"; and that "the creation was made subject to vanity in the hope that it would be delivered from its bondage to corruption into the freedom of the glory of the sons of God."

We may go further. We may maintain that the anticipation of an individual Messiah has its root in universal human nature. We not only feel a dissatisfaction with the present condition of society, but with the character of every individual in society; yea, with our own character as degenerate and imperfect. No one fully expresses in his life his ideal conception of what a man ought to be. No one acts and lives in perfect harmony with the holy voice within him. Thus there arises within us the ideal of a perfect man, — of one whose whole manner of thinking, feeling, and acting is in perfect harmony with the spirit of God; that is, we form the idea of the Messiah of God. But as we cannot find such a Messiah around us or within us, it is natural to look for him in the same future in which we looked for the regeneration of society. From such a future perfect man it would be natural to look for the regeneration of society, at least in certain ages of the world, when abstract principles are not distinctly apprehended and their power understood. For we learn from observation how much the improvement of society and the advancement of intellectual and moral light have depended on gifted individuals, who from time to time have appeared on the earth. From this view it appears that the coming of such a person as Jesus was not only, in some sense, a fulfilment of the expectations of the Jews, but of "the desire of nations."

The Messianic idea was however developed in a very high

degree, and in a peculiar form, among the Jews. This happened from the same reason that the spirit of prophecy, in general, on all subjects to which it applied itself, was developed in a far higher degree than among other nations. But from the preceding remarks it will be perceived that the Messianic predictions of the Hebrew prophets are not so peculiar and anomalous as they have sometimes been supposed to be.

The Messianic predictions originated less immediately in ideas of earthly retribution, and were less suggested by the circumstances of the times, than the other predictions of the Hebrew prophets. They partook more of an ideal character than common predictions, and sprung more from the general faith of the nation as the peculiar people of God, and from the general convictions and spirit of the prophets. It will be found, however, that the Messianic predictions, as well as those relating to other subjects, always had a practical object with reference to the contemporaries of the writers, and were not designed by their authors for the special use of distant ages. They always had the practical object of reviving the drooping spirits of the nation in calamitous times, of keeping the people from despair of help from their God, and thus from casting off their faith and trust in him.

We now come to the inquiry what the Messianic predictions of the Jewish prophets were. It will be convenient to consider, — 1. What was the glorious state of things in the future, which they predicted; and 2. What was the instrumentality by which it was to be effected. Under the first head we may make a subdivision of the prophetic expectations: — 1. The purely religious; 2. The political and religious united.

I. The general religious expectations, or predictions. These were founded on the correct view that truth has an almighty power, and must finally obtain a triumphant and universal dominion over the minds of men. The prophets were convinced of the truth and power of their religion, and hence of its tendency to extend itself beyond the bounds of their own nation. Consequently they could not fail of entertaining the firm expectation that the time would come when every form of idolatry should perish, and give place to faith in the true God, and thus the religion of Israel be received by all the heathen nations. Among passages of this import are

Is. xviii. 7, &c., where it is predicted that the Ethiopians, whose country was regarded as one of the remotest from Palestine, should bring presents to the temple of Jehovah at Jerusalem.

> "At that time shall gifts be brought to Jehovah of hosts
> From a people tall and fair,
> From a people terrible from the first and onward,
> A mighty, victorious nation,
> Whose land is divided by rivers,
> To the dwelling-place of Jehovah of hosts, to Mount Zion."

In Is. xxiii. 17, 18, the same thing is predicted of the Tyrians, viz. that their wealth should be consecrated to the service of Jehovah at Jerusalem.

> "But her gain and her hire shall be holy to Jehovah,
> It shall not be treasured, nor laid up in store;
> But it shall be for them that dwell before Jehovah
> For abundant food and for splendid clothing."

In Is. xix. 19 – 21, the same thing is predicted of Egypt.

> "In that day shall there be five cities in the land of Egypt
> Speaking the language of Canaan
> And swearing by Jehovah of hosts;
> One of them shall be called the City of the Sun.
> Thus shall Jehovah be made known to Egypt,
> And the Egyptians shall know Jehovah in that day,
> And shall offer to him sacrifices and oblations;
> They shall make vows to Jehovah and perform them."

This confident expectation of the acknowledgment of Jehovah as the true God, in other words, of the extension and establishment of the kingdom of Heaven among men, is carried still further by some of the later prophets. Thus, Zeph. ii. 11:—

> "Jehovah will be terrible against them;
> For he will destroy all the gods of the earth
> And before him shall worship, every one from his place,
> All the islands of the nations."

So also iii. 9:—

> "Then will I again bestow upon the nations pure lips,
> So that they shall all of them call on the name of Jehovah,
> And serve him with one consent.

From beyond the rivers of Ethiopia
My suppliants, the sons of my dispersed ones, shall bring my offering."

So in Jer. iii. 17: —

"For then shall Jerusalem be called the throne of Jehovah,
And all the nations shall resort to it;
They shall resort to Jehovah, to Jerusalem,
And shall no more walk after the perverseness of their evil hearts."

See also xvi. 19 – 21; Zech. viii. 20 – 23, xiv. 16.

But perhaps the strongest and purest hopes of the universal spread of the religion of Jehovah are expressed by an unknown prophet, in religious insight the most distinguished of all the prophets, who wrote a short time before the close of the exile at Babylon, and whose work has been erroneously ascribed to Isaiah. Thus, Is. xlii. 1, 4: —

"Behold my servant, whom I uphold,
My chosen, in whom my soul delighteth;
I have put my spirit upon him;
He shall cause laws to go forth to the nations. . . . .
He shall not fail, nor become weary,
Until he shall have established justice in the earth,
And distant nations shall wait for his law."

So in xlix. 6: —

"He said, It is a small thing that thou shouldst be my servant
To raise up the tribes of Jacob,
And to restore the preserved of Israel;
I will also make thee the light of the nations,
That my salvation may reach the ends of the earth."

So in li. 4: —

"For a law shall proceed from me,
And I will establish my statutes for the light of the nations."

See also lx. 5, 6, and lxvi. 18 – 23.

In all the preceding passages it is predicted that all the nations shall be united with Israel by a common religious faith, — by the knowledge and worship of Jehovah. Perhaps a certain degree of political superiority on the part of the Jews is implied in them. But the predictions are probably as purely religious as Jews of the age when they were written could make.

II. Having spoken of the purely religious and moral expectations of the prophets relating to the period which may be called Messianic, I come now to those of a temporal nature, i.e. those in which a national, political, or physical element is mingled with the religious and moral. A lover of truth will not ignore any part of the predictions of the prophets.

I will, however, first speak of the state of things which according to the prophets would immediately precede the Messianic times. It was to be a time of national purification and reformation, brought about by the retributive judgments of God. The people were to become righteous before they became prosperous. Thus Jer. iii. 12, 13, 14, &c.: —

" Return, O rebellious Israel, saith Jehovah!
I will not turn a frowning face upon you ;
Though I have rejected you,
Yet will I receive you again,
One from a city and two from a nation,
And I will bring you to Zion."

This work of national purification and reformation is represented as being brought about by Jehovah's inflicting punishment on his people by means of heathen nations, through which he destroys the incorrigibly wicked from the midst of his people, and brings the remainder to a better mind. Thus, Is. i. 25, 26: —

" And I will again turn my hand toward thee,
And wholly purge away thy dross,
And take away all thy alloy.
And I will restore thee judges, as at the first,
And counsellors, as at the beginning.
Thou shalt be called the city of righteousness, the faithful city."

So, ch. iv. 2-6: —

" In that day shall the increase of Jehovah be glorious and honorable,
And the fruit of the land excellent and beautiful,
For them that have escaped of Israel.
All that remain in Zion,
And all that are left in Jerusalem,
Shall be called holy;
When the Lord shall have washed away the filth of the daughters of Zion,
And have removed the blood of Jerusalem from the midst of her,
By a spirit of judgment and a spirit of destruction,

Then shall Jehovah create upon the whole extent of mount Zion, and upon
her places of assembly,
A cloud and smoke by day,
And the brightness of a flaming fire by night;
Yea, for all that is glorious there shall be a shelter;
There shall be a tent by day for a shadow from the heat,
And for a refuge and shelter from the storm and rain."

To the disciplinary punishments by which the Jewish nation was to be prepared for its condition of blessedness and glory, the exile at Babylon belongs. In this exile the chastised people would repent of their transgressions and turn to Jehovah with their whole hearts. Thus, Jer. xxiv. 5 – 7: "Thus saith Jehovah, the God of Israel: As these good figs, so will I regard the captives of Judah, whom I have sent out of this place into the land of Chaldea for their good; and I will bring them again to this land; and I will build them up, and not pull them down; and I will plant them, and not pluck them up. And I will give them a heart to know me, that I am Jehovah; and they shall be my people, and I will be their God; for they shall return to me with their whole heart." See also xxix. 10 – 14, l. 5; Is. xl. — lxvi.; Ezek. vi. 8 – 10, xx. 38; Zeph. iii. 9 – 13.

The prophets after the captivity still retain the expectation of the purification of the Jewish nation before the Messianic times by the chastising judgments of God. Mal. iii. 1 – 3.

In regard to the time when the glorious Messianic state of the Jewish nation should commence, the prophets do not appear to have definite views. It is represented as following the purifying judgments of God on the nation at no distant period. Different prophets have different times in view at no great distance in their own future. Thus Isaiah, Jeremiah, the unknown author of Is. xl. — lxvi., Malachi, the author of the Book of Daniel, who lived in different periods, some of them in periods distant from each other, evidently regard the Messianic future as equally near to their own time. Isaiah iv. 2 – 5, and especially viii. 1 — ix. 7 seems to expect it soon after a hostile invasion which was threatened in his time. But Jeremiah * and the misnamed Isaiah † expect it to succeed the return from the captivity at Babylon, so as to belong to the same current of events. But Malachi, who wrote long after the return

* Jer. xxxii., xxxiii. † Is. liv. &c.

from the captivity, still expects it at no distant period, and the author of the Book of Daniel, who wrote about 175 A. C., expects it to follow immediately the death of Antiochus Epiphanes.

Having spoken of what was immediately to precede the Messianic period, and of the time when the prophets expected it to arrive, I now come to speak of the Messianic state itself, with reference to its national, political and physical characteristics. The prophets all unite in describing it as an inexpressibly happy and glorious temporal condition of the Jewish nation with respect to its government, its internal concerns, and its foreign relations. How any one can read the Hebrew prophets and not come to this conclusion would be an utter mystery to me, did I not know that the exploded doctrine of an allegorical sense affects the interpretations of many expositors who have nominally abandoned it.

1. The prophets set forth that the remnant left in Judea shall be the stem or nucleus of a flourishing state, to which accessions shall be made by the return of the exiled Israelites from all quarters of the earth. See Is. iv. 2, 5, 6, vi. 13. Micah vii. 11, 12 says: —

> "The day cometh when thy walls are to be built;
> In that day shall the decree be far removed.
> In that day shall they come to thee
> From Assyria and the cities of Egypt,
> And from Egypt to the river,
> From sea to sea, from mountain to mountain."

See also ii. 12; Amos ix. 11 – 15; Is. xi. 11, &c., xlix. 9 – 12; Jer. xxiii. 7 – 8, xxix. 14, xxxii. 37 – 44; Ezek. xxxvii. 21 – 25.

2. It is predicted that the extent and population of the renovated nation shall be very great. Thus, Is. liv. 1: —

> "Sing, O thou barren, that didst not bear!
> Break forth into singing, and shout for joy, thou that wast not in travail!
> For more are the children of the desolate,
> Than of the married woman, saith Jehovah.
> Enlarge the place of thy tent,
> And let the canopy of thy habitation be extended!
> Spare not; lengthen thy cords,
> And make fast thy stakes!
> For on the right hand and on the left shalt thou burst forth with increase;
> And thy posterity shall inherit the nations,
> And people the desolate cities."

Is lx. 22:—

"The little one shall become a thousand,
And the small one a strong nation;
I, Jehovah, will hasten it in its time."

See also xlix. 19–21; Ezek. xxxvi. 37, 38; Zech. viii. 4, 5.

3. The internal political condition of the nation shall be one of the highest prosperity and glory. See Is. xi., xii.; Ezek. xxxvii. 22, &c.; Jer. iii. 18.

4 The moral and religious condition of the nation shall be in the highest degree satisfactory. Thus, Is. xxxii. 15:—

"Until the spirit be poured upon us from on high,
And the wilderness become a fruitful field,
And the fruitful field be esteemed a forest.
Then shall justice dwell in the wilderness,
And righteousness in the fruitful field.
And the effect of righteousness shall be peace,
And the fruit of righteousness quietness and security forever"

See also liv. 13, lix. 21. Is. lx. 18, 21 says:—

"Violence shall no more be heard in thy land,
Wasting or destruction within thy borders;
Thou shalt call thy walls Salvation,
And thy gates Praise.
Thy people shall be all righteous," &c.

Jer. xxxi. 31–34:—

"Behold, the days come, saith Jehovah,
That I will make with the house of Israel,
And with the house of Judah, a new covenant;
But this is the covenant which I will make with the house of Israel;
After those days, saith Jehovah, I will put my law into their inward parts,
And upon their hearts will I write it;
And I will be their God,
And they shall be my people.
And they shall teach no more,
Every man his neighbor, and every man his brother,
Saying, Know Jehovah!
For they shall all know me,
From the least of them even to the greatest of them, saith Jehovah"

See also Joel ii. 28, 29.

5. The physical condition of the country shall be in the highest degree favorable. The prophets seem to labor for expressions by

which to set forth its state of more than paradisiacal felicity. Thus, Joel iii. 18:—

> "In that day shall the mountains drop down new wine,
> And the hills shall flow with milk,
> And all the streams of Judah shall flow with water."

See also Zech. xiv. 8. Is. xxx. 25, 26 says:—

> "And on every lofty mountain,
> And on every high hill,
> Shall be brooks and streams of water.
> Then shall the light of the moon be as the light of the sun,
> And the light of the sun shall be sevenfold,
> As the light of seven days."

See also Is. xli. 18; Jer. xxxi. 12; Ezek. xxxiv. 27, 29; Amos ix. 13; Is. lx., lxi., lxv. 17–25.

6. The political condition of Israel with respect to foreign nations shall be in the highest degree satisfactory. They shall no more be under the yoke of oppression from abroad. Is. ix. 3, 4; Ezek. xxxiv. 28, xxxvi. 15; Joel iii. 17; Is. liv. 17. So far from being molested or oppressed by foreign nations, Israel shall in the Messianic times annex, make tributary, or destroy foreign nations on all sides, and to a great extent. Thus, Is. xi. 14:—

> "But they shall fly upon the shoulders of the Philistines at the sea; 77
> Together shall they plunder the children of the East;
> Edom and Moab shall be their prey,
> And the sons of Ammon shall be subject to them."

See also Joel iii. 9–17; Amos ix. 12; Obad. 19, 20; Zeph. ii. 9. Is. xlix. 23 says:—

> "Kings shall be thy nursing fathers,
> And queens thy nursing mothers,
> And their faces shall they bow down before thee,
> And lick the dust of thy feet."

Is. lx. 11, 12 says:—

> "Thy gates shall be open continually;
> They shall not be shut by day or by night,
> That the treasures of the nations may be brought to thee,
> And that their kings may come with their retinues.
> For that nation and that kingdom
> Which will not serve thee shall perish;
> Yea, those nations shall be utterly destroyed.

See also Zech. xiv. 14.

There seems also to be predicted a signal destruction of heathen nations which opposed Israel. See Is. xxiv. 21; Ezek. xxviii. 26; Mic. v. 8, 9; Hag. ii. 6. The most complete descriptions of this destruction of the nations seem to be in Joel, ch. iii., and Zech., ch. xiv.

7. The duration of the happy state of things in the Messianic period of the Jewish nation was to be perpetual. See Jer. xxiv. 6; Ezek. xxxvii. 25. Joel iii. 20 says:—

> "But Judah shall be inhabited forever,
> And Jerusalem from generation to generation."

So Is. lxi. 8. Mic. iv. 7 says:—

> "I will make the halting a remnant,
> And the far scattered a strong nation;
> And Jehovah shall reign over them in mount Zion,
> Henceforth even forever."

So Jer. xxxii. 40.

Such in a small compass is the picture which the prophets present of the happy and glorious temporal condition of the Jewish nation in the Messianic times,—a condition which was to endure forever. Much more to the same effect might be quoted. That every line of these predictions of temporal felicity and glory to the Jewish nation is to be understood literally, cannot be maintained. For they were uttered by those who were poets as well as prophets, in the most glowing state of feeling and imagination. We must expect therefore a certain exuberance and exaggeration in their descriptions. We must read the prophets as poets, rather than as dogmatic theologians. To the province of poetry, perhaps, belongs the representation that the wild beasts are to become tame, that the stars are to shine brighter, that the light of the moon is to be as the light of the sun, and that Jehovah will create new heavens and a new earth. We may not be able in every case to draw the exact line between what the writers would have regarded as imaginative embellishment, and what as the express objects of their faith. Common sense, however, applied to their interpretation, will prevent frequent mistakes. But that the amount of the predictions of the prophets, as they and their contemporaries must have understood them, is to set forth a flourishing and glorious condition of the Jewish nation, a condition of righteousness and peace, a condition of political prosperity and power, and a condition of superiority and triumph over all other nations, seems to me so plain that he who opens his eyes may see it, and that he who runs may read it. If we set aside the conscious meaning of the prophets, and regard their thoughts as mere types or prefigurations of the future, of course they may denote one thing in the tenth century, another in the sixteenth, another in the nineteenth, and another at some future time.

III. Having now spoken of the purely moral and religious predictions of the prophets, and of those in which a certain political element and a certain outward condition of the Jewish nation are introduced, I now come to speak of the instrumentality by which such a glorious future of the Jewish nation in both respects was to be effected. The prophets Joel, Zephaniah, Nahum, and Habakkuk all predict the glorious future times called Messianic, but do not indicate the particular human instrumentality by which they supposed it would be effected.

The prophets Hosea, Amos, Isaiah, Micah, Jeremiah, Ezekiel, and Zechariah represent a Jewish king as the instrument by which the glorious condition of the nation and of the world was to be introduced. It may be that Haggai, iii. 20, &c., and Malachi should be added. This appears from the names which are applied to him, the offices which he bears, and the work which he is said to perform. Merely referring to Hosea iii. 5, and Amos ix. 11, which are not very full and free from doubt, the first clear and definite description of the future Messiah which, without allegorical interpretation, I find in the whole Old Testament, occurs in Is. ix. 6. Here we read, that, after a time of great distress to the Jewish nation, Jehovah will bring them joy and peace by raising up to them a wise and mighty prince, who shall, by the help of God, establish and extend his dominion over the house of David forever.

"For to us a child is born,
To us a son is given,
And the government shall be upon his shoulder,
And he shall be called
Wonderful, counsellor, mighty potentate,
Everlasting father, prince of peace;

His dominion shall be great,
And peace without end shall be upon the throne of David and his kingdom,
To fix and establish it
Through justice and equity,
Henceforth and forever.
The zeal of Jehovah of hosts will do this."

This passage is at the close of a prediction of considerable length; and the plain meaning of the language as describing a literal temporal king of the Jewish nation is wholly favored by the connection. All the epithets given to this personage are attributes of royalty. When it is said that "to us," i. e. to the nation, "a child is born," "a son is given," the meaning evidently is a child at the head of the nation, a royal child, a king's son. Then it is said expressly, that "the government shall be upon his shoulder," i. e. the government of the Jewish nation, as the connection requires. Then follow epithets denoting his wisdom as a king. *Mighty potentate*, or *mighty God*, (it is of no consequence which rendering is adopted,) denotes his power. It is also said that he should be *the everlasting father*, i. e. perpetual benefactor of his people, and *the prince of peace*, i. e. one who, having overcome the enemies of the state, should be the author of peace and prosperity. To understand the epithets of this passage in a spiritual sense is wholly inconsistent with its connection with the longer passage of which it is the conclusion.

In Is. xi. there is another striking description of the Messiah, which evidently represents him as a king clothed with temporal power. See verses 1, 4, 10, 11, 14. Such must have been the conception of the prophet.

The next prediction of the Messiah occurs in Is. xxxii., which begins,

"Behold! a king shall reign in righteousness!
And princes shall rule with equity," &c.

Some have doubted whether this passage be a prediction of the Messiah. But it is generally supposed to be such, and, I think, correctly. The common version has for the caption of the chapter, "The blessings of Christ's kingdom." But if the passage relate to the Messiah, the first verse evidently describes him as a temporal king. Such must have been the conception of the prophet.

The next passage descriptive of the Messiah in the order of time is a celebrated one in Micah, who was a contemporary of Isaiah. See ch. v. 2, &c.

> "But thou, Bethlehem Ephratah,
> Who art small to be among the thousands of Judah,
> Out of thee shall he come forth for me to be ruler in Israel,
> Whose origin is from the ancient age, from the days of old.
> 4 He shall stand and rule in the strength of Jehovah,
> In the majesty of Jehovah his God;
> And they shall dwell in security;
> For he shall be great even to the ends of the earth.
> 5 And he shall be peace.
> When the Assyrian shall come into our land,
> To trample on our palaces, &c.
> 6 Thus shall he deliver us from the Assyrian when he cometh into our land,
> And treadeth in our borders."

Of this passage it is sufficient to remark, that the connection in which it stands supports the plain meaning of the language, which describes the Messiah as king of Israel, subduing, at the head of the nation, the Assyrians and other enemies. There is in Micah no other passage referring to the Messiah, unless it be ii. 13. If this refer to him, it is in perfect harmony with ch. v. 2, &c.

The next prophet who has given a prediction of the Messiah is Jeremiah. In ch. xxiii. 6, after speaking of calamitous times of the Jewish nation, the prophet says:

> "Behold, the days are coming, saith Jehovah,
> When I will raise up from David a righteous Branch,
> And a king shall reign and prosper,
> And shall maintain justice and equity in the land.
> In his days Judah shall be saved,
> And Israel shall dwell securely;
> And this is the name which shall be given him,
> Jehovah-is-our-salvation."

Now the verses preceding and following this passage strongly confirm the plain meaning of the official and symbolical names given to the Messiah in this passage. He is expressly called a king, and the offices of a king are ascribed to him. The symbolical names "Branch" and "Jehovah-is-our-salvation" are given him to denote that he was to be of the royal family of David, and that Jehovah would save or deliver the people of Israel from exile and other calamities by his instrumentality. Nothing occurs in the passage to show that the regal epithets applied to him are to be understood in a figurative or spiritual sense. It is only by allegorical interpretation that such a sense can be extracted from it.

The only other passage in Jeremiah which speaks of the Messiah is ch. xxxiii. 14, &c.:

"Behold, the days come, saith Jehovah,
That I will perform that good thing
Which I have spoken concerning the house of Israel,
And concerning the house of Judah.
In those days and at that time
Will I cause to grow up from David a righteous Branch,
Who shall maintain justice and equity in the land;
In those days shall Judah be saved,
And Israel shall dwell securely;
And this is the name which shall be given her,
Jehovah-is-our-salvation."

This passage is somewhat less explicit than the last. But the symbolical names applied to the Messiah, as well as the literal term, "king," and the connection of the passage with what precedes and follows, show that the prophet conceived of him as a temporal king at the head of the Jewish nation, the author to it of temporal peace and prosperity. There is no other passage relating to the Messiah in Jeremiah.

We now come to Ezekiel, who first speaks of the Messiah in ch. xxxiv. 23, 24: "And I will raise up one shepherd over them, and he shall feed them, even my servant David; he shall feed them, and he shall be their shepherd. And I, Jehovah, will be their God, and my servant David a prince among them." Who can doubt that the prophet was here thinking of a literal king, who should rule the Jewish nation in the spirit of David? In ch. xxxvii. 25, Ezekiel again predicts the Messiah, in language so similar to that of the last passage that I need not recite it. I am not aware that there is any other reference to the Messiah in Ezekiel.

The next prophet who speaks of the Messiah is Zechariah, ch. iii. 8: "For, behold, I will cause to come my servant, the Branch."

The symbolic name "Branch" seems to be used to indicate a royal descendant from the house of David. This is confirmed by ch. vi. 12, 13:

> "Behold, a man whose name is the Branch,
> He shall spring up from his place,
> And he shall build the temple of Jehovah,
> And he shall bear the majesty,
> And sit and rule upon his throne,
> And be a priest upon his throne.
> And the counsel of peace shall be between them both."

Nothing can be plainer than that the Messiah, as here described, was regarded by the prophet as a temporal king, who should build the temple of Jehovah, and promote the will of Jehovah by advancing the peace of the Jewish people, uniting in his person the office of king and priest, as was sometimes the case with ancient kings.

The next passage is in ch. ix. 8–10:

> "And I will encamp about my house, as about a stronghold,
> Against him that passeth by and him that returneth,
> And no oppressor shall pass through them any more;
> For now have I seen with mine eyes.
> Rejoice greatly, O daughter of Zion,
> Shout, O daughter of Jerusalem!
> Behold, thy king cometh to thee;
> He is just and victorious,
> Mild, and riding upon an ass,
> Even upon a colt, the foal of an ass.
> And I will cut off the chariot from Ephraim,
> And the horse from Jerusalem;
> And the battle-bow shall be cut off.
> And he shall speak peace to the nations;
> And his dominion shall be from sea to sea,
> And from the river to the ends of the earth."

In this beautiful passage the Messiah is expressly called a king, and the attributes and actions of a temporal king are ascribed to him. He is a king, who shall give peace to the Jewish nation; who shall break the battle-bow, and cause the horse and the chariot to disappear. But from a comparison of the connection in verses thirteenth and fourteenth, and from other passages, especially ch. xiv., the prophet would seem to expect peace in Judæa, not from the dissemination of pacific principles, but rather from the victories of the Messiah over all other nations, and the extension of political power over them, so that the Jews would have no need of weapons of war with which to defend themselves.

These three are all the references to the Messiah in Zechariah. There are, indeed, two other passages which by some have been supposed to refer to the Messiah, but with no good reason. The first is in ch. xiii. 7:

"Awake, O sword, against my shepherd,
Even against the man who is my fellow, saith Jehovah of hosts!
Smite the shepherd, and let the sheep be scattered!
I will also turn my hand against the lambs."

Now if the passage last quoted in ch. ix., relating to the perpetual peace of Israel, the destruction of weapons of war, and the extension of the dominion of the Messiah, be a genuine prediction of Zechariah, it follows that what is said of the smiting of the shepherd and the scattering of the sheep must refer to calamitous times of the Jewish nation and its rulers *before* the coming of the Messiah. When he should come, according to the predictions not only of Zechariah, but of all the other prophets, there was to be victory, prosperity, and peace.

The other passage in Zechariah is in ch. xii. 10:

"Then will I pour upon the house of David,
And upon the inhabitants of Jerusalem,
A spirit of supplication and of prayer;
And they shall look to me whom they pierced," &c.

But the obvious meaning of the prophet in this passage is, that the speaker, Jehovah, and not the future Messiah, was pierced by the neglect and disobedience of the Jews, or by the persecution of his prophets. Calvin, in his note on the passage as quoted in John xix. 37, says, "God here speaks in the manner of men, signifying that he is wounded by the wickedness of his people, and especially by the obstinate contempt of his word, as a man is mortally wounded when his heart is pierced."

The prophet Malachi may possibly refer to the Messiah in ch. iii. 1:

"And the Lord whom ye seek shall suddenly come to his temple;
And the messenger of the covenant whom ye desire,
Behold, he shall come, saith Jehovah of hosts.

But who shall abide the day of his coming?
And who shall stand when he appeareth?
For he shall be like the fire of the refiner,
And like the soap of the fuller.
And he shall sit as a refiner and purifier of silver,
And he shall purify the sons of Levi,
And shall refine them as gold and silver,
That, being holy to Jehovah, they may bring an offering in righteousness."

Whether this passage, if it refer to the Messiah, represents his office to be that of a king after the type of David, or a prophet after the type of Elijah, seems doubtful. If it represents him as a prophet, it is the only passage in the Old Testament which gives such a representation. All the other prophets represent him as a king.

In the Book of Daniel, the character of which is not material in this inquiry, there is only one passage which can be regarded as predicting a personal Messiah by an unbiassed interpreter, namely, ch. vii. 13, 14: "I saw in the night visions, and, behold, one like a son of man came with the clouds of heaven, and came to the aged person, and they brought him near before him. And there was given him dominion, and glory, and a kingdom, that all people, nations, and languages should serve him; his dominion is an everlasting dominion, which shall not pass away, and his kingdom shall not be destroyed."

In a former edition I expressed the opinion that this passage relates to a personal Messiah. This is by far the most common opinion, and may be the correct one. If so, it harmonizes with the passages adduced from the other prophets, which represent the Messiah as a temporal king. For even on the supposition that the prophet pictures him as a superhuman being, which is doubtful, his dominion is represented as succeeding four great monarchies, and nothing is said to show that the dominion which is given to "one like a son of man" is different in its nature from that of the four preceding monarchies, or any other than a perpetual earthly dominion.

But on further investigation it appears to me that the common explanation of this passage is exceedingly doubtful. It is, in my view, more probable that the phrase *son of man* does not here refer to the Messiah. It is rather a symbol of the Jewish people.

In the former part of the chapter Daniel is represented as seeing in the night visions four animals, namely, a lion, a bear, a leopard, and another terrible beast unnamed, symbolizing four empires; namely, 1. the Babylonian, 2. the Median, 3. the Medo-Persian, and 4. that of Alexander and his successors. In close connection he is represented as seeing in the night visions one like a son of man, and as seeing dominion given to him by God. Now, as the four animals seen in the night visions are symbols denoting four empires, it seems probable that the one like a son of man is also a symbol, denoting the Jewish nation. Thus there would be five successive symbols, four beasts and one man. This interpretation seems also to be confirmed by the explanation of the night visions which is given by the angel. For when he had informed Daniel that the four beasts denoted kingdoms or nations, he says in verse twenty-seventh, that, after the destruction of the fourth or Macedonian empire, "the sovereignty and dominion and power over all kingdoms under the whole heaven shall be given to the people of the saints of the Most High." Here, instead of the symbol, "a son of man," we seem to have the thing symbolized, namely, the people of the saints of the Most High, that is, the Jewish people. Admitting, therefore, that the common interpretation of the phrase *son of man* in the passage is entitled to respect, it is most probable that it denotes the Jewish nation, just as the lion denoted the Babylonian, the bear the Median, the leopard the Medo-Persian, and an unnamed beast the Macedonian. This interpretation in its primary application was adopted in ancient times by Ephræm Syrus,* though he supposed that it had a second and complete fulfilment in Jesus Christ. In modern times, Paulus, Jahn, Wegscheider, Baumgarten-Crusius, and Hitzig have maintained the same explanation. So also Dorner, Von der Person Christi, p. 63. Grotius interpreted the phrase *son of man* in the same symbolic way, but supposed that it referred to the Roman empire. As to the representation that the symbol of the Jewish empire came with the clouds of heaven, it may be well understood as denoting that its source was in God,—that God would be the mighty and irresistible agent in setting it up, as the supreme national king of the Jews, according to ch. ii. 44: "But in the days of

* Ephræm Syri Opera, Vol. II. p. 215.

these kings shall the God of heaven set up a kingdom which shall never be destroyed," &c.

I have thus brought forward *all* the passages which occur in the prophetic writings relating to an individual Messiah as the instrumentality for introducing the glorious future condition of the Jewish nation and of the world. Nor do I think that any other predictions of an individual Messiah in the whole of the Old Testament, except those which I have brought forward, can be found, without resorting to allegorical interpretation, or double senses. There are four Psalms, respecting which there may be some doubt whether they be predictions of the Messiah or not; viz. Ps. ii., xlv., lxxii., and cx. If they do relate to him, they clearly ascribe to him the office and character of a triumphant temporal king. The same remarks apply to the prediction in Numb. xxiv. 17, by the Moabite prophet Balaam. But the balance of probability is against the Messianic character of those Psalms. It is not difficult to explain how it happened that the instrumentality for bringing about the glorious Messianic future, both as regards the religious and moral, as well as the political element of it, should by most of the prophets be represented as a king. All the predictions of a personal Messiah were made after the establishment of the government by kings. The prophets, who were the historians of the nation, knew very well the vast influence exercised by kings not only in regard to the national prosperity and glory, but also in regard to the establishment and extension of religion and morals. They could conceive of no higher instrumentality by which a religious and political reformation united could be accomplished, than by a wise and pious king. They knew from their national history, that when wise, righteous, and religious kings had governed, then idolatry had been suppressed, true religion had been established and extended, and the nation had prospered; in fine, that the religious and political condition of the nation had depended very much on the good or bad character of the king. We have only to read the books of Kings and Chronicles to see that such must have been the views of the prophets who lived under the kings. From no single prophet or priest could they expect so much for the regeneration of the nation in its religious, moral, and political condition, as from a king. For it depended on the king to encourage true prophets and holy priests, or the reverse.

It is also easy to explain why the prophets should represent tho king who was to bring in the glorious future times as a son or descendant of David, and why he should sometimes be called by the very name of David. David was the king who, according to the judgment of the prophets as expressed in the historical books, ruled according to the strictest theocratic principles, and performed with the greatest fidelity what Jehovah commanded. See, for example, 1 Kings ix. 5, xiv. 8, xv. 5. Succeeding kings are approved or condemned according as they did or did not resemble David, and conduct themselves like David, their father. In a word, David was regarded as the model theocratic ruler, the promoter and extender of the religion of Jehovah. See 1 Kings xv. 4; 2 Kings viii. 19, xix. 34. The prophets, therefore, who lived under the kings, were naturally led to expect, as the head of the pure theocracy in the future glorious Messianic times, a king, a descendant of David; as it were, David himself arisen in one of his posterity. Besides, the family of David had always been the reigning family at Jerusalem; so that, if David had been less eminent than he was, still one of his descendants must have been represented as the Messiah, when once the Messiah was regarded as a temporal king.

In a similar way is to be explained the prediction in Micah v. 2, that Bethlehem should be honored as the source from which the Messiah should come forth. Bethlehem was the family seat of the race of David, 1 Sam. xvii. 12, and consequently whoever looked for a king of the race of David would represent him as about to come from Bethlehem. To say that he was to originate in Bethlehem, was the same thing as to say that he would proceed from the family of David.

In regard to the attributes or character of the Messiah, as conceived of by the prophets, they are what constituted the prophetic ideal of a perfect Hebrew king. He was to be strong and mighty, wise and pious, righteous and merciful. See Is. ix. 6, &c., xi. 2, 3, &c.; Jer. xxiii. 5; Mic. v. 3; Zech. xii. 3. By some, the Messiah has been supposed to be represented by the prophets as a supernatural being, or even as the Supreme Being. This opinion has been generally rejected by the best scholars of all denominations. The passages which have been supposed to favor this view are Is. ix. 6; Dan. vii. 13; Mal. iii. 1; Jer. xxiii. 5; and a few others of less note. For a refutation of this view, see my notes on the passages, and especially an article of mine in the Christian Examiner for January, 1836.

The extent of the dominion of the Messiah, the work which he was to perform, the time of his coming, and the duration of his reign, are implied in what has been said, pp. xxvi. *et seq.*, concerning the predicted Messianic times. The Messiah was to be the head of the Jewish nation and the world, in the glorious condition which he had introduced. In reference to the two classes of predictions relating to the Messianic times, viz. those purely religious, relating to the establishment and extension of true religion, or the worship and service of Jehovah among men, and those in which a political element was included, the Messiah was to be God's representative and instrument in the accomplishment of both. He was to be the founder of the universal spiritual kingdom of God, and, at the same time, of the political dominion and temporal prosperity and glory of the Jewish nation, as above described, pp. xxvi. *et seq.*

Respecting the time of the coming of the Messiah, as understood by the prophets, the remarks hold good which were made, p. xxv., respecting the predicted time of the glorious future condition of the Jewish nation. So far as the prophets indicate any opinion respecting the time of the Messiah's coming, they seem to have expected that he would come after certain great national judgments, which they supposed would take place either in their own day, or in no distant period from it. See Is. viii.—ix. 6. Some of the prophets seem to have supposed that the Messiah would come after a return of the Jews from exile. See Mic. iv., v.; Jer. xxiii. 5–8; Ezek. xxxvii. 21–25; Zech. vi. 12, 13, compared with iii. 8. They evidently had no uniform expectation on the subject. Each expected it at no distant period in his own future.

We have thus seen that all the prophets whose writings we have examined, with the exception of Malachi, whose language is too ambiguous to authorize a confident opinion, represent the Messiah as the temporal king of the Jewish nation.

But is there no other instrumentality mentioned by any prophet, by which the glorious future period of the Jewish nation and of the world was to be introduced? It appears to me that there is; namely, that described by an unknown prophet, the greatest of all the Jewish prophets, who lived near the close of the exile at Babylon, and wrote the composition included in Is. xl.-lxvi. His prediction, fairly interpreted in its connection, and by his own use of language, indicates that by the "Servant of Jehovah," who should introduce the glorious future condition of the Jewish nation, and in some degree of the world, he had in view not an individual Messiah, but a collective body, the Jewish church, the better part of the Jewish nation, the true Israel, i. e. the Jewish nation considered as the true and faithful servant of Jehovah.

The passage which at once arrests attention among the utterances of this great unknown prophet is Is. lii. 13-liii., of which the following is a careful translation.

"Behold, my servant shall prosper;
He shall be lifted up, and set on high, and greatly exalted.
As many were amazed at the sight of him, —
So disfigured and scarcely human was his visage,
And so unlike that of a man was his form, —
So shall he cause many nations to exult on account of him;
Kings shall shut their mouths before him.
For what had never been told them shall they see,
And what they never heard shall they perceive.
"Who hath believed our report,
And to whom hath the arm of Jehovah been revealed?
For he grew up before him like a tender plant;
Like a sucker from a dry soil;
He had no form nor comeliness, that we should look upon him,
Nor beauty, that we should take pleasure in him.
He was despised and forsaken of men,
A man of sorrows, and acquainted with disease;
As one from whom men hide their faces,
He was despised, and we esteemed him not
But he bore our diseases,
And carried our pains,
And we esteemed him stricken from above,
Smitten of God, and afflicted.
"But he was wounded for our transgressions;
He was bruised for our iniquities;
For our peace was the chastisement upon him,
And by his stripes are we healed.
All we like sheep were going astray;
We turned every one to his own way,

And Jehovah laid upon him the iniquity of us all.
He was oppressed that was already afflicted,
Yet he opened not his mouth ;
As a lamb that is led to the slaughter,
And as a sheep before her shearers is dumb,
He opened not his mouth.
By oppression and punishment he was taken away,
And who in his generation would consider
That he was cut off from the land of the living,
That for the transgression of my people he was smitten?
His grave was appointed with the wicked,
And with the rich man was his sepulchre,
Although he had done no injustice,
And there was no deceit in his mouth.
It pleased Jehovah severely to bruise him;
But when he has made his life a sacrifice for sin,
He shall see posterity; he shall prolong his days,
And the pleasure of Jehovah shall prosper in his hand.
Free from his sorrows, he shall see and be satisfied;
By his knowledge shall my righteous servant lead many to righteousness,
And he will bear their iniquities.
Therefore will I give him his portion with the mighty,
And with heroes shall he divide the spoil,
Because he poured out his soul unto death,
And was numbered with transgressors;
Because he bore the sin of many,
And made intercession for transgressors."

This passage is a very remarkable one, whatever instrumentality may be denoted by the " Servant of Jehovah." For it sets forth in a clear and emphatic manner the moral good and the general happiness which the writer conceived to be produced by the sufferings of the righteous. The resemblance, in some particulars, of the fortunes, character, and work of the Servant of God to those of our Saviour, is so striking that no one can fail to be impressed by it. The great body of Christians have been in the habit of regarding the passage as a miraculous prediction of the sufferings, death, and burial of Jesus of Nazareth. Any individual would be reluctant to oppose the general voice, were it not for the fact, that, owing to unfounded principles of interpretation, hundreds of passages in the Old Testament have from the earliest times with equal confidence been applied to Christ, which no well-informed interpreter can now apply to him in the sense which was in the mind of the writer. On many accounts the passage deserves a very careful consideration.

In view of the passages which I have heretofore quoted from the Prophets, as descriptive of the coming and office of the Messiah, there arises at once a difficulty in the way of applying to him this remarkable description of the Servant of God. The difficulty is in accounting for the fact, that in every other passage in which the Messiah is introduced he is represented as prosperous, mighty, victorious, and that in this passage alone he should be represented as a sufferer. How remarkable that, if the prophets had regarded the Messiah as a sufferer, not one of them should have alluded to so important a circumstance, except the writer of this single passage! It is still more remarkable, when we consider that the very work of the Servant of God is represented in this description as in a considerable degree accomplished by his sufferings. Compare the passage, for instance, with the first prediction of the Messiah in Is. ix. 6. Here we find that, after a description of the great national distress, the writer goes on to say that it shall not continue. "For unto us a child is born," &c. Not a word is said here of the Messianic king's being in distress. Everything is of an opposite character, from his very birth. The same is true of every other prophetic description of the Messiah. This consideration cannot but raise a presumption against the common interpretation of the term Servant of Jehovah in ch. liii. It is not absolutely conclusive, because it might be said that the author of the passage entertained a different view from the rest of the prophets.

Perhaps it may be asked whether there is any actual inconsistency between the passage under consideration relating to the sufferings of the Servant of God, and the prophetic descriptions of the Messiah as a prosperous and triumphant temporal king. There certainly is no inconsistency in the representation that a monarch is at one time in adversity, and at another in prosperity. History informs us of many monarchs who have arrived at royalty by the path of trial, persecution, and suffering of various kinds. This was the case with David, from whom the prophets borrow some traits in their delineations of the Messiah. They might, therefore, have conceived of the Messiah as having arrived at the throne of the Jewish nation, and qualified himself to be their religious and moral reformer, the benefactor of their nation and the extender of their empire and their religion over foreign nations, by having passed through the ordeal of trial and suffering. But, though there is no inconsistency between the description of the Servant of God in a state of suffering, and the representation of the Messiah as a prosperous and victorious king in the other prophets, does it not still remain unaccountable, that not one of the latter should have alluded to any suffering condition of the Messiah previous to his prosperous and triumphant state as a king? This question has the greater force when we consider that the suffering condition of the Servant of God, as described in Is. lii. 13 – liii., was to have a very important agency in the accomplishment of his work.

On the other hand, the passage under consideration relating to the sufferings of the Servant of God is in one sense Messianic. For the Servant of God was evidently regarded by the writer as the instrumentality which God would use in introducing the glorious Messianic times. The result of the work of the suffering Servant of God is the same which in other prophets is ascribed to the prosperous Messiah. No other prophet has set forth the glorious future condition of the Jewish nation and of the world with respect to religion, morals, temporal felicity, and glory in more glowing colors than has this unknown prophet in the exile, the un-genuine Isaiah; and all this glorious future is ascribed by him to the instrumentality of the "Servant of God." Thus, in ch. xlii. 1, 4, 6:

> "Behold my servant, whom I uphold,
> My chosen, in whom my soul delighteth;
> I have put my spirit upon him;
> He shall cause law to go forth to the nations. . . .
> He shall not fail, nor become weary,
> Until he shall have established justice in the earth,
> And distant nations shall wait for his law. . . .
> I, Jehovah, have called thee for salvation;
> I will hold thee by the hand;
> I will defend thee and make thee a covenant to the people,
> A light to the nations."

Again in ch. xlix. 6, 7:

"He said, It is a small thing that thou shouldst be my servant
To raise up the tribes of Jacob,
And to restore the preserved of Israel;
I will also make thee the light of the nations,
That my salvation may reach the ends of the earth.
Thus saith Jehovah, the Redeemer of Israel, his Holy One,
To him that is despised by men, abhorred by the people,
To the servant of tyrants:
Kings shall see, and stand up,
Princes, and they shall pay homage,
On account of Jehovah, who is faithful,
The Holy One of Israel, who hath chosen thee."

So in ch. liv. we have a glowing description of the glorious condition of the Jewish nation which was to follow the sufferings and work of the Servant of God, as described in ch. liii. So, in the chapters following, the same consequences are ascribed to his sufferings and work which, in the other prophets, are ascribed to a triumphant temporal king, to whom no sufferings are ascribed.

Hence, if it be assumed that the predictions of the prophets are objective, that is, that all the prophets had in view a particular historical person, whose actions and fortunes they miraculously foresaw, as if they were looking back upon history, then it will follow that the Servant of God in his humiliation and his sufferings designates the same person with the mighty potentate and victorious king of the other prophets. For the consequences of the work of both are the same. If, on the other hand, it be admitted, as the truth demands, that all the predictions of the Messianic king are subjective, merely setting forth the ideal of the prophetic mind, no one of the prophets pretending to have knowledge of the actions, life, or fortunes of any particular future person, then it will follow that the prophets may have supposed that the glorious future of the Jewish nation might be brought about by very different instrumentalities. Those prophets who lived under kings would naturally suppose that it would be brought about by a king. Malachi, who lived in the time of Nehemiah, might suppose that it would be effected by a prophet like Elijah, or one greater than Elijah. The author of the passage under consideration, Is. lii. 13 – liii., who lived near the close of the Jewish exile, when there was no king and no prospect of one, and when everything seemed to depend upon the virtue and piety of the Jewish people and their disposition to return from exile, might suppose the better part of the Jewish nation, the Jewish church, the true Israel, to be the instrumentality by which the glorious future times would be introduced. One class of prophets might suppose the administration, the virtues, and the victories of a king to be the chief means of accomplishing the work, and another might attribute the same work to the self-denial, the virtues, and the sufferings of the better part of the nation. The conception of the latter class would be partly objective and partly ideal. The past condition of the Jewish church, the people of God, would be actual; but its future condition might be ideal in the mind of the prophet.

The question now recurs, What was the actual instrumentality which the prophet had in view in the passage quoted from Is. lii. 13 – liii.? In other words, what is the meaning of the phrase Servant of God in that passage? Does it denote an individual, or a collective body? Now, in order to understand the expression, it is necessary, agreeably to universally acknowledged laws of interpretation, to consider the subject of the whole composition of which it forms a part. As it would be impossible to understand the meaning of any expression in one verse or chapter of an epistle of Paul without examining the use of the same expression in other parts of it, so it is impossible to know what is meant by the phrase Servant of God in Isaiah liii. without considering the use of the phrase in the whole composition of which that chapter is a part, and without considering the subject and design of the whole composition, and the connection of the passage under consideration with what immediately precedes and follows it. It is generally admitted that the last twenty-seven chapters of Isaiah form one continuous discourse or piece of composition, and relate principally to one subject. Those who think that it consists of three or four discourses, — 1. xl. – xlviii.; 2. xlix. – lx.; 3. lxi. – lxiii. 6; 4. lxiii. 7 – lxvi., — yet maintain that they all relate to one principal subject, and were written by the same author, at nearly the same time. There has been some difference of opinion as to what this subject is. Three opinions have been supported by different commentators.

1. The first, the most obvious and the best supported, is, that the subject of the whole composition Is. xl. – lxvi. is the deliver-

ance of the Jewish nation from the exile in Babylon, and the state of prosperity and glory which it was to enjoy soon after its return to its own land. The writer is supposed to have lived near the close of the exile at Babylon, and of course to have taken this time as his stand-point. His design was to encourage his contemporaries, to whom his discourse was addressed, to return to Palestine, by predicting their deliverance and their restoration to a high degree of prosperity and glory, so that religious light and Divine favor should through them be extended to all nations.

2. The opinion of Bishop Lowth and others coincides with, and establishes, the preceding view in part. He maintains that the first and main subject of the whole composition is the political restoration of the Jews from the captivity at Babylon, and the subsequent state of things in Judæa. But he thinks that the composition "is a plain instance of the mystical allegory, or double sense of prophecy." "The redemption from Babylon is clearly foretold; and at the same time is employed as an image to shadow out a redemption of an infinitely higher and more important nature." See Lowth's note on xl. 1. Lowth, like the supporters of the first opinion, makes the time of the exile the stand-point of the writer, and finds a reference to Christianity only in the allegorical sense. He also supposes, in many cases, a sudden transition from the meaning, which the common laws of language establish, to the allegorical sense, and from the latter to the former, which is in the highest degree arbitrary. Those who cannot admit an allegorical or double sense will be led by Lowth himself to the first-mentioned opinion.

3. Other interpreters, among whom the most celebrated is Vitringa, exclude entirely the meaning which the common laws of language give to the passage, and the principal subject which naturally presents itself to the reader, and suppose the whole passage to be an allegorical prediction of the deliverance of the world from the bondage of sin by Jesus Christ. These critics maintain that the prophet takes for his sole stand-point the wilderness of Judæa and the time of the preaching of John the Baptist.

Besides the insuperable objection to this theory arising from the improbability that a Jewish prophet, overlooking his contemporaries and their circumstances, should choose his position in a period and state of things which would not exist until many ages after he wrote, it is also to be observed that this theory of Vitringa supposes a use of language by the prophet which could not possibly be understood by his contemporaries, or even by the prophet himself. It does not extract the writer's meaning from his language, but puts one into it of which he could have had no conception. It is founded wholly on the allegorical or double sense.

I do not think it necessary, by a careful analysis of the passage (Is. xl.–lxvi.), to prove, what has been made evident by Bishop Lowth, that the return of the Jews from the captivity at Babylon and the glorious condition of the Jewish nation, and through it of the world, is what was in the prophet's mind. Whoever rejects mystical and allegorical senses must come to this conclusion.

The design of the discourse under consideration appears to me equally evident with the main subject of it. It was to raise the spirits of the Jewish people in exile, to awaken in them a desire to return to their native land, to inspire them with courage and resolution to overcome the obstacles which were in the way, and to induce them to abandon the sins which prevented the Divine favor.

It may be supposed, as seems to be implied in the exhortations of the prophet, that among the Jews at Babylon there was an opposing party of the irreligious and idolatrous, who thought they might as well remain in Babylonia where they were; that there was another portion who were indolent or indifferent, and needed to be aroused; and that only the remaining portion, perhaps a minority, consisted of the true and faithful Israelites who sighed for the enjoyment of their religious privileges in their native land. Such being the state of things among the exiles, it was evidently the design of the prophet to say a word in season to the different classes of them, in order to qualify them for a return from exile, to stir them up to exertion, and to inspire them with confidence in Jehovah.

The prophecy or discourse under consideration, Is. xl.–lxvi., is one of the most interesting in the Old Testament. If it do not contain, strictly speaking, the sublimest poetry, it does at least contain the loftiest eloquence, and the most spiritual and comprehensive views of religion, which are to be found in any of the sacred books before Christ. It is one incessant stream of fervent and stirring thoughts. But it has been much misunderstood on account of want of attention to the subject and design of the writer, and especially on account of the false supposition that, instead of addressing his contemporary exiles at Babylon, he was writing to men in general in all subsequent ages.

In this discourse there is frequent mention of a " Servant of God " who had, and was to have, great influence in the accomplishment of the glorious things predicted for the Jewish nation and the world. Now as ch. liii. forms a component of this whole discourse, which has one main subject and design, how evident is it that it can only be understood by viewing it in its connection with the discourse of which it forms a part! If chapters lii. and liv. relate to the Jewish nation, to its deliverance from exile, and to its expansion and prosperity, how contrary is it to all just laws of interpretation to suppose that ch. liii. relates to an entirely different subject viz. the spiritual deliverance of those who were *not* the Jewish nation! Especially in regard to the phrase " Servant of God," how absurd is it to suppose that it means one thing in ch. lii. 13 – liii., and altogether another in all the other parts of the discourse where it occurs!

In regard to the meaning of the phrase itself, independent of any particular application, it may denote one who serves the Lord with the obedience of his heart and life, i. e. a pious and good man; or it may be applied in an official sense to one who is raised up by the Deity for the accomplishment of a particular work. I apprehend that the phrase is employed in the passages we are about to examine in both these senses united. The " Servant of God " denotes one truly devoted to the service of God, and one employed by God for the accomplishment of his purposes.

With these preliminary remarks let us now examine the use of the phrase " Servant of God " in every place where it occurs in Is. xl. – lxvi., in order to see what meaning the *usus loquendi* of the writer requires it to have in lii. 13 – liii.

The first passage in which the phrase occurs, is in ch. xli. 8 – 17, where it is so closely defined that there can be no mistake about its meaning: —

"But thou, O Israel, my servant,
Thou, Jacob, whom I have chosen,
Offspring of Abraham, my friend!
Thou, whom I have led by the hand from the ends of the earth,
And called from the extremities thereof,
And said to thee, 'Thou art my servant,
I have chosen thee, and not cast thee away!'
Fear not, for I am with thee;
Faint not, for I, thy God, will strengthen thee.
I will help thee, and sustain thee with my right hand of salvation!"

In this passage no one can doubt that the Servant of God denotes the Jewish nation, regarded as the chosen people of God. The nation is very distinctly personified as a single man, as the offspring of Abraham, as one whom Jehovah took by the hand. It is the more necessary to attend to this representation by which the people of God is undeniably represented as an individual person, because in other passages the representation has been thought too harsh to be admitted. It is also to be observed, that, when the Jewish people is represented as the Servant of Jehovah, it is described as worthy of the name, as the true Israel, whom God will not cast away.

The next passage in which the expression occurs is at the beginning of the next chapter, xlii. 1 – 7: —

"Behold my servant, whom I uphold,
My chosen, in whom my soul delighteth,
I have put my spirit upon him;
He shall cause law to go forth to the nations.
He shall not cry aloud, nor lift up his voice,
Nor cause it to be heard in the street.
The bruised reed shall he not break,
And the glimmering flax shall he not quench;
He shall send forth law according to truth.
He shall not fail, nor become weary,
Until he shall have established justice in the earth,
And distant nations shall wait for his law.
"Thus saith God Jehovah,
Who created the heavens and stretched them out,
Who spread forth the earth, and that which springeth forth from it,
Who gave breath to the people upon it,
And spirit to them that walk thereon:
I, Jehovah, have called thee for salvation;

I will hold thee by the hand;
I will defend thee, and make thee a covenant to the people,
A light to the nations;
To open the blind eyes;
To bring out the prisoners from the prison,
And them that sit in darkness out of the prison-house."

Now this passage occurs in close connection with the preceding chapter. It is a part of the same discourse. What reason, then, can be given why the phrase Servant of God should not have the same meaning in this passage as in that. When the prophet represents the Deity as saying without explanation, "Behold my servant, whom I uphold," the laws of interpretation require us to believe that he refers to the same servant Jacob, the chosen Jewish people, more definitely described in the preceding chapter. The same epithet must be supposed to relate to the same subject, unless some decisive reason, arising out of the connection, can be given for a different application of it. But in this passage we find no such reason. On the contrary, we find confirmation of the impression that the phrase must mean the chosen people of God in ch. xlii. as well as in ch. xli. God is said, in the first verse, to put "his spirit" upon his servant. But this is just what is promised in ch. lix. 21, where it is said:

"My spirit which is upon thee,
And my words which I have put in thy mouth,
They shall not depart from thy mouth,
Nor from the mouth of thy sons,
Nor from the mouth of thy sons' sons, saith Jehovah,
From this time forth forever."

So it is said of the whole nation, "They shall be all taught of God." The Servant of God is also said to "cause law to go forth to the nations." But this corresponds exactly to the promise made to Abraham, "In thy race or posterity shall all the families of the earth be blessed."

The representation, then, that the people of God, having the spirit of God, should be a mediator and a prophet to the nations, is perfectly agreeable to the phraseology of this writer.

Of this we have strong confirmation in verses 18 – 22 of this chapter, such as leaves no doubt of the meaning of the phrase "my servant" in the first seven verses: —

"Hear, O ye deaf!
And look, ye blind, and see!
Who is blind, if not my servant?
And who so deaf as my messenger, whom I send?
Who so blind as the friend of God,
So blind as the servant of Jehovah?
Thou seest many things, but regardest them not;
Thou hast thine ears open, but hearest not!
It pleased Jehovah for his goodness' sake
To give him a law, great and glorious;
And yet it is a robbed and plundered people," &c.

Here, I suppose, all will admit that it is the people of God which is called the servant, friend, and messenger of Jehovah; his messenger to defend the cause of religion and to give light to the nations, and yet indifferent and blind in regard to the indications of Divine Providence having reference to their restoration, and consequently remaining a robbed and plundered people. The servant who is deaf and blind is also, in verse eighteenth, addressed in the plural number, — "Hear, O ye deaf! and look, ye blind," &c. But if in verses 18 – 22 the Servant of God denotes the people of God, I do not see how we can escape the conclusion, that it has the same meaning in the first seven verses of this same chapter. No writer would employ a phrase in such a close connection, and with such similar accompaniments, without attaching to it the same meaning. Neither is it easy to see in what sense the epithets "deaf" and "blind" could be applied to Jesus Christ. It may also be remarked that the explanation of ch. xlii. 1, as denoting the people of God, is the most ancient explanation of the passage which is now extant. The Sept. version interpolates "Jacob" and "Israel" into the first verse.

Ἰακὼβ, ὁ παῖς μου, ἀντιλήψομαι αὐτοῦ·
Ἰσραὴλ, ὁ ἐκλεκτός μου, προσεδέξατο αὐτὸν ἡ ψυχή μου.

We now proceed to the next chapter, xliii. Here, at the beginning of the chapter, we still find the Supreme Being represented as addressing his chosen people, personified as a single man: —

"But now thus saith Jehovah, that created thee, O Jacob,
That formed thee, O Israel:
Fear not, for I have redeemed thee;
I have called thee by name; thou art mine!"

In the same strain God is represented as speaking, until we come to verse tenth, where He says: —

"Ye are my witnesses, saith Jehovah,
And my servant whom I have chosen,
That ye may know and believe me,
And understand that I am He.
Before me was no God formed,
And after me there shall be none."

Israel is here addressed at the same time in the singular and the plural. "Ye are my witnesses," and "ye are my servant whom I have chosen." The passage thus corresponds with, and confirms, the previous representation of Israel as a collective body personified as an individual, and constituted God's servant for the purpose of knowing that of which foreign nations were ignorant, and bearing witness of it.

We now come to ch. xliv. Here, in verses 1, 2, we read:

"Yet now hear, O Jacob, my servant,
And Israel, whom I have chosen;
Thus saith Jehovah, thy Creator,
He that formed thee, and hath helped thee from thy birth:
Fear not, O Jacob, my servant,
Jeshurun, whom I have chosen."

Then in the eighth verse: —

"Ye are my witnesses;
Is there a God beside me?
Yea, there is no other rock; I know not any."

Here Israel, the people of God, is still represented as an individual prophet, having God's spirit, his chosen servant, as bearing witness for God, &c.

Now turn to ch. xlviii. 20: —

"Come ye forth from Babylon, flee ye from the land of the Chaldæans
with the voice of joy!
Publish ye this, and make it known;
Let it resound to the ends of the earth!
Say, 'Jehovah hath redeemed his servant Jacob.'"

The people of God is still personified as a single man, the Servant of God.

Then, two verses beyond, in ch xlix. 1 – 9, we have the following remarkable passage: —

"Listen to me, ye distant lands;
Attend, ye nations from afar!
Jehovah called me at my birth;
In my very childhood he called me by name.
He made my mouth like a sharp sword;
In the shadow of his hand did he hide me;
He made me a polished shaft;
In his quiver did he hide me.
He said to me, Thou art my servant;
Israel, in whom I will be glorified.
Then I said, I have labored in vain;
For naught, for vanity have I spent my strength;
Yet my cause is with Jehovah,
And my reward with my God.
And now thus saith Jehovah,
Who formed me from my birth to be his servant,
To bring Jacob to him again,
And that Israel might be gathered to him, —
For I am honored in the eyes of Jehovah,
And my God is my strength, —
He said, It is a small thing that thou shouldst be my servant
To raise up the tribes of Jacob,
And to restore the preserved of Israel;
I will also make thee the light of the nations,
That my salvation may reach the ends of the earth.
Thus saith Jehovah, the Redeemer of Israel, his Holy One,
To him that is despised by men, abhorred by the people,
To the servant of tyrants:
Kings shall see, and stand up,
Princes, and they shall pay homage
On account of Jehovah, who is faithful,
The Holy One of Israel, who hath chosen thee.
Thus saith Jehovah:
In the time of favor will I hear thee;
And in the day of deliverance will I help thee;
I will preserve thee, and make thee a mediator for the people,
To restore the land, to distribute the desolated inheritances;
To say to the prisoners, Go forth!
To them that are in darkness, Come to the light!
They shall feed in the ways,
And on all high places shall be their pasture."

It is evident that the same "Servant of God," his chosen people, is here represented by the prophet as speaking in the first person. The personification is here carried to such an extreme, that it is no wonder that there has been some doubt as to the subject introduced as speaking. But the passage stands in so close a connection with the preceding representations which have been adduced, that we are obliged to regard the Servant of God, who is the speaker in it, as denoting the same people of God, the true Israel, personified as before. If the passage stood by itself, it would indeed be hardly credible that the Jewish church should be personified to such an extent as to be represented as a prophet speaking in the first person, having a mouth like a sharp sword, and called by name by the Deity from birth. But we must remember that the personification is almost as strong in the other passages which have been cited, where there can be no doubt that the people of God is denoted,—xli. 8, 9, xlii. 1–4, xliii. 1, &c., xliv. 1–3, xlvi. 3. Besides, in verse third, we have a direct intimation that it is the people of God which is represented as speaking:—

> " He said to me, Thou art my servant;
> Israel, in whom I will be glorified."

I do not see how the term Israel can be applied to an individual prophet. It is constantly used in this discourse, as throughout the Old Testament, to denote the people of God. So forcible is this consideration, that some critics, without the least authority of manuscripts or versions, have actually expunged the word "Israel" from the verse. Besides, no individual Jewish prophet would be spoken of as sent to "the nations" in the first instance, but only to the Jews, or to "the nations" in connection with the Jews. It would also have been extravagant for the writer to say of himself, or any Jewish prophet, "Kings shall see and stand up, princes, and they shall pay homage." In regard to the Messiah, no prophet could have introduced him so abruptly, and represented him as speaking before he had any personal existence as Messiah. The context, the *usus loquendi* relating to the term "Servant of God," and the very name "Israel" in the third verse, all lead to the conclusion that it is the people of God, the Jewish church, which is represented as speaking.

There is, indeed, an apparent difficulty in the way of this conclusion, which however disappears on examination. It is presented in verse 5:—

> "And now thus saith Jehovah,
> Who formed me from my birth to be his servant,
> To bring Jacob to him again,
> And that Israel might be gathered to him," &c.

Here it may be asked, If the Servant of God denote the people of God, the Jewish church, how is it that this people is said to bring Jacob again, &c.? Is not the Servant of God here distinguished from the nation of Israel? The answer is, that when the Jewish people is personified as an individual prophet, and called the servant, or the messenger, or the friend of God, it denotes the righteous Jewish people, Israel worthy of the name, the true Israel. The people of God is represented partly in an actual, partly in an ideal sense. This emphatic use of Israel is indicated in the third verse. So St. Paul says, "They are not all Israel that are of Israel." It follows of course, when a community is personified as an individual, that it should be understood now in a wider, now in a narrower sense. So the Christian Church sometimes denotes the holy church in the sight of God, "the pillar and ground of the truth," and sometimes all the individuals of every character who, in some sense, may be said to belong to it. That the true Israel, the genuine people of God, the righteous part of the Jewish nation, should be distinguished from the members of the nation at large, considered as individuals of every description of character, is just what might be expected. It arises from the very nature of the personification. Sometimes the ideal, the elect, the God-inspired Israel is denoted by the term, and sometimes the actual descendants of Jacob.

On the whole, therefore, it is by far the most probable opinion that in ch. xlix. 1–9, as in the preceding passages, the Servant of God denotes the people of God, the true Israel. So Doederlein, Gesenius, Rosenmueller, and Dr. Alexander, with a qualification.

We now come to ch. l. 4–10. Here one is tempted by the very extraordinary extent to which the personification is carried to suppose, with Calvin, Grotius, Knobel, and others, that the prophet for once speaks as the Servant of God in his own name, and refers to his own persecutions as an individual. Without having so much confidence in relation to the meaning of the phrase in this passage, as in all the rest in which the "Servant of God" is mentioned, I still think it most agreeable to the connection to understand it in the same way as ch. xlix. 1 – 9, and the preceding citations, that is, as denoting the people of God, the true Israel. So Maurer and Ewald explain it. No doubt the prophet regarded himself as belonging to this collective body, and as having great influence in it. Hence, in personifying it as an individual speaking in the first person, his own personality might unconsciously predominate more than was in strict harmony with the figure of speech which he was employing. Dr. Alexander admits that the people of God is, *in part*, referred to here.

Thus I have examined every passage in which the phrase "Servant of God" is used in the whole discourse, Is. xl. – lxvi., with the view of determining its meaning in ch. lii. 13 – liii. 12. It has been seen, that in all the passages but one, and most probably in this one, it denotes the people of God, the genuine Israel in distinction from the mere descendants of Jacob. This genuine Israel was called from the very infancy of the nation to be the servant of Jehovah in bearing witness of his existence and perfections to the world. Now from this use of the phrase in other parts of the composition it seems to be an irresistible conclusion, according to the established laws of language, that it must have the same meaning in ch. lii. 13 – liii., unless a decided intimation is given by the writer of a change of meaning. We have no more right to interpret a passage independent of its connection with the composition of which it forms a part, or to give to a phrase a meaning which is not established by its use in other parts of the composition, than we have to make light mean darkness, or darkness light. When, therefore, in lii. 13, the prophet represents the Deity as saying,

> "Behold, my servant shall prosper;
> He shall be lifted up, and set on high, and greatly exalted," —

we are obliged by the use of language, *usus loquendi*, in the passages which have been adduced, to suppose that he refers to the same servant, the same people of God, of which it is said in xlii. 10, "It is a robbed and plundered people," and in xliii. 10, "Ye are my witnesses, and my servant whom I have chosen," and which in xlix. 3 is expressly called "Israel, in whom I will be glorified." This people of God, this better part of the nation, under the guidance of the prophets, was disposed to return from exile, and to incite and prepare the whole nation for a restoration from captivity.

This meaning of the phrase "Servant of God" is not only supported by the writer's use of language, and by the connection of lii. 13–liii. with the preceding and following chapters, but also by several indications in the description of the Servant of God in ch. liii., taken in connection with the circumstances under which the author wrote.

1. The sufferings and persecutions of the Servant of God in this passage are represented as past. It is only his prosperity and glory that are represented as future. Thus:—

> lii. 14. "As many *were* amazed at the sight of him."
> liii. 2. "He *grew* up before him like a tender plant."
> 3. "He *was* despised and forsaken of men."
> 6. "All we like sheep *were* going astray.
> We *turned* every one to his own way;
> But Jehovah laid upon him the iniquity of us all."
> 9. "His grave *was* appointed with the wicked," &c.

On the other hand, the prosperity and glory of the Servant of God are future:—

> lii. 13. "Behold, my servant *shall* prosper," &c.
> 15. "So *shall* he cause many nations to exult," &c.
> liii. 10. "He *shall see* posterity," &c.
> 12. "Therefore *will* I give him his portion," &c.

It is evident, then, that the prophet represents the Servant of God as already existing in a low condition; that his sufferings are present or past, and have been observed by the writer and his contemporaries. The stand-point of the prophet is between the suffering condition of the Servant of God, and his glory. He predicts no sufferings. Here, too, there is no room for the application of the Hebrew idiom, that the prophets, in order to express emphasis or certainty in predictions, sometimes use the present or past tense instead of the future. This will not explain why the sufferings should all be represented as past, and the prosperity and glory as all future. If, then, the Servant of God is represented as actually living in a low condition in the time of the prophet; if his sufferings are represented as present or past, and his prosperity and glory as future; and if what is said of the Servant of God can be applied to no individual in the time of the prophet,—then it follows that it refers to the same people of God, the Jewish church, called his servant in the preceding chapters, who had suffered grievous afflictions and persecutions in the exile at Babylon, and were now to be restored to their native land, exalted to prosperity, and employed as God's instrument for extending the light of religion and love to the nations of the earth.

2. There is one part of the description which shows very conclusively that by the Servant of God is meant not an individual man, but a body of men personified. It is that which represents him as dying and buried, and yet as one who should "see posterity," and "prolong his days," and "have his portion with the mighty," and "divide the spoil with heroes." Here, there can be no reference to a resurrection from death. The connection shows that the writer had no such conception in his mind. He plainly represents the Servant of God as prospering *on earth* after his humiliation and death; as "causing kings to shut their mouths before him"; as having posterity on earth, and dividing the spoil with heroes. Now if the Servant of God denote the people of God, the righteous part of the nation, then some of their number might be represented as dying in Babylon, and thus making their graves with the wicked, while the holy people itself, the organ of God's spirit, the elect agent of his plans, might have an immortal existence, be restored from exile, attain to prosperity and glory, and give light and righteousness to the nations.

3. The most remarkable part of the description of the Servant of God is that in which the unrighteous and irreligious Jews are represented as saying of him: "He bore our diseases and carried our pains"; "he was wounded for our transgressions, and bruised for our iniquities"; "by his stripes we are healed"; "Jehovah hath laid upon him the iniquity of us all"; "he hath made his life a sacrifice for sin," — "bore the sin of many, and was numbered with transgressors." This is certainly very remarkable language, whether relating to an individual or to a body of men. But it is plain that the prophet is speaking of the past, and not of the future. It is to be regretted that we have not a history of the precise condition of the Jews in Babylon during the captivity, so that we might be able to judge how applicable the language above quoted was to the religious and righteous part of the Jewish nation, the elect Israel of God. It is easy to suppose, however, from

the circumstances of the case, from intimations of the writer in other parts of the discourse (l. 4 – 10), and from indications in the Psalms, such as cxxxvii., that the most religious and patriotic Jews in the captivity at Babylon were most ridiculed and oppressed by their Babylonian tyrants; that it was of them that their oppressors demanded to hear "one of the songs of Zion" in a strange land. It is also evident from such passages as lxvi. 5, that many of the captives became indifferent to their native land. Their moral and religious condition may be compared to that of their ancestors, whom Moses led out of Egypt. Such being the case, it would be natural for the prophet to represent the true and righteous servants of God among the exiles, — such as were animated with the spirit of the prophet himself, and labored to inspire a spirit of religion and patriotism in the idolatrous Jews, and were ridiculed for it, and perhaps in some instances suffered martyrdom for it, — it would be natural, I say, for the prophet, by a figure of speech common both in the Old Testament and the New, to represent such righteous servants of God as "bearing the sins" of the idolatrous and indifferent Hebrews, whom they labored and suffered to inspire with the spirit of religion, and with a desire to return to their native land. The more faithful these righteous men were, the more were they ridiculed and persecuted at Babylon. By their peculiar oppressions there can be no doubt that many of them came to an untimely end. At any rate, the whole Jewish nation is represented as punished with captivity on account of their sins; and, of course, the pious and righteous among them suffered, not for their own sins, but for those of the community with which they were connected. It was also for the sake of the righteous servants of God, that he is represented as restoring the nation to their own land. Thus in ch. lxv. 8, 9: —

"Thus saith Jehovah:
As when juice is found in a cluster,
Men say, "Destroy it not, for a blessing is in it";
So will I do, for the sake of my servants, and will not destroy the whole;
I will cause a stem to spring forth from Jacob,
And from Judah a possessor of my mountains;
My chosen shall possess the land,
And my servants shall dwell there."

We also read, that ten righteous men would have been the salvation of Sodom, and that Ezekiel* "bore the iniquity" of the house of Israel. See also Matt. viii. 17. We also read: "I will give Egypt for thy ransom, Ethiopia and Seba for thee. I will give men for thee, and nations for thy life."† In the Arabian Nights Entertainments, as translated by Mr. Lane, we constantly meet such language as "I will be thy ransom," meaning, I will risk my life to save yours. It cannot, therefore, be regarded as an extravagant or very uncommon use of metaphorical language, that the people of God, the righteous part of the Jewish nation, laboring, suffering, and dying in exile, should be represented as "wounded" for the transgressions of others, and "bruised for their iniquities"; as receiving the stripes by which the people were healed, and offering themselves a sacrifice for their deliverance. It is at least certain that this metaphorical language would, in the time of the prophet and his contemporaries, be just as appropriate and intelligible when applied to a body of righteous servants of God, as when applied to an individual. The idea of the literal sacrifice of a single man would have been as abhorrent to the feelings of the prophet as that of the literal sacrifice of a body of men. Thus, from all the considerations which have been adduced, the conclusion is that the humiliation and exaltation of the Servant of God in Is. lii. 13 – liii. 12 denote the humiliation and exaltation of the people of God, the Jewish church, or that part of the Jewish nation which was true to its name and calling.

Having thus given a positive view of what the passage does mean, it is not necessary to examine the various explanations which suppose the Servant of God to denote an individual, whether Jeremiah, Isaiah, Cyrus, or any other. I will only observe, that the Messiah is in no other passage of the Old Testament represented as a sufferer, but only as prosperous and triumphant. It is also to be observed, that, however suitable some parts of the language may be to describe the life, sufferings, and death of Jesus Christ, yet other parts of it cannot be so applied without manifest violence. Thus kings are represented as personally doing homage to the Servant of God, and "shutting their mouths before him." The Servant of God is also represented as having "his grave with the wicked," and yet as "seeing posterity, and dividing the spoil

* Ch. iv.

† Is. xliii. 3, 4.

with the strong." This was not true of Christ in the obvious sense of the writer, and it is not easy to see how it can be true of any individual servant of God. But if the phrase have, as we have explained it, a collective sense, and denote the people of God, then some of its members might die while the community continued to live. Then, as we have before seen, the sufferings of the Servant of God are all represented as past in the time of the writer. How, then, could they be regarded by him as relating to Jesus of Nazareth? The application of the passage to Christ would also require an entire separation of it from its connection with all which precedes and follows it in the discourse contained in Is. xl.-lxvi. Whether the passage may be applied to Christ in the allegorical or double sense, a sense not in the mind of the writer, is another question, which it is not my purpose to discuss. Unconscious types or prefigurations of Christ are to be found in Moses, David, Jeremiah, Socrates, and others. But no more distinct type of the Saviour can be found than the Servant of God as described by the evangelical prophet. The ideas of self-denial and self-sacrifice, and of victory or salvation effected not only in spite of the sufferings and ignominy of the instrument, but by means of them, are set forth with the greatest clearness. It is one of many passages in the Old Testament which sets the seal of condemnation on the elaborate and unqualified contrasts which some of our modern preachers have drawn between Judaism and Christianity. Noon does not follow morning more naturally than Christianity followed the inspired utterances of the unknown Jewish prophet, the greatest, in a religious point of view, of the wonderful succession of the holy men of God who have spoken as they were moved by the Holy Ghost for the instruction of the world.

The opinion that "the Servant of God," in the passage we have been examining, denotes a community, and not an individual, has been maintained with different modifications by the Jewish critics Aben-Ezra, Jarchi, Kimchi, and Abarbanel; also by Rosenmüller, Eichhorn, Dr. Priestley, Seiler, Gesenius, Paulus, Maurer, Knobel, Ewald, Hitzig, and others.

I have thus endeavored to set forth the origin, the nature, and the subject-matter of the Messianic predictions. I have brought forward all the passages of the Old Testament which, in my view, relate to the Messiah, and have examined a considerable number of passages which, by some interpreters, have been supposed to relate to him, but which seem to me to have been misinterpreted or misapplied.

I now come to the subject of the fulfilment of the Messianic predictions, — a subject to which great importance has been attached in the Christian Church, and which has been by some regarded as one of the pillars on which the truth of Christianity rests. On this account I have endeavored to be very careful and thorough in the examination of the Messianic predictions, in order to find out what they are, and what they mean. It appears to me very injurious to Christianity, and promotive of infidelity, to insist upon a kind of proof which will not stand the test of critical examination. Our religion has abundant evidence on which it rests, as on a rock against which the gates of hell can never prevail. The effect of referring young inquirers to a kind of evidence which, in a period of deeper inquiry, may sink beneath their feet, is to impair their confidence in that which is solid and genuine.

It has been a prevalent view, especially among English writers, that the Messianic predictions were designed and promulgated by God through the prophets, for the express purpose of characterizing the person of an extraordinary messenger, whom he was at a future time to raise up for the redemption of the world, so that, when he came, these predictions might constitute a miraculous attestation to his Divine mission. Accordingly, the course of many writers on the evidences of Christianity has been to show in the particular events, actions, and sufferings of the personal life of Jesus such a coincidence with the predictions of the prophets of the Old Testament as proves miraculous foresight in them, such as Omniscience alone could impart or exercise.

On this view two remarks may be made, before, by a review of the life of Jesus, we endeavor to ascertain what the fulfilment of the Messianic predictions by him actually was.

The first remark is, that it is difficult to perceive how the circumstance that an event or act in the life of Jesus corresponds to a prediction of it by a prophet, affords evidence of the Divine mission of the former. If the prediction be beyond human foresight, implying miraculous foreknowledge in the prophet, it is easy to understand how it proves the Divine mission of the predicter; but not how it proves any such thing in regard to the *subject* of the prediction. Suppose, for instance, that King Cyrus or the Pope of Rome was the subject of a miraculous prediction. Such a prediction would not prove the Divine mission of King Cyrus or of the Pope of Rome, but only of the prophet who made the prediction. It is the author, not the subject, of a miraculous prediction, who is shown to have had special intercourse with Heaven. Suppose that any Hebrew prophet had predicted any miracle of Jesus, such as the resurrection of Lazarus from the dead. Who does not see that it is only the resurrection of Lazarus itself by the instrumentality of Jesus, that proves anything concerning his relations to the Deity? The prediction of the event would only prove the miraculous knowledge of the ancient prophet.

My second remark is, that it appears from a general survey of the Messianic predictions in the Old Testament, that they are in their very nature *subjective*, not *objective*, so far at least as the prophetic writers are concerned. These predictions are indefinite, general, and, in some degree, various. The prophets, in writing them, could not have supposed that they had foresight of the particular actions or events in the life of an historical person. The whole aspect and purport of their predictions show that what they did was to predict that a glorious state of things would be brought about by such instrumentalities as they, in their circumstances, would naturally conceive to be the most effectual for the purpose. A king, a descendant of David, who would of course be born in Bethlehem, would be such an instrumentality in the time of Isaiah or Micah. To another prophet, writing near the close of the exile in Babylon, the Jewish church collectively, or the righteous part of the nation, rather than a single individual, might appear to be the instrumentality for the same purpose. To Malachi a single prophet of transcendent powers might seem to be the great deliverer. If, then, the instrumentalities for affecting the glorious condition of the Jewish nation and the world might be various, and represent only the subjective views of the prophets, — if the prophets themselves never supposed that they had objective foresight of the actions or events in the life of any future historical person, — then it follows of course that no historical person could have fulfilled their predictions in the sense which many have maintained; namely, that of performing particular acts, and experiencing particular events, whether joyous or afflictive, which had been miraculously foreseen. The prophets never imagined that they had any such objective foresight, independent of natural indications. This appears, as has been said, from an examination of their predictions themselves, independently of any comparison of them with the actions and life of Jesus. Their predictions were subjective, not objective. Whether the Deity himself, who raised up the prophets, may have had an historical person in view, to which their subjective predictions tended or pointed, is another question, — a question which cannot be decided by any rules of interpretation. The mind of the prophets alone can be ascertained by the interpretation of language. I can see no objection to the supposition that it was revealed to the mind of Christ that he was the instrument for accomplishing the great moral and religious purposes of God which the prophets had unfolded.

With these preliminary remarks, we come to the question in what sense and in what degree Christ himself claimed to fulfil their predictions, and especially their predictions relating to the kingdom of God. For it is a truth which can neither be doubted nor denied, that Jesus connected the whole plan of his mission and ministry with the predictions of the prophets. He claimed to fulfil in some sense their predictions, and especially their predictions relating to the kingdom of God. He claimed to be a king, the head of the kingdom which the prophets had predicted as about to be established in the world.

Now, in order to perceive in what sense and in what degree Jesus claimed to fulfil the Messianic predictions, it is necessary to call in mind the threefold classification of them which we have before considered: — 1. Those exclusively religious and moral in their nature. 2. Those in which a political element was mingled. 3. Those which relate to the instrumentality by which the things predicted were to be effected.

It has been shown in relation to the first class of predictions that the Hebrew prophets, trusting in the power of truth and in the promises made by God to the fathers of their nation, had expressed the confident expectation, that is, had predicted, that the time would come when the kingdom of God would be universally established on earth; when the Supreme Being, who in their time was known and worshipped only in Israel, would be known and worshipped by all nations; when all men would feel and acknowledge their obligation to govern their lives by his will; when the moral and religious knowledge already established in Israel by the Divine Spirit would be greatly increased there, and also be diffused throughout the world; when the light of truth, proceeding from Israel, should enlighten the whole human race.

Now we know from the New Testament that it was these moral and religious predictions alone which Jesus regarded himself as sent from the Father to accomplish in their literal sense. The design of his mission, as set forth by him, was strictly a moral and religious design. When, therefore, he claimed to be the Messiah, and to fulfil the predictions of the prophets relating to the Messiah, his meaning must have been, that he was the instrument, raised up and sent by God, to accomplish the moral and religious predictions of the prophets. That he was this instrument he knew by the revelation of the spirit of God in his own soul. To others he gave evidence of it in various ways. In claiming to be the Messiah, it could not have been the meaning of Jesus, that he was the identical historical person, performing the same historical acts, meeting with the same incidents, suffering the same identical trials, which the prophets foresaw; because, as we have seen, the prophets never had, nor pretended to have, any such foresight of an historical individual. It is amply sufficient to justify the claim of Jesus to be the Messiah, to be "him of whom Moses in the law and the prophets did write," if he was appointed by God to bless all the families of the earth by accomplishing the predictions of the prophets respecting the extension of the knowledge of God and of his laws. The political element in the predictions of the prophets Jesus could not regard himself as called by God to fulfil, or believe that he fulfilled, in a literal sense, but only in an analogous and higher sense. That the prophets had connected a political element with their predictions of the regeneration of the

Jewish nation and the world, Jesus regarded as evidence of their imperfection, when compared with the humblest Christian.* He never doubted or denied that they had cherished expectations of such an outward political kingdom. He felt that it was his mission to fulfil the essential moral and religious expectations of the prophets, separated from whatever was outward and political in them.

The evidence of the preceding statements is to be found, first, in what we know of the design and plan of Jesus, and secondly, in some of his particular declarations.

I. The design and plan of Jesus were moral, spiritual, and universal. His object was to diffuse the knowledge of God and of duty to the whole human race, and not to effect any political object relating to the Jewish nation or to himself. He asserts that the great design of his manifestation was to bear witness to the truth. "For this end was I born, and for this end have I come to the world, to bear witness to the truth. Every one who is of the truth listens to my voice," † — i. e. obeys me, or is my subject. "This is life eternal, that they may know thee, the only true God, and Jesus Christ whom thou hast sent." ‡ "I have made known thy name to the men whom thou hast given me out of the world." "I have made known to them thy name, and will make it known." § In John viii. 12, he calls himself the light of the world, which is come that no one might remain in darkness, but have the light of life; and in xii. 46, "I have come a light into the world, that whosoever believeth in me may not abide in darkness." But it is scarcely necessary to bring an array of passages to show, what all the discourses of Jesus, from the Sermon on the Mount to the last words which he uttered, fully prove, that his plan was purely of a moral and spiritual nature. All attempts to show that, at any period of his life, he had a different one, have proved futile and vain. The universality of this plan or aim is equally manifest. He embraced in it the whole family of man. In addition to the passages already quoted from John, we find in Luke xxiv. 47, "that repentance and forgiveness of sins should be proclaimed in his name among all the nations";

* See Matt xi. 1 – 11.

† John xviii. 37.

‡ John xvii. 3.

§ Ib. xvii. 6, 26.

and in Matt. xxiv. 14, "And this gospel of the kingdom shall be proclaimed in all the world for a witness to all the nations"; and in xxvi. 13, "wherever this gospel shall be proclaimed in the whole world"; and in Mark xvi. 15, "Go ye into all the world, and proclaim the gospel to the whole creation."

If, then, the plan of Jesus was purely moral and religious, and also universal, then it is manifest that he neither could, nor supposed that he could, accomplish in the strict and proper sense any of the predictions of the prophets except those which were moral and religious in their nature, and related to all mankind. He could not, in a literal sense, accomplish those which predicted a happy and glorious political condition of the Jewish nation under the Messiah as an earthly king. In these expectations he must have regarded the prophets as being in error. This is evident, not only from what has been stated respecting the purely spiritual design of his mission, but also from clear intimations of his own, especially in Matt. xi., where we find him casting a degree of disparagement upon John the Baptist, and making him less than the least under the Christian dispensation. It is evident from the connection, that the cause of his disparaging John was, that the latter, as a Jewish prophet, regarded the kingdom of God as in part a political kingdom,* and the Messiah as a political king, who was to found his kingdom as much by an outward triumph over his foes as by moral influence. And yet Jesus with emphasis pronounces John to be the greatest of all the prophets of the Jewish dispensation. How plainly does his language concerning John show in what light he regarded the predictions of the more ancient and less illumined prophets! How plain is it, that he regarded them as entertaining imperfect and erroneous conceptions of the nature of his kingdom! And if this be so, how plain is it that he did not regard their predictions as arising from miraculous foresight of the events of his life! For if they had had such miraculous objective foresight, they could not have mistaken a private man who had not where to lay his head for a glorious and triumphant temporal king. I regard this passage in Matthew as highly important as a proof of the light in which Jesus regarded the predictions of the prophets.

* So Neander in his Life of Christ, § 135. So also Lightfoot, Meyer and De Wette, *ad loc.*

Let us now, in contrast with what has been maintained to be the moral, religious, and universal plan of Jesus, suppose, for the sake of illustrating the subject, that the prophets, in order to give characteristics by which the men of future times might know the Messiah, had delineated the actual personal history of Jesus; and that he had believed it to be the design, or even one design, of his ministry to act it out. Who cannot perceive that the tendency of such an impression on his mind would have been to produce a formal, imitative, artificial, unoriginal character, inferior to that of the prophets themselves, and as different as possible from what we know the character of Christ to have been? Some have supposed that Jesus rode into Jerusalem on an ass in order by that particular act to fulfil a prediction of the prophets relating to himself personally. Who could not do such an outward thing as that? And what sort of character would a man acquire who should regard it as the mission of his life to do things of that kind in conformity with a prescribed program?

It appears, then, from what we know of the design and plan of Jesus, as well as from some more particular intimations, that when he claimed to fulfil the predictions of the prophets, or of the Old Testament, his meaning was that he was the instrument raised up by God to accomplish their moral and religious predictions relating to the extension and establishment of the knowledge of God and his laws in the world, and to the establishment of a religious community. This is all which Jesus could design to fulfil in the sense of literal accomplishment.

II. But did not Jesus claim to fulfil predictions of another description? Did he not claim to be the founder of a kingdom, and to be a king, — a greater king than David? Did he not claim to found such a kingdom, and to be such a Messiah, as should fulfil the predictions of the prophets in which the political element predominates? Certainly he did. But it by no means follows that he undertook to fulfil them in a literal sense, or in the sense which the prophets attached to their language. Their temporal and political expectations relating to their nation and to the Messiah he well knew; but as they did not harmonize with his moral and religious plan, he could not realize them in the sense in which the prophets cherished and expressed them. He must, in order to be consistent, have regarded the national and political predictions of the prophets as containing a portion of imperfection and error. For they had predicted, as we have seen, a state of pre-eminent glory and felicity for their nation under the Messianic king. The germ of essential and universal truth which was included in these predictions, and which harmonized with his moral and religious plan, that he undertook to realize and perfect. This germ was the fundamental idea of theocratic government; the idea that Jehovah was to be their Supreme Ruler, and that all nations would in fellowship with Israel be subject to his dominion, and serve him as the only God. Jesus had only to remove from the theocratic predictions of the prophets their partial, exclusive, political element, to bring them into harmony with his spiritual and universal plan.

Thus, in a certain sense of the word "fulfilment," a sense recognized in the Gospels, and found in the dictionaries, Jesus could regard himself as fulfilling the political theocratic predictions of the prophets, as well as those which were purely moral and religious. In one sense of the word "fulfil," it means to perfect that which is incomplete, to supply something better in place of that which is imperfect, to fill up that which is deficient. Thus our Saviour says, Matt. v. 17: "Think not that I came to destroy the law or the prophets; I came not to destroy, but to fulfil." It may be that he refers here only to the preceptive part both of the prophets and the law. How, then, did he fulfil the preceptive part of the Law and the Prophets? Not certainly by re-enacting and enforcing the identical precepts contained in the Old Testament, but rather by giving higher, broader, and more spiritual precepts in their place; i. e. by completing and perfecting the morality of the ancient times, — by giving a system which would accomplish the end which the Law and the Prophets aimed at.

Now in the same sense of the word "fulfil" Jesus might claim to fulfil the national theocratic predictions of the prophets; namely, by effecting something analogous to what these imported, but more comprehensive, higher, and better. This he undertook to do by excluding from them what was political, partial, and national, as belonging to the imperfect and erroneous conceptions of the prophets, and by retaining only the idea of the reign of Jehovah over the whole human race and over the human heart, which was the most essential element in those predictions. By establishing the kingdom of God, the empire of truth and duty, of moral and religious principle, the worship of the Father in spirit and in truth, not in Jerusalem or Gerizim only, but throughout the earth, — not by long journeys, a splendid temple, and pompous rites, but in spirit and in truth, — our Saviour conceived that he was fulfilling even the theocratic predictions of the prophets. This was a fulfilment, not because it was in all respects the very thing which the prophets had predicted, but something purer, more comprehensive, higher, and better. His enemies might accuse him of destroying the prophets by regarding the outward political element in their predictions as imperfect and erroneous. He says that by so doing he was not destroying, but fulfilling.

I will, on account of the importance of the subject, go into some particulars for the sake of illustration, though at the risk of repetition.

1. The prophets had predicted that Jehovah would deliver his people from the yoke of political slavery, and from the temporal misery which had been brought upon them by victorious foreign enemies. Jesus claimed to fulfil this prediction by accomplishing a higher, better, and wider deliverance than the prophets had fully conceived. He found the whole Jewish and heathen world under the dominion of error and sin, slaves in a religious and moral sense, and claimed to be commissioned by God to redeem them from this condition. Thus John iii. 17: "For God sent not his Son into the world to condemn the world, but that the world through him might be saved." John viii. 34-36: "Jesus answered, Whoso committeth sin is a servant of sin. And the servant abideth not in the house forever; but the Son abideth forever. If the Son, therefore, shall make you free, ye shall be free indeed." It seems to be the very design of Christ in this last verse, to contrast the freedom which he promised with that which the prophets had predicted. He fulfilled their predictions of political freedom, not by the offer of the thing itself, but of something higher and better, — of moral freedom, freedom from sin.

2. The prophets had predicted that Jehovah would again be

reconciled with his penitent and reformed people of the Jewish nation; that he would dwell in the midst of them, and never more forsake them; that he would be their God, and that they should be his people. Jesus undertook to fulfil this prediction in a higher and more comprehensive sense than had entered the minds of the prophets. He found the whole world in a state of alienation from God by sin, and regarded it as his mission to bring them back to their offended sovereign, — to bring them into an intimate relation to him, making them sons of God, looking to him with confidence as a father. "But as many as received him, to them gave he power to become sons of God, even to them that believe on his name; who were born, not of blood, nor of the will of the flesh, nor of the will of man, but of God." (John i. 12, 13.) "That they all may be one; as thou, Father, art in me, and I in thee, that they also may be one in us." (John xvii. 21.)

3. The prophets had predicted that, when Jehovah had redeemed his people from their oppressions and reconciled them to himself, he would confer upon them great temporal felicity. Jesus fulfilled this prediction by giving his followers, not the very thing predicted, but something higher and better than temporal felicity; — a blessedness which may be enjoyed by the poor, by the weak, by the persecuted; a participation in the kingdom of heaven through spiritual fellowship with God in this world, which would be the foretaste and pledge of endless blessedness with him in heaven. "Peace I leave with you, my peace I give unto you; not as the world giveth, give I unto you." (John xiv. 27.)

4. Finally, the prophets had predicted the restoration of the Jewish nation to a flourishing condition as a state, and its continuance in imperishable splendor among the nations of the earth. How far Jesus was from fulfilling, or designing to fulfil, this prediction according to the conceptions of the prophets themselves, is plain from the fact that he came predicting the destruction, and not the glory, of the Jewish nation. But in one sense of the term "fulfil," to which we have referred, Jesus fulfilled even this prediction. He fulfilled it by establishing something higher and better, — by founding a spiritual community inwardly united by a common faith and by fraternal love, existing in imperfection in this world, but attaining to perfection in the world to come. Men

cannot observe its rise and its progress as those of an outward empire; for it has its seat in the inward life. "The kingdom of God cometh not with observation; neither shall they say, Lo here! or, Lo there! for, behold, the kingdom of God is within you." (Luke xvii. 20, 21.) But a sign of its presence is the conflict with evil. "But if I cast out demons by the spirit of God, then is the kingdom of God already come to you." (Matt. xii. 28.) It has no political objects; for it is not of this world. "My kingdom is not of this world: if my kingdom were of this world, then would my servants fight that I should not be delivered to the Jews; but now is my kingdom not from hence." (John xviii. 36.) In this spiritual community of Christ there are no distinctions of rank, as in political communities. "Ye know that the princes of the Gentiles exercise dominion over them, and they that are great exercise authority upon them. But it shall not be so among you; but whosoever will be great among you, let him be your minister; and whosoever will be chief among you, let him be your servant." What is outward, relating to time, place, and form, is unimportant. A pious, devoted heart is everything. "The true worshippers shall worship the Father in spirit and in truth." (John iv. 23.) The members of this community are they who come to God and to his Son, and remain true to them in heart and life, whether on earth or in heaven. It is destined to be, not only an eternal, but a universal kingdom. Religious and moral truth shall draw to it one after another, till at last it shall bring all under its dominion. "The kingdom of heaven is like to a grain of mustard-seed, which a man took and sowed in his field: which is the least indeed of all seeds; but when it is grown, it is the greatest among herbs, and becometh a tree, so that the birds of the air come and lodge in its branches." (Matt. xiii. 31, 32.)

To denote this invisible spiritual community, Jesus uses the old theocratic expression, "kingdom of God," or "kingdom of heaven," though he represents it not as a nation, but as a family of God. Jehovah, as the head of the old outward theocracy, was called king. At the head of the new community of Christ he is called father. The members of the old theocracy were subjects or servants; those of the new Christian community were sons of God. The religious bond between God and the old theocracy was the fear of Jehovah; that between him and the community of Christ is childlike faith; the chief duty in the one is righteousness; in the other, love. Thus, under Christ, the fulfiller of the old theocracy, every family in heaven and earth is united to one common Father by faith, and held together by one common bond of love.

Thus, in general and in various particulars it has been shown how Jesus fulfilled the theocratic, as well as the moral and religious expectations of the prophets. He aimed to realize the essential fundamental ideas which were shrouded in their imperfect, erroneous, partial, political conceptions, by introducing into the world something having a certain analogy to them, but higher, more spiritual, and more comprehensive. Thus it was that Jesus came not to destroy, but to fulfil, the prophets.

I now come to the third class of the Messianic predictions, namely, those relating to the theocratic king himself. Though the explanation of these is essentially the same as that of the last class, there is an advantage in examining those relating to the Messiah himself separately, on account of the passages in the New Testament which belong to the subject. The object is to explain in what sense Jesus claimed to fulfil in his own person the predictions of the prophets relating to the theocratic king of the Jewish nation, the Messiah.

What those predictions were, we have seen. We have found that, according to nearly all the prophets, the Messiah was not only to be filled with the spirit of God, and qualified to extend the knowledge of Jehovah in the world, but also to be a wise and mighty temporal king of the house of David, who would exalt the Jewish nation to a high degree of prosperity and glory. He was not only to establish and extend the kingdom of God among men, and cause truth and righteousness to prevail under his influence, but he was to do it as a wise, virtuous, mighty, and victorious temporal king. We have found, by an examination of all the passages relating to the Messiah in the Old Testament, that they admitted of no other interpretation. We have also been unable to find any passage in which an individual Messiah was represented by any Hebrew prophet as in a low condition, or as suffering and dying. This ought to be admitted as the sure result of scientific criticism, whatever bearing it may have on New Testament interpretation.

Still Jesus claimed to be the Messiah virtually and by intimation in the beginning of his ministry, and more fully and explicitly in a subsequent part of it. In Matt. xvi. 17, he gives high commendation to Peter for his declaration, " Thou art the Christ, the son of the living God" ; and affirms that it was revealed to him not by flesh and blood, but by his father in heaven. In ch. xxvi. 63, Pilate adjures him by the living God to say whether he was the Christ, and his answer under oath is, " I am." So in ch. xxvii. 11, in answer to the question of Pilate, " Art thou the King of the Jews?" he replies, "I am." So in the Gospel of John he is represented as solemnly affirming the same thing to the woman of Samaria (iv. 26) ; to the blind man, who was restored to sight (ix. 37, &c.) ; and to Pilate (xviii. 37).

It is equally plain in what sense Jesus claimed to be a king and to be the Messiah. He did not claim to be the Messianic king in the outward, partial, political sense of the term, as the prophets anticipated and his countrymen expected. He advised his countrymen to pay tribute to Cæsar. (Matt. xxii. 21.) He refuses to decide a controversy relating to property, saying, " Who made me a ruler or a divider over you?" (Luke xii. 14.) He withdraws into retirement, when the people would compel him to be king. (John vi. 15.) He affirms expressly that his kingdom is not of this world ; by which he evidently means to deny, not that this world is the place where his kingdom is to exist, but only that his kingdom is of the same nature with the kingdoms of this world. What is specially to be noted is, that Jesus expects to accomplish his plan and the great purposes of his mission, not by wealth, by armies, by victories, but by poverty, by desertion, by martyrdom, and above all, by the destruction of the Jewish nation rather than by its political pre-eminence. How could he have thought of raising the Jews as a nation to the prosperity and glory predicted by the prophets, when in so emphatic a manner he himself predicted the destruction of Jerusalem and the temple as a means of establishing his kingdom? (Matt. xxiv. ; Luke xix. 43, 44.)

So much for denial. He also states positively in what sense he does claim to be a king ; namely, as a source of moral and religious influence, as an authoritative teacher of the truth, an authorized expounder of the laws according to which the retributions of eternity will be determined. The community of which he is king by spiritual influence alone is one the members of which receive him as the source of life and peace by genuine faith, as they are drawn to him by the Father, and who feel bound to each other only by the cords of love. The most explicit passage to this effect is that in John xviii. 37. Pilate says to him, "Art thou a king then?" Jesus answered, "Yes, I am a king; for this end was I born, and for this end came I into the world, that I might bear witness to the truth. Every one who is of the truth listens to my voice," or "is my subject." All the regard which Jesus claims is of a moral and religious nature. He claims to be Lord of the sabbath (Matt. xii. 8). He is greater than the temple (Matt. xii. 6), and reforms it (John ii. 16). He releases his disciples from the obligation of stated fasts (Matt. ix. 14-16). He asserts his right to forgive sins (Matt. ix. 6). All his discourses are of a moral and religious nature. When he speaks of coming in his kingdom, i. e. coming to reign at a future time, before some of his contemporaries should taste of death (Matt. xvi. 27, 28, xxiv. 31), it is not with human forces, or the parade of earthly grandeur, but in the glory of his Father and with the holy angels. Whatever may be the meaning of his coming in his kingdom after his resurrection and ascension, all must admit that it was not as an earthly, victorious king, conquering by means of mighty armies and polished weapons, as the Hebrew prophets supposed the Messiah would come.

If, then, Jesus claimed to be a king both on earth and in heaven only by spiritual influence, by being "anointed with the holy spirit and with power," having no helper but the spirit of the Almighty, how could he suppose that he fulfilled the predictions of the prophets respecting an outward Messianic king? If the Jewish prophets predicted a temporal Messiah, how could Jesus suppose that he was fulfilling their predictions?

The answer to this question makes some repetition necessary, but not, I hope, without adding light to the subject. I say, then, that Jesus claimed to be the predicted Messiah for more reasons than one.

I. Because the Messiah of the prophets was to be not *merely* a temporal king, but also the minister of Jehovah for promoting the cause of religion and righteousness, and for extending the knowledge of him and his laws, not only among the Jews, but to the ends of the earth. Jesus could thus connect his mission and plan with the moral and religious part of the office of the predicted Messianic king. He could feel himself inspired and commissioned by the Almighty to accomplish the moral and religious part of the office of the Messiah, while he regarded the outward and earthly royalty, with which the prophets invested him, as belonging to their imperfect and erroneous conceptions. In being God's minister for regenerating the world by extending the knowledge of God and his laws, he believed that he was fulfilling all that was essential in the predictions concerning the Messiah. With him the inward, the spiritual, the eternal, was everything; the outward, the gross, the temporal, comparatively nothing. The Jews, the contemporaries of our Saviour, with their low and selfish views, fixed their minds almost exclusively on the outward temporal grandeur with which the prophets had invested the Messiah, and on the temporal deliverance and exaltation of their nation, which they believed that he would effect. Jesus, on the contrary, regarded a spiritual dominion in the world, the governing of mankind by the moral and spiritual power of his religion, the bestowal of the privileges of sons of God on *all* who should believe in his name, the admission to the vision of God of all the pure in heart, as the fulfilment of all that was of much consequence in the offices ascribed by the ancient prophets of his nation to the Messiah. Thus it was that Jesus claimed to be the Messiah, in the first place, because it was revealed to his mind by the spirit of God that he was qualified and commissioned to accomplish the purely moral and religious work assigned by the prophets of the Old Testament to the Messianic king.

II. In regard to our Saviour's claim to be a king, as predicted by the prophets, we must call to mind the second sense of the term "fulfil"; namely, to supply that which is defective, to complete that which is imperfect, to elevate that which is low. Jesus, then, claimed to be a king, because he sustained an office *analogous* to the kingly office which the prophets predicted, but higher, more spiritual, and more comprehensive, answering to the fundamental Divine idea of royalty, namely, influence over the minds of men. Dominion over the mind and spirit is analogous in the effects produced by it to dominion by means of outward displays of power. But it is of a higher, more comprehensive, and more permanent character. Jesus, by bearing witness to the truth, by drawing all men to him by the powerful influence of being lifted up on the cross, by casting out the prince of this world through a religion established by self-denial and death, by vanquishing evil through the Comforter or Helper which was to come in his name after his death, by being the authoritative promulgator and expounder of the laws of Divine retribution and Divine acceptance, felt that he sat upon a far higher throne than that of David, — that he was a king analogous to the reputed ancestor of the Messiah, but with a more real, more beneficent, more extensive, and more lasting dominion. He might thus claim to be the Messiah, though he had not been the subject of objective or miraculous prediction. He was *the Anointed*, — "anointed with the holy spirit and with power" to accomplish the best purposes which the prophets supposed would be accomplished by the Messiah, though he came not arrayed in robes of royalty as their imaginations had represented him; though his religion was established in the world by the destruction, rather than by the prosperity and glory, of the Jewish nation; and though he completed his work by martyrdom and not by victory. It was this spiritual conception of the Messiah which Jesus designed to awaken in the minds of the Jews in the conversation recorded in Matt. xxii. 41 – 44.*

In accordance with these views, it is remarked by one whose writings are held in high estimation among Christians of nearly every denomination, the learned and truthful Neander: "The fulfilment of prophecy in the manifestation and labors of Christ necessarily involved the destruction of the prophetic veil and covering of the Messianic idea." † And again: "The fact that Christ places the Baptist *above* the prophets, who were the very culmi-

* See an exposition of this passage in the Christian Examiner for January, 1836, p. 277.

† Life of Christ, § 56.

nating point of the old covenant, and yet so far *below* the members of the new development of the kingdom, exhibits in the most striking way possible his view of the distance between the Old preparatory Testament and the New. The authority of Christ himself, therefore, is contradicted by those who expect to find the truth revealed by him already developed in the Old Testament. If in John we are to distinguish the fundamental truth which he held, and which pointed to the New Testament, from the limited and sensuous form in which he held it, much more, according to Christ's words, are we bound to do this in the Old Testament generally, and in its Messianic elements especially." *

If these views be correct, the question arises, With what views did our Saviour refer to the predictions of the Old Testament with so much emphasis and frequency as a confirmation of his mission, and as testifying of him.

The answer is, Because such a reference to the prophetic writings presented, to all who acknowledged their authority, though not miraculous *evidence*, yet a strong *argument* in favor of Christianity, — an argument drawn from resemblance and analogy, and the completion of the Divine purposes, intimated and begun to be completed in the ancient dispensation. The Jews charged Christ with opposition to Moses and the prophets, and even with blasphemy against God, in the claims which he made. "We know," said they, "that God spake to Moses, but as for this man, we know not whence he is." (John ix. 29.) This supposed opposition to Moses and the prophets by our Saviour was the main thing which led the Jews to reject and crucify him. It was, therefore, very much to the purpose of Jesus to show that in all essential respects there was a perfect harmony between him and Moses and the prophets; that in regard to the essential designs and plans of God as intimated in the Old Testament, — in regard to the end of the law and the principal object for which the prophets were raised up, — he came not to destroy, but to fulfil; to accomplish some things foreseen by the prophets, and to fill out, develop, and perfect what was imperfect and gross in their conceptions. We at the present day regard it as a strong argument in favor of Christianity, when we show that its truths are

* Life of Christ, § 135.

analogous to the light of reason, — to all that we can discover in the elder Scripture writ by God's own hand. In the same way Jesus exhibited a strong argument to the Jews in all those resemblances and analogies which he found between his religion and that of Moses, and in all that accomplishment of the purposes of God by the extension of the knowledge of him and of his laws which he effected by his mission, his life, and his death. It may be regarded as one design of the appearance of Moses and Elijah conversing with our Saviour in his transfiguration, if it be a real transaction, to show that there was a perfect harmony between him and the two most venerated prophets of the ancient dispensation, and that he came to complete the work which they had begun. So we find frequent references made by Christ to passages which are not predictions but only records of facts, on account of the analogy which such facts bore to his life and death. Thus he is the living bread,* and not the manna which could not save from death; his blood is that of the new covenant, as the old was ratified by blood; he was to be lifted up on the cross, † as Moses lifted up the serpent in the wilderness upon a pole; he was to be betrayed by a sharer of his table, even as an ancient servant of God complained, "My familiar friend in whom I trusted, who did eat of my bread, he hath lifted up his heel against me." ‡ Such analogies and comparisons were adapted to recommend his religion to thoughtful Jews.

Still more might he expect to recommend his religion and his moral precepts to the Jews, when he showed that a great extension of the knowledge of God and his laws had been predicted by the prophets of the Old Testament, which it was his mission to effect; and when he maintained that, by the establishment of the empire of truth and duty in the hearts of men, he fulfilled the essential, the Divine idea even of the theocratic predictions of the prophets. "He thus," in the language of Neander, "distinguished the kernel from the perishable shell, the Divine idea from its temporary veil, the truth which lay in germ in the Old Testament from the contracted form in which it presented itself to Old Testament minds."

We thus see that our Saviour's appeals to the Old Testament

* John vi. 32. † John iii. 14. ‡ Ps. xli. 9; John xiii. 18.

presented to all who acknowledged its authority an argument in favor of his religion, — an argument from analogy, and the fulfilment of the Divine purposes and plans, — an argument which does not depend on the prophet's miraculous foresight of contingent circumstances and events. Christ thus engrafted his religion on that of the Old Testament, and the new covenant was the fulfilment of the old, but not in the technical sense which some have maintained.

The ministry of the prophets was confined to their own nation. They were the immediate messengers of Jehovah to Israel. But God in his providence had appointed for them a work of greater comprehension than that for which they consciously labored. They were to be the pioneers to prepare the way for a wider and nobler kingdom of God than that which they aimed to establish over Israel, — a kingdom which was to include the whole of humanity. That strong sense of the relation of the sons of Israel to God, which they aimed to strengthen in their own nation, was one day to be established between God and all souls. The greatest of the prophets, the fulfiller of the prophetic institution, he who came not to destroy but to perfect, was to establish in the faith and life of mankind the prophetic ideal of the kingdom of God, extended, purified, elevated, and spiritualized, and thus accomplish for the whole world what the prophets sought to accomplish for the Jewish nation.

These holy men of old, then, rise in dignity when we regard them as in a measure, what John the Baptist was by way of eminence, the forerunners of Jesus, and pioneers of the universal kingdom of God. One has only to leave out of the prophetic dispensation what is national, outward, and particular, and retain the purely religious ideas belonging to it in their general truth and significance, in order to regard them in this light, and to assign them an important part in the history and advancement of the religion of the Mediator of the new covenant.

An examination of all the instances in the New Testament in which the writers have been supposed to cite, or to represent Christ as citing, passages from the Old Testament as fulfilled in a more special sense than is here supposed allowable, or in a typical or allegorical sense, would carry us too far into the province of

New Testament interpretation, and require far more space than is consistent with the limits of this already extended Introduction. I have no doubt that the writers of the New Testament, agreeably to the hermeneutical logic of their age, interpreted the Old Testament allegorically. It is possible that our Saviour did the same. But it is also possible that he may have risen above his contemporaries in this respect, as he did in respect to all the essential principles of religion and morals. It is doubtful whether any clear and decided instance of allegorical interpretation occurs in his discourses, even as they are handed down to us by allegorical interpreters. It cannot, at any rate, be shown that an exact knowledge of historical or exegetical criticism was more essential to the mission of Christ as the light and life of men, than a knowledge of mathematics, of astronomy, or geology. Of course the arguments of the Apostles had weight with those who agreed with the writers in the validity of their mode of interpretation. But such arguments can have no weight as miraculous evidence with those who regard the historico-grammatical as the only true interpretation, or who insist that the Bible is to be interpreted as having a single sense, on the same principles as all other books.

It is not my purpose to discuss the validity of allegorical interpretation. I will only make two remarks in relation to it.

I. If the New Testament writers did find an allegorical sense in the Old Testament, — a sense confessedly not in the minds of the prophets, — such a fact would not affect our interpretation of the prophetic writings. For the meaning which was in the mind of the prophets must be at least the foundation on which any other sense, if there be any other, must rest. I have undertaken to give only the sense of the writings of the prophets as it existed in their minds, and must have been understood by their contemporaries. If there were in the words of the prophet a sense of which he himself was unconscious, and which existed only in the mind of the Omniscient, still the prophet's own conceptions would be as limited, imperfect, and fallible as they have been represented to be. The allegorical sense, not being known to the prophet himself, but only to God, could be known by a modern reader only through an immediate subsequent Divine revelation to his own soul. For instance, if the brazen serpent, or the miraculous manna, or the water brought by Moses from the rock of Horeb, or the paschal lamb, or the sin-offering, were expressly designed by the Deity to be actual predictions of Christ, still no one can maintain that Moses and his contemporaries regarded the brazen serpent as anything more than a means of effecting a cure of the body, or the manna and the water as more than means for satisfying hunger and thirst. Our Saviour himself says, "Moses gave you not the bread from heaven." * So the paschal lamb and the sin-offering could not have been regarded by Moses and his contemporaries as denoting the future sacrifice of a man. Such an idea would have filled their minds with horror. The typical sense of Old Testament facts could, then, be of no use to the writers and their contemporaries. The same remarks apply to the allegorical sense of predictions. It was useless to those who lived at the time when they were made.

II. The typical sense of Old Testament facts, and the allegorical sense of predictions, can be of little use to those who live after Christ has come. Certainly it cannot be *evidence* for a revelation from God. For it requires an immediate revelation from God to tell us what the allegorical sense is. But after we are satisfied that we have an immediate revelation from God in the teachings of Christ, what need have we of the allegorical sense of the Old Testament as evidence of that revelation? It is nothing but a sophism, a vicious arguing in a circle, first to adduce the Christian revelation as evidence of the allegorical sense, and then adduce the allegorical sense to prove the reality of the Christian revelation. Is it not strictly true, then, that so far as the evidences of Christianity are concerned, before the Christian revelation was made, the typical or allegorical sense was useless, and that after it was made it was needless? Allegorical interpretation takes away infallible authority from the Scriptures as completely as rationalistic.

It is not necessary to deny, however, that believing pious Christians may find pleasure, or even edification, from what is called the typical or allegorical sense of the Old Testament. But it is probable that the pleasure and edification are derived from the resemblance and analogy which exist between the Old Testament and

* John vi. 32.

the New, and the gradual development and fulfilment of the Divine purposes, which were brought to their consummation in Christ. This is without doubt a pleasing subject of contemplation. Still, however, the typical and allegorical sense cannot, even if real, be very important even as a means of edification to the believing Christian. After we have obtained Christ himself, the substance in place of the shadow, the true bread, the living water, the sacrifice which can take away sin, and are in the actual possession and enjoyment of "the good things to come," we cannot expect to gain much by going back to the types and symbols of an earlier age. "Moses gave you not the bread from heaven. But my Father giveth you the true bread from heaven." "Among those that are born of women there hath not arisen a greater than John the Baptist; but he that is least in the kingdom of heaven is greater than he."

In illustrating the subject of prophecy in this Introduction, I have derived considerable aid from Knobel's *Der Prophetismus der Hebräer*, Breslau, 1837. In my notes on the Prophets it has been my principal aim to explain their language. To illustrate their utterances by an exposition of the historical circumstances from which each of them received its character, on the model of the admirable commentary of Gesenius on Isaiah, would have required a work of much greater size. In connection with the historical parts of the Old Testament, and the well-known Antiquities of Josephus, the History of the Jews by Dean Milman, relating to the times in which the prophets lived and wrote, though not sufficiently full, is a good book of reference. Dr. Davidson's Introduction to the Old Testament contains a good deal of Jewish history, and ought to be in the possession of every Biblical student. It contains a condensed statement of the views of nearly all the distinguished theologians of Germany who have written on the Old Testament, in connection with his own opinions of the various subjects which are discussed. The treatise on Inspiration by Tholuck, a translation of which may be found in my Collection of Theological Essays, will well repay perusal.

CAMBRIDGE, June 13, 1865.

NOTE TO THE INTRODUCTION.

(See p. viii.)

I AM glad to be able to quote in support of this view the authority of one who has so enviable a reputation, wherever the English language is spoken, as Dr. Arnold of Rugby.

"It is an unwarranted interpretation of the term Inspiration, to suppose that it is equivalent to a communication of the Divine perfections. Surely many of our words and many of our actions are done by the inspiration of God's Spirit, without whom we can do nothing acceptable to God. Yet does the Holy Spirit so inspire us as to communicate to us his own perfections? Are our best words or works utterly free from error and sin? All inspiration, then, does not destroy the human and fallible part in the nature which it inspires; it does not change man into God. . . . . The difference between the inspiration of the common and perhaps unworthy Christian, who merely said that Jesus was the Lord, and that of Moses, or St. Paul, or St. John, is almost to our eyes beyond measuring. Still the position remains, that the highest degree of inspiration given to man has still suffered to exist along with it a portion of human fallibility and corruption. . . .

"Now, then, consider the Epistles of the blessed Apostle St. Paul, who had the spirit of God so abundantly that never, we may suppose, did any merely human being enjoy a larger share of it. Endowed with the Spirit as a Christian, and daily receiving grace more largely as he became more and more ripe for glory; endowed with the Spirit's extraordinary gifts most eminently; favored also with an abundance of revelations, disclosing to him things ineffable and inconceivable, — are not his writings most truly called inspired? Yet this great Apostle expected that the world would come to an end in the generation then existing." *

The importance of the subject will justify me in citing a passage from another distinguished light of the Church, so regarded by all Protestant Christians. Martin Luther, in his comment on Gal. ii. 11, says: "Here let other men debate whether an Apostle may sin or no. This say I, that we ought not to make Peter's fault less than it was indeed. The prophets themselves have sometimes erred and been deceived. Nathan of his own spirit said unto David that he should build the house of the Lord. But

* Sermons on the Christian Life, p. 487.

this prophecy was by and by after corrected by a revelation from God that it should not be David, because he was a man of war and had shed much blood; but his son Solomon should build up the house of the Lord. So did the Apostles err also. For they imagined that the kingdom of Christ should be carnal and worldly. See Acts i., where they asked of Christ, saying, Lord wilt thou, &c. And Peter, although he had heard this command of Christ, Go ye into all the world, &c., would not have gone to Cornelius if he had not been admonished by a vision. And in this matter he not only did err, but committed a great sin; and if Paul had not resisted him, all the Gentiles which believed would have been constrained to receive circumcision and to keep the Law. The believing Jews would also have been confirmed in their opinion; to wit, that the observation of these things was necessary to salvation; and by this means they would have received the Law instead of the Gospel, Moses instead of Christ. And of all this great enormity and horrible sin Peter by this dissimulation would have been the only occasion. Therefore we may not attribute to the saints such perfection as though they could not sin."

As to the distinction which has sometimes been made between the *writings* and the *speech* of prophets, as if the former were of greater authority than the latter, it is altogether unfounded in the Scriptures. For one instance where the prophets are said to be inspired as writers, there are at least a hundred where they are represented as inspired speakers. Nor do the Scriptures speak of two kinds of inspiration from God.

If it should still appear to any one strange that the prophets, even under the influence of the spirit of God, should claim in a manner so emphatic that their utterances were the word of God, and that they should prefix "Thus saith the Lord" to nearly all their discourses, let him consider that nearly all these discourses have for their object the establishment of the primary truths of religion and the most obvious duties of life, — "the quickening up of our minds to a more lively converse with those eternal truths of reason, which commonly lie buried in so much fleshly obscurity within us that we discern them not"; and that even now in modern times, according to the most approved philosophy, these primary truths of religion, these elementary principles of duty, are regarded as revealed to the mind by God, and immediately seen by the eyes of the soul. In other words, there are intuitive perceptions of truth and duty in all men, which are rightly acknowledged as an immediate, primary revelation from God. It is a very common figure of speech to call these intuitions the voice of God within us. The excellent old English writer, John Smith, the author more than two hundred years ago of the only English treatise on prophecy which I regard as of much value, says: "The souls of men are as capable of conversing with truth, though it do not naturally arise from the fecundity of their own understandings, as they are with any sensible and external objects. And as our sensations carry the notions of material things to our understandings which before were unacquainted with them, so there is some analogical way whereby the knowledge of Divine truth may also be revealed to us. For so we may call as well that historical truth of corporeal and material things, which we are informed of by our senses, truth of revelation, as that Divine truth which we now speak of; and therefore we may have as certain and infallible a way of being acquainted with the one as with the other. And God, having so contrived the nature of our souls that we may converse one with another, and inform one another of things we knew not before, would not make us so deaf to his Divine voice, that breaks the rocks and rends the mountains asunder, — he would not make us so undisciplinable in Divine things, — as that we should not be capable of receiving any impressions from himself of those things which we were before unacquainted with. And this way of communicating truth to the souls of men is originally nothing else but prophetical or enthusiastical; and so we may take notice of the general nature of prophecy." * If, then, the elements of religious truth and duty may be represented as a revelation from the Deity to the intuitive mind of man, it is easy to see how the prophets, with their views of the operations of the spirit of God, and of their own gifts and office under the theocratic government of his people, might honestly and intelligently speak as the representatives of God, and as uttering his word. Nor would they thus lay claim to infallibility any more than religious philosophers of modern times lay claim to infallibility when they maintain the elementary principles of religion and morals to be an immediate revelation from God to the souls of men. This connection of infallibility with inspiration, this entire separation of the natural from the supernatural, is a theological figment of more modern times.

John Milton speaks of abilities to write like Pindar and Callimachus as "the inspired gift of God, rarely bestowed, but yet to some (though most abuse) in every nation." Speaking also of the Paradise Lost which he had in contemplation, he says that it is "a work not to be raised from the heat of youth, or the vapors of wine, like that which flows at waste from the pen of some vulgar amorist, or the trencher fury of a rhyming parasite, nor to be obtained by the invocation of Dame Memory, and her Siren daughters, but by devout prayer to that Eternal Spirit who can enrich with all utterance and knowledge, and sends out his seraphim with the hallowed fire of his altar to touch and purify the lips of whom he pleases." †

The late Professor Stuart of Andover, who deserves much credit, not only as a Biblical scholar, but as a reformer in theology, has given a general view of inspiration substantially, but not wholly, in accordance with mine. In his Commentary on the Apocalypse, Vol. I. p. 167, he writes as follows: "I do not apprehend that *inspiration*, whatever aid it gave a writer in the way of illumination and guidance, changed the peculiarities of that writer's

* See Smith, in Watson's Tracts, Vol. IV. p. 298, or Select Discourses of John Smith, Cambridge, 1859.

† See the Reason of Church Government, &c., Book II., Introd.

style, or hindered the full and proper exercise of his logical and rhetorical powers. The result of all my researches into the nature of inspiration is a full belief that its influence is rather to be considered as resulting in a *state* than in an *act*. What I mean is, that by inspiration the state or condition of him who is the subject of it is affected; his mind is enlightened respecting things proper to be said, of which he was before totally or partially ignorant; his views and affections are elevated; his powers of mind are in a degree quickened and heightened; things sensual and deluding and degrading recede, and for the time being cease to annoy him; and his judgment as to what he is to communicate becomes not only more discerning, but more sound and safe. The *inspired* John, for example, is the same individual as the *uninspired* John, and retains all the innocent peculiarities of his character and habitudes; but the inspired John is elevated, enlightened, quickened, keen of discernment even to such a degree that future things can be seen from his elevated condition, and he is so guided by all the combinations of influence upon him, that he will communicate nothing but truth. Were I to choose a simile for illustration, I should say that the inspired man ascends an intellectual and moral eminence so high that his prospect widens almost without bounds, and what is altogether hidden from ordinary men is more or less distinctly within his view."

To this statement of Professor Stuart I see little to object, except to a part of the sentence which asserts that the inspired man will communicate *nothing but* truth. This assertion appears to me mere theological assumption, not only not supported, but contradicted by Scriptural facts. For that there are some errors in the writings of the Prophets, the Evangelists, and the Apostles, is a demonstrable truth. The writer of the Apocalypse, in reference to whom the learned Professor made his remarks, represents things as *shortly* to come to pass, which have not come to pass yet, after a lapse of more than eighteen centuries, and which never can come to pass, according to any just interpretation of his language. Dr. Arnold's statement is in much better accordance with well-known Scriptural and historical facts, when he says "that the highest degree of inspiration given to man has still suffered to exist along with it a portion of human fallibility and corruption."

In fact St. Paul himself seems to have sanctioned this view of the fallibility of the prophets, when he says, concerning the Christian prophets of his time, who uttered with the authority of inspiration their warnings and encouragements and exhortations, and enforced the truths of Christianity with supernatural energy, in 1 Cor. xiv. 32, "The spirits of the prophets are subject to prophets." On this passage Mr. Poole, the well-known author of the *Synopsis Criticorum*, in a note borrowed from Calvin, remarks: "But here ariseth a difficulty, how the gifts of the Holy Spirit, flowing immediately from the Spirit, should be subject to any human judgment or censure. That indeed they could not be, if the Divine revelation to this or that man were full and perfect, and ran as clearly in the stream always as it was in the fountain. But God giveth his spirit to us but by measure; and in the exercise of his gifts there is always *aliquid humani*, something of our own, and this maketh them subject to the prophets; viz. whether what they pretended to have from the spirit of God were indeed from it, yes or no. . . . . Here he showeth the principle that any prophet's speech is not so certain, or at least not more certain, than this, that nothing which is confusion can come from God." See also Calvin, *ad loc.*

If, instead of the above explanation, which is also that of Theodoret, Chrysostom, Calovius, Bengel, Beza, and many others, ancient and modern, we take that of most recent expositors, — viz. that the Divine spirit which inspires the prophets is subject to the control of the prophets' own will, so that they can speak, or refrain from speaking, as they choose, — I think that quite as strong an inference may be drawn from the passage in favor of the views which I have maintained. But as the gift of discernment of spirits is mentioned in ch. xii. in immediate connection with the prophetic gift, and as in verse 29 it is said, "Let the prophets speak two or three, and let the others *judge*," it seems to me that the older explanation has quite as good a claim to acceptance as the more recent one. Especially as there may perhaps be some force in Bishop Middleton's remark, that, if Paul had meant to say that the spirits of the prophets were subject to themselves, he would grammatically have used the article before the repeated word *prophets*, and have written τοῖς προφήταις ὑποτάσσεται. Both meanings, however, are so agreeable to the connection, that one cannot decide very confidently which is correct.

After all, the authority of names is only a subsidiary consideration. The proof of the fallibility of apostles and prophets is the actual errors which are found in their writings.

To deny infallibility to the writings of prophets, evangelists, and apostles is by no means to deprive them of authority. On the contrary, they come to us not only with an authority of their own, but with that of all the human hearts which have been converted, strengthened, and comforted by them for eighteen centuries. Divine Providence has given them vast authority in the education of mankind. But this authority, like that of the Great Teacher, the chief corner-stone on which prophets, evangelists, and apostles built, extends only to the essential principles of religion and morality which are able to make us wise unto salvation, and not to matters of scientific criticism, hermeneutical logic, the causes and cure of disease, chronology, astronomy, or geology. No one at the present day would think of pouring wine into a fresh wound on account of the commendation which Jesus gave to the good Samaritan for so doing. These matters did not fall within the province of Christ's mission. They were safely left to the progressive reason of mankind.

In the same way, it is not necessary to deny authority, in regard to some ideas, to the Church; for instance, the Catholic, the Lutheran, the Methodist, or the Unitarian churches. The individual reason is strengthened in its convictions when they are in accordance with the belief of any great church. Even in criticism, the very essence of which is the judgment of the individual, every sound inquirer keeps in mind the fallibility of his own reason, and has more confidence in his conclusions when they are supported by the authority of a large number of learned, honest, unbiassed searchers after truth. Still the question what church shall be allowed the greatest weight of authority, and how much authority is to be allowed to any church, or to all churches, and to what subjects the authority extends, must be decided by the reason of the individual under the influence of the Divine spirit. No church can stand between the individual soul and its Creator at the day of judgment, and therefore the individual soul must in the last resort decide in all matters of faith and practice.

So it is with respect to the conscience. The individual must in the last resort follow his own conscience, as the best guide which he has, however fallible and imperfect it may be; but he must do so not in contemptuous disregard of authority, but with a just estimation of it.

We might illustrate this subject of authority by reference to the Common or the Civil Law. Who can deny that they have vast authority in the administration of justice throughout the world? Our governors and judges do not deny the authority of the Common or the Roman Law, when they deny the infallibility of either. Allowing that the law, according to either of these systems, is founded in right reason, and has "its seat in the bosom of God," yet may it not be overruled? Is not allowance made for the growth of reason?

It is feared by many, that, in denying infallibility to the Scriptures, we take away one of the supports of morality. The other side of the question has been overlooked. It has not been considered how far this doctrine of infallibility has been the support of wrong-doing in the Christian Church. But I think it can be demonstrated that practices, now generally regarded as inhuman and inconsistent with the spirit of Christ, have found their strongest support in this doctrine of the absolute infallibility of the Scriptures. The infliction of horrible penalties for religious opinion, the principle of retaliation in criminal jurisprudence, the cruelties in the punishment of witchcraft, and the custom of chattel slavery, have prevailed under the supposed sanction of the Scriptures. If they are regarded in all their utterances as an infallible guide, they do give that sanction. The Southern Christian teachers of every name who united in proclaiming slavery to be sanctioned by the Bible were not only honest, but right, if the Scriptures in every part are regarded as an infallible standard of truth and duty, without the least mixture of human error. The old expositors of the Scriptures, who wrote before the modern agitation of the subject of slavery, — an agitation excited, as I think, by the Holy Spirit of God in the human reason and the human heart, — give abundant support to the Southern religious teachers. While I admit this, however, I should still maintain that the spirit of the prophets, as well as of Christ and St. Paul, fairly deduced from all which they uttered or wrote, is clearly and strongly against slavery in every form.

It would be strange, indeed, if in the present advanced state of society Christians should not, in respect to the *application* of the essential principles and spirit of Christian morality to many outward usages, have juster and clearer views than the Apostle of the Gentiles.

If it still be asked how we are to distinguish the word of God in the Scriptures from the imperfections and errors mixed up with it, I reply, By the reason of the individual. The same Holy Spirit which inspired prophets and apostles *to speak* and *write* is still living and present to illuminate and strengthen the reason of hearers and readers *to judge*, and to separate the eternal truth from the errors and imperfections which, imbibed from the age in which they lived, clung to the greatest prophets, such as John the Baptist, and the chiefest Apostles, such as Paul. "He that is spiritual judgeth all things." (1 Cor. ii. 15.)

There is limited, yet trustworthy, but no absolute, infallible authority whatever for man. God is infallible. But every human interpreter and all collective bodies of human interpreters of Divine manifestations are fallible. The human senses, the human intellect, the human memory, oral tradition, and historical records are all fallible. Yet by their aid we may attain not only faith, but knowledge. The light which it has pleased God to bestow upon us is amply sufficient to guide us to the blessedness for which we were designed, in this world and that which is to come. Whether the necessities or the interests of humanity would be better promoted by an infallible standard of doctrine and duty, either in a written volume, in a church, or a single individual, is a question which it is not worth while to discuss. What God has done, not what it is necessary or useful for him to do, is the important concern for us. Who shall undertake to prescribe to the Creator the best method for the enlightenment and improvement of the world? Undoubtedly there is a part of our nature which inclines us to seek repose in an outward, infallible standard. But it may well be doubted whether this is the highest part of our nature. It seems rather to be a selfish love of ease and quiet, an aversion to action and progress, a desire to escape anxiety, suspense, and labor, rather than to attain to truth and perfection. The result is rather an arbitrary suppression of doubt, than a genuine exercise of faith. "If I go not away," says the Great Teacher, "the Helper will not come." It well deserves to be considered whether it is not an actual fact, that those Christians enjoy a stronger as well as a purer faith, who, giving up the doctrine of Scriptural infallibility as a dream, conceding to authority its just weight, yet guarding against its undue influence, feel bound to trust their own reason under the guidance of the Holy Spirit, as the supreme judge, believing that to deny reason is to deny God.

JOEL.

INSCRIPTION.

1 The word of Jehovah, which came to Joel, the son of Pethuel.

I.

A description of the desolation of the land of Judah by locusts.— Ch. I. 2-20.

2 Hear this, ye old men;
Give ear, all ye inhabitants of the land!
Hath such a thing happened in your days,
Or even in the days of your fathers?
3 Tell ye your children of it,
And let your children tell their children,
And their children another generation!
4 That which the gnawing-locust left hath the swarming-locust eaten,
And that which the swarming-locust left hath the licking-locust eaten,
And that which the licking-locust left hath the consuming-locust eaten.

5 Awake, ye drunkards, and weep!
Howl, all ye drinkers of wine,
For the new wine, which is snatched from your mouths!
6 For a nation hath come up on my land,
Strong, and not to be numbered;
Their teeth are the teeth of the lion;
They have the jaw-teeth of the lioness.
7 They have made my vine a desolation,
And my fig-tree a broken branch;

They have made it quite bare, and cast it away;
The branches thereof are made white.

8 Lament ye, like a bride,
Clothed in sackcloth for the husband of her youth!
9 The flour-offering and the drink-offering are cut off from the house of Jehovah;
The priests, the servants of Jehovah, mourn.
10 The field is laid waste;
The ground mourneth,
For the corn is laid waste;
The new wine is dried up;
The oil languisheth.

11 Lament, O ye husbandmen,
Howl, O ye vine-dressers,
For the wheat and the barley,
For the harvest of the field hath perished!
12 The vine is dried up,
And the fig-tree languisheth;
The pomegranate, the palm-tree, and the apple-tree,—
All the trees of the field, are withered;
Yea, joy is withered away from the sons of men.

13 Gird yourselves with sackcloth and mourn, ye priests!
Howl, ye ministers of the altar!
Come, lie all night in sackcloth, ye ministers of my God,
For the flour-offering and the drink-offering are withholden from the house of your God!
14 Appoint ye a fast, proclaim a solemn assembly!
Gather the elders and all the inhabitants of the land
Into the house of Jehovah, your God,
And cry unto Jehovah!

15 Alas, alas the day!
For the day of Jehovah is near;
Even as destruction from the Almighty doth it come.
16 Is not our food cut off from before our eyes,
Yea, joy and gladness from the house of our God?
17 The seeds are rotten under their clods,
The storehouses are laid desolate, the garners are destroyed;

For the corn is withered.
18 How do the beasts groan,
How do the herds of oxen wander perplexed,
Having no pasture!
The flocks of sheep also are destroyed.
19 To thee, O Jehovah, do I call,
For a fire hath devoured the pastures of the desert,
And a flame hath burned all the trees of the field!
20 The beasts of the field, also, cry unto thee,
For the streams of water are dried up,
And a fire hath devoured the pastures of the desert!

II.

A similar desolation by locusts threatened. — Exhortation to repentance. — Promises of future abundance, of religious light, and of triumph over enemies. — CH. II., III.

1 BLOW ye the trumpet in Zion;
Sound an alarm in my holy mountain!
Let all the inhabitants of the land tremble!
For the day of Jehovah cometh, for it is near!
2 A day of darkness, and gloominess,
A day of clouds, and thick darkness.
As the morning light spreadeth itself upon the mountains,
There cometh a numerous people and a strong;
Like them there have been none of old time,
And after them there shall not be,
Even to the years of many generations.
3 A fire devoureth before them,
And behind them a flame burneth;
The land is as the garden of Eden before them.
And behind them a desolate wilderness!
Yea, nothing escapeth them.

4 Their appearance is like the appearance of horses,
And like horsemen do they run;
5 Like rattling chariots they leap on the tops of the mountains;
Like the crackling flame of fire, which devoureth stubble;

Like a mighty host set in battle array.
6 Before them the people tremble,
And all faces gather blackness.
7 They run like mighty men;
They climb the wall like warriors;
They march every one on his way;
They change not their paths.
8 One doth not thrust another;
They march every one in his path,
And though they rush among weapons, they are not wounded.
9 They run through the city;
They run upon the wall;
They go up into the houses;
They enter in at the windows, like a thief.
10 The earth quaketh before them,
And the heavens tremble:
The sun and the moon are darkened,
And the stars withdraw their shining.
11 Jehovah uttereth his voice before his army;
For very great is his host;
Yea, it is mighty, executing his word;
The day of Jehovah is great, and very terrible;
Who shall be able to bear it?

12 Yet even now, saith Jehovah,
Turn ye to me with all your heart,
With fasting, with weeping, and with mourning!
13 And rend your hearts, and not your garments,
And turn to Jehovah your God,
For he is gracious and merciful,
Slow to anger, and of great kindness,
And repenteth of a threatened evil.
14 Who knoweth but he will turn and repent,
And leave a blessing behind him,
Even a flour-offering and a drink-offering for Jehovah your God.

15 Blow ye the trumpet in Zion;
Appoint ye a fast; proclaim a solemn assembly!
16 Gather the people; appoint a congregation;
Assemble the elders;

Gather the children and the sucklings!
Let the bridegroom come forth from his chamber,
And the bride from her nuptial bed!
17 Let the priests, the servants of Jehovah,
Weep between the porch and the altar,
And say, Spare thy people, O Jehovah,
And give not thine inheritance to reproach,
And to be a by-word to the nations!
Why should they say among the nations,
Where is their God?

18 Then will Jehovah be zealous for his land,
And have compassion on his people,
19 Yea, Jehovah will answer, and say to his people,
Behold, I will send you corn,
And new wine, and oil, and ye shall be satisfied therewith;
And I will no more make you a reproach among the nations.
20 I will remove far from you the northern host,
And I will drive it into a dry and desolate land;
Its van toward the Eastern sea,
And its rear toward the Western sea.
And its scent shall come up,
And its ill savor shall come up,
Because it hath done great things.
21 Fear not, O land, exult and rejoice,
For Jehovah hath done great things!
22 Fear not, O ye beasts of the field,
For the pastures of the desert spring up,
For the tree beareth its fruit;
The fig-tree and the vine yield their strength!
23 And, O ye sons of Zion, exult,
And rejoice in Jehovah your God!
For he giveth you the former rain in just measure,
And causeth showers to come down upon you,
Even the former rain, and the latter rain, as aforetime.
24 And the threshing-floors shall be full of wheat,
And the vats shall overflow with new wine and oil.
25 And I will restore to you the years
Which the swarming-locust hath eaten,
The licking-locust, the consuming-locust, and the gnawing-locust,

My great army, which I sent among you.
26 Ye shall eat in plenty, and be satisfied,
And praise the name of Jehovah your God,
Who hath dealt wondrously with you;
And my people shall never be put to shame.
27 Ye shall know that I am in the midst of Israel,
And that I am Jehovah, your God, and none else;
And my people shall never be put to shame.

28 And it shall come to pass afterward,
That I will pour out my spirit upon all flesh;
And your sons and your daughters shall prophesy;
Your old men shall dream dreams,
Your young men shall see visions.
29 Upon the men-servants also, and upon the handmaids,
Will I pour out my spirit in those days.

30 And I will show wonders in the heavens and in the earth;
Blood and fire, and pillars of smoke.
31 The sun shall be turned into darkness,
And the moon into blood,
Before the day of Jehovah cometh,
The great and the terrible day.
Then whoever calleth on the name of Jehovah shall be delivered;
32 For upon mount Zion, and in Jerusalem, shall be deliverance,
As Jehovah hath spoken;
And among the remnant, whom Jehovah shall call.

1 For behold, in those days and at that time,
When I shall bring back the captives of Judah and Jerusalem,
2 I will assemble all the nations,
And will bring them down into the valley of Jehoshaphat,
And there will I contend with them for my people and inheritance, Israel;
Because they scattered them among the nations,
And divided my land among themselves.
3 Yea, they cast lots for my people,
And gave a boy for a harlot,

And sold a damsel for wine to drink.
4 What have ye to do with me, O Tyre and Sidon,
And all the borders of Philistia?
Will ye retaliate on me?
Or will ye do anything against me?
Swiftly and speedily will I bring back your doings upon your own head.
5 Ye have taken my silver and my gold,
And have carried into your palaces my precious, goodly things;
6 The sons also of Judah, and the sons of Jerusalem,
Ye have sold to the Grecians,
That ye might remove them far from their border.
7 Behold, I will raise them out of the place whither ye have sold them,
And I will return your injury upon your own head;
8 I will sell your sons and your daughters into the hand of the sons of Judah,
And they shall sell them to the Sabeans, to a nation afar off;
For Jehovah hath spoken it.

9 Proclaim ye this among the nations:
"Prepare war! Stir up the mighty ones!
Let all the warriors draw near; let them come up!"
10 Beat your ploughshares into swords,
And your pruning-hooks into spears;
Let the weak say, I am strong!
11 Assemble yourselves and come, all ye nations round about;
Gather yourselves together!
Thither, O Jehovah, bring down thy mighty ones!
12 Let the nations rise and come up to the valley of Jehoshaphat!
For there will I sit to judge all the nations around.

13 Put ye in the sickle, for the harvest is ripe;
Come and tread, for the wine-press is full;
The vats overflow;
For their wickedness is great!
14 The multitudes, the multitudes in the valley of judgment!

For the day of Jehovah is near in the valley of judgment.
15 The sun and the moon are darkened,
And the stars withdraw their shining.

16 Jehovah also will roar from Zion,
And utter his voice from Jerusalem;
The heavens and the earth shall shake.
But Jehovah will be a refuge to his people;
A strong-hold to the sons of Israel.
17 Then shall ye know that I am Jehovah your God,
Dwelling in Zion, my holy mountain;
And Jerusalem shall be holy;
Strangers shall pass through her no more.

18 In that day shall the mountains drop down new wine,
And the hills shall flow with milk,
And all the streams of Judah shall flow with water.
A fountain shall come forth from the house of Jehovah,
That shall water the valley of Shittim.

19 Egypt shall be a waste,
And Edom a desolate wilderness,
For their violence against the sons of Judah;
For they shed innocent blood in their land.
20 But Judah shall be inhabited for ever,
And Jerusalem from generation to generation.
21 And I will avenge their blood, which I have not avenged,
And Jehovah will dwell upon Zion.

AMOS.

INSCRIPTION.

1 The words of Amos, one of the shepherds of Tekoa,
which he prophesied concerning Israel in the days of
Uzziah king of Judah, and in the days of Jeroboam, the
son of Joash, king of Israel, two years before the earth
quake. He said:—

I.

Threats of punishment against several foreign states, and against Judah and Israel.—CH. I., II.

2 JEHOVAH will roar from Zion,
And utter his voice from Jerusalem;
The habitations of the shepherds shall mourn,
And the top of Carmel shall wither.

3 Thus saith Jehovah;
For three transgressions of Damascus,
And for four, will I not turn away its punishment;
For they thrashed Gilead with thrashing-wains of iron.
4 I will send a fire upon the house of Hazael,
Which shall devour the palaces of Benhadad.
5 I will also break the bar of Damascus,
And I will destroy the inhabitant from the valley of Aven,
And him that holdeth the sceptre from Beth-Eden,
And the people of Syria shall be led captive to Kir:
Jehovah hath said it.

6 Thus saith Jehovah:
For three transgressions of Gaza,
And for four, I will not turn away its punishment;

For they led captive all that fell into their hands,
And delivered them up to Edom.
7 But I will send a fire upon the wall of Gaza,
Which shall devour her palaces.
8 And I will destroy the inhabitant from Ashdod,
And him that holdeth the sceptre from Ashkelon;
And I will turn my hand against Ekron,
And the residue of the Philistines shall perish.
The Lord, Jehovah, hath said it.

9 Thus saith Jehovah:
For three transgressions of Tyre,
And for four, will I not turn away its punishment;
Because they delivered up all their captives to Edom,
And remembered not the brotherly covenant.
10 But I will send a fire on the wall of Tyre,
Which shall devour her palaces.

11 Thus saith Jehovah:
For three transgressions of Edom,
And for four, will I not turn away his punishment;
For he pursued his brother with the sword,
And cast off all pity,
And his anger tore perpetually;
Yea, he kept his wrath forever.
12 But I will send a fire upon Teman,
Which shall devour the palaces of Bozrah.

13 Thus saith Jehovah:
For three transgressions of the children of Ammon,
And for four, will I not turn away their punishment;
For they ripped up the women with child of Gilead,
That they might enlarge their border.
14 But I will kindle a fire on the wall of Rabbah,
Which shall devour her palaces,
Amid the war-shout in the day of battle,
In a whirlwind in the day of the storm.
15 Their king shall go into captivity,
He and his princes together, saith Jehovah.

1 Thus saith Jehovah:
For three transgressions of Moab,

And for four, will I not turn away his punishment;
For he burned the bones of the king of Edom into lime;
2 But I will send a fire on Moab,
Which shall devour the palaces of Kirioth;
And Moab shall die amid tumults,
Amid the war-shout, and the sound of the trumpet.
3 I will destroy the judge from the midst of him,
And slay all the princes with him, saith Jehovah.

4 Thus saith Jehovah:
For three transgressions of Judah,
And for four, will I not turn away their punishment;
For they have despised the law of Jehovah,
And have not kept his statutes,
And their idols have caused them to err,
After which their fathers walked.
5 But I will send a fire upon Judah,
Which shall devour the palaces of Jerusalem.

6 Thus saith Jehovah:
For three transgressions of Israel,
And for four, will I not turn away their punishment.
For they sell the righteous for silver,
And the needy for a pair of shoes;
7 They pant for the dust of the earth on the head of the poor,
And pervert the cause of the afflicted.
The son and the father go in to the same damsel,
To dishonor my holy name.
8 They lay themselves down upon pledged garments
Near every altar;
And drink wine, procured by fines,
In the house of their gods.

9 Yet I destroyed the Amorites before them,
Who were tall as the cedars,
And strong as the oaks.
I destroyed their fruit above,
And their roots beneath.
10 I brought you up from the land of Egypt,
And led you in the desert forty years,
That ye might possess the land of the Amorite.

11 Of your sons also I raised up prophets,
And of your young men Nazarites;
Is it not even so, O ye sons of Israel? saith Jehovah.
12 But ye gave the Nazarites wine to drink,
And commanded the prophets,
Saying, Prophesy not!

13 Behold, I will press you down,
As a wagon presseth down that is full of sheaves.
14 And flight shall fail the swift,
And the strong shall not exert his strength,
And the mighty shall not save his life,
15 And he that handleth the bow shall not stand,
And the swift of foot shall not save himself,
And the horseman shall not escape with his life.
16 He that is strong in heart among the mighty
Shall, in that day, flee away naked, saith Jehovah.

II.

Punishment threatened against the whole race of the Hebrews on account of injustice, luxury, and idolatry.— CH. III.

1 HEAR these words, which Jehovah speaketh against you, ye sons of Israel;
Against the whole family which I brought up out of the land of Egypt!

2 You only have I known of all the families of the earth;
Therefore will I punish you for all your iniquities.
3 Can two walk together,
Unless they agree together?
4 Will the lion roar in the forest,
When he seeth no prey?
Will the young lion cry aloud from his den,
If he have seized nothing?
5 Can a bird fall into a snare upon the earth,
Where none is set for him?
Will a snare spring up from the ground,
When it hath caught nothing?

6 Shall a trumpet be blown in the city,
And the people not be afraid?
Shall there be evil upon a city,
And Jehovah not have done it?
7 Surely the Lord Jehovah doeth nothing,
But he revealeth his secret
To his servants the prophets.
8 When the lion roareth, who will not fear?
When the Lord Jehovah speaketh, who will not prophesy?

9 Proclaim ye, in the palaces in Ashdod,
And in the palaces in the land of Egypt,
And say, Assemble yourselves upon the mountains of Samaria;
Behold the great tumults in the midst of her,
And the oppressions within her!
10 For they have no care to do right, saith Jehovah;
They treasure up rapine and robbery in their palaces.
11 Therefore thus saith the Lord Jehovah:
An enemy shall encompass the land,
And shall bring down thy strength from thee,
And thy palaces shall be plundered.

12 Thus saith Jehovah:
As the shepherd taketh out of the lion's mouth
Two legs, or a portion of an ear,
So shall the children of Israel be taken out,
Who in Samaria sit in the corners of their sofas,
And upon their damask couches.

13 Hear ye, and testify to the house of Jacob,
Saith the Lord, Jehovah, God of hosts!
14 In the day when I punish the transgressions of Israel,
Then will I punish the altars of Bethel;
The horns of the altar shall be cut off,
And fall to the ground.
15 And I will smite the winter-house together with the summer-house,
And the houses of ivory shall be destroyed,
And the great houses shall be brought to the ground, saith Jehovah.

III.

Rebuke of oppression, luxury, and idolatry.—CH. IV.

1 HEAR these words, O ye kine of Bashan,
That are on the mountain of Samaria;
That oppress the poor; that crush the needy;
That say to your master, Bring, and let us drink!

2 The Lord Jehovah hath sworn by his holiness;
Behold, the days shall come upon you
When ye shall be taken away with hooks,
And your residue with fishing-hooks.
3 And ye shall go out at the breaches, every one right forward,
And ye shall be thrown into a castle, saith Jehovah.

4 Go, now, to Bethel, and transgress;
At Gilgal multiply transgression!
Bring your sacrifices every morning,
And your tithes every three years!
5 Burn a thank-offering from your extortions,
And proclaim the free-will offerings; publish them abroad!
For this is your delight, ye sons of Israel,
Saith the Lord, Jehovah.

6 I also have caused cleanness of teeth in all your cities,
And want of bread in all your places;
And yet ye have not returned to me, saith Jehovah.

7 I also have withholden from you the rain three months before the harvest;
I have caused it to rain upon one city,
And upon another city have I not caused it to rain;
One piece of ground hath been rained upon,
And another, upon which I have not caused it to rain, hath withered.
8 Two or three cities have gone to one city,
To drink water, and have not been satisfied;
And yet ye have not returned to me, saith Jehovah.

9 I have smitten you with blasting and mildew;
The locust hath devoured your many gardens,
Your vineyards, your fig-trees, and your olive-trees;
Yet have ye not returned to me, saith Jehovah.

10 I have sent among you the pestilence after the manner of Egypt;
I have slain your young men with the sword,
And your horses have I led into captivity;
I have made the smell of your camps to come up into your nostrils;
And yet ye have not returned to me, saith Jehovah.

11 I have overthrown some of you, as God overthrew Sodom and Gomorrah;
And ye were as a firebrand plucked out of the burning;
And yet ye have not returned to me, saith Jehovah.
12 Therefore thus will I deal with thee, O Israel!
Yet since I will thus deal with thee,
Prepare to meet thy God, O Israel!
13 For behold, he formed the mountains, and created the wind;
He declareth to man what is his thought;
He maketh the morning darkness,
And walketh upon the high places of the earth;
Jehovah, God of hosts, is his name.

IV.

Dissuasive from idolatry. Admonition to return to God. Threats of punishment. — CH. V.

1 HEAR these words, which I utter concerning you;
This lamentation, O house of Israel!

2 She is fallen, she shall rise no more,
The virgin of Israel!
She is prostrate on her own ground, there is none to raise her up!
3 For thus saith the Lord Jehovah;
The city which sent out a thousand shall have a hundred left,

And that which sent out a hundred shall have ten left,
To the house of Israel.

4 For thus saith Jehovah to the house of Israel:
Seek ye me, and ye shall live!
5 Seek not Bethel,
And go not to Gilgal,
And pass not over to Beersheba!
For Gilgal shall surely go into captivity,
And Bethel shall come to naught.
6 Seek Jehovah, and ye shall live!
Lest he rush like a fire on the house of Joseph,
And it devour, and there be none to quench it in the house of Israel.
7 Ye who turn justice into wormwood,
And cast righteousness down to the ground.
8 Seek him, that made the Pleiads and Orion;
That changeth death-like darkness into morning,
And darkeneth day into night;
That calleth up the waters of the sea,
And poureth them out upon the face of the earth;
Jehovah is his name!
9 Who sendeth sudden destruction upon the strong,
And bringeth desolation upon the fortress.

10 They hate him that pleadeth in the gate,
And abhor him that speaketh uprightly.
11 Since, then, ye trample upon the poor,
And take from him presents of wheat,
Though ye build houses of hewn stone, ye shall not dwell in them;
Though ye plant pleasant vineyards, ye shall not drink their wine.
12 For I know that your sins are many,
And your transgressions manifold,
Ye who afflict the righteous, and take a bribe,
And oppress the poor in the gate!
13 Therefore the wise man shall be silent at that time,
For it shall be an evil time.

14 Seek ye good, and not evil, that ye may live;
Then shall Jehovah, the God of hosts, be with you, as ye boast.

15 Hate ye evil, and love good,
And establish justice in the gate;
It may be that Jehovah, the God of hosts, will have pity upon the remnant of Joseph.
16 Thus saith Jehovah, the God of hosts, the Lord:
In all the streets shall there be wailing,
And in all the highways shall they cry, Alas! alas!
They shall call the husbandmen to mourning,
And those who are skilful in lamentation to wailing,
17 And in all vineyards shall be sounds of woe,
For I will pass through the midst of thee, saith Jehovah.

18 Woe unto them that ask for the day of Jehovah!
What is the day of Jehovah to you?
It shall be darkness, and not light.
19 As if a man fled from a lion,
And a bear met him;
Or went into a house and leaned his hand on a wall,
And a serpent bit him;
20 So shall the day of Jehovah be darkness, and not light,
Even thick darkness, and no brightness in it.

21 I hate, I despise your feasts;
I have no delight in your solemn assemblies.
22 When ye offer me burnt-offerings and flour-offerings,
I will not accept them;
And upon the thank-offerings of your fatlings I will not look.
23 Take ye away from me the noise of your songs,
And the music of your harps let me not hear!
24 Let justice flow forth as waters,
And righteousness as a mighty stream!
25 Did ye offer me sacrifices and offerings
In the wilderness, for forty years, O house of Israel?
26 But ye bore the tabernacle of your king,
And the shrine of your images,
The star of your god, which ye made for yourselves.
27 Therefore will I cause you to go into captivity beyond Damascus,
Saith Jehovah, whose name is the God of hosts.

V.

Woes denounced against the luxurious and oppressive aristocracy of Israel. — CH. VI.

1 WOE to them that dwell at ease in Zion;
That feel secure upon the mountain of Samaria;
The honorable men of the chief of the nations,
To whom the house of Israel resort!
2 Pass over to Calneh, and see;
And thence go to great Hamath;
Then go down to Gath of the Philistines:
Are they better than these kingdoms,
Or is their border greater than your border?
3 Woe to them, that put far away the day of evil,
And bring near the seat of oppression;
4 That lie upon beds of ivory,
And stretch themselves upon their couches;
That eat lambs from the flock,
And calves from the stall;
5 That chant to the sound of the harp,
And invent for themselves instruments of music, like David;
6 That drink wine in bowls,
And anoint themselves with the most precious perfumes,
But grieve not for the destruction of Joseph!
7 Therefore now shall they go captive at the head of the captives;
Yea, the shouting of them that stretch themselves upon their couches shall cease.

8 The Lord Jehovah hath sworn by himself,
Thus saith Jehovah, the God of hosts:
I abhor the pride of Jacob,
And I hate his palaces;
I will give up the city, and all that is therein.
9 And if ten men remain in one house,
These also shall die.
10 A man's relative, or a burner of the dead, shall take him up,
To carry his bones out of the house,

And he shall say to him that is in the innermost part of
the house,
Is there yet any one with thee?
And he shall answer, No one!
Then shall he say, Keep silence!
For we may not make mention of the name of Jehovah.
11 For behold Jehovah hath commanded,
And he will smite the great house with breaches,
And the small house with clefts.

12 Shall horses run upon rocks,
Or will one plough rocks with oxen,
That ye change justice into hemlock,
And the fruit of equity into wormwood,
13 Ye that rejoice in a thing of naught,
And say, Have we not acquired dominion by our own
strength?
14 Behold, O house of Israel, saith Jehovah, the God of hosts,
I will raise against you a nation,
That shall oppress you from Hamath
Even to the brook of the desert.

VI.

Israel threatened with destruction. — CH. VII. 1-9.

1 THE Lord Jehovah showed me this vision:
Behold, he formed locusts
In the beginning of the shooting up of the latter growth;
Behold, it was the latter growth after the king's mowing.
2 And when they had devoured the grass of the land,
Then said I, O Lord Jehovah, forgive, I beseech thee!
How shall Jacob stand?
For he is small!
3 Jehovah repented of this;
It shall not be, said Jehovah.

4 The Lord Jehovah also showed me this vision:
Behold, the Lord Jehovah commanded the fire to execute
judgment;

And it devoured the great deep,
And it devoured the fields.
5 Then said I, O Lord Jehovah, desist, I beseech thee!
How shall Jacob stand?
For he is small!
6 Jehovah repented of this;
This also shall not be, said the Lord Jehovah.

7 He also showed me this vision:
Behold, the Lord stood upon a wall, built with a plumb-line,
And in his hand was a plumb-line;
8 And Jehovah said to me, What seest thou, Amos?
And I said, A plumb-line.
And the Lord said, Behold I will set a plumb-line in the midst of my people Israel;
I will not spare them any more.
9 The high places of Isaac shall be desolate,
And the sanctuaries of Israel shall be laid waste,
And I will rise against the house of Jeroboam with the sword.

VII.

Amos is ordered to depart from the kingdom of Israel. Answer of the prophet. — CH. VII. 10-17.

10 THEN sent Amaziah, the priest of Bethel,
To Jeroboam, the king of Israel, and said:
Amos conspireth against thee in the midst of the house of Israel;
The land is not able to bear all his words.
11 For thus hath Amos said:
Jeroboam shall die by the sword,
And Israel shall surely be led captive from their own land.

12 And Amaziah said to Amos,
Go, thou seer! flee into the land of Judah!
There eat thy bread, and there prophesy!
13 But prophesy no more at Bethel,

IX.

Destruction and restoration of Israel. — CH. IX.

1 I SAW the Lord standing by the altar; and he said:
Smite the capital, so that the thresholds shall tremble!
Break them in pieces upon the heads of all of them!
And their residue will I slay with the sword.
He that fleeth of them shall not flee from danger,
And he that escapeth of them shall not escape into safety.
2 Though they dig down to the under-world,
Thence shall my hand take them;
Though they climb up to heaven,
Thence will I bring them down.
3 Though they hide themselves on the top of Carmel,
There will I search for them, and take them away;
Though they hide themselves from mine eyes in the bottom of the sea,
There will I command the serpent, and he shall bite them.
4 Though they go into captivity before their enemies,
There will I command the sword, and it shall slay them;
I will set mine eyes upon them for evil, and not for good.

5 For the Lord Jehovah of hosts
Is he, that toucheth the earth, and it shall melt,
And all that dwell therein shall mourn;
All of it shall rise in waves like a river,
And shall be overflowed, as by the river of Egypt;
6 He that buildeth his upper rooms in the heavens,
And foundeth his arch upon the earth, —
That calleth the waters of the sea,
And poureth them out upon the face of the earth, —
Jehovah is his name.

7 Are ye not as the Ethiopians to me, O children of Israel? saith Jehovah.
Did I not bring Israel from the land of Egypt,
And the Philistines from Caphtor, and the Syrians from Kir?

8 Behold, the eyes of the Lord Jehovah are upon the sinful kingdom,
And I will destroy it from the face of the earth;
Yet will I not utterly destroy the house of Jacob, saith Jehovah.
9 For, behold, I will command,
And I will sift the house of Israel among all the nations,
As one sifteth corn with a sieve,
And not a grain shall fall upon the ground.
10 But all the sinners of my people shall die by the sword,
Who say, Evil shall not approach, nor fall upon us.

11 In that day I will raise up the fallen tabernacle of David,
And I will close up the breaches thereof,
And raise up its ruins,
And I will build it, as in the days of old.
12 That they may possess the remnant of Edom,
And all the nations, which shall be called by my name.
Thus saith Jehovah, who doeth this.
13 Behold the days come, saith Jehovah,
That the plougher shall draw near to the reaper,
And the treader of grapes to the sower of the seed;
And the mountains shall drop new wine,
And all the hills shall melt.
14 I will bring back the captives of my people Israel,
And they shall build the desolate cities, and shall inhabit them;
And they shall plant vineyards, and drink their wine;
They shall also make gardens, and eat their fruit.
15 I will plant them in their land,
And they shall no more be rooted up from the land which I have given them,
Saith Jehovah, thy God.

For it is the king's sanctuary,
And it is the king's abode.

14 Then answered Amos, and said to Amaziah:
I was no prophet, nor the son of a prophet;
I was a shepherd, and a gatherer of sycamore fruit.
15 And Jehovah took me from the flock;
And Jehovah said to me,
Go, prophesy to my people Israel!
16 Now, therefore, hear the word of Jehovah:
Thou sayest, Prophesy not against Israel,
And speak no word against the house of Isaac!
17 Therefore thus saith Jehovah:
"Thy wife shall be put to shame in the city,
And thy sons and daughters shall fall by the sword;
Thy land shall be divided by the line,
And thou shalt die in a polluted land,
And Israel shall surely be led captive from his own land."

VIII.

Israel ripe for destruction. — CH. VIII.

1 THE Lord Jehovah showed me this vision:
Behold a basket of ripe fruits!
2 And he said, Amos, what seest thou?
And I said, A basket of ripe fruits.
Then said Jehovah to me, The destruction of my people
Israel is ripe;
I will not spare them any more.
3 The songs of the palace shall be shrieks in that day,
Saith the Lord Jehovah.
There shall be many dead bodies in every place,
And they shall be cast forth in silence.

4 Hear this, ye that pant to oppress the needy,
And to destroy the poor of the land.
5 That say, When will the new moon be gone, that we
may sell corn,
And the Sabbath, that we may set forth wheat,

Making the ephah small, and the shekel heavy,
And falsifying the balances for deceit,
6 That we may buy the poor for silver,
And the needy for a pair of shoes,
And sell the refuse of the wheat?
7 Jehovah hath sworn by the glory of Jacob:
Surely I will never forget any of their deeds.
8 Shall not the land tremble for this,
And shall not all that dwell therein mourn?
Shall not all of it rise in waves like a river,
And be swept from its place, and overflowed, as by the river of Egypt!
9 It shall come to pass in that day, saith the Lord Jehovah,
That I will cause the sun to go down at noon,
And will darken the land in the clear day.
10 I will turn your feasts into mourning,
And all your songs into lamentation;
I will bring sackcloth upon all loins,
And baldness upon all heads.
I will fill the land with mourning, as for an only son,
And its end shall be as a day of bitter woe.

11 Behold, the time cometh, saith the Lord Jehovah,
That I will send a famine upon the land;
Not a famine of bread, nor a thirst for water,
But of hearing the word of Jehovah.
12 And men shall wander from sea to sea,
And from the north even to the east shall they run to and fro,
To seek an answer from Jehovah, and shall not find it.
13 In that day shall the fair virgins, and the young men, faint for thirst,
14 Who swear by the sin of Samaria,
And say, By the life of thy God, O Dan!
And, By the worship of Beersheba!
They shall fall, and shall rise no more!

HOSEA.

INSCRIPTION.

1 The word of Jehovah, which came to Hosea, the son of
Beeri, in the days of Uzziah, Jotham, Ahaz, and Hezekiah, kings of Judah, and in the days of Jeroboam, the son of Joash, king of Israel.

I.

The idolatry of Israel symbolically represented. Her punishment, and restoration to favor. — CH. I. 2 — II. 1.

2 The beginning of the word of Jehovah by Hosea. Je-
hovah said to Hosea: Go, and take thee a wife of lewd-
ness, and children of lewdness; for the land hath committed
great lewdness; it is false to Jehovah.
3 So he went, and took Gomer, the daughter of Diblaim;
4 and she conceived and bore him a son. And Jehovah
said to him, Call his name Jezreel; for yet a little while,
and I will avenge the blood of Jezreel upon the house of
Jehu, and will bring the kingdom of the house of Israel to
5 an end. Yea, in that day will I break the bow of Israel
in the valley of Jezreel.
6 And she conceived again, and bore a daughter. And
God said to him, Call her name Unpitied; for I will no
more have pity upon the house of Israel, but will surely
7 take them away. But upon the house of Judah will I
have pity, and will save them by Jehovah their God; I
will not save them by bow, nor by sword, nor by battle,
nor by horses, nor by horsemen.

8 Then she weaned her daughter Unpitied, and conceived,
9 and bore a son. And God said, Call his name Not-my-
people. For ye are not my people, and I will not be
your God.
10 Yet the number of the children of Israel shall be as the
sand of the sea, which cannot be measured, or numbered;
and in the place where it was said to them, Ye are not my
people, there shall it be said to them, Ye are the sons of
11 the living God. Then shall the sons of Judah and the
sons of Israel be gathered together, and shall appoint to
themselves one head, and shall come up out of the land.
1 For great shall be the day of Jezreel. Call ye your
brethren My-people; and your sisters Pitied.

II.

The same subject. — CH. II. 2–23.

2 CONTEND ye with your mother, contend!
For she is not my wife,
Nor am I her husband;
That she put away lewdness from her face,
And adultery from her breasts,
Lest I strip her naked,
And expose her, as when she was born;
3 Lest I make her as the desert, and like a parched land,
And kill her with thirst.
4 Upon her sons also I will not have pity,
For they are the sons of lewdness.
5 For their mother hath been guilty of lewdness;
She that bore them hath brought upon herself shame;
For she said, I will go after my lovers,
Who give me my food and my water,
My wool and my flax, my oil and my strong drink.
6 Therefore, behold, I will hedge up her way with thorns,
And I will enclose her with a wall,
So that she shall not find her paths.
7 When she followeth after her lovers, she shall not over-
take them;
When she seeketh them, she shall not find them

Then shall she say, I will go back to my former husband;
For then it was better with me than now.

8 For she did not consider that I gave her corn, and wine,
and oil,
And multiplied silver unto her,
And gold, of which they made images of Baal.
9 Therefore will I take back my corn in its time,
And my new wine in its season,
And I will take away my wool and my flax,
Which covered her nakedness.
10 And now will I reveal her shame before the eyes of her
lovers,
And none shall deliver her out of my hand.
11 And I will cause all her joy to cease;
Her feasts, and new moons, and sabbaths,
And all her festal days.
12 I will destroy her vines, and her fig-trees,
Of which she said, These are my hire,
Which my lovers have given me;
And I will make them a forest,
And the wild beasts shall eat them.
13 I will punish her for the days of the Baals,
When she burned incense to them,
And decked herself with her rings and her jewels,
And went after her lovers,
And forgot me, saith Jehovah.

14 Therefore, behold, I will allure her,
And will lead her to the desert,
And will speak kindly to her;
15 And thence will I give her her vineyards,
And the valley of Achor for a door of hope;
And there shall she sing, as in the days of her youth;
As in the day when she came up from the land of Egypt.
16 At that time, saith Jehovah,
Thou shalt call me, MY HUSBAND;
Thou shalt no more call me, MY BAAL;
17 For I will take away the name of the Baals out of her
mouth,
And their name shall no more be uttered.
18 At that time will I make for them a covenant

With the beasts of the forest, and with the birds of heaven,
And with the creeping things of the ground.
The bow and the sword and the battle will I break from the land,
And I will cause them to lie down in safety.
19 I will betroth thee to me forever;
Yea, I will betroth thee to me in righteousness, and in justice,
And in kindness, and in tender love.
20 Yea, I will betroth thee to me in faithfulness,
And thou shalt know Jehovah.

21 At that time will I hear, saith Jehovah;
I will hear the heavens;
And they shall hear the earth,
22 And the earth shall hear the corn, and the new wine, and the oil,
And they shall hear Jezreel.
23 And I will plant her for myself in the land;
And I will have pity upon her that was called Unpitied;
And I will say to them called Not-my-people, Thou art my people;
And they shall say, Thou art my God.

III.

Israel's idolatry, desolation, and subsequent restoration. — CH. III.

1 AND Jehovah said to me, Go again, love a woman that
is loved by another, and is an adulteress; even as Jeho-
vah loveth the sons of Israel, who turn themselves to
2 other gods, and love raisin-cakes. So I bought her for me
for fifteen shekels of silver, and a homer and a half of
3 barley. And I said to her, Thou shalt wait for me many
days; thou shalt not play the harlot, and thou shalt not
4 be with any man; so will I also wait for thee. For the
sons of Israel shall abide many days without a king, and
without a prince, and without a sacrifice, and without an
5 image, and without an ephod, and without teraphim. Af-

terward shall the sons of Israel return, and seek Jehovah
their God, and David their king, and turn with fear to
Jehovah and his goodness in future times.

IV.

Various judgments denounced against the wickedness and idolatry of Israel. — CH. IV.

1 HEAR the word of Jehovah, ye sons of Israel!
For Jehovah hath a controversy with the inhabitants of the land;
For there is no truth, nor mercy, nor knowledge of God in the land.
2 Perjury, and falsehood, and murder,
And theft, and adultery have broken forth,
And blood reacheth to blood.
3 Therefore shall the land mourn,
And every one that dwelleth therein shall languish,
Together with the beasts of the forest, and the birds of heaven;
Yea, even the fishes of the sea shall perish.
4 Yet let no man rebuke, and let no man reprove;
For thy people are like those that contend with the priest.
5 Therefore shalt thou fall by day,
And the prophet shall fall with thee by night,
And I will destroy thy mother.
6 My people is destroyed for lack of knowledge;
Since thou hast rejected knowledge,
I will also reject thee, so that thou shalt no more be my priest;
Since thou hast forgotten the law of thy God,
I also will forget thy children.
7 As they have become great, so have they sinned against me;
I will change their glory into shame.
8 They feed upon the sins of my people,
And incline their hearts to their iniquity.
9 And it shall be, as with the people, so with the priest;
I will punish them for their ways,

And requite them for their doings.
10 They shall eat and shall not be satisfied;
They shall commit fornication, and shall not increase,
For they have left off giving heed to Jehovah.

11 Fornication and wine and new wine take away the understanding;
12 My people ask counsel of their stocks,
And their staff revealeth to them.
For the spirit of fornication causeth them to err;
Yea, they commit fornication, forsaking their God.
13 On the tops of the mountains they sacrifice,
And on the hills they burn incense,
Under the oak, and the poplar, and the terebinth,
Because their shade is pleasant.
Therefore your daughters commit fornication,
And your daughters-in-law commit adultery;
14 I will not punish your daughters, when they commit fornication,
Nor your daughters-in-law, when they commit adultery;
For ye yourselves go aside with harlots,
And sacrifice with prostitutes;
Therefore the people that hath not understanding shall fall.

15 Though thou play the harlot, O Israel,
Yet let not Judah offend!
Come ye not to Gilgal,
Neither go ye up to Bethaven.
And swear ye not, saying, As Jehovah liveth!
16 For like a refractory heifer is Israel become refractory,
Therefore will Jehovah feed them, like a lamb in a wide place.
17 Ephraim is joined to idols;
Let him alone!
18 When their carousal is over,
They give themselves up to lasciviousness;
Their rulers love shame.
19 The wind hath bound them up with its wings,
And they shall be brought to shame on account of their sacrifices.

V.

Complaint of the idolatry of Israel and Judah. — CH. V. 1-7.

1 HEAR ye this, O ye priests,
And hearken, O house of Israel,
And give ear, O house of the king!
For judgment is coming upon you,
Because ye have been a snare at Mizpah,
And an outspread net upon Tabor.
2 By their sacrifices they commit deep transgression,
And I will bring chastisement upon them all.
3 I know Ephraim,
And Israel is not hidden from me;
For thou committest fornication, O Ephraim,
And Israel is defiled.
4 They will not frame their doings
To return to their God;
For a spirit of fornication is within them,
And they have no regard to Jehovah.
5 The pride of Israel testifieth to his face;
Therefore shall Israel and Ephraim fall in their iniquity;
Judah also shall fall with them.
6 With their flocks and with their herds shall they go to seek Jehovah,
And shall not find him;
He hath withdrawn himself from them.
7 They have been false to Jehovah,
For they have begotten strange children;
Now shall the new moon consume them with their possessions.

VI.

Israel and Judah threatened with punishmeut. — CH. V. 8 — VI. 3.

8 BLOW ye the trumpet in Gibeah,
And the cornet in Ramah;
Cry aloud at Bethaven!
Look behind thee, O Benjamin!

9 Ephraim shall be desolate in the day of rebuke;
Among the tribes of Israel do I make known what is sure.
10 The princes of Judah are like them that remove the land-mark;
I will pour out my wrath upon them like water.

11 Ephraim is oppressed; he is crushed with punishment,
Because he willingly walked after the decree.
12 I am as a moth to Ephraim,
And as rottenness to the house of Judah.
13 When Ephraim saw his sickness,
And Judah his wound,
Then went Ephraim to the Assyrian,
And Judah sent to the hostile king;
But he will not be able to heal you,
Nor will he cure you of your wound.
14 For I will be as a lion to Ephraim,
And as a young lion to the house of Judah.
I, even I, will tear, and will depart;
I will take away, and none shall rescue.
15 I will go back to my place,
Till they have suffered for their sin, and seek my face,
In their affliction they will seek me early.
1 "Come, and let us return to Jehovah!
For he hath torn, and he will heal us;
He hath smitten, and he will bind us up.
2 After two days will he revive us,
On the third day he will raise us up,
And we shall live in his presence.
3 Let us, therefore, know him;
Let us ever strive to know Jehovah,
His coming forth is sure as the morning;
He will come to us like the rain,
Like the latter rain which watereth the earth."

VII.

Expostulation with Israel and Judah on account of their want of piety. — CH. VI. 4 — 11.

4 O EPHRAIM, what shall I do to thee?
O Judah, what shall I do to thee?
For your goodness is like the morning cloud,
And like the early dew, which vanisheth away.
5 Therefore I have hewn them by the prophets,
I have slain them by the words of my mouth,
And my judgments have gone forth like the light.
6 For I desired mercy, and not sacrifice,
And the knowledge of God rather than burnt-offerings.
7 But they, after the manner of men, have transgressed the covenant;
Even therein have they dealt unfaithfully with me.
8 Gilead is a city of them that do iniquity;
She is full of footsteps of blood.
9 As troops of robbers lying in wait for a man, so is the company of priests;
They murder in the way to Shechem;
Yea, they commit heinous wickedness.
10 I have seen a horrible thing in the house of Israel;
There Ephraim committeth fornication,
Israel is polluted.
11 For thee also, O Judah, a harvest is appointed.

VIII.

Complaint of corrupt manners, violence, and political misconduct. — CH. VII.

1 WHEN I was about to deliver my people from captivity,
When I would have healed Israel,
Then the iniquity of Ephraim was discovered,
And the wickedness of Samaria;
For they practise fraud,

And the thief entereth in,
And the band of robbers spoileth without.
2 And they think not in their hearts,
That I remember all their wickedness.
Now shall their doings encompass them;
They are before my face.
3 With their wickedness they gladden the king,
And with their falsehoods the princes;
All of them are adulterers;
4 They are as an oven heated by the baker;
He ceaseth to stir the fire,
Until the dough which he hath kneaded be leavened.
5 On the feast-day of our king, the princes are sick with the heat of wine,
And he stretcheth out his hand with revilers.
6 For they make ready their heart like an oven, while they lie in wait;
All night the baker sleepeth;
In the morning it gloweth like a flaming fire.
7 They all glow as an oven;
They have devoured their judges;
All their kings have fallen;
And none among them calleth upon me.
8 Ephraim hath mixed himself with the nations;
Ephraim is a cake not turned.
9 Strangers have devoured his strength,
And he knoweth it not;
Yea, gray hairs are sprinkled upon him,
Yet he knoweth it not.
10 The pride of Israel testifieth to his face;
Yet do not they return to Jehovah their God,
Nor seek him, for all this.
11 Ephraim is like a silly dove, without understanding;
They call upon Egypt; they go to Assyria.
12 When they go, I will spread my net over them;
As birds of heaven will I bring them down.
I will chastise them, as hath been proclaimed in their congregation.
13 Woe to them, for they have wandered from me!
Destruction upon them, for they have rebelled against me!
Though I myself would redeem them, they speak falsely to me.

14 They cry not to me from their heart,
But howl upon their beds;
For corn and wine they assemble themselves;
They rebel against me.
15 I have chastened them; I have also strengthened their arms;
Yet do they devise evil against me.
16 They return, but not to the Most High;
They are like a deceitful bow;
Their princes shall fall by the sword for the haughtiness of their tongues;
This shall be their reproach in the land of Egypt.

IX.

Complaint of idolatry in Israel, and threats of punishment on account of their reliance upon foreign nations. — CH. VIII.

1 PUT the trumpet to thy mouth!
Like an eagle cometh an enemy against the house of Jehovah,
Because they have transgressed my covenant,
And have rebelled against my law.
2 They shall say to me,
My God, we know thee, we, thine Israel!
3 Israel hath cast away what is good;
The enemy shall pursue him.
4 They have set up kings, but not by me;
They have made princes, and I knew it not.
Of their silver and their gold have they made themselves idols,
That they may be brought to destruction.
5 An abomination is thy calf, O Samaria!
Mine anger is kindled against them;
How long will it be ere they can attain to purity!
6 For from Israel it came;
The workman made it, and it is no God;
Yea, into fragments shall the calf of Samaria be broken.
7 They have sown the wind,
And they shall reap the whirlwind.

They shall have no standing harvest;
The ear shall yield no meal;
If perchance it yield, strangers shall devour it.
8 Israel is swallowed up;
Soon shall they become among the nations
As a vessel which no one desireth.
9 For they have gone up to Assyria,
Like a solitary wild-ass;
Ephraim hireth lovers;
10 But though they hire among the nations,
Soon will I gather the nations against them;
Then shall they rest a little while from the burden of their king, and their princes!
11 Ephraim hath built many altars for sin,
Therefore shall he have altars for sin.
12 Though I write for him many laws,
They are accounted as a strange thing;
13 As to the sacrifices which they should offer me, they slay flesh and eat it;
Jehovah hath no pleasure in them.
Now will he remember their iniquity,
And punish their sins;
To Egypt shall they return.
14 For Israel hath forgotten his Maker, and builded palaces,
And Judah hath multiplied fenced cities;
But I will send a fire upon his cities,
And it shall devour his palaces.

X.

Punishment threatened on account of idolatry in Israel. — CH. IX. 1-9.

1 REJOICE not, O Israel,
Exult not, like the nations!
For thou committest fornication, forsaking thy God;
Thou lovest hire on every corn-floor.
2 The floor and the vat shall not feed them,
And the new wine shall deceive them.
3 They shall not dwell in the land of Jehovah;
To Egypt shall Ephraim go back,
And eat unclean things in Assyria.

4 They shall pour out no offerings of wine to Jehovah,
Nor shall their sacrifices please him;
They shall be to them as the bread of mourners;
All that eat thereof shall be polluted.
Their bread shall be for their own hunger;
It shall not come into the house of Jehovah.
5 What will ye do in the festal day,
In the day of the feast of Jehovah?
6 For, behold, they go forth from a wasted land;
Egypt shall gather them;
Memphis shall bury them;
The precious places of their silver,
Nettles shall possess them;
Thorns shall spring up in their habitations.
7 The days of visitation are come;
The days of retribution are come —
Israel shall know that the prophet was foolish,
That the man of the spirit was mad —
For the greatness of thy iniquity, and thy great hatred.
8 If Ephraim seek an answer from my God,
The prophet is as the snare of the fowler in all his ways,
A net in the house of his God.
9 They have deeply corrupted themselves, as in the days of
Gibeah;
He will remember their iniquity;
He will requite their sins.

XI.

Israel threatened with destruction. — CH. IX. 10 — 17.

10 I FOUND Israel as grapes in the wilderness;
As the early fruit on the fig-tree, at its first time of bearing,
I saw your fathers.
But they went to Baal Peor,
And separated themselves to shame,
And had abominable idols according to their love.
11 The glory of Ephraim shall fly away as a bird;
They shall not bring forth, nor bear in the womb, nor
conceive;

12 Yea, if they bring up children, I will utterly bereave
them;
Yea, woe to them when I depart from them!
13 I have seen Ephraim planted, like Tyre, in a rich pasture,
Yet shall Ephraim bring out his children to the murderer.
14 Give them, O Jehovah! What wilt thou give them?
Give them a miscarrying womb,
And dry breasts!
15 All their wickedness is in Gilgal;
Yea, there have I hated them for the wickedness of their
doings;
I will drive them from my house;
I will love them no more;
All their princes are revolters.
16 Ephraim is smitten;
Their root is dried up; they shall bear no fruit;
Yea, though they should beget children,
I will destroy the beloved fruit of the womb.
17 My God shall cast them away,
Because they have not hearkened to him,
And they shall be wanderers among the nations.

XII.

Punishment of idolatry and other vices of Israel. — CH. X.

1 ISRAEL is a luxuriant vine,
That bringeth forth fruit;
But according to the abundance of his fruit hath he
abounded in altars;
According to the goodness of his land hath he made
goodly images.
2 Their heart is divided; now shall they suffer for it;
He will break down their altars,
And destroy their images.
3 For soon shall they say, We have no king,
Because we fear not Jehovah;
What can a king do for us?
4 They utter empty words,

Swearing falsely, making covenants,
And now judgment springeth up, as hemlock in the furrows of the field.
5 For the calf of Bethaven shall the inhabitants of Samaria be in fear;
Yea, its people shall grieve for it,
And its priests shall tremble for it,
Because its glory has departed from it.
6 It shall be carried to Assyria,
As a present to the hostile king.
Ephraim shall be covered with confusion,
And Israel shall be ashamed of his doings.
7 Samaria shall be brought to destruction;
Her king shall be as a twig upon the waters.
8 The high places of Aven, the sin of Israel, shall be destroyed;
The thorn and the thistle shall come up on their altars.
And they shall say to the mountains, Cover us!
And to the hills, Fall on us!

9 More than in the days of Gibeah hast thou sinned, O Israel!
There they stood;
The battle in Gibeah against the sons of iniquity did not overtake them.
10 Now will I chastise them according to my pleasure,
And the nations shall be gathered together against them,
When I shall bind them for their two iniquities.
11 Ephraim is a trained heifer, that loveth to tread out the corn;
But I will lay the yoke upon her fair neck;
I will cause Ephraim to draw,
Judah shall plough, Jacob shall harrow.

12 Sow for yourselves to righteousness, and ye shall reap according to your piety;
Break up your fallow ground;
For it is a time to seek Jehovah,
Till he come and rain righteousness upon you.
13 Ye plough wickedness, ye shall reap injustice;
Ye shall eat the fruit of falsehood.
Because thou trustest in thy way, in the multitude of thy mighty men,

14 There shall arise a tumult among thy people,
And all thy fortresses shall be destroyed,
As Shalman destroyed Betharbel in the day of battle,
When the mother was dashed in pieces with her children.
15 Such things shall Bethel bring upon you
Because of your great wickedness.
In the morning shall the king of Israel be destroyed.

XIII.

Israel's ingratitude, and its punishment. Promise of restoration. — CH. XI. 1 — 11.

1 WHEN Israel was a child, I loved him,
And called my son out of Egypt.
2 But they turned away from those that called them,
They sacrificed to images of Baal;
They burned incense to idols.
3 I helped Ephraim to go,
Yea, I took them up in my arms;
Yet they marked not that I healed them.
4 I drew them with human cords, with bands of love;
I was to them as those who lift up the yoke from their jaws;
I dealt gently with them, and gave them food.
5 They shall no more go down to Egypt;
For the Assyrian shall be their king,
Because they refuse to return to me.
6 The sword shall fall upon their cities,
It shall consume their bars, and devour
Because of their devices.
7 For my people persevere in turning away from me;
Though they are called to the Most High,
None will exalt him.

8 How shall I give thee up, Ephraim?
How shall I abandon thee, Israel?
How shall I make thee as Admah?
How shall I set thee as Zeboim?
My heart is changed within me;
Yea, my compassion is kindled.

9 I will not execute the fierceness of mine anger ;
I will not again destroy Ephraim ;
For I am God, and not man,
The Holy One in the midst of thee,
And I will not come in anger.
10 They shall walk after Jehovah, when he shall roar like a lion,
When he shall roar, then shall their sons hasten from the west ;
11 They shall hasten as a bird from Egypt,
And as a dove from the land of Assyria,
And I will place them in their houses, saith Jehovah.

XIV.

Rebuke of Israel and Judah on account of their wickedness. — Ch. XI. 12 — XII.

12 Ephraim compasseth me about with falsehood,
And the house of Israel with deceit ;
Judah also is inconstant toward God,
Toward the holy and faithful one.
1 Ephraim feedeth on wind, and followeth after the east wind ;
Every day he multiplieth falsehood and violence ;
They make a league with Assyria,
And oil is carried into Egypt.
2 Therefore Jehovah hath a controversy with Judah.
And he will punish Jacob for his ways,
And requite him according to his doings.
3 In the womb he took his brother by the heel,
And in his strength he contended with God ;
4 Yea, he contended with the angel, and prevailed ;
He wept, and made supplication to him.
At Bethel he found him,
And there he spake with us.
5 And Jehovah, the God of hosts,
Jehovah is his name.
6 Therefore turn thou to thy God ;
Observe mercy and justice,
And hope in thy God always !

7 He is a Canaanite; in his hands are the balances of deceit;
He loveth to oppress.
8 Yet Ephraim saith, Lo, I have become rich;
I have found myself substance;
In all my earnings can be found no transgression in which there is guilt.
9 Yet I, Jehovah, have been thy God from the land of Egypt;
I will again cause thee to dwell in tents, as in the days of the solemn feast.
10 I have also spoken to the prophets,
And I have given many visions,
And by the prophets I have used similitudes.
11 Behold, Gilead is full of iniquity;
Surely they have become corrupt;
In Gilgal they sacrifice oxen,
And their altars are like the heaps in the furrows of the field.
12 Jacob fled into the country of Syria,
And Israel served for a wife,
And for a wife he kept sheep.
13 By a prophet Jehovah brought up Israel out of Egypt,
And by a prophet was he preserved.
14 Ephraim hath provoked his Lord most bitterly;
Therefore will he leave his blood upon him,
And recompense to him his reproach.

XV.

The destruction of Israel threatened. — Ch. XIII.

1 Once when Ephraim spake, there was trembling; he was exalted in Israel;
But he offended through Baal, and died.
2 And now they sin more and more,
And have made to themselves molten images;
Of their silver by their skill have they made idols;
All of it is the work of artificers.

They say concerning them,
Whoever will sacrifice, let him kiss the calves!
3 Therefore shall they be as the morning cloud,
And as the early dew, which passeth away;
As chaff driven with a whirlwind from the thrashing-floor,
And as smoke from the chimney.
4 Yet I, Jehovah, have been thy God from the land of Egypt,
And thou hast known no God but me;
Yea, there was no saviour besides me.
5 I cared for thee in the desert,
In the land of great drought.
6 As they were fed, so they were filled;
They were filled, and their heart was lifted up;
Therefore they forgot me.
7 Therefore have I become to them as a lion;
As a leopard I watch for them in the way;
8 I will meet them as a bear bereaved of her whelps,
And I will rend the caul of their heart,
And there will I devour them as a lioness;
The wild beast shall tear them.
9 It hath been thy destruction, O Israel,
That against me, against thy help, thou hast rebelled!
10 Where is now thy king?
Let him save thee in all thy cities!
And where thy judges,
In regard to whom thou saidst, Give me a king and princes!
11 I gave thee a king in mine anger,
And I have taken him away in my wrath.
12 The iniquity of Ephraim is treasured up;
His guilt is laid up in store.
13 The pangs of a travailing woman shall come upon him;
He is an unwise son,
For else would he not tarry long in the place of the breaking forth of children.

14 I will ransom them from the power of the grave;
I will redeem them from death;
O death, where is thy plague?
O grave, where is thy destruction?
Repentance is hidden from mine eyes.

15 Though he be fruitful among his brethren,
An east wind shall come,
A wind of Jehovah shall come up from the desert,
And his spring shall become dry,
And his fountain shall be dried up,
And the treasure of all his pleasant vessels shall be spoiled.
16 Samaria shall suffer for her guilt,
For she hath rebelled against her God.
They shall fall by the sword;
Their infants shall be dashed in pieces,
And their women with child shall be ripped up.

XVI.

An exhortation to repentance, and promise of the future favor of God.—Ch. XIV.

1 Return, O Israel, to Jehovah thy God;
For thou hast fallen by thine iniquity.
2 Take with you words,
And return to Jehovah, saying,
"Forgive all our iniquity, and receive us graciously,
And we will render to thee the sacrifices of our lips!
3 Assyria shall not help us;
We will not ride on horses;
And no more will we say to the work of our hands,
Ye are our Gods!
For from thee the fatherless obtaineth mercy."

4 "I will heal their rebellion; I will love them freely;
For my anger is turned away from them.
5 I will be as the dew to Israel;
He shall blossom as the lily,
And strike his roots like Lebanon.
6 His sprouts shall spread forth,
And his beauty shall be as the olive-tree,
And his fragrance as Lebanon.
7 They that dwell under his shadow
Shall revive as the corn;

They shall shoot forth as the vine;
Their name shall be like the wine of Lebanon.
8 Ephraim shall say, What have I more to do with idols?
I will hear him; I will care for him;
I will be like a green cypress-tree;
From me shall thy fruit be found."

9 Who is wise, that he may understand these things,
Prudent, that he may know them?
For the ways of Jehovah are right,
And the righteous walk in them;
But in them transgressors stumble.

ISAIAH.

INSCRIPTION.

1 The visions of Isaiah, the son of Amoz, which he saw
concerning Judah and Jerusalem, in the days of Uzziah, Jotham, Ahaz, and Hezekiah, kings of Judah.

I.

Remonstrance against the depravity of the times. — CH. I. 2-31.

2 HEAR, O ye heavens, and give ear, O earth!
For Jehovah speaketh:
"I have nourished and brought up children,
And they have rebelled against me.
3 The ox knoweth his owner,
And the ass his master's crib;
But Israel doth not know;
My people do not consider."

4 Ah, sinful nation! a people laden with iniquity!
A race of evil-doers! degenerate children!
They have forsaken Jehovah; they have despised the Holy One of Israel;
They have gone backward.
5 Where can ye be smitten again,
Since ye renew your rebellion?
The whole head is sick, and the whole heart faint;
6 From the sole of the foot even to the head, there is no soundness in it;
It is all bruises, and stripes, and fresh wounds,

Neither pressed, nor bound up, nor softened with ointment.
7 Your country is desolate;
Your cities are burnt with fire;
Your ground, strangers devour it before your eyes;
It is become desolate, destroyed by an enemy.
8 And the daughter of Zion is left as a shed in a vineyard,
As a hut in a garden of cucumbers,
As a besieged city.
9 Had not Jehovah of hosts left us a small remnant,
We had soon become as Sodom;
We had been like to Gomorrah.

10 Hear ye the word of Jehovah, ye princes of Sodom!
Give ear to the instruction of our God, ye people of Gomorrah!
11 What to me is the multitude of your sacrifices? saith Jehovah;
I am satiated with burnt-offerings of rams, and the fat of fed beasts;
In the blood of bullocks and of lambs and of goats I have no delight.
12 When ye come to appear before me,
Who hath required this of you, to tread my courts?
13 Bring no more false oblations!
Incense is an abomination to me,
The new moon also, and the sabbath, and the calling of the assembly;
Iniquity and festivals I cannot endure.
14 Your new moons and your feasts my soul hateth;
They are a burden to me;
I am weary of bearing them.
15 When ye spread forth your hands,
I will hide mine eyes from you;
Yea, when ye multiply prayers, I will not hear;
Your hands are full of blood!
16 Wash you; make you clean;
Put away your evil doings from before mine eyes;
17 Cease to do evil;
Learn to do well;
Seek justice; relieve the oppressed;
Defend the fatherless; plead for the widow!

18 Come, now, and let us argue together, saith Jehovah.
Though your sins be as scarlet, they shall be as white as snow;
Though they be red as crimson, they shall be like wool.
19 If ye be willing and obedient,
Ye shall consume the good of the land.
20 But if ye refuse, and be rebellious,
The sword shall consume you;
For the mouth of Jehovah hath said it.

21 How is the faithful city become a harlot,
She that was full of equity!
Once justice dwelt in her, but now murderers!
22 Thy silver is become dross;
Thy wine is adulterated with water.
23 Thy princes are faithless, companions of thieves;
Every one of them loveth gifts, and seeketh rewards;
They render not justice to the fatherless,
And the cause of the widow cometh not before them.

24 Wherefore, thus saith the Lord, Jehovah of hosts, the Mighty One of Israel:
Ha! I will ease me of mine adversaries,
And avenge me of mine enemies.
25 And I will again turn my hand toward thee,
And wholly purge away thy dross,
And take away all thy alloy.
26 And I will restore thee judges, as at the first,
And counsellors, as at the beginning.
Then shalt thou be called the city of righteousness, the faithful city.
27 Through justice shall Zion be delivered,
And her reformed sons through righteousness.
28 But destruction shall fall at once on the rebels and sinners;
Yea, they that forsake Jehovah shall be consumed.
29 For ye shall be ashamed of the terebinths in which ye delighted;
Ye shall blush for the gardens which ye loved;
30 And ye shall be as a terebinth-tree whose leaves are withered,
And as a garden in which is no water.

31 The strong shall become tow,
And his work a spark of fire;
Both shall burn together,
And none shall quench them.

II.

INSCRIPTION.

1 The word, which was revealed to Isaiah, the son of Amoz, concerning Judah and Jerusalem.

Promises of glorious future times, when distant nations shall voluntarily subject themselves to the religion and laws of the people of Jehovah. But the Jewish nation must first be purified from their various vices by the just judgments of God. — CH. II., III., IV.

2 It shall come to pass in the last days,
That the mountain of the house of Jehovah shall be established at the head of the mountains,
And exalted above the hills;
And all nations shall flow unto it.
3 And many kingdoms shall go, and shall say,
"Come, let us go to the mountain of Jehovah,
To the house of the God of Jacob,
That he may teach us his ways,
And that we may walk in his paths!"
For from Zion shall go forth a law,
And the word of Jehovah from Jerusalem.
4 He shall be a judge of the nations,
And an umpire of many kingdoms;
And they shall beat their swords into ploughshares,
And their spears into pruning-hooks;
Nation shall not lift up the sword against nation,
Neither shall they learn war any more.

5 O house of Jacob, come ye,
And let us walk in the light of Jehovah!
6 For thou hast forsaken thy people, the house cf Jacob,
Because they are full of the East,

And are sorcerers, like the Philistines,
And strike hands with a foreign race!
7 Their land is full of silver and gold,
And there is no end to their treasures;
Their land is full of horses,
And there is no end to their chariots;
8 Their land is full of idols;
They bow down to the work of their own hands, —
To that which their own fingers have made.
9 Therefore shall the mean man be bowed down,
And the great man be brought low;
And thou wilt not forgive them!

10 Go into the rock, hide yourselves in the dust,
From the terror of Jehovah, and the glory of his majesty!
11 The proud looks of man shall be humbled,
And the loftiness of mortals shall be brought low;
Jehovah alone shall be exalted in that day.
12 For Jehovah of hosts holdeth a day of judgment
Against all that is proud and lofty;
Against all that is exalted, and it shall be brought low;
13 Against all the cedars of Lebanon, the high and the exalted,
And against all the oaks of Bashan;
14 Against all the lofty mountains,
And against all the high hills;
15 Against every lofty tower,
And against every high wall;
16 Against all the ships of Tarshish,
And against all their beautiful flags.
17 The pride of man shall be humbled;
The loftiness of mortals shall be brought low;
Jehovah alone shall be exalted in that day.

18 The idols shall wholly pass away;
19 And men shall go into clefts of the rocks, and caves of the earth,
From the terror of Jehovah, and the glory of his majesty,
When he ariseth to make the earth tremble.

20 At that time shall men cast away their idols of silver and their idols of gold,
Which they have made to worship,
To the moles and the bats;
21 Fleeing into caves of the rocks, and clefts of the craggy rocks,
From the terror of Jehovah, and the glory of his majesty,
When he ariseth to make the earth tremble.
22 Trust, then, no more in man,
Whose breath is in his nostrils!
For what account is to be made of him!

1 For behold, the Lord, Jehovah of hosts,
Taketh away from Jerusalem and from Judah every stay and support;
The whole stay of bread, and the whole stay of water;
2 The mighty man, and the warrior,
The judge, the prophet, the diviner, and the sage,
3 The captain of fifty, and the honorable man,
The counsellor, the expert in arts, and the skilful in charms.
4 And I will make boys their princes,
And children shall rule over them.
5 And the people shall oppress one another,
Man striving against man, and neighbor against neighbor;
The boy shall behave himself insolently toward the aged,
And the base toward the honorable.
6 Then shall a man take hold of his brother in his father's house, [and say,]
Thou hast yet clothing,
Be thou our ruler,
And take this ruin into thy hands!
7 But in that day shall he lift up his hand, and say:
I am no healer;
In my house is neither bread nor raiment;
Make not me ruler of the people!
8 For Jerusalem tottereth, and Judah falleth,
Because their tongues and their deeds are against Jehovah,
To provoke his holy eyes.

9 Their very countenance witnesseth against them;
They publish their sin like Sodom; they hide it not;
Woe to them, for they bring evil upon themselves!
10 Say ye of the righteous that it shall be well with him,
For he shall eat the fruit of his doings.
11 Woe to the wicked, it shall be ill with him,
For the work of his hands shall be repaid him!
12 As for my people, children are their oppressors,
And women rule over them.
O my people, thy leaders cause thee to err,
And destroy the way in which thou walkest!

13 Jehovah standeth up to maintain his cause;
He standeth up to judge his people.
14 Jehovah entereth into judgment with the elders of his people, and their princes:
"So then ye have consumed the vineyard;
The plunder of the poor is in your houses!
15 What mean ye, that ye crush my people,
And grind the faces of the poor?"
Saith Jehovah, the Lord of hosts.

16 Thus, also, saith Jehovah:
Because the daughters of Zion are haughty,
And walk with outstretched necks,
And glance their eyes wantonly,
Mincing their steps as they go,
And tinkling with their foot-clasps,
17 Therefore will the Lord make their heads bald,
And Jehovah will expose their nakedness.
18 In that day shall the Lord take from them
The ornaments of the foot-clasps, and the net-works, and the crescents;
19 The ear-rings, and the bracelets, and the veils;
20 The turbans, and the ankle-chains, and the belts;
The perfume-boxes, and the amulets;
21 The finger-rings, and the nose-jewels;
22 The embroidered robes, and the tunics, and the cloaks, and the purses;
23 The mirrors, and the linen shifts, and the head-bands, and the large veils.
24 And instead of perfume there shall be corruption;

Instead of a belt, a rope;
Instead of curled locks, baldness;
Instead of a wide mantle, a covering of sackcloth;
Fire-scars instead of beauty.
25 Thy men shall fall by the sword,
Yea, thy mighty men in battle;
26 Her gates shall lament and mourn,
And she, being desolate, shall sit upon the ground.

1 In that day shall seven women lay hold of one man, saying:
We will eat our own bread,
And wear our own garments,
Only let us be called by thy name,
And take away our reproach!

2 In that day shall the increase of Jehovah be glorious and honorable,
And the fruit of the land excellent and beautiful,
For them that have escaped of Israel.
3 All that remain in Zion,
And all that are left in Jerusalem,
Shall be called holy;
Every one that is written down for life in Jerusalem.
4 When the Lord shall have washed away the filth of the daughters of Zion,
And have removed the blood of Jerusalem from the midst of her,
By a spirit of judgment and a spirit of destruction,
5 Then shall Jehovah create upon the whole extent of mount Zion, and upon her places of assembly,
A cloud and smoke by day,
And the brightness of a flaming fire by night;
Yea, for all that is glorious there shall be a shelter;
6 There shall be a tent by day for a shadow from the heat,
And for a refuge and shelter from the storm and rain.

III.

Parable of Jehovah's vineyard. Woes denounced against various forms of wickedness. CH. V.

1 LET me sing now a song respecting my friend,
A song respecting my friend touching his vineyard.
My friend had a vineyard
On a very fruitful hill;
2 He digged it, and cleared it of stones,
And planted it with the choicest vine,
And built a tower in the midst of it,
And hewed out a wine-press therein;
Then he looked that it should bring forth its grapes,
But it brought forth sour grapes.
3 And now, O inhabitants of Jerusalem, and men of Judah,
Judge ye between me and my vineyard!
4 What could have been done for my vineyard
That I have not done for it?
Why, then, when I looked that it should bring forth its grapes,
Brought it forth sour grapes?
5 But come now, and I will tell you
What I mean to do with my vineyard.
I will take away its hedge, and it shall be eaten up;
I will break down its wall, and it shall be trodden down;
6 And I will make it a waste;
It shall not be pruned, nor digged,
But shall grow up into thorns and briers;
I will also command the clouds
That they shed no rain upon it.

7 The vineyard of Jehovah of hosts is the house of Israel,
And the men of Judah the plant of his delight.
He looked for justice, and behold, bloodshed!
For righteousness, and behold, outcry!

8 Woe to them that join house to house,
That add field to field,

Till there is no place left,
And they dwell alone in the land.
9 To mine ear hath Jehovah of hosts revealed it:
Surely many houses shall become a desolation,
The great and the fair ones, without an inhabitant.
10 Yea, ten acres of vineyard shall yield a single bath of wine,
And a homer of seed shall produce but an ephah.

11 Woe to them that rise early in the morning to follow strong drink, —
Who sit late in the night that wine may inflame them!
12 And the lyre and the harp, the tabret and the pipe, and wine, are at their feasts,
But they regard not the work of Jehovah,
Nor attend to the operation of his hands.
13 Therefore shall my people be led captive, when they think not of it;
Their honorable men shall be famished with hunger,
And their rich men parched with thirst.
14 Therefore doth the under-world enlarge its greedy throat,
And stretch open its mouth without measure,
And down go her nobility and her wealth,
Her busy throng, and all that was joyful within her.
15 The mean man shall be bowed down,
And the great man shall be brought low,
And the eyes of the haughty shall be humbled;
16 Jehovah of hosts shall be exalted through judgment;
Yea, God, the Holy One, shall be sanctified through righteousness.
17 Then shall the lambs feed, as in their own pasture,
And the deserted fields of the rich shall strangers consume.

18 Woe to them that draw calamity with cords of wickedness,
And punishment as with wagon-traces, —
19 Who say, Let him make speed, let him hasten his work, that we may see it!
Let the purpose of the Holy One of Israel draw near and be fulfilled, that we may know it!
20 Woe to them that call evil good, and good evil,

That put darkness for light, and light for darkness,
That put bitter for sweet, and sweet for bitter!
21 Woe to them that are wise in their own eyes,
And prudent in their own conceit!
22 Woe to them that are valiant to drink wine,
And men of might to mingle strong drink!
23 That clear the guilty for a reward,
And take away from the righteous his right!
24 Therefore, as fire devours stubble,
And as the withered grass sinks into the flame,
So their root shall become rottenness,
And their blossom shall fly up like dust.
For they have despised the law of Jehovah of hosts,
And contemned the word of the Holy One of Israel.
25 Therefore is the anger of Jehovah kindled against his people;
He stretcheth forth his hand against them, and smiteth them, so that the mountains tremble,
And their carcasses are as dung in the midst of the streets;
For all this his anger is not turned away,
But his hand is stretched out still.

26 He lifteth up a banner for the nations afar off,
He whistleth for them from the ends of the earth,
And behold, they haste, and come swiftly.
27 None among them is weary, and none stumbleth;
None slumbereth nor sleepeth;
The girdle of their loins is not loosed,
Nor the latchet of their shoes broken.
28 Their arrows are sharp,
And all their bows bent;
The hoofs of their horses are like flint,
And their wheels like a whirlwind.
29 Their roaring is like the roaring of the lion;
They roar like young lions;
They roar, and seize the prey;
They bear it away, and none can rescue it.
30 Yea, in that day shall they roar against them like the roaring of the sea;
And if one look to the land, behold darkness and sorrow,
And the light is darkened by its clouds.

IV.

The call of Isaiah to the prophetical office. — Ch. VI.

1 In the year in which King Uzziah died, I saw the
Lord sitting on a throne high and lifted up, and the train
of his robe filled the temple.
2 Around him stood seraphs; each one of them had six
wings; with two he covered his face, with two he covered
3 his feet, and with two he did fly. And one called to
another, and said:

Holy, holy, holy is Jehovah of hosts;
The whole earth is full of his glory.

4 And the foundations of the thresholds were shaken
with the voice of their cry. And the temple was filled
5 with smoke. Then I said, Alas for me! I am undone!
For I am a man of unclean lips, and dwell among a peo-
ple of unclean lips, and mine eyes have seen the King,
6 Jehovah of hosts. Then flew one of the seraphs to me,
having in his hands a glowing stone, which he had taken
with the tongs from the altar. And he touched my
7 mouth, and said, Behold, this toucheth thy lips, and thine
iniquity is taken away, and thy sin is expiated.

8 And I heard the voice of the Lord, saying,
Whom shall I send, and who will go for us?
And I said: Behold, here am I; send me!
9 And he said:
Go, and say thou to this people,
Hear ye, indeed, but understand not;
See ye, indeed, but perceive not!
10 Make the heart of this people gross;
Make their ears dull, and blind their eyes;
That they may not see with their eyes, nor hear with their ears,
Nor perceive with their hearts, and turn, and be healed.
11 Then said I, How long, Lord? He said:
Until the cities be laid waste, so that there be no inhabitant,
And the houses, so that there be no man,

And the land be left utterly desolate;
12 Until Jehovah have removed the men far away,
And there be great desolation in the land.
13 And though there be a tenth part remaining in it,
Even this shall again be destroyed;
Yet as when the terebinth and the oak are cut down,
Their stem remaineth alive,
So shall a holy race be the stem of the nation.

V.

A prediction of the ill-success of the designs of the Israelites and Syrians against Judah, and of the subsequent ruin of Judah by the Assyrians, with whom Ahaz wished to form an alliance. — CH. VII.

1 IN the time of Ahaz, the son of Jotham, the son of
Uzziah, king of Judah, Rezin, king of Syria, and Pekah,
the son of Remaliah, king of Israel, came up against Je-
rusalem to besiege it; but he could not prevail against it
2 And when it was told the house of David, that the
Syrians had encamped in Ephraim, his heart was moved,
and the hearts of his people, as the trees of the forest are
moved with the wind.
3 Then said Jehovah to Isaiah, Go forth to meet Ahaz,
thou and Shear-Jashub thy son, at the end of the aque-
duct of the upper pool, in the way to the fuller's field;
4 and say to him:

Take heed, and be quiet!
Fear not, neither let thy heart be faint
On account of the two tails of these smoking firebrands,
On account of the fierce wrath of Rezin with the Syrians, and of the son of Remaliah,
5 Because Syria deviseth evil against thee,
Ephraim and the son of Remaliah, saying,
6 "Let us go up against Judah, and besiege the city,
And take it,
And set a king in the midst of it,
Even the son of Tabeal."

7 Thus saith the Lord Jehovah:
"It shall not stand, neither shall it be;
8 But the head of Syria shall still be Damascus,
And the head of Damascus, Rezin;
[And within threescore and five years shall Ephraim be
broken, that he be no more a people.]
9 And the head of Ephraim shall still be Samaria,
And the head of Samaria, the son of Remaliah.
If ye will not believe, neither shall ye thrive."

10 Jehovah spake also again to Ahaz:
11 "Ask thee a sign of Jehovah, thy God;
Ask it from below, or in the height above!"
12 And Ahaz said, I will not ask; I will not tempt Jeho-
13 vah! Then he said,
Hear ye now, O house of David!
Is it too small a thing for you to weary men,
That ye should weary my God also?
14 Therefore shall Jehovah himself give you a sign:
Behold, the damsel shall conceive, and bear a son,
And she shall call his name Immanuel.
15 Milk and honey shall he eat,
Until he learn to refuse the evil, and choose the good;
16 For before this child shall have learned to refuse the evil
and choose the good,
The land shall become desolate,
On account of whose two kings thou art in terror.
17 Yet Jehovah shall bring upon thee, and upon thy people,
and upon thy father's house,
Days such as have not been
Since Ephraim revolted from Judah.
[Even the king of Assyria.]
18 And it shall come to pass in that day
That Jehovah shall whistle for the fly that is at the end
of the streams of Egypt,
And the bee that is in the land of Assyria.
19 And they shall come, and light all of them
In the desolate valleys, and fissures of the rocks,
And upon all hedges, and upon all pastures.
20 In that day shall Jehovah shave, with a razor hired be-
yond the river, [with the king of Assyria,]
The head, and the hair of the feet;

Yea, even the beard shall he take away.
21 And it shall come to pass in that day,
That a man shall keep a young cow, and two sheep;
22 And for the abundance of milk which they produce, shall he eat cheese;
For milk and honey shall all eat
Who are left in the land.
23 And it shall come to pass in that day,
That every place where stood a thousand vines, worth a thousand shekels of silver,
Shall be covered with briers and thorns.
24 With arrows and with bows shall men go thither;
For all the land shall become briers and thorns.
25 All the hills that were digged with the mattock
Shall no one approach through fear of briers and thorns;
They shall be for the pasturage of oxen,
And the trampling of sheep.

VI.

Another prophecy, a little later than the preceding, concerning the destruction of Ephraim and the Syrians, and the invasion of Judah by the Assyrians, with a description of the subsequent glorious and prosperous condition of the Jewish nation under the reign of a wise, mighty, and peaceful prince; referring, as some suppose, to Hezekiah, the son of Ahaz, who was then about twelve years old, or as others with much greater probability believe, to the Messiah. — CH. VIII. 1 — IX. 7.

1 AND Jehovah said to me, Take thee a great tablet, and
with a man's writing-instrument write on it, Hasteth-the-
2 prey, Speedeth-the-spoil. And I took with me faithful
witnesses, Uriah the priest, and Zechariah, the son of
3 Berechiah. I went in to the prophetess, and she conceived
and bore a son. Then said Jehovah to me, Call his name,
4 Hasteth-the-prey, Speedeth-the-spoil. For before the
child shall learn to say, My father, and My mother, the
riches of Damascus and the spoil of Samaria shall be
borne away before the king of Assyria.

5 Moreover, Jehovah spake to me again, saying:
6 Because this people despiseth
The soft-flowing waters of Siloah,
And rejoiceth in Rezin, and the son of Remaliah,
7 Therefore, behold, the Lord bringeth upon them the strong and mighty waters of the river;
[The king of Assyria and all his glory.]
He shall rise above all his channels,
And go over all his banks.
8 And he shall pass through Judah, overflowing and spreading;
Even to the neck shall he reach,
And his stretched-out wings shall fill the whole breadth of thy land, O Immanuel!

9 Rage, ye nations, and despair!
Give ear, all ye distant parts of the earth!
Gird yourselves, and despair!
Gird yourselves, and despair!
10 Form your plan, and it shall come to naught;
Give the command, and it shall not stand;
For God is with us.
11 For thus spake Jehovah to me with a strong hand,
Instructing me not to walk in the way of this people:
12 Call not everything a confederacy which this people calleth a confederacy;
Fear ye not what they fear,
Neither be afraid!
13 Jehovah of hosts, sanctify ye him;
Let him be your fear, and let him be your dread!
14 And he shall be to you a sanctuary;
But a stone of stumbling, and a rock to strike against,
To the two houses of Israel,
A trap and a snare to the inhabitants of Jerusalem.
15 And many among them shall stumble;
They shall fall, and be broken;
They shall be ensnared and taken.
16 Bind up the revelation,
Seal the word, with my disciples!

17 I will, therefore, wait for Jehovah,
Who now hideth his face from the house of Jacob;

Yet will I look for him.
18 Behold, I, and the children which Jehovah hath given me,
Are signs and tokens in Israel
From Jehovah of hosts, who dwelleth upon mount Zion.

19 And when they shall say to you,
"Inquire of the necromancers and the wizards,
That chirp, and that murmur,"
[Then say ye,] "Should not a people inquire of their God?
Should they inquire of the dead for the living?"
20 To the word, to the revelation!
If they speak not according to this,
For them no bright morning shall arise.
21 They shall pass through the land distressed and famished;
And when they are famished, they shall be enraged, and curse their king and their God,
And look upward.
22 And if they look to the earth,
Behold distress and darkness, fearful darkness!
And into darkness shall they be driven.

1 But the darkness shall not remain where now is distress;
Of old he brought the land of Zebulon and the land of Naphtali into contempt;
In future times shall he bring the land of the sea beyond Jordan, the circle of the gentiles, into honor.

2 The people that walk in darkness behold a great light;
They who dwell in the land of death-like shade,
Upon them a light shineth.
3 Thou enlargest the nation;
Thou increasest their joy;
They rejoice before thee with the joy of harvest,
With the joy of those who divide the spoil.
4 For thou breakest their heavy yoke,
And the rod that smote their backs,
And the scourge of the taskmaster,
As in the day of Midian.
5 For every greave of the warrior in battle,
And the war-garment rolled in blood,
Shall be burned; yea, it shall be food for the fire.

6 For to us a child is born,
To us a son is given,
And the government shall be upon his shoulder,
And he shall be called
Wonderful, counsellor, mighty potentate,
Everlasting father, prince of peace;
7 His dominion shall be great,
And peace without end shall be upon the throne of David and his kingdom,
To fix and establish it
Through justice and equity,
Henceforth and forever.
The zeal of Jehovah of hosts will do this.

VII.

Israel, considered as distinct from Judah, is threatened with destruction on account of their perseverance in various vices. — CH. IX. 8 — X. 4.

1.

8 THE Lord sendeth a word against Jacob;
It cometh down to Israel.
9 His whole people shall feel it,
Ephraim, and the inhabitants of Samaria,
Who say in pride and arrogance of heart,
10 "The bricks are fallen down, but we will build with hewn stones;
The sycamores are cut down, but we will replace them with cedars."
11 Jehovah will raise up the enemies of Rezin against them,
And will arm their adversaries;
12 The Syrians before, the Philistines behind,
Who shall devour Israel with wide jaws.
For all this his anger is not turned away,
But his hand is stretched out still.

2.

13 The people turn not to him that smiteth them;
Neither do they seek Jehovah of hosts.

14 Therefore shall Jehovah cut off from Israel the head and the tail,
The palm-branch and the rush, in one day.
15 [The aged and the honorable are the head,
And the prophet that speaketh falsehood is the tail.]
16 For the leaders of this people lead them astray,
And they that are led by them go to destruction.
17 Therefore shall the Lord have no joy in their young men,
And on their orphans and widows he shall have no compassion;
For they are all profane, and evil-doers;
Every mouth speaketh folly.
For all this his anger is not turned away,
But his hand is stretched out still.

3.

18 For wickedness burneth like a fire,
It consumeth the briers and thorns,
And it kindleth the thicket of the forest,
So that it goeth up in columns of smoke.
19 Through the wrath of Jehovah of hosts is the land burned,
And the people are food for the fire;
No one spareth another.
20 They consume on the right hand, and yet are hungry;
They devour on the left, and are not satisfied;
Every one devoureth the flesh of his arm.
21 Manasseh is against Ephraim, and Ephraim against Manasseh,
And both together against Judah.
For all this his anger is not turned away,
But his hand is stretched out still.

4.

1 Woe to them that make unrighteous decrees,
That write oppressive decisions,
2 To turn away the needy from judgment,
And rob the poor of my people of their right;
That the widows may become their prey,
And that they may plunder the orphans.
3 What will ye do in the day of visitation,
And in the desolation which cometh from afar?
To whom will ye flee for help,

And where will ye leave your glory?
4 Forsaken by me, they shall sink down among the prisoners,
And fall among the slain.
For all this his anger is not turned away,
But his hand is stretched out still.

VIII.

Prediction of the destruction of the Assyrian invading army, and of glory and felicity to the remnant of Israel under the Messiah's reign. — CH. X. 5 — XII.

5 WOE to the Assyrian, the rod of mine anger,
The staff in whose hands is the instrument of my indignation!
6 Against an impious nation I will send him,
And against a people under my wrath I will give him a charge
To gather the spoil, and seize the prey,
And to trample them under foot like the mire of the streets.
7 But he doth not so purpose,
And his heart doth not so intend;
But to destroy is in his heart,
And to cut off a multitude of nations.
8 For he saith, "Are not my princes altogether kings?
9 Is not Calno as Carchemish?
Is not Hamath as Arpad?
Is not Samaria as Damascus?
10 As my hand hath seized the kingdoms of the idols,
Whose graven images were more numerous than those of Jerusalem and Samaria,
11 Behold! as I have done to Samaria and her idols,
So will I do to Jerusalem and her images."
12 But when the Lord hath accomplished his whole work upon Mount Zion and Jerusalem,
Then will he punish the fruit of the proud heart of the king of Assyria,
And the arrogance of his lofty eyes.
13 For he hath said: "By the strength of my hand I have done it,

And by my wisdom; for I am wise;
I have removed the bounds of nations,
I have plundered their treasures;
As a hero have I brought down them that sat upon thrones.
14 The riches of the nations hath my hand seized, as a nest;
As one gathereth eggs that have been left,
So have I gathered the whole world.
And there was none that moved the wing,
Or that opened the beak, or that chirped."
15 Shall the axe boast itself against him that heweth with it?
Or shall the saw magnify itself against him that moveth it?
As if the rod should wield him that lifteth it!
As if the staff should lift up him that is not wood!
16 Wherefore the Lord, the Lord of hosts, shall send upon his fat ones leanness,
And under his glory shall he kindle a burning, like the burning of a fire.
17 The light of Israel shall be a fire,
And his Holy One a flame,
Which shall burn and devour his thorns and briers in one day.
18 The glory of his forest and of his fruitful field
From the spirit even to the flesh shall he consume;
It shall be with them as when a sick man fainteth.
19 The remaining trees of the forest shall be few,
So that a child may write them down.

20 In that day shall the remnant of Israel, and they that have escaped of the house of Jacob, no more lean upon him that smote them;
They shall lean upon Jehovah, the Holy One of Israel, in truth.
21 The remnant shall return, the remnant of Jacob, to the mighty Potentate;
22 For though thy people, O Israel, be as the sand of the sea,
Only a remnant of them shall return.
The devastation is decreed;
It shall overflow with righteousness
23 For devastation and punishment doth the Lord, Jehovah of hosts, execute in the midst of the whole land.

24 Yet thus saith the Lord, Jehovah of hosts:
Fear not, O my people, that dwellest in Zion, because of the Assyrian!
With his rod indeed shall he smite thee,
And lift up his staff against thee in the manner of Egypt;
25 But yet a very little while, and my indignation shall have past,
And my anger shall destroy them.
26 Jehovah of hosts shall raise up against him a scourge,
As he smote Midian at the rock of Horeb,
And as he lifted up the rod against the sea;
Yea, he shall lift it up, as in Egypt.
27 In that day shall his burden be removed from thy shoulder,
And his yoke from thy neck;
Yea, thy yoke shall be broken, as that of a fat steer.

28 He is come to Aiath; he passeth through Migron;
In Michmash he leaveth his baggage;
29 They pass the strait;
At Geba they make their night-quarters;
Ramah trembleth;
Gibeah of Saul fleeth.
30 Cry aloud, O daughter of Gallim!
Hear, O Laish!
Alas, poor Anathoth!
31 Madmenah hasteth away;
The inhabitants of Gebim take to flight.
32 Yet one day shall he rest at Nob,
Then shall he shake his hand against the mount of the daughter of Zion,
The hill of Jerusalem.

33 But behold! the Lord, Jehovah of hosts, shall lop the branches with fearful force,
And the high of stature shall be cut down,
And the lofty shall be brought low.
34 He shall hew the thickets of the forest with iron,
And Lebanon shall fall by a mighty hand.

1 Then shall spring forth a shoot from the stem of Jesse,
And a sprout grow up from his roots.

2 The spirit of Jehovah shall rest upon him,
The spirit of wisdom and understanding,
The spirit of counsel and might,
The spirit of the knowledge and of the fear of Jehovah.
3 He shall take delight in the fear of Jehovah;
He shall not judge by the sight of his eyes,
Nor decide by the hearing of his ears.
4 But with righteousness shall he judge the poor,
And decide with equity for the afflicted of the land;
He shall smite the earth with the rod of his mouth;
With the breath of his lips shall he slay the wicked.
5 Righteousness shall be the girdle of his loins,
And faithfulness the girdle of his reins.
6 Then shall the wolf dwell with the lamb,
And the leopard shall lie down with the kid;
The calf, and the young lion, and the fatling shall be together,
And a little child shall lead them.
7 The cow and the bear shall feed together,
Together shall their young lie down,
And the lion shall eat straw like the ox.
8 The suckling shall play upon the hole of the asp,
And the new-weaned child lay his hand on the hiding-place of the basilisk.
9 They shall not hurt nor destroy in all my holy mountain;
For the land shall be full of the knowledge of Jehovah,
As the waters cover the depths of the sea.
10 In that day shall the shoot of Jesse stand as a banner to the nations,
And to him shall the gentiles repair,
And his dwelling-place shall be glorious.
11 In that day shall Jehovah the second time stretch forth his hand
To recover the remnant of his people,
That remaineth, from Assyria, and from Egypt,
And from Pathros, and from Ethiopia, and from Elam,
And from Shinar, and from Hamath,
And from the islands of the sea.
12 He shall set up a banner to the nations,
And gather the outcasts of Israel,
And bring together the dispersed of Judah,
From the four extremities of the earth.

13 Then shall the jealousy of Ephraim depart,
And the enmity in Judah be at an end;
Ephraim shall not be jealous of Judah,
And Judah shall not contend with Ephraim.
14 But they shall fly upon the shoulders of the Philistines at the sea;
Together shall they plunder the children of the East;
On Edom and Moab shall they lay their hand,
And the sons of Ammon shall be subject to them.
15 Then will Jehovah utterly destroy the tongue of the Egyptian sea,
And shake his hand over the river with a mighty wind,
And smite it into seven streams,
So that men may go over it dry-shod.
16 And it shall be a highway for the remnant of the people,
Which shall remain, from Assyria,
As there was to Israel,
When he came up from the land of Egypt.

1 In that day shalt thou say,
"I will praise thee, O Jehovah, for, though thou hast been angry with me,
Thine anger is turned away, and thou comfortest me.
2 Behold, God is my salvation;
I will trust, and will not be afraid;
For Jehovah is my glory, and my song;
It is he who was my salvation."
3 Ye shall draw waters with joy from the fountains of salvation;
4 And in that day ye shall say,
"Give thanks to Jehovah; call upon his name;
Make known his deeds among the people;
Give praises, for his name is exalted!
5 Sing to Jehovah, for he hath done glorious things;
Be this known in all the earth!
6 Cry aloud, shout for joy, O inhabitant of Zion,
For great is the Holy One of Israel in the midst of thee!"

IX.

Prophecy concerning the destruction of Babylon, and the deliverance of the Jews. — CH. XIII. — XIV. 23.

1 A PROPHECY concerning Babylon, which Isaiah, the son of Amoz, saw.

2 Upon the bare mountain lift up a banner;
Cry aloud to them, wave the hand,
That they may enter the gates of the tyrants!
3 I have given orders to my consecrated ones,
Yea, I have called upon my mighty ones to execute mine anger,
My proud exulters!

4 The noise of a multitude upon the mountains, like that of a great people!
The tumultuous noise of kingdoms, of nations gathered together!
Jehovah of hosts mustereth his army for battle.
5 They come from a distant country,
From the end of Heaven,
Jehovah and the instruments of his indignation,
To lay waste the whole land.

6 Howl ye, for the day of Jehovah is at hand!
Like a destruction from the Almighty, it cometh;
7 Therefore shall all hands hang down,
And every heart of man shall melt.
8 They shall be in consternation;
Distress and anguish shall lay hold of them;
As a woman in travail shall they writhe;
They shall look upon one another with amazement;
Their faces shall glow like flames.

9 Behold! the day of Jehovah cometh,
Terrible, full of wrath and burning indignation,
To make the land a waste,
And to destroy the sinners out of it.

10 For the stars of heaven, and the constellations thereof,
Shall not give their light;
The sun shall be darkened at his going forth,
And the moon shall withhold her light.
11 For I will punish the world for its guilt,
And the wicked for their iniquity.
I will put an end to the arrogance of the proud,
And I will bring down the haughtiness of the tyrants.
12 I will make men scarcer than gold;
Yea, men than the gold of Ophir.
13 Therefore I will make the heavens tremble,
And the earth shall be shaken out of her place,
In the anger of Jehovah of hosts,
In the day of his burning indignation.
14 Then shall they be like a chased doe;
Like a flock, which no one gathereth together;
Every one shall turn to his own people,
And every one flee to his own land.
15 Every one that is overtaken shall be thrust through,
And every one that is caught shall fall by the sword.
16 Their children shall be dashed to pieces before their eyes;
Their houses shall be plundered, and their wives ravished.

17 Behold, I stir up against them the Medes,
Who make no account of silver,
And as to gold, they do not regard it.
18 Their bows shall strike down the young men,
And on the fruit of the womb they shall have no compassion;
Their eye shall not pity the children.
19 So shall Babylon, the glory of kingdoms,
The proud ornament of the Chaldeans,
Be like Sodom and Gomorrah, which God overthrew,
20 It shall never more be inhabited;
Nor shall it be dwelt in through all generations.
Nor shall the Arabian pitch his tent there,
Nor shall shepherds make their folds there.
21 But there shall the wild beasts of the desert lodge,
And owls shall fill their houses;
And ostriches shall dwell there,
And satyrs shall dance there.
22 Wolves shall howl in their palaces,

And jackals in their pleasant edifices.
Her time is near,
And her days shall not be prolonged.

1 For Jehovah will have compassion upon Jacob,
And will again set his love upon Israel,
And cause them to rest in his own land.
And strangers shall join themselves to them,
And cleave to the house of Jacob.
2 The nations shall take them and bring them to their own place;
And the house of Israel shall possess them, in the land of Jehovah,
As servants and as handmaids;
They shall take captive their captors,
And they shall rule over their oppressors.
3 So when Jehovah shall have given thee rest
From thy sorrow and thy distress,
And from the hard bondage
Which was laid upon thee,
4 Then shalt thou utter this song over the king of Babylon, and say,
"How hath the tyrant fallen,
The oppression ceased!
5 Jehovah hath broken the staff of the wicked,
The rod of the tyrants,
6 That smote the people in anger,
With a continual stroke,
That lorded it over the nations in wrath
With unremitted oppression.
7 The whole earth is at rest, is quiet;
They break forth into singing.
8 Even the cypress-trees exult over thee,
And the cedars of Lebanon:
'Since thou art fallen,
No feller cometh up against us.'
9 The under-world is in commotion on account of thee,
To meet thee at thy coming;
It stirreth up before thee the shades, all the mighty of the earth;
It arouseth from their thrones all the kings of the nations;
10 They all accost thee, and say,

'Art thou, too, become weak as we?
Art thou become like us?'
11 Thy pomp is brought down to the grave,
And the sound of thy harps.
Vermin have become thy couch,
And worms thy covering.
12 How art thou fallen from heaven,
O Lucifer, son of the morning!
How art thou cast down to the ground,
Thou that didst trample upon the nations!
13 Thou saidst in thy heart, 'I will ascend to heaven,
Above the stars of God will I exalt my throne;
I will sit upon the mount of assembly in the recesses of the north.
14 I will ascend above the height of the clouds;
I will be like the Most High.'
15 But thou art brought down to the grave,
To the depths of the pit.
16 They that see thee gaze upon thee, and view thee attentively, (and say,)
'Is this the man that made the earth tremble,
That shook kingdoms,
17 That made the world a wilderness,
And laid waste its cities,
And sent not his captives to their homes?'
18 All the kings of the nations, yea, all of them,
Lie down in glory, each in his own sepulchre;
19 But thou art cast forth without a grave,
Like a worthless branch;
Covered with the slain, who are pierced by the sword,
Who go down to the stones of the pit,
Like a carcass trampled under foot.
20 Thou shalt not be joined with them in the grave,
Because thou hast destroyed thy country,
And slain thy people;
The race of evil-doers shall nevermore be named.
21 Prepare ye slaughter for his children,
For the iniquity of their fathers,
That they may no more arise, and possess the earth,
And fill the world with enemies!"

22 For I will arise against them, saith Jehovah of hosts,

And I will cut off from Babylon the name and remnant,
Posterity and offspring, saith Jehovah.
23 I will make her the possession of the porcupine, and pools of water;
Yea, I will sweep her away with the besom of destruction, saith Jehovah of hosts.

X.

Fragment concerning the destruction of the Assyrians. — CH. XIV. 24-27.

24 JEHOVAH of hosts hath sworn, saying,
Surely, as I have devised, so shall it come to pass;
The purpose which I have formed, that shall stand,
25 To crush the Assyrian in my land,
And to trample him on my mountains.
Then shall his yoke depart from them,
And his burden be removed from their shoulders.
26 This is the purpose which is formed concerning all the earth,
And this the hand which is stretched out over all the nations.
27 For Jehovah of hosts hath decreed, and who shall disannul it?
And his hand is stretched out, and who shall turn it back?

XI.

Prophecy against the Philistines. — CH. XIV. 28-32.

28 IN the year in which Ahaz the king died came this prophecy.

29 Rejoice not, all Philistia,
Because the rod that smote thee is broken,
For from the root of a serpent shall come forth a basilisk,

And his fruit shall be a flying, fiery serpent.
30 Then shall the most wretched of the poor feed quietly,
And the needy shall lie down in security;
For I will kill thy root with famine,
And thy remnant shall be slain.
31 Howl, O gate! cry aloud, O city!
O Philistia, thou meltest away in terror!
For from the north cometh a smoke,
And there is no straggler in their hosts.
32 What answer shall be given to the messengers of the nations?
That Jehovah hath founded Zion,
And in her shall the poor of his people find refuge.

XII.

The destruction of Moab. — CH. XV., XVI.

1 THE prophecy concerning Moab.

Yea! in the night of assault was Ar of Moab a ruin!
In the night of assault was Kir of Moab a ruin!
2 They go up to the temple, and to Dibon, to weep upon the high places;
Upon Nebo and upon Medeba doth Moab howl;
On every head is baldness,
And every beard is shorn.
3 In their streets they gird themselves with sackcloth;
On the tops of their houses and in their public walks every one howleth,
And melteth away with weeping.
4 Heshbon and Elealah utter a cry;
Even to Jahaz is their voice heard;
Therefore the warriors of Moab shriek aloud;
Their hearts tremble within them.
5 My heart crieth out for Moab,
Whose fugitives wander to Zoar, to Eglath-shelishijah;
For they ascend the heights of Luhith weeping,
And in the way of Horonaim they raise the cry of destruction.

6 For the waters of Nimrim are desolate;
The grass is withered; the tender plant faileth;
There is no green thing left.
7 Wherefore the remnant of their substance and their wealth
They shall carry to the brook of willows.

8 For the cry encompasseth the borders of Moab;
Even to Eglaim reacheth her wailing,
To Beer-Elim her howling.
9 For the waters of Dimon are full of blood;
For I bring new evils upon Dimon;
Upon him that escapeth of Moab will I send a lion,
Even upon him that remaineth in the land.

1 Send ye the lambs to the ruler of the land,
From Selah through the wilderness
To the mount of the daughter of Zion!
2 For as a wandering bird,
As a forthdriven nest,
So shall be the daughters of Moab
At the fords of Arnon; [saying,]
3 "Offer counsel; give decision.
Make thy shadow at noonday like the darkness of night.
Hide the outcasts;
Betray not the fugitives.
4 Let my outcasts dwell with thee, [O Zion!]
Be thou to them a covert from the spoiler!
For the extortion is at an end,
The spoiling ceaseth.
The oppressors are consumed from the land.
5 Then shall your throne be established through mercy,
And upon it shall sit in the house of David
A judge searching for justice, and prompt in equity."

Answer of the Jews.

6 "We have heard of the pride of Moab; he is very proud;
His haughtiness, and his pride, and his insolence,
His vain boastings."

7 Therefore shall Moab howl for Moab;

Every one shall howl;
For the ruins of Kir-hares shall ye mourn,
In deep affliction.
8 For the fields of Heshbon languish,
The lords of the nations break down the choicest shoots of the vine of Sibmah,
They reached even to Jazer; they wandered into the desert;
Her branches were spread out; they crossed the sea.
9 Therefore I will weep, like Jazer, for the vine of Sibmah;
I will water thee with my tears, O Heshbon and Elealah,
For upon thy summer fruits, and thy harvest, the war-shout is fallen.
10 Gladness and joy are driven from the fruitful field,
And in the vineyards is no singing nor shouting;
The treaders tread out no wine in their vats;
I have made the vintage-shouting to cease.
11 Therefore shall my bowels sound like a harp for Moab,
And my inward parts for Kir-hares.
12 And it shall come to pass that though Moab present himself,
Though he weary himself upon his high places,
And go up to his sanctuary to pray,
Yet shall he not prevail.
13 This is the word which Jehovah spake concerning
14 Moab of old. But now saith Jehovah:
Within three years, like the years of a hireling,
The glory of Moab shall be put to shame,
With all his great multitude;
And the remnant shall be very small, and without strength.

XIII.

Against Ephraim and Damascus. — CH. XVII. 1-11.

1 THE prophecy concerning Damascus.

Behold, Damascus shall be no more a city;
It shall become a heap of ruins.

2 The cities of Aroer shall be forsaken;
They shall be pastures for flocks,
Which shall lie down, and none shall make them afraid.
3 The fortress shall cease from Ephraim,
And the kingdom from Damascus, and the rest of Syria;
It shall be with them as with the glory of the children of Israel,
Saith Jehovah of hosts.
4 In that day shall the glory of Jacob sink away,
And the fatness of his flesh become leanness.
5 And it shall be as when the harvest-man gathereth the corn,
And reapeth the ears with his arm;
Yea, as when one gleaneth ears in the valley of Rephaim.
6 There shall be left in it only a gleaning, as in the olive-harvest,
Two or three berries on the top of the highest bough,
Four or five on the fruitful branches,
Saith Jehovah, the God of Israel.

7 In that day shall a man have regard to his Maker,
And his eyes shall look to the Holy One of Israel.
8 He shall not look to the altars, the work of his hands,
Nor have respect to that which his fingers have made,
The images of Astarte and the Sun-pillars.
9 In that day shall his fortified cities be like ruins in the forests, or on the mountain tops,
Which the enemy left, in flight from the children of Israel;
And the land shall be a desolation.
10 For thou hast forgotten the God of thy salvation,
And hast not been mindful of the rock of thy strength;
Therefore though thou plant beautiful plants,
And set shoots from a foreign soil,
11 When thou hast planted them, though thou hedge them in,
And in the morning bring thy plants to the blossom,
Yet shall the harvest flee away,
In the day of pain and desperate sorrow.

XIV.

A description of the sudden destruction of Sennacherib's army near Jerusalem, which leads the prophet to speak of the Ethiopians, and of their conversion to Jehovah through the display of his power in favor of the Jews. — CH. XVII. 12 — XVIII.

12 ALAS! a tumult of many nations!
They rage with the raging of the sea.
Alas! a roaring of kingdoms!
They roar with the roaring of mighty waters.
13 Like the roaring of mighty waters do the nations roar;
HE rebuketh them, and they flee away,
Driven like the chaff of the mountains before the wind,
Like stubble before the whirlwind.
14 At the time of evening, behold, terror!
Before morning, behold, they are no more!
This is the portion of them that spoil us,
And the lot of them that plunder us.

1 Ho! thou land of rustling wings,
Beyond the rivers of Ethiopia!
2 That sendest thy messengers upon the sea,
In reed-boats upon the face of the waters:
Go, ye swift messengers, to a nation tall and fair,
To a people terrible from the first and onward,
To a mighty, victorious people,
Whose land is divided by rivers!
3 All ye inhabitants of the world, ye that dwell on the earth,
When the standard is lifted up on the mountains, behold!
When the trumpet is sounded, hear!
4 For thus hath Jehovah said to me:
"I will sit still, and look on from my dwelling-place,
Like a serene heat when the sun shineth,
Like a dewy cloud in the heat of harvest."
5 But before the vintage, when the bud is gone,
And the blossom is ripening into a swelling grape,
He shall cut off the shoots with pruning-hooks,
And the branches he shall take away and cut down.
6 They shall be left together to the ravenous birds of the mountains,

And to the wild beasts of the earth.
The ravenous birds shall summer upon it,
And every wild beast of the earth shall winter upon it.
7 At that time shall gifts be brought to Jehovah of hosts
From a nation tall and fair,
From a people terrible from the first and onward,
A mighty, victorious people,
Whose land is divided by rivers,
To the dwelling-place of Jehovah of hosts, to mount Zion.

XV.

Political and physical calamities brought upon the Egyptians by Jehovah. They turn to him, and regain their prosperity. — CH. XIX.

1 THE prophecy concerning Egypt.

Behold, Jehovah rideth upon a swift cloud,
And cometh to Egypt;
The gods of Egypt tremble at his presence,
And the heart of Egypt melteth within her.
2 "I will set the Egyptians against the Egyptians;
Brother shall fight against brother,
And neighbor against neighbor;
City against city,
And kingdom against kingdom.
3 The spirit of Egypt shall fail within her,
And her devices I will bring to naught.
Then shall they consult the idols, and the sorcerers,
And the necromancers, and the wizards.
4 But I will give up the Egyptians to the hands of a cruel lord,
And a fierce king shall rule over them,"
Saith the Lord, Jehovah of hosts.
5 Then shall the waters fail from the river,
Yea, the river shall be wasted and dried up.
6 The streams shall become putrid;
The canals of Egypt shall be emptied and dried up;
The reed and the rush shall wither.
7 The meadows by the river, by the borders of the river,

And all that groweth by the river,
Shall wither, be blasted, and be no more.
8 Then shall the fishermen mourn;
All they that cast the hook into the river shall lament,
And they that spread nets upon the face of the waters shall languish.
9 They, also, that work in flax,
And they that weave white linen, shall be confounded.
10 Her pillars are broken down,
And all who labor for hire are grieved in heart
11 Surely the princes of Zoan are fools;
The wise counsellors of Pharaoh have been stupid in their counsels.
How, then, can ye say to Pharaoh,
"I am the son of the wise,
The son of ancient kings"?
12 Where are they now, thy wise men?
Let them tell thee now, so that men may know it,
What Jehovah of hosts hath determined concerning Egypt!
13 The princes of Zoan are become fools;
The princes of Noph are deceived,
Even the chiefs of her tribes have caused Egypt to err.
14 Jehovah hath mingled within her a spirit of perverseness,
And they have caused Egypt to err in all her works,
As a drunkard staggereth in his vomit.
15 There shall be nothing which can be done by Egypt,
By the head, or the tail, the palm-branch, or the rush.
16 In that day shall the Egyptians be like women;
They shall tremble and fear
On account of the shaking of the hand of Jehovah of hosts,
Which he shall shake against them.
17 The land of Judah shall be a terror to Egypt;
Every one to whom it is mentioned shall tremble
On account of the purpose of Jehovah of hosts,
Which he hath determined against them.
18 In that day there shall be five cities in the land of Egypt
Speaking the language of Canaan,
And swearing by Jehovah of hosts;
One of them shall be called the City of the Sun.
19 In that day there shall be an altar to Jehovah in the midst of the land of Egypt,

And in the border of it a pillar to Jehovah,
20 Which shall be a sign and a witness
For Jehovah of hosts in the land of Egypt,
That they cried to Jehovah on account of their oppressors,
And he sent them a saviour, and a defender, who delivered them.
21 Thus shall Jehovah be made known to Egypt,
And the Egyptians shall know Jehovah in that day,
And shall offer him sacrifices and oblations;
They shall make vows to Jehovah, and perform them.
22 Thus Jehovah will smite Egypt; he will smite and heal her;
They shall return to Jehovah;
Therefore will he hear and heal them.
23 In that day shall there be a highway from Egypt to Assyria,
And the Assyrian shall come into Egypt,
And the Egyptian into Assyria,
And the Egyptians shall worship with the Assyrians.
24 In that day shall Israel be the third
In connection with Egypt and Assyria,
A blessing in the midst of the earth.
25 Jehovah of hosts shall bless them, and say,
Blessed be Egypt, my people,
And Assyria, the work of my hands,
And Israel, my inheritance!

XVI.

Against the trust of Israel in Egypt and Ethiopia. — Ch. XX.

1 In the year in which Tartan, being sent by Sargon,
the king of Assyria, came to Ashdod, and fought against
2 Ashdod, and took it, at that time spake Jehovah through
Isaiah the son of Amoz in this manner: Go, and loose the
sackcloth from thy loins, and put off thy shoes from thy
feet. And he did so, walking naked and barefoot.
3 And Jehovah said: As my servant Isaiah hath walked
naked and barefoot three years, a sign and a token for
4 Egypt and Ethiopia, so shall the king of Assyria lead the

captives of Egypt, and prisoners of Ethiopia, young and
old, naked and barefoot, with their hind parts uncovered,
5 to the shame of the Egyptians. Then shall they be
afraid and ashamed on account of Ethiopia their trust, and
6 of Egypt their glory. The inhabitant of this coast shall
say in that day, "Behold, so is it with them in whom we
trusted, and to whom we fled for help, that we might be
delivered from the king of Assyria. How then shall we
escape?"

XVII.

The destruction of Babylon by the Medes and Persians. — CH. XXI. 1-10.

1 THE prophecy concerning the desert of the sea.

As storms which rush along through the south,
So it cometh from the desert,
From the terrible land.
2 A grievous vision was revealed to me;
The plunderer plundereth, and the destroyer destroyeth.
"Go up, O Elam! Besiege, O Media!
All sighing do I make to cease."
3 Therefore are my loins full of pain;
Pangs have seized me, as the pangs of a woman in travail;
For convulsions I cannot hear;
For anguish I cannot see.
4 My heart panteth,
Terror hath seized upon me;
The evening of my desire is changed into horror.
5 The table is prepared; the watch is set;
They eat; they drink;
"Arise, ye princes!
Anoint the shield!"
6 For thus said the Lord unto me:
"Go, set a watchman,
Who shall declare what he seeth."
7 And he saw a troop, horsemen in pairs,
Riders on asses, and riders on camels,

And he watched with the utmost heed.
8 Then he cried like a lion:
"My Lord, I stand continually upon the watch-towe the daytime,
And keep my post all the night;
9 And behold, there cometh a troop,
Horsemen in pairs."
Again also he lifted up his voice, and said:
"Fallen, fallen is Babylon,
And all the graven images of her gods are cast broken t the ground."
10 O my threshing, and the corn of my floor!
What I have heard from Jehovah of hosts, the God of Israel,
That have I declared to you.

XVIII.

Prophecy concerning Dumah.— CH. XXI. 11, 12.

11 THE prophecy concerning Dumah.

A voice came to me from Seir:
"Watchman, what of the night?
Watchman, what of the night?"
12 The watchman saith:
"Morning cometh, and also night.
If ye will inquire, inquire!
Return, come!"

XIX.

Prophecy against the Arabians.— CH. XXI. 13-17.

13 THE prophecy against the Arabians.

In the thickets of Arabia shall ye lodge,
O ye caravans of Dedan!

14 The inhabitants of the land of Tema
Bring water to the thirsty;
They come to meet the fugitive with bread.
15 For they flee from swords,
From the drawn sword,
And from the bent bow,
And from the fury of war.
16 For thus saith the Lord to me:
Within one year, according to the years of a hireling,
Shall all the glory of Kedar be consumed.
17 The remainder of the mighty bowmen of the sons of Kedar shall be diminished;
For Jehovah, the God of Israel, hath said it.

XX.

Addressed to the inhabitants of Jerusalem, when their city was besieged.— CH. XXII. 1-14.

1 THE prophecy concerning the valley of vision.

What aileth thee now,
That all thine inhabitants are gone up to the house-tops?
2 Thou that wast full of noise,
A tumultuous city, a joyous city!
Thy slain fall not by the sword;
They are not slain in battle.
3 All thy leaders flee together,
By the bowmen are they bound;
All found within thee are made captive together,
Even they who have fled from afar.
4 Therefore, say I, look away from me, that I may weep bitterly;
Strive not to comfort me for the desolation of the daughter of my people!
5 For a day of trouble, of desolation, and of perplexity cometh
From the Lord, Jehovah of hosts, in the valley of vision.
They break down the walls;
The cry reacheth to the mountains.

6 Elam beareth the quiver,
With chariots full of men, and with horsemen;
Kir uncovereth the shield.
7 Thy fairest valleys, [O Jerusalem,] are full of chariots;
The horsemen set themselves in array against the gate;
8 The veil of Judah is torn from her.
But in such a day ye look to the armor of the house of the forest;
9 Ye mark how many are the breaches of the city of David,
And collect the waters of the lower pool;
10 Ye number the houses of Jerusalem,
And ye break down the houses to prepare the wall;
11 Ye make a reservoir between the two walls for the waters of the old pool;
But ye look not to Him who hath done this;
Ye regard not Him that hath prepared this from afar.
12 The Lord, Jehovah of hosts, calleth you this day
To weeping and to lamentation,
To baldness and to girding with sackcloth.
13 But, behold, joy and gladness,
Slaying oxen and killing sheep,
Eating flesh and drinking wine!
"Let us eat and drink,
For to-morrow we die!"
14 Therefore it hath been revealed in my ears by Jehovah of hosts;
"This iniquity shall not be forgiven you, till ye die,"
Saith the Lord, Jehovah of hosts.

XXI.

The fall of Shebna, the prefect of the palace, and the promotion of Eliakim in his place. — CH. XXII. 15-25.

15 THUS saith the Lord, Jehovah of hosts:
Go in to this steward,
To Shebna, who is over the household, and say,
16 What hast thou here, and whom hast thou here,
That thou here hewest thee out a sepulchre, —
That thou hewest out thy sepulchre on high,

And gravest out a habitation for thyself in the rock?
17 Behold, Jehovah will cast thee headlong with a mighty thrust;
18 He will violently roll thee together like a ball;
Like a ball will he hurl thee into a wide country.
There shalt thou die;
And there shall be thy splendid chariots,
Thou disgrace of the house of thy lord!
19 I will drive thee from thy post,
And from thy station I will pull thee down.
20 In that day I will call my servant,
Even Eliakim, the son of Hilkiah;
21 I will clothe him with thy robe,
And bind thy girdle around him;
Thy government will I commit to his hand,
And he shall be a father to the inhabitants of Jerusalem,
And to the house of Judah.
22 I will lay the key of the house of David upon his shoulder;
He shall open, and none shall shut,
And he shall shut, and none shall open.
23 I will fasten him as a peg in a sure place,
And he shall be a glorious seat for his father's house.
24 Upon him shall hang all the glory of his father's house,
The offspring and the offshoots;
Every small vessel, from the goblet even to all the pitchers.
25 In that day, saith Jehovah of hosts,
The peg that was once fastened in a sure place shall be moved;
It shall be cut down, and fall,
And the burden which was upon it shall come to the ground.
For Jehovah hath said it.

XXII.

Prophecy of the destruction of Tyre. — Ch. XXIII

1 The prophecy concerning Tyre.

Howl, ye ships of Tarshish!
For it is laid waste;
No house, no entrance is left!
From the land of the Chittæans were the tidings brought
to them.
2 Be amazed, ye inhabitants of the sea-coast,
Which the merchants of Sidon, that pass over the sea, did
crowd!
3 Upon the wide waters, the corn of the Nile,
The harvest of the river, was her revenue;
She was the mart of the nations.
4 Be thou ashamed, O Sidon, for the sea hath spoken,
The fortress of the sea hath spoken thus:
"I have not travailed, nor brought forth children;
I have not nourished youths, nor brought up virgins."
5 When the tidings shall reach Egypt,
They shall be filled with anguish at the tidings concerning
Tyre.
6 Pass ye over to Tarshish;
Howl, ye inhabitants of the sea-coast!
7 Is this your joyous city,
Whose antiquity is of ancient days?
Now her own feet bear her
To sojourn far away.
8 Who hath purposed this against Tyre,
The dispenser of crowns,
Whose merchants are princes,
Whose traders the nobles of the earth?
9 Jehovah of hosts hath purposed it,
To bring down the pride of all glory,
To humble the nobles of the earth.
10 Go over thy land like the Nile, O daughter of Tarshish!
Now thy bonds are broken.
11 He hath stretched out his hand over the sea,

He hath made the kingdoms tremble;
Jehovah hath given commandment concerning Canaan
To destroy her strong holds.
12 He hath said, Thou shalt no more rejoice,
Thou ravished virgin, daughter of Sidon!
Arise, pass over to the Chittæans;
Yet even there shalt thou have no rest.
13 Behold the land of the Chaldæans,
Who, not long ago, were not a people,—
The Assyrian assigned it to the inhabitants of the wilderness,—
They raise their watch-towers;
They destroy her palaces;
They make her a heap of ruins.
14 Howl, ye ships of Tarshish!
For your stronghold is destroyed.

15 And it shall come to pass in that day,
That Tyre shall be forgotten seventy years,
According to the days of one king;
But at the end of seventy years
It shall be with Tyre as in the song of the harlot:
16 "Take thy lyre, go about the city,
O harlot, long forgotten;
Make sweet melody; sing many songs,
That thou mayst again be remembered!"
17 At the end of seventy years shall Jehovah show regard to Tyre,
And she shall return to her hire,
And play the harlot with all the kingdoms of the world,
That are upon the face of the earth.
18 But her gain and her hire shall be holy to Jehovah;
It shall not be treasured, nor laid up in store;
But it shall be for them that dwell before Jehovah,
For abundant food, and for splendid clothing.

XXIII.

Desolation of the land, return of the Jews from exile, and the destruction of Babylon. — CH. XXIV. — XXVII.

1 BEHOLD, Jehovah emptieth and draineth the land;
Yea, he turneth it upside down, and scattereth its inhabitants.
2 As with the people, so is it with the priest;
As with the servant, so with the master;
As with the maid, so with the mistress;
As with the buyer, so with the seller;
As with the borrower, so with the lender;
As with the usurer, so with the giver of usury.
3 The land is utterly emptied and utterly plundered;
For Jehovah hath spoken this word.
4 The land mourneth, and withereth;
The world languisheth, and withereth;
The nobles of the people of the land do languish.
5 The land was polluted under its inhabitants,
Because they transgressed the law, they violated the statutes,
They broke the everlasting covenant.
6 Therefore a curse devoured the land;
Its inhabitants suffered for their guilt;
Therefore are the inhabitants of the land consumed with heat,
And few of the men are left.
7 The new wine mourneth;
The vine languisheth;
All that were of a joyful heart do sigh;
8 The mirth of tabrets ceaseth;
The noise of them that rejoice is at an end;
The joy of the harp ceaseth.
9 No more do they drink wine with the song;
Strong drink is bitter to them that use it.
10 The city of desolation is broken down;
Every house is closed, so that none can enter.
11 There is a cry for wine in the streets;
All gladness is departed;

The mirth of the land is gone;
12 Desolation is left in the city,
And the gate is smitten into ruins.
13 Yea, thus shall it be in the land, in the midst of the people,
As when the olive-tree has been shaken;
As the gleaning, when the vintage is ended.
14 These shall lift up their voice, and sing;
Yea, for the majesty of Jehovah they shall shout from the sea.
15 Wherefore praise ye Jehovah in the East,
The name of Jehovah, the God of Israel, in the isles of the sea!
16 From the end of the earth we hear songs:
"Glory to the righteous!"
But I cry, Alas, my wretchedness, my wretchedness! woe is me!
The plunderers plunder; the plunderers seize the spoil.
17 The terror, the pit, and the snare
Are upon thee, O inhabitant of the land!
18 Whoso fleeth from the terror shall fall into the pit,
And whoso escapeth from the pit,
He shall be taken in the snare;
For the floodgates of heaven are opened,
And the foundations of the earth tremble.
19 The earth is utterly broken down;
The earth is shattered in pieces;
The earth is violently moved from her place.
20 The earth reeleth like a drunkard,
It moveth to and fro like a hammock;
For her iniquity lieth heavy upon her,
And she shall fall and rise no more.
21 In that day will Jehovah punish the host of the high ones that are on high,
And the kings of the earth upon the earth.
22 They shall be thrown together bound into the pit,
And shall be shut up in the prison,
But after many days shall they be visited.
23 The moon shall be confounded, and the sun ashamed,
When Jehovah of hosts shall reign in mount Zion and Jerusalem,
And his glory shall be before his ancients.

1 O Jehovah, thou art my God;
I will exalt thee; I will praise thy name,
For thou hast done wonderful things;
Thine ancient purposes are faithfulness and truth.
2 Thou hast made the city a heap;
The fortified city a ruin.
The palace of the barbarians is to be no more a city;
It shall never be built again.
3 Therefore shall mighty kingdoms praise thee;
The cities of the terrible nations shall honor thee;
4 For thou hast been a defence to the poor;
A defence to the needy in his distress;
A refuge from the storm, a shadow from the heat,
When the rage of tyrants was like a storm against a wall.
5 As heat in a dry land is made to vanish,
So thou puttest down the tumult of the barbarians;
As heat is allayed by a thick cloud,
So the triumph of the tyrants is brought low.

6 Then in this mountain shall Jehovah of hosts prepare for all nations
A feast of fat things, and wines kept on the lees;
Of fat things full of marrow, of wines kept on the lees well refined.
7 He will destroy in this mountain the covering that was cast over all people,
And the veil that was spread over all nations.
8 He will destroy death forever;
The Lord Jehovah will wipe away the tears from all faces,
And the reproach of his people will he take away from the whole earth;
For Jehovah hath said it.
9 In that day shall men say, "Behold, this is our God;
We waited for him, and he hath saved us;
This is Jehovah, for whom we waited;
Let us rejoice and exult in his salvation."
10 For the hand of Jehovah shall rest upon this mountain,
And Moab shall be trodden down in his place,
As straw is trodden down in a dung-pool.
11 And he shall stretch out his hands in the midst of it,
As the swimmer stretcheth out his hands to swim,
But God shall put down his pride,

Together with the devices of his hands.
12 And the high bulwarks of thy walls will he lay low;
He will bring them down to the ground; he will lay them in the dust.

1 In that day shall this song be sung in the land of Judah:
"We have a strong city;
His aid doth God appoint for walls and bulwarks.
2 Open ye the gates,
That the righteous nation may enter in,
The nation that keepeth the truth.
3 Him that is of a steadfast mind
Thou wilt keep in continual peace,
Because he trusteth in thee.
4 Trust ye in Jehovah forever,
For the Lord Jehovah is an everlasting rock.
5 For he hath brought down the inhabitants of the fortress;
The lofty city he hath laid low;
He hath laid her low even to the ground;
He hath levelled her with the dust.
6 The foot trampleth upon her,
The feet of the poor, the steps of the needy.
7 The way of the upright is a smooth way;
Thou, O most righteous, doth level the path of the upright!
8 In the way of thy judgments, O Jehovah, we have waited for thee;
The desire of our souls is to thy name, and to the remembrance of thee.
9 My soul longeth for thee in the night,
And my spirit within me seeketh thee in the morning;
For when thy judgments are in the earth,
The inhabitants of the world learn righteousness.
10 Though favor be shown to the wicked,
He will not learn righteousness;
In the land of uprightness will he deal unjustly,
And have no regard to the majesty of Jehovah.
11 Thy hand, O Jehovah, is lifted up, yet do they not see;
But they shall see with shame thy zeal for thy people;
Yea, fire shall devour thine adversaries.
12 Thou, O Jehovah, wilt give us peace;
For all our works thou doest for us.

13 O Jehovah, our God, other lords have had dominion over
us besides thee;
Only through thee do we call upon thy name.
14 They are dead, they shall not live;
They are shades, they shall not rise.
For thou hast visited and destroyed them,
And caused all the memory of them to perish.

15 "Thou wilt enlarge the nation, O Jehovah!
Thou wilt enlarge the nation; thou wilt glorify thyself;
Thou wilt widely extend all the borders of the land.
16 O Jehovah, in affliction they sought thee;
They poured out their prayer, when thy chastisement was
upon them.
17 As a woman with child, when her delivery is near,
Is in anguish, and crieth aloud in her pangs,
So have we been, far from thy presence, O Jehovah!
18 We have been with child; we have been in anguish,
Yet have, as it were, brought forth wind.
To the land we bring no deliverance;
Nor are the inhabitants of the land born.
19 O might thy dead live again,
Might the dead bodies of my people arise!
Awake, and sing, ye that dwell in the dust!
For thy dew is like the dew upon plants,
And the earth shall bring forth her dead."

20 Come, my people, enter into thy chambers,
And shut thy doors behind thee;
Hide thyself for a little moment,
Until the indignation be overpast!
21 For behold, Jehovah cometh forth from his place,
To punish the inhabitants of the earth for their iniquity;
And the earth shall disclose her blood,
And shall no longer cover her slain.

1 In that day will Jehovah punish with his sword,
His hard, and great, and strong sword,
The leviathan, that fleet serpent,
Even the leviathan, that winding serpent;
Yea, he will slay the monster, that is in the sea.
2 In that day, sing ye thus concerning the vineyard:

3 "I, Jehovah, am its guardian;
I will water it every moment;
That no one may assault it,
I will watch it day and night.
4 There is no fury in me;
But let me find the thorns and thistles in battle.
I will go against them,
And burn them up together,
5 Unless they take hold of my protection,
And with me make peace,
And make peace with me."

6 In coming days shall Jacob take root,
And Israel flourish and bud forth,
And fill the world with fruit.
7 Did he smite Israel, as he smote those that smote him?
Was he slain as those that slew him?
8 In measure, by sending her away, didst thou punish her,
Taking her away in the rough tempest, in the day of the east wind.
9 By this, therefore, is the iniquity of Jacob expiated,
And this is wholly the fruit of the removal of his sin,
That He has made the stones of the altar like limestones broken in pieces,
And that the images of Astarte and the sun-pillars no more stand.
10 For the fortified city is desolate,
An habitation forsaken, deserted like a wilderness;
There doth the calf feed, and there doth he lie down,
And consume her branches.
11 When her boughs are withered, they are broken off;
Women come, and burn them;
For it was a people of no understanding;
Therefore he that made him had not mercy on him,
And he that formed him showed him no favor.
12 But it shall come to pass in that day,
That Jehovah shall gather fruit
From the stream of the Euphrates to the river of Egypt,
And ye shall be gathered, one by one, ye children of Israel!
13 In that day shall a great trumpet be sounded,
And they shall come who are lost in the land of Assyria,

And are outcasts in the land of Egypt,
And shall worship Jehovah upon the holy mountain in Jerusalem.

XXIV.

The kingdom of Ephraim or Israel threatened with destruction, on account of its depravity. A favorable state of things is promised to Judah, which, however, is afterwards to be destroyed on account of the intemperance, disobedience, and impiety of the people, especially of the higher classes. — CH. XXVIII.

1 Woe to the proud crown of the drunkards of Ephraim,
To the fading flower, his glorious beauty,
At the head of the rich valley of a people stupefied with wine.
2 Behold a strong, a mighty one from the Lord
Like a storm of hail, like a destructive tempest,
Like a flood of mighty, overflowing waters,
With violence shall dash it to the ground.
3 It shall be trodden under foot,
The proud crown of the drunkards of Ephraim.
4 And the fading flower, their glorious beauty,
At the head of the rich valley,
Shall be as the early fig before the time of harvest,
Which whoso seeth plucketh immediately,
And swalloweth as soon as it is in his hand.

5 In that day shall Jehovah of hosts
Be a glorious crown, and a beautiful diadem to the residue of his people;
6 A spirit of judgment to him that sitteth in judgment,
And of strength to them that drive back the enemy to their gates.
7 But even these stagger through wine,
And reel through strong drink;
The priest and the prophet stagger through strong drink
They are overpowered with wine;
They stumble through strong drink;
They reel in vision,
They stagger in judgment.

8 For all their tables are full of filthy vomit,
So that there is no place clean.
9 "Whom," say they, "will he teach knowledge,
And to whom will he impart instruction?
To the weaned from the milk?
To those just taken from the breast?
10 For it is precept upon precept, precept upon precept,
Command upon command, command upon command,
A little here, and a little there."
11 Yea, with stammering lips and a strange tongue
He shall indeed speak to this people;
12 He that said to them,
"This is the way of rest, give rest to the weary;
This is the way of safety";
But they would not hear.
13 Then shall the word of Jehovah be indeed to them
"Precept upon precept, precept upon precept,
Command upon command, command upon command,
A little here, and a little there,"
So that they shall go on, and fall backwards, and be broken,
And be snared and caught.
14 Wherefore hear ye the word of Jehovah,
Ye scoffers, who rule this people in Jerusalem!
15 Since ye say,
"We have entered into a covenant with death,
And with the under-world have we made an agreement,
The overflowing scourge, when it passeth through, shall not reach us;
For we have made falsehood our refuge,
And in deceit we have hidden ourselves."
16 Therefore thus saith the Lord Jehovah:
Behold, I have laid in Zion as a foundation a stone,
A tried stone, a precious corner-stone, a sure foundation;
He that trusteth shall not flee away.
17 I will make justice a line,
And righteousness a plummet,
And the hail shall sweep away the refuge of falsehood,
And the waters shall overwhelm its hiding-place;
18 And your covenant with death shall be broken,
And your agreement with the under-world shall not stand;
When the overflowing scourge shall pass through,

By it shall ye be beaten down.
19 As often as it passeth through, it shall bear you away;
For every morning shall it pass through,
By day and by night;
Even to hear the rumor of it shall be terrible.
20 Yea, the bed is too short for one to stretch himself on it,
And the covering too narrow for one to wrap himself in it.
21 For Jehovah will rise up, as in mount Perazim;
He will be moved with anger, as in the valley of Gibeon,
To perform his act, his strange act,
And to execute his work, his strange work.
22 Now, therefore, be ye no longer scoffers,
Lest your bands become stronger;
For destruction and punishment have been revealed to me
From Jehovah of hosts concerning the whole land!

23 Give ear, and listen to my voice,
Attend, and hearken to my words!
24 Is the ploughman always ploughing in order to sow?
Is he always opening and harrowing his field?
25 When he hath made the face thereof even,
Doth he not then scatter the dill, and cast abroad the cumin,
And sow the wheat in rows,
And the barley in its appointed place,
And the spelt in his border?
26 Thus his God rightly instructeth him,
And giveth him knowledge.
27 The dill is not beaten out with the thrashing-sledge,
Nor is the wheel of the wain rolled over the cumin;
But the dill is beaten out with a staff,
And the cumin with a rod.
28 Bread-corn is beaten out,
Yet doth not the husbandman thrash it without limi
He driveth over it the wheels of the wain,
And the horses, yet doth he not utterly crush it.
29 This also proceedeth from Jehovah of hosts;
He is wonderful in counsel,
Excellent in wisdom.

XXV.

The siege and deliverance of Jerusalem. Reproofs of infidelity and impiety. — CH. XXIX.

1 WOE to Ariel, to Ariel,
The city where David dwelt!
Add year to year,
Let the festivals go round,
2 Then will I distress Ariel;
Mourning and sorrow shall be there;
Yet shall she be to me as Ariel [the lion of God].
3 I will encamp against thee round about,
And I will lay siege against thee with a mound,
And I will raise towers against thee.
4 Thou shalt be brought down, and speak from the ground,
And thy speech shall be low from the dust;
Thy voice shall be like that of a spirit under ground,
And thy speech shall chirp as from the dust.

5 Yet shall the multitude of thine enemies be like fine dust;
The multitude of the terrible like flying chaff;
It shall take place suddenly, in a moment.
6 From Jehovah of hosts cometh the visitation
With thunder, and earthquake, and great noise,
With storm and tempest,
And flames of devouring fire.
7 As a dream, a vision of the night,
Shall be the multitude of all the nations
That fight against Ariel,
That fight against her and her fortress,
And distress her.
8 As a hungry man dreameth, and lo! he eateth,
But awaketh and is still hungry;
And as a thirsty man dreameth, and lo! he drinketh,
But awaketh, and lo! he is faint and thirsty;
So shall it be with the multitude of all the nations
That fight against mount Zion.
9 Be in amazement and be amazed!
Be blinded and be blind!

They are drunk, but not with wine;
They stagger, but not with strong drink!
10 For Jehovah hath poured upon you a spirit of slumber;
He hath closed your eyes, the prophets,
And covered your heads, the seers;
11 And so every vision is to you as the words of a sealed book,
Which is given to a man that is skilled in writing,
Saying, "Read this, I pray thee";
But he answereth, "I cannot, for it is sealed."
12 Or, if he give it to one that is not skilled in writing,
Saying, "Read this, I pray thee,"
He answereth, "I am not skilled in writing."
13 Therefore saith the Lord,
Since this people draweth near to me with their mouth,
And honoreth me with their lips,
While their heart is far from me,
And their worship of me is according to the commandments of men,
14 Therefore, behold, I will proceed to deal marvellously with this people;
Marvellously and wonderfully,
For the wisdom of their wise men shall perish,
And the prudence of the prudent shall be hid.
15 Woe to them that hide deep their purposes from Jehovah,
Whose work is in darkness;
That say, Who seeth us? Who knoweth us?
16 Alas, your perverseness!
Is the potter to be esteemed as the clay,
That the work should say of its maker, He made me not?
And the thing formed say of him that formed it,
He hath no understanding?

17 Is it not yet a very little while,
And Lebanon shall be changed to a fruitful field,
And the fruitful field be esteemed a forest.
18 And in that day shall the deaf hear the words of the book,
And out of mist and darkness shall the eyes of the blind see.
19 The afflicted shall exceedingly rejoice in Jehovah,
And the poor shall exult in the Holy One of Israel.
20 For the oppressor hath come to naught; the scoffer is destroyed;

And all that watched for iniquity are cut off;
21 Who condemned a man in his cause,
And laid snares for him who defended himself in the gate,
And with falsehood caused the righteous to fail.
22 Therefore concerning the house of Jacob thus saith Jehovah,
He that redeemed Abraham:
No more shall Jacob be ashamed,
And no more shall his face grow pale.
23 For when his children behold the work of my hands in the midst of them,
They shall honor my name.
They shall honor the Holy One of Jacob,
And reverence the God of Israel.
24 They that erred in spirit shall come to understanding,
And the obstinate shall receive instruction.

XXVI.

The prophet condemns attempts to form an alliance with Egypt, and reproves the fondness for war, and the want of piety in the people. Piety will lead to prosperity. The Assyrians to be destroyed. — CH. XXX.

1 WOE to the rebellious children, saith Jehovah,
Who form plans, and not from me,
And make covenants without my spirit,
That they may add sin to sin!
2 Who go down into Egypt,
Without inquiring at my mouth,
To seek refuge in Pharaoh's protection,
And to trust in the shadow of Egypt!
3 The protection of Pharaoh shall be your shame;
Your trust in the shadow of Egypt your confusion.
4 For their princes are at Zoan,
Their ambassadors have arrived at Hanes.
5 But they are all ashamed of a people that do not profit them;
That are no help and no profit,
But only a shame and a reproach.
6 The loaded beasts go southward,

Through a land of anguish and distress,
Whence come forth the lioness, and the fierce lion,
The viper, and the flying fiery serpent;
On the shoulders of young asses they carry their wealth,
And on the bunches of camels their treasures,
To a people that will not profit them!
7 Vain and empty is the help of Egypt;
Wherefore I call her, The Blusterer that sitteth still.
8 Go now, write this on a tablet before them;
Note it down upon a book,
That it may remain for future times,
A testimony forever!
9 For this is a rebellious people, false children;
Children who will not hear the law of Jehovah;
10 Who say to the seers, "See not!"
And to the prophets, "Prophesy not right things;
Speak to us smooth things,
Prophesy falsehood!
11 Turn aside from the way,
Depart from the path,
Remove from our sight the Holy One of Israel!"
12 Wherefore thus saith the Holy One of Israel:
Since ye despise this word,
And trust in oppression and perverseness,
And lean thereon,
13 Therefore shall this iniquity be to you
Like a breach ready to give way,
That swelleth out in a high wall,
Whose fall cometh suddenly, in an instant.
14 It is broken like a potter's vessel,
Which is dashed in pieces and not spared,
So that among its fragments not a sherd is found to take up fire from the hearth,
Or to dip water from the cistern.
15 For thus said the Lord Jehovah, the Holy One of Israel
By a return and by rest shall ye be saved;
In quietness and confidence is your strength;
16 But ye would not.
Ye said, "No! we will bound along upon horses";
Truly ye shall bound along in flight.
"We will ride upon swift coursers";
But they shall be swift that pursue you.

17 A thousand shall flee at the rebuke of one,
And ten thousand at the rebuke of five,
Till what remains of you shall be as a beacon on the top of a mountain,
As a banner upon a hill.
18 And yet will Jehovah wait to be gracious to you,
And yet will he arise to have mercy upon you;
For Jehovah is a righteous God;
Happy are all they who wait for him!

19 For, O people of Zion, that dwellest in Jerusalem,
Thou shalt not always weep!
He will be very gracious to thee at the voice of thy cry;
No sooner shall he hear it, than he will answer thee.
20 Though Jehovah hath given thee the bread of distress, and the water of affliction,
Yet shall thy teachers be hidden from thee no more;
But thine eyes shall see thy teachers.
21 And thine ears shall hear a voice behind thee,
Saying, "This is the way, walk ye in it!"
When ye turn aside to the right hand, or to the left.
22 Ye shall treat as defiled the silver coverings of your graven images,
And the golden clothing of your molten images,
Ye shall cast them away as an unclean thing;
Away! shall ye say to them.
23 Then will he give rain for thy seed,
With which thou shalt sow the ground,
And the bread-corn, the produce of the land, shall be rich and nourishing;
Then shall thy cattle feed in large pastures.
24 The oxen also, and the young asses, that till the ground,
Shall eat well-seasoned provender,
Which hath been winnowed with the shovel and the fan.
25 And on every lofty mountain,
And on every high hill,
Shall be brooks and streams of water,
In the day of the great slaughter,
When the towers fall.
26 Then shall the light of the moon be as the light of the sun,
And the light of the sun shall be sevenfold,
[As the light of seven days,]

When Jehovah bindeth up the bruises of his people,
And healeth the wound which they have received.

27 Behold, the name of Jehovah cometh from afar,
His anger burneth, and violent is the flame,
His lips are full of indignation,
And his tongue like a devouring fire.
28 His breath is like an overflowing torrent,
That reacheth even to the neck;
He will toss the nation with the winnowing-fan of destruction;
He will put a bridle upon the jaws of the people, that shall lead them astray.
29 But ye shall then sing as in the night of a solemn festival;
Your heart shall be glad, like his who marcheth with the sound of the pipe
To the mountain of Jehovah, to the rock of Israel.
30 Jehovah will cause his glorious voice to be heard,
And the blow of his arm to be seen,
With furious anger, and flames of devouring fire;
With flood, and storm, and hailstones.
31 For by the voice of Jehovah shall the Assyrian be beaten down;
He will smite him with the rod.
32 And as often as the appointed rod shall strike,
Which Jehovah shall lay heavily upon him,
It shall be accompanied with tabrets and harps;
And with fierce battles will he fight against him.
33 For long hath the burning place been prepared;
Yea, for the king hath it been made ready;
The pile is made deep and broad;
There is fire and wood in abundance;
The breath of Jehovah, like a stream of brimstone, kindle it.

XXVII.

Against an alliance with Egypt, and in favor of trusting in Jehovah.—CH. XXXI.

1 Woe to them that go down to Egypt for help,
And put their trust in horses,
And confide in chariots, because they are many,
And in horsemen, because their number is great,
But look not to the Holy One of Israel,
And resort not to Jehovah.
2 Yet he, too, is wise;
He will bring evil, and not take back his words;
He will arise against the house of the evil-doers,
And against the help of them that do iniquity.
3 The Egyptians are men, and not God,
And their horses are flesh, and not spirit.
When Jehovah shall stretch forth his hand,
Then shall the helper fall, and the helped be overthrown;
And they shall all perish together.
4 For thus hath Jehovah said to me:
As when the lion and the young lion growl over their prey,
And a multitude of shepherds is called forth against him,
By their noise he is not terrified,
Nor by their tumult disheartened;
So shall Jehovah of hosts come down to fight for mount Zion, and her hill.
5 As birds hover over their young,
So shall Jehovah of hosts defend Jerusalem;
He will defend and deliver, spare and save.

6 Turn, O ye children of Israel,
To him from whom ye have so deeply revolted!
7 For in that day shall every one cast away his idols of silver and his idols of gold,
Which your hands have made for sin.
8 The Assyrian shall fall by a sword not of man,
Yea, a sword not of mortal shall devour him;
He shall flee before the sword,
And his young warriors shall be slaves.

9 Through fear shall he pass beyond his stronghold,
And his princes shall be afraid of the standard.
Thus saith Jehovah, who hath his fire in Zion,
And his furnace in Jerusalem.

XXVIII.

A happy state of things is to succeed the calamities of the Jewish nation.—Ch. XXXII.

1 Behold! a king shall reign in righteousness,
And princes shall rule with equity.
2 Every one of them shall be a hiding-place from the wind,
And a shelter from the tempest;
As streams of water in a dry place,
As the shadow of a great rock in a weary land.
3 The eyes of them that see shall no more be blind,
And the ears of them that hear shall hearken.
4 The heart of the rash shall gain wisdom,
And the tongue of the stammerer learn to speak plainly.
5 The vile shall no more be called liberal,
Nor the niggard said to be bountiful;
6 For the vile will still utter villany,
And his heart will devise iniquity;
He will practise deception, and speak impiety against God;
He will take away the food of the hungry,
And deprive the thirsty of drink.
7 The instruments also of the niggard are evil;
He plotteth mischievous devices,
To destroy the poor with lying words,
Even when the cause of the needy is just.
8 But the liberal deviseth liberal things,
And in liberal things will he persevere.

9 Arise, hear my voice, ye women that are at ease!
Give ear to my speech, ye careless daughters!
10 One year more, and ye shall tremble, ye careless women!
For the vintage shall fail; the harvest shall not come.
11 Tremble, O ye that are at ease!

Be in dismay, ye careless ones!
Strip you, make you bare, gird ye sackcloth upon your loins!
12 They shall smite themselves on their breasts,
On account of the pleasant fields,
On account of the fruitful vine.
13 Upon the land of my people shall come up thorns and briers;
Yea, upon all the houses of joy in the joyous city.
14 For the palace shall be forsaken;
The tumult of the city shall be solitary;
The fortified hill and the tower shall be dens forever;
The joy of wild-asses, the pasture of flocks;
15 Until the spirit from on high be poured upon us,
And the wilderness become a fruitful field,
And the fruitful field be esteemed a forest.
16 Then shall justice dwell in the wilderness,
And righteousness in the fruitful field.
17 And the effect of righteousness shall be peace,
And the fruit of righteousness quiet and security forever.
18 Then shall my people dwell in peaceful habitations,
In secure dwellings, in quiet resting-places.
19 But the hail shall descend, and the forest shall fall;
And the city shall be brought very low.
20 Happy ye who sow beside all waters;
Who send forth thither the feet of the ox and the ass!

XXIX.

The destruction of the Assyrian army, and the security of the Jews under the protection of God. — CH. XXXIII.

1 WOE to thee, thou spoiler, who hast not been spoiled!
Thou plunderer, who hast not been plundered!
When thou hast ceased to spoil, thou shalt be spoiled;
When thou hast finished plundering, they shall plunder thee.

2 O Jehovah, have mercy upon us! in thee do we trust;
Be thou our strength every morning,

Our salvation in the time of trouble.
3 At the voice of thy thunder the people flee;
When thou dost arise, the nations are scattered.

4 Your spoil shall be gathered, as the locust gathereth;
As the locust runneth, so shall they run upon it.
5 Jehovah is exalted;
Yea, he dwelleth on high;
He filleth Zion with justice and righteousness.
6 There shall be security in thy times;
Wisdom and knowledge shall be thy store of prosperity,
And the fear of Jehovah, this shall be thy treasure!

7 Behold, the mighty men cry without:
The ambassadors of peace weep bitterly.
8 The highways are desolate;
The traveller ceaseth;
He breaketh the covenant; he despiseth the cities;
Of men he maketh no account.
9 The land mourneth and languisheth;
Lebanon is put to shame, and withered away;
Sharon is like a desert,
And Bashan and Carmel are stripped of their leaves.
10 Now will I arise, saith Jehovah,
Now will I exalt myself,
Now will I lift myself up.
11 Ye shall conceive chaff, and bring forth stubble;
Your own wrath is the fire which shall devour you.
12 The nations shall be burnt into lime;
Like thorns cut down, they shall be consumed with fire.
13 Hear, ye that are far off, what I have done;
Mark, ye that are near, my power!
14 The sinners in Zion are struck with dread;
Terror hath seized upon the unrighteous:
"Who among us can dwell in devouring fire?
Who among us can dwell in everlasting flames?"

15 He that walketh in righteousness,
And speaketh that which is right,
That despiseth the gain of oppression,
And shaketh his hands from bribery,
That stoppeth his ears, so as not to hear of blood,

And shutteth his eyes, so as not to behold iniquity,
16 He shall dwell on high;
The strongholds of rocks shall be his defence;
His bread shall be given him;
His water shall not fail.
17 Thine eyes shall see the king in his glory
They shall survey a wide-extended land.
18 Thy heart shall meditate on the past terror:
"Where now is the scribe? Where the weigher of trib ute?
Where he that numbered the towers?"
19 Thou shalt see no more a fierce people,
A people of a dark language, which thou couldst not hear,
And of a barbarous tongue, which thou couldst not understand;
20 Thou shalt see Zion, the city of our solemn feasts;
Thine eyes shall behold Jerusalem, as a quiet habitation.
A tent that shall never be moved,
Whose stakes shall never be taken away,
And whose cords shall never be broken.
21 For there the glorious Jehovah will be to us
Instead of rivers and broad streams,
Which no oared galley shall pass,
And no gallant ship go through.
22 For Jehovah is our judge; Jehovah is our lawgiver;
Jehovah is our king; it is he that will save us.

23 Thy ropes hang loose;
They cannot hold the mast-socket,
Nor can they spread the sail.
Then shall a great spoil be divided;
Even the lame shall take the prey.
24 No inhabitant shall say, I am sick;
The people that dwell therein shall be forgiven their iniquity

XXX.

The destruction of the enemies of the Jews, especially of Edom, and the restoration of the Jews to their native land from the captivity at Babylon. — CH. XXXIV., XXXV.

1 DRAW near, O ye nations, and hear!
Attend, O ye people!
Let the earth hear, and all that is therein;
The world, and all that springs from it!
2 For the wrath of Jehovah is kindled against all the nations,
And his fury against all their armies;
He hath devoted them to destruction;
He hath given them up to slaughter.
3 Their slain shall be cast out;
From their carcasses their stench shall ascend,
And the mountains shall flow down with their blood.
4 And all the hosts of heaven shall melt away;
And the heavens shall be rolled up like a scroll,
And all their host shall fall down,
As the withered leaf falleth from the vine,
As the blighted fruit from the fig-tree.
5 For my sword hath become drunk in heaven;
Behold, upon Edom shall it descend,
Upon the people under my curse, for vengeance.
6 The sword of Jehovah is full of blood;
It is covered with fat,
With the blood of lambs and goats,
With the fat of the kidneys of rams;
For Jehovah holdeth a sacrifice in Bozrah,
And a great slaughter in the land of Edom.
7 The wild buffaloes shall fall down with them,
And the bullocks with the bulls;
The land shall be drunk with blood,
And the ground enriched with fat.
8 For Jehovah holdeth a day of vengeance,
A year of recompense in the cause of Zion.
9 Her streams shall be turned into pitch,
And her dust into brimstone,
And her whole land shall become burning pitch.

10 Day and night it shall not be quenched;
Its smoke shall ascend forever;
From generation to generation it shall lie waste;
None shall pass through it for ever and ever.
11 The pelican and the hedgehog shall possess it;
The heron aud the raven shall dwell in it;
Over it will he draw the measuring-line of destruction.
And the plummet of desolation.
12 Her nobles — none are there, who may proclaim a kingdom,
And all her princes have come to naught.
13 Thorns shall spring up in her palaces;
Nettles and thistles in her strongholds.
She shall become a habitation for jackals,
A court for ostriches.
14 The wild-cats shall fall upon the wolves,
And the satyr shall call to his fellow;
There also shall the night-spectre light,
And find a place of rest.
15 There also shall the arrow-snake make her nest, and lay her eggs;
She shall hatch them, and gather her young under her shadow:
There also shall the vultures be gathered together,
Every one with her mate.
16 Search ye the book of Jehovah, and read!
Not one of these shall fail;
Not one shall want her mate;
For His mouth, it shall command,
And His spirit, it shall gather them.
17 He shall cast the lot for them;
His hand shall divide it for them with a line;
They shall possess it forever;
From generation to generation shall they dwell therein.

1 The wilderness and the parched land shall be glad,
And the desert rejoice and blossom as the rose;
2 It shall blossom abundantly, and exult with joy and singing;
The glory of Lebanon shall be given to it;
The beauty of Carmel and Sharon;
They shall behold the glory of Jehovah,

The majesty of our God;
3 Strengthen ye the weak hands,
And confirm the tottering knees!
4 Say ye to the faint-hearted, "Be ye strong; fear ye not;
Behold your God!
Vengeance cometh, the retribution of God;
He will come and save you!"
5 Then shall the eyes of the blind be opened,
And the ears of the deaf be unstopped.
6 Then shall the lame leap like the hart,
And the tongue of the dumb shall sing;
For in the wilderness shall waters break forth,
And streams in the desert.
7 The glowing sands shall become a pool,
And the thirsty ground springs of water;
In the habitation of jackals, where they lie,
Shall be a place for reeds and rushes.
8 And a path shall be there, and a highway,
And it shall be called the holy way;
No unclean person shall pass over it; it shall be for them alone;
He that goeth in this way, though a fool, shall not err therein.
9 No lion shall be there,
Nor shall any ravenous beast go up thereon;
It shall not be found there;
But the redeemed shall walk there.
10 Yea, the ransomed of Jehovah shall return;
They shall come to Zion with songs;
Everlasting joy shall be upon their heads;
They shall obtain joy and gladness,
And sorrow and sighing shall flee away.

XXXI.

Narrative of certain transactions which took place during the reign of Hezekiah. — CH. XXXVI. — XXXIX.

1 In the fourteenth year of King Hezekiah, Sennacherib,
king of Assyria, came up against all the fortified cities

2 of Judah, and took them. And the king of Assyria sent
Rabshakeh from Lachish to Jerusalem, with a great army,
against King Hezekiah, and he halted at the aqueduct of
3 the upper pool, in the highway to the fuller's field. Then
came forth to him Eliakim, the son of Hilkiah, who was
over the palace, and Shebna the scribe, and Joah, the son
of Asaph, the annalist.

4 And Rabshakeh said to them, Say ye to Hezekiah,
Thus saith the great king, the king of Assyria: What a
5 confidence is this which thou cherishest! Thou sayest,
(but it is vain talk,) "I have counsel and strength for
war." In whom, then, dost thou trust, that thou rebellest
6 against me? Behold, thou trustest in that broken reed-
staff, Egypt, on which if a man lean, it will pierce his
hand, and go through it. Such is Pharaoh, king of Egypt,
7 to all that trust in him. But if ye say to me, "We trust
in Jehovah, our God," — is it not he whose high places
and whose altars Hezekiah hath taken away, and com-
manded Judah and Jerusalem to worship before this altar?
8 Engage, now, with my master, the king of Assyria! and
I will give thee two thousand horses, when thou art able
9 to provide for thyself riders for them. How, then, canst
thou resist a single captain, one of the least of the servants
of my master? Yet thou trustest in Egypt, on account of
10 her chariots and her horsemen. And am I now come up
without Jehovah against this land to destroy it? Jehovah
hath said to me, "Go up against this land and destroy it!"

11 Then said Eliakim and Shebna and Joah to Rabshakeh:
Speak, we beseech thee, to thy servants in the Aramaic
language, for we understand it; and speak not to us in the
Jewish language, in the hearing of the people that are
12 upon the wall. But Rabshakeh said, Hath my master sent
me to speak these words to thy master and to thee only,
and not to the people who sit upon the wall, to eat their
own dung, and to drink their own urine with you?

13 Then Rabshakeh stood and cried with a loud voice in
the Jewish language, and said, Hear ye the words of the
14 great king, the king of Assyria. Thus saith the king:
Let not Hezekiah deceive you, for he will not be able to
15 deliver you. And let not Hezekiah persuade you to trust

in Jehovah, saying, "Jehovah will certainly deliver us.
This city shall not be delivered into the hands of the king
16 of Assyria." Hearken not to Hezekiah; for thus saith
the king of Assyria: Make peace with me, and come out
to me; and ye shall every one eat of his own vine, and
every one of his own fig-tree, and ye shall every one drink
17 the waters of his own cistern, until I come, and take you to
a land like your own land; a land of corn, and of new wine,
18 a land of bread and of vineyards. Be not persuaded by
Hezekiah, when he saith, "Jehovah will deliver us."
Have the gods of the nations delivered every one his own
19 land from the hand of the king of Assyria? Where are
the gods of Hamath and of Arphad? Where are the gods
of Sepharvaim? And did the gods deliver Samaria from
20 my hand? Who is there among all the gods of these
lands, that hath delivered his land out of my hand, that
21 Jehovah should deliver Jerusalem out of my hand? But
the people held their peace, and answered him not a word;
for the king's command was, "Answer him not."

22 Then came Eliakim, the son of Hilkiah, that was over
the palace, and Shebna the scribe, and Joah, the son of
Asaph, the annalist, to Hezekiah, with their clothes rent,
and told him the words of Rabshakeh.

1 And when the king, Hezekiah, heard it, he rent his
clothes, and covered himself with sackcloth, and went into
2 the house of Jehovah. And he sent Eliakim, who was
over the palace, and Shebna the scribe, and the elders of
the priests, covered with sackcloth, to Isaiah the prophet,
3 the son of Amoz. And they said to him, Thus saith Hez-
ekiah: This day is a day of distress, of rebuke, and of con-
tempt; for the children have come to the birth, and there
4 is not strength to bring forth. It may be that Jehovah,
thy God, will hear the words of Rabshakeh, whom the
king of Assyria, his master, hath sent to reproach the liv-
ing God, and to revile him with the words which Jehovah,
thy God, hath heard. Do thou, therefore, lift up thy
prayer for the remnant of the people, that is yet left
5 And the servants of King Hezekiah came to Isaiah.

6 And Isaiah said to them, Thus shall ye say to your

master: Thus saith Jehovah: Be not afraid on account
of the words which thou hast heard, with which the ser-
7 vants of the king of Assyria have blasphemed me. Be-
hold, I will put a spirit within him, so that he shall hear
a rumor, and return to his own land; and I will cause
him to fall by the sword in his own land.

8 Then Rabshakeh returned, and found the king of As-
syria warring agaist Libnah, for he had heard that he
9 had departed from Lachish. Then he heard concerning
Tirhakah, king of Ethiopia, that it was said, "He is come
forth to war against thee." And when he heard it, he sent
10 messengers to Hezekiah and said, Thus shall ye say to
Hezekiah, the king of Judah: Let not thy God, in whom
thou trustest, deceive thee, saying, Jerusalem shall not be
11 given into the hand of the king of Assyria. Behold, thou
hast heard what the kings of Assyria have done to all
the lands; how they have utterly destroyed them. And
12 shalt thou be delivered? Did the gods of the nations
which my father destroyed, deliver them? Gozan, and
Haran, and Rezeph, and the children of Eden in Telassar?
13 Where is the king of Hamath, and the king of Arphad,
and the king of the city of Sepharvaim, of Henah, and of
Ivah?

14 And Hezekiah received the letter from the hand of the
messengers, and read it. Then he went up to the house
15 of Jehovah, and spread it before Jehovah. And Heze-
16 kiah prayed before Jehovah, saying, O Jehovah of hosts,
God of Israel, who sittest between the cherubs, thou alone
art the God of all the kingdoms of the earth; thou hast
17 made heaven and earth. Incline thine ear, O Jehovah,
and hear; open thine eyes, O Jehovah, and see; and hear
all the words of Sennacherib, which he hath sent to re-
18 proach the living God. In truth, O Jehovah, the kings
of Assyria have destroyed all the nations, and their lands,
19 and have cast their gods into the fire; for they were not
gods, but the work of men's hands, wood and stone; and
20 they have destroyed them. But do thou, O Jehovah, our
God, save us from his hand, that all the kingdoms of the
21 earth may know that thou alone art Jehovah. Then Isa-
iah, the son of Amoz, sent to Hezekiah, saying, Thus saith

Jehovah, the God of Israel: Whereas thou hast prayed
to me on account of Sennacherib, the king of Assyria,
22 This is the word which Jehovah hath spoken against him.

The virgin, the daughter of Zion, despiseth thee; she laugheth thee to scorn;
The daughter of Jerusalem shaketh her head after thee.
23 Whom hast thou reproached, and reviled,
And against whom hast thou exalted thy voice,
And lifted up thine eyes on high?
Against the Holy One of Israel.
24 By thy servants hast thou reproached the Lord, and said:
"With the multitude of my chariots have I ascended the heights of the mountains, the extremities of Lebanon;
I have cut down its tall cedars, and its choice cypress-trees;
I have come to its utmost height, to its garden forest.
25 I have digged and drunk water,
And with the sole of my feet will I dry up all the rivers of Egypt."
26 Hast thou not heard, that of old I ordained it,
And from ancient times purposed it?
Now have I brought it to pass,
That thou shouldst convert fortified cities into ruinous heaps.
27 Therefore were their inhabitants of little strength;
They were dismayed and confounded;
They were as the grass of the field, and the green herb;
As grass upon the house-top, and as corn blasted, before it is grown up.
28 I know thy sitting down, thy going out, and thy coming in,
And thy rage against me.
29 Because thy rage against me, and thy insolence, is come up into my ears,
I will put my ring into thy nose,
And my bridle into thy lips,
And turn thee back by the way in which thou camest.

30 And this shall be the sign to thee;
Eat this year that which groweth of itself,
And in the second year that which groweth of itself,
And in the third year ye shall sow and reap,

And plant vineyards, and eat the fruit thereof.
31 And the remnant of the house of Judah, that have escaped,
Shall again strike root downward,
And bear fruit upward.
32 For from Jerusalem shall go forth a remnant,
And they that have escaped from mount Zion.
The zeal of Jehovah of hosts will perform this.

33 Therefore thus saith Jehovah of hosts concerning the king of Assyria;
He shall not come into this city,
Nor shoot an arrow into it;
He shall not present a shield before it,
Nor cast up a mound against it.
34 By the way in which he came, by the same shall he return,
And into this city shall he not come, saith Jehovah.
35 For I will defend this city, and deliver it,
For mine own sake, and for my servant David's sake.

36 Then an angel of Jehovah went forth, and smote in the
camp of the Assyrians a hundred and eighty-five thousand
men; and when the people arose early in the morning,
37 behold they were all dead corpses. Then Sennacherib,
king of Assyria, decamped, and went away, and returned,
38 and dwelt at Nineveh. And as he was worshipping in the
temple of Nisroch, his god, he was slain with the sword
by his sons Adrammelech and Sharezer, who escaped in-
to the land of Ararat. And Esarhaddon, his son, reigned
in his stead.

1 In those days was Hezekiah sick unto death; and Isa-
iah the prophet, the son of Amoz, came to him, and said to
him, Set thy house in order, for thou shalt die, and not
2 live. Then Hezekiah turned his face toward the wall,
3 and made his supplication to Jehovah. And he said, I
beseech thee, O Jehovah, remember now how I have
walked before thee in truth, and with a perfect heart, and
have done that which is good in thine eyes! And Heze-
4 kiah wept bitterly. Then came the word of Jehovah to
5 Isaiah, Go in and say to Hezekiah, Thus saith Jehovah,
the God of David thy father: I have heard thy prayer;
I have seen thy tears. Behold, I will add to thy life fif-

6 teen years. And I will deliver thee and this city from
the hand of the king of Assyria, and I will defend this
7 city. And this shall be the sign to thee from Jehovah,
8 that Jehovah will do that which he hath spoken. Behold,
I will cause the shadow upon the dial, which hath gone
down upon the dial of Ahaz with the sun, to go back ten
degrees. So the sun went back ten degrees, which de-
grees it had gone down.

9 The writing of Hezekiah, king of Judah, when he had been sick, and had recovered from his sickness.

10 I said: "Now, in the quiet of my days, shall I go down to the gates of the under-world;
I am deprived of the residue of my years."
11 I said: "No more shall I see Jehovah,
Jehovah in the land of the living.
I shall behold man no more
Among the inhabitants of stillness.
12 My habitation is torn away and removed from me,
Like a shepherd's tent;
My life is rolled up as by the weaver;
He cutteth me off from the thrum;
Between morning and night wilt thou make an end of me!"
13 I waited till morning, and like a lion
Did he crush all my bones;
"Between morning and night wilt thou make an end of me!"
14 Like a swallow or a crane, so did I twitter;
I did mourn as a dove;
Mine eyes failed with looking upward;
"O Lord, I am in distress; O, deliver me!"

15 What shall I say?
He promised it, and he hath done it;
I will walk humbly all my life
On account of the bitterness of my soul.
16 Lord, it is thus that men live;
From thee alone cometh the life of my spirit;
Thou hast restored me, and caused me to live.
17 Behold, my anguish is changed into ease;

In love thou hast delivered me from the pit of destruction;
Thou hast cast all my sins behind thy back.
18 For the under-world cannot praise thee;
The realms of death cannot celebrate thee;
They that go down to the pit cannot wait for thy faithfulness.
19 The living, the living praise thee, as I do this day;
The father to the children shall make known thy faithfulness.
20 Jehovah hath saved me;
Therefore will we sing our songs with stringed instruments,
All the days of our life,
In the house of Jehovah.

21 Now Isaiah had said, let them take a lump of figs,
and bruise them, and lay them upon the ulcer, and he
22 shall recover. Hezekiah also had said, What is the sign
that I shall go up to the house of Jehovah?

1 At that time Merodach Baladan, the son of Baladan,
king of Babylon, sent a letter and a present to Hezekiah,
for he had heard that he had been sick and was recovered.
2 And Hezekiah was delighted with them, and showed the
embassy his treasure-house, the silver, and the gold, and
the spices, and the precious oil, and his whole armory,
and all that was found in his treasures. There was nothing
in his house, nor in all his dominion, which Hezekiah
did not show them.

3 Then came Isaiah the prophet to King Hezekiah, and
said to him, What did these men say, and whence did
they come to thee? And Hezekiah said, They came to
4 me from a distant country, from Babylon. Then said he,
What have they seen in thy house? And Hezekiah answered:
All that is in my house have they seen. There
is nothing in my treasures which I have not shown them.
5 Then said Isaiah to Hezekiah, Hear the word of Jehovah
6 of hosts. Behold, the days shall come, when all that is
in thy house, and that thy fathers have treasured up to
this day, shall be carried away to Babylon. Nothing

7 shall be left, saith Jehovah. And of thy sons, which shall
issue from thee, which thou shalt beget, shall they take
away, and they shall be eunuchs in the palace of the king
of Babylon. Then said Hezekiah to Isaiah, Good is the
word of Jehovah, which thou hast spoken. For, said he,
there shall be peace and security in my days.

XXXII.

Consolation, admonition, and exhortation, addressed to the Jews. The restoration of the Jews from the captivity at Babylon through the agency of Cyrus, and the subsequent improvement and glory of their nation. The conversion of some foreign nations to the worship of Jehovah, and the destruction of others.

1.

The prophet encourages the Hebrew nation in exile, and persuades them to put themselves under the guidance of Jehovah, by contrasting the power and wisdom of Jehovah with the impotence of idols. — CH. XL.

1 COMFORT ye, comfort ye, my people,
Saith your God.
2 Speak ye encouragement to Jerusalem, and declare to her,
That her hard service is ended;
That her iniquity is expiated;
That she hath received from the hand of Jehovah
Double for all her sins.

3 A voice crieth:
"Prepare ye in the wilderness the way of Jehovah;
Make straight in the desert a highway for our God!
4 Every valley shall be exalted,
And every mountain and hill be made low;
The crooked shall become straight,
And the rough places plain.
5 For the glory of Jehovah shall be revealed,
And all flesh shall see it together;
For the mouth of Jehovah hath spoken it."

6 A voice said, Proclaim!
And I said, What shall I proclaim?
All flesh is grass,
And all its comeliness as the flower of the field.
7 The grass withereth, the flower fadeth,
When the breath of Jehovah bloweth upon it.
Truly the people is grass.
8 The grass withereth, the flower fadeth,
But the word of our God shall stand forever.

9 Get thee up on the high mountain,
O thou that bringest glad tidings to Zion;
Lift up thy voice with strength, thou that bringest glad tidings to Jerusalem;
Lift it up; be not afraid;
Say to the cities of Judah, Behold your God!
10 Behold, the Lord Jehovah shall come with might,
And his arm shall rule for him;
Behold, his reward is with him,
And his recompense before him.
11 He shall feed his flock like a shepherd;
He shall gather up the lambs in his arms,
And carry them in his bosom,
And gently lead the nursing ewes.

12 Who hath measured the waters in the hollow of his hand,
And meted out the heavens with his span,
And gathered the dust of the earth into a measure,
And weighed the mountains in scales,
And the hills in a balance?
13 Who hath searched out the spirit of Jehovah,
Or, being his counsellor, hath taught him?
14 With whom took he counsel, and who instructed him,
And taught him the path of justice,
And taught him knowledge,
And showed him the way of understanding?
15 Behold, the nations are as a drop from a bucket,
And are accounted as the small dust of the balance;
Behold, he taketh up the isles as a very little thing,
16 And Lebanon is not sufficient for fire,
Nor its beasts for a burnt-offering.

17 All the nations are as nothing before him;
They are accounted by him as less than nothing, and vanity.
18 To whom then will ye liken God,
And what likeness will ye compare unto him?
19 The workman casteth an image,
And the smith overlayeth it with gold,
And casteth for it silver chains.
20 He that is too poor to make an oblation
Chooseth a piece of wood that will not rot;
He seeketh for himself a skilful artificer,
To prepare an image that shall not be moved.
21 Do ye not know?
Have ye not heard?
Hath it not been declared to you from the beginning?
Have ye not considered the foundations of the earth?
22 It is He that sitteth above the circle of the earth,
And the inhabitants are to him as grasshoppers;
That stretcheth out the heavens as a canopy,
And spreadeth them out as a tent to dwell in;
23 That bringeth princes to nothing,
And reduceth the rulers of the earth to vanity.
24 Yea, scarcely are they planted, scarcely are they sown,
Scarcely hath their stem taken root in the ground,
When He bloweth upon them and they wither,
And the whirlwind beareth them away like stubble.
25 To whom then will ye liken me,
And to whom shall I be compared?
Saith the Holy One.
26 Lift up your eyes to the heavens, and behold!
Who hath created these?
He draweth forth their host by number,
He calleth them all by name;
Through the greatness of his strength and the mightiness of his power,
Not one of them faileth to appear.
27 Why sayest thou, O Jacob, and speakest, O Israel,
"My way is hidden from Jehovah,
My cause passeth by before my God"?
28 Do ye not know?
Have ye not heard?
Jehovah is an everlasting God,

The creator of the ends of the earth;
He fainteth not, nor is he weary;
His understanding is unsearchable.
29 He giveth power to the faint;
To the feeble abundant strength.
30 The youths shall faint and be weary,
And the young warriors shall utterly fall.
31 But they that trust in Jehovah shall renew their strength;
They shall mount up with wings like eagles;
They shall run and not be weary;
They shall walk and not faint.

2.

Superiority of Jehovah over other gods. He will defend Israel. — CH. XLI

1 KEEP silence, and hear me, ye distant lands,
Ye nations, gather your strength!
Let them come near; then let them speak;
Let us go together into judgment.

2 Who hath raised up from the region of the East
Him whom victory meeteth in his march?
Who hath subdued nations before him,
And given him dominion over kings?
Who made their swords like dust,
And their bows like driven stubble?
3 He pursued them, and passed in safety,
By a path which his foot had never trodden.
4 Who hath wrought and done it?
I, who have called the generations from the beginning,
I, Jehovah, the first;
And with the last also am I.

5 Distant nations saw it, and were afraid;
The ends of the earth, and trembled;
They drew near, and came together.
6 One helped another,
And said to him, "Be of good courage!"
7 The carpenter encouraged the smith,
He that smoothed with the hammer him that smote on the anvil,

And said, "The soldering is good,"
And he fastened it with nails that it might not fall.

8 But thou, O Israel, my servant,
Thou, Jacob, whom I have chosen,
Offspring of Abraham, my friend!
9 Thou, whom I have led by the hand from the ends of the
earth,
And called from the extremities thereof,
And said to thee, "Thou art my servant,
I have chosen thee, and not cast thee away!"
10 Fear not, for I am with thee;
Faint not, for I, thy God, will strengthen thee;
I will help thee, and sustain thee, with my right hand of
salvation!
11 Behold, all who are enraged against thee
Shall be ashamed and confounded;
All that contend with thee
Shall come to nothing and perish.
12 Thou shalt seek and not find
Them that contend with thee;
They shall come to nothing, and be no more,
Who make war against thee.
13 For I, Jehovah, am thy God, that holdeth thee by the
right hand,
That saith to thee, "Fear not, I am thy helper!"
14 Fear not, thou worm Jacob, thou feeble people of Israel!
I am thy helper, saith Jehovah;
Thy redeemer is the Holy One of Israel.
15 Behold, I will make thee a thrashing-wain, sharp and new,
With double edges;
Thou shalt thrash the mountains, and beat them small,
And make the hills as chaff.
16 Thou shalt winnow them, and the wind shall carry them
away,
And the whirlwind shall scatter them.
But thou shalt rejoice in Jehovah,
And glory in the Holy One of Israel.

17 When the poor and needy seek water, and there is none,
And their tongue is parched with thirst,
I, Jehovah, will hear them;

I, the God of Israel, will not forsake them.
18 I will open rivers upon the bare hills,
And fountains in the midst of the valleys;
I will make the wilderness a pool of water,
And the dry land springs of water.
19 I will plant in the wilderness the cedar and the acacia,
The myrtle and the olive-tree;
I will place in the desert the cypress,
The plane-tree and the larch together.
20 That they may see, and know,
And consider, and understand together,
That the hand of Jehovah hath done this,
And that the Holy One of Israel hath created it.

21 Bring forward your cause, saith Jehovah;
Produce your strong reasons, saith the king of Jacob.
22 Let them produce them, and show us what shall happen!
Tell us what ye have predicted in times past,
That we may consider, and know its fulfilment!
Or declare to us things that are to come!
23 Let us hear what shall happen in future times,
That we may know whether ye are gods;
Do something, be it good or evil,
That we may be astonished, and see it together!
24 Behold, ye are less than nothing,
And your work is less than naught;
An abomination is he that chooseth you!

25 I have raised up one from the north, and he cometh;
From the rising of the sun he calleth upon my name;
He trampleth upon princes as upon mortar;
As the potter treadeth down the clay.
26 Who hath declared this from the beginning, that we might know it,
And long ago, that we might say, It is true?
There was not one that foretold it, not one that declared it,
Not one that heard your words.
27 I first said to Zion, Behold! behold them!
And I gave to Jerusalem a messenger of glad tidings.
28 I looked, but there was no man;
Even among them, but there was none that gave counsel;

I inquired of them that they might give an answer;
29 But behold, they are all vanity;
Their works are nothing;
Wind and emptiness are their molten images.

3.

Description of the Servant of God. Deliverance promised. — CH. XLII.

1 BEHOLD my servant, whom I uphold,
My chosen, in whom my soul delighteth,
I have put my spirit upon him;
He shall cause law to go forth to the nations.
2 He shall not cry aloud, nor lift up his voice,
Nor cause it to be heard in the street.
3 The bruised reed shall he not break,
And the glimmering flax shall he not quench;
He shall send forth law according to truth.
4 He shall not fail, nor become weary,
Until he shall have established justice in the earth,
And distant nations shall wait for his law.

5 Thus saith God Jehovah,
Who created the heavens and stretched them out,
Who spread forth the earth, and that which springeth forth from it,
Who gave breath to the people upon it,
And spirit to them that walk thereon:
6 I, Jehovah, have called thee for salvation;
I will hold thee by the hand;
I will defend thee, and make thee a covenant to the people,
A light to the nations;
7 To open the blind eyes,
To bring out the prisoners from the prison,
And them that sit in darkness out of the prison-house.
8 I am Jehovah, that is my name;
And my glory will I not give to another,
Nor my praise to graven images.
9 The former things, behold! they are come to pass,
And new things do I now declare;
Before they spring forth, I make them known to you.

10 Sing to Jehovah a new song;
His praise to the ends of the earth;
Ye that go down upon the sea, and all that fill it;
Ye distant coasts, and ye that dwell therein!
11 Let the desert cry aloud, and the cities thereof;
The villages, that Kedar inhabiteth;
Let the inhabitants of the rock sing;
Let them shout from the top of the mountains!
12 Let them give glory to Jehovah,
And proclaim his praise in distant lands!
13 Jehovah shall march forth like a hero;
Like a mighty warrior shall he rouse his indignation,
He shall cry aloud; he shall shout the war-cry,
And show himself mighty against his enemies.
14 "I have long held my peace;
I have been still and refrained myself;
But now will I cry like a woman in travail;
I will destroy and swallow up at once.
15 I will lay waste mountains and hills,
And dry up all their herbs.
I will make the river solid land,
And dry up the pools of water.
16 Then will I lead the blind in a way which they know not,
And in unknown paths will I guide them;
I will make darkness light before them,
And crooked paths straight;
These things will I do for them, and not forsake them."

17 Then shall they be turned back, and be put to shame,
Who trust in graven images;
Who say to molten images,
"Ye are our gods!"

18 Hear, O ye deaf!
And look, ye blind, and see!
19 Who is blind, if not my servant?
And who so deaf as my messenger, whom I send?
Who so blind as the friend of God,
So blind as the servant of Jehovah?
20 Thou seest many things, but regardest them not;
Thou hast thine ears open, but hearest not!
21 It pleased Jehovah for his goodness' sake

To give him a law, great and glorious;
22 And yet it is a robbed and plundered people;
They are all of them bound in prisons,
And hid in dungeons;
They have become a spoil, and none delivereth;
A prey, and none saith, "Restore!"

23 Who is there among you that will give ear to this,
That will listen and attend for the time to come?
24 Who gave Jacob to be a spoil,
And Israel to plunderers?
Was it not Jehovah, against whom we sinned,
In whose ways we would not walk,
And whose laws we would not obey?
25 Therefore hath he poured out upon Israel the fury of his wrath, and the violence of war;
It kindled a flame around about him, yet he did not regard it;
It set him on fire, yet he laid it not to heart.

4.

Promise of deliverance. — Ch. XLIII.

1 But now thus saith Jehovah, that created thee, O Jacob,
That formed thee, O Israel:
Fear not, for I have redeemed thee;
I have called thee by name; thou art mine!
2 When thou passest through waters, I will be with thee;
And through rivers, they shall not overflow thee;
When thou walkest through fire, thou shalt not be burned,
And the flame shall not consume thee.
3 For I am Jehovah, thy God,
The Holy One of Israel, thy saviour.
I will give Egypt for thy ransom,
Ethiopia and Seba for thee.
4 Because thou art precious in my sight,
Because thou art honored, and I love thee,
Therefore will I give men for thee,
And nations for thy life.
5 Fear not, for I am with thee!
I will bring thy children from the East,

And gather thee from the West.
6 I will say to the North, "Give them up!"
And to the South, "Withhold them not!
Bring my sons from afar,
And my daughters from the ends of the earth;
7 Every one that is called by my name,
That I have created for my glory,
That I have formed and made!"
8 Bring forth the blind people, having eyes,
And the deaf, having ears.
9 Let all the nations be gathered together,
And the kingdoms be assembled!
Who among them hath declared this,
And can show us former predictions?
Let them produce their witnesses that they are right;
That men may hear, and say, It is true!
10 Ye are my witnesses, saith Jehovah,
And my servant whom I have chosen,
That ye may know and believe me,
And understand that I am He.
Before me was no god formed,
And after me there shall be none.
11 I, I am Jehovah,
And besides me there is no saviour.
12 I have declared and have saved;
I made it known, when there was no strange god among
you;
Ye are my witnesses, saith Jehovah,
That I am God.
13 Even from the beginning of time I have been He,
And none can rescue from my hand;
I undertake, and who can hinder?

14 Thus saith Jehovah,
Your redeemer, the Holy One of Israel;
For your sakes have I sent to Babylon,
And caused all her fugitives,
And the Chaldeans, to descend to the ships of their delight.
15 I, Jehovah, am your Holy One,
The creator of Israel, your king.

16 Thus saith Jehovah, —

He that made a way in the sea,
And a path in the mighty waters,
17 That caused the chariot and the horse, the army and the forces, to march forth;
There they lay down together; they rose no more;
They were extinguished; they were quenched like a torch; —
18 Remember not the former things;
The things of old regard no more!
19 Behold, I do a new thing;
Now shall it spring forth; yea, ye shall see it.
Behold, I make a way in the wilderness,
And streams in the desert;
20 The beasts of the forest shall honor me,
The jackals and the ostriches;
For I make rivers in the wilderness
And streams in the desert,
To give drink to my people, my chosen.
21 This people, which I have formed for myself
Shall make known my praise.

22 Yet thou hast not called upon me, O Jacob,
So as to have wearied thyself for me, O Israel!
23 Thou hast not brought me thy lambs for a burnt-offering,
Nor honored me with thy sacrifices;
I have not burdened thee with oblations,
Nor wearied thee with incense;
24 Thou hast bought me no sweet-smelling reed with silver,
Neither hast thou satisfied me with the fat of thy sacrifices;
With thy sins hast thou burdened me,
And wearied me with thine iniquities.
25 I, I myself, blot out thy transgressions for my own sake,
And will not remember thy sins.
26 Put me in remembrance; let us plead together;
Speak that thou mayst justify thyself.
27 Thy forefathers sinned,
And thy teachers were rebellious against me;
28 Therefore have I profaned the princes of the sanctuary,
And given up Jacob to a curse,
And Israel to reproach.

5.

The weakness of idols. The mission of Cyrus for the deliverance of the Jews. — CH. XLIV., XLV.

1 YET now hear, O Jacob, my servant,
And Israel, whom I have chosen;
2 Thus saith Jehovah, thy Creator,
He that formed thee, and hath helped thee from thy birth
Fear not, O Jacob, my servant,
O Jeshurun, whom I have chosen.
3 For I will pour water upon the thirsty land,
And streams upon the dry ground.
I will pour out my spirit on thy children,
And my blessing on thine offspring;
4 And they shall grow up, as among grass;
As willows by the water-brooks.
5 One shall say, "I belong to Jehovah";
Another shall call upon the name of Jacob;
Another shall write upon his hand, Jehovah's!
And praise the name of Israel.
6 Thus saith Jehovah, the King of Israel,
His redeemer, Jehovah of hosts:
I am the first, and I the last,
And besides me there is no God.
7 Who like me hath proclaimed the future, —
Let him declare it, and set it in order before me! —
Since I established the people of old?
Let them make known the future, even that which is to come!
8 Fear ye not, neither be ye afraid!
Have I not declared and made it known to you of old?
Ye are my witnesses;
Is there a God beside me?
Yea, there is no other rock; I know not any.
9 They that make a graven image are all of them vanity,
And their valued works are profitable for nothing;
They are their own witnesses;
They neither see nor understand,
So that they may be ashamed.
10 Who hath formed a god,
And cast a graven image, that is profitable for nothing?
11 Behold, all his fellows shall be ashamed;

The workmen are themselves mortal men;
They shall all be assembled; they shall stand up;
They shall tremble, and be put to shame together!

12 The smith prepareth an axe in the coals,
And fashioneth it with hammers,
And worketh it with his strong arm;
He becometh hungry, and his strength faileth;
He drinketh no water, and is faint.
13 The carpenter stretcheth out the line;
He marketh out the form of it with the sharp tool;
He formeth it with planes;
He marketh it with the compass;
He maketh it in the figure of a man,
With the beauty of a man,
To dwell in a house.
14 He heweth him down cedars;
He taketh the ilex and the oak;
He chooseth for himself among the trees of the forest;
He planteth the ash, and the rain matureth it;
15 These are fuel for man;
He taketh thereof and warmeth himself;
He kindleth with it, and baketh bread;
A god also he formeth of it, and worshippeth it;
A graven image, and falleth down before it.
16 Half of it he burneth with fire;
With half of it he eateth flesh;
He roasteth meat, and satisfieth himself;
He also warmeth himself, and saith,
Aha! I am warm; I feel the fire.
17 Of the residue he maketh a god, even his graven image;
He falleth down before it and worshippeth it,
And prayeth to it, and saith,
"Deliver me, for thou art my God!"
18 They know not, neither understand;
For their eyes are closed up, that they cannot see,
And their hearts, that they cannot understand.
19 None considereth in his mind,
Or hath knowledge and understanding to say:
"Half of it I have burned with fire;
I have also baked bread on the coals of it;
I have roasted flesh and have eaten;

And shall I make the remnant an abomination?
Shall I fall down before the stock of a tree?"
20 He toileth for ashes;
A deluded heart turneth him aside,
So that he cannot deliver himself, and say,
"Is there not a lie in my right hand?"
21 Remember these things, O Jacob,
O Israel, for thou art my servant!
I formed thee; thou art my servant;
O Israel, I will not forget thee.
22 I have caused thy transgressions to vanish like a cloud,
And thy sins like a mist;
Return to me, for I have redeemed thee!

23 Sing, O ye heavens, for Jehovah hath done it;
Shout, O ye depths of the earth!
Break forth into song, ye mountains!
Thou forest, and every tree therein!
For Jehovah hath redeemed Jacob,
And glorified himself in Israel.

24 Thus saith Jehovah, thy Redeemer,
Even he that formed thee from the womb;
I am Jehovah, who made all things;
Who stretched out the heavens alone;
Who spread out the earth by myself;
25 Who frustrateth the signs of deceivers,
And maketh the diviners mad;
Who putteth the wise men to shame,
And maketh their knowledge folly;
26 Who establisheth the word of his servant,
And performeth the purpose of his messengers;
Who saith of Jerusalem, "She shall be inhabited,"
And of the cities of Judah, "They shall be built,"
And, "Her desolated places I will restore."
27 Who saith to the deep, "Be dry!
I will dry up thy streams!"
28 Who saith of Cyrus, "He is my shepherd;
He shall perform all my pleasure";
Who saith of Jerusalem, "She shall be built,"
And of the temple, "Her foundation shall be laid."

1 Thus saith Jehovah to his anointed,
To Cyrus, whom I hold by his right hand,
To subdue nations before him,
And ungird the loins of kings;
To open before him the two-leaved gates,
And the doors shall not be shut.
2 I will go before thee,
And make the high places plain;
I will break in pieces the gates of brass,
And cut in sunder the bars of iron.
3 I will give thee the treasures of darkness,
And hidden riches of secret places,
That thou mayst know that I am Jehovah
Who calleth thee by name, the God of Israel.
4 For the sake of Jacob, my servant,
And Israel, my chosen,
I have called thee by thy name;
I have spoken to thee as a friend, though thou hast not known me.
5 I am Jehovah, and none else;
There is no God besides me;
I have girded thee, though thou hast not known me.
6 That men may know from the rising of the sun,
And from the West, that there is none besides me;
I am Jehovah, and none else.
7 I form the light, and create darkness;
I make peace, and create evil;
I, Jehovah, do all these things.
8 Pour forth, ye heavens, from above;
Ye clouds, shower down prosperity!
Let the earth open, and bring forth salvation;
Yea, let righteousness spring up together!
I, Jehovah, create it.

9 Woe to him that contendeth with his Maker!
A potsherd of the potsherds of the earth!
Shall the clay say to him that fashioneth it, What makest thou?
Or thy work say of thee, He hath no hands?
10 Woe to him that saith to his father,
Why dost thou beget?
Or to his mother, Why dost thou bring forth?

11 Thus saith Jehovah, the Holy One of Israel, and his Maker,
Ask of me concerning things to come;
My children, the work of my hands, leave them to me!
12 I made the earth,
And created man upon it;
My hands spread out the heavens,
And all their host did I arrange.
13 I have raised him up for salvation,
And I will make all his ways plain;
He shall build my city, and release my captives,
Not for price, and not for ransom,
Saith Jehovah of hosts.
14 Thus saith Jehovah:
The wealth of Egypt and the merchandise of the Ethiopians and Sabeans, men of stature,
Shall come over to thee, and be thine;
They shall follow thee; in chains shall they pass along;
They shall fall down to thee, and make supplication to thee:
"In thee alone is God, and there is none else;
There is no other God."
15 Truly thou art a God that hidest thyself,
O God of Israel, the saviour!
16 They shall all be ashamed and confounded,
They shall go to confusion together,
That are makers of idols.
17 But Israel shall be saved by Jehovah with an everlasting salvation;
Ye shall never be ashamed, nor confounded.

18 For thus saith Jehovah, who created the heavens;
The God that formed the earth and made it; he that made it firm;
He created it not in vain; he formed it to be inhabited:
I am Jehovah, and none else.
19 I have not spoken in secret, in a dark place of the earth;
I have not said to the race of Jacob, Seek ye me in vain!
I, Jehovah, speak truth; I declare that which is right.
20 Assemble yourselves and come;
Gather yourselves together, ye that are escaped of the nations!

They are without understanding, who carry about with
them the wood of their graven image,
And pray to a god that cannot save.
21 Proclaim ye, and bring them near,
And let them take counsel together:
Who hath made this known from ancient time?
Who hath declared it of old?
Is it not I, Jehovah, besides whom there is no God?
A God that uttereth truth, and giveth salvation; there is
none besides me.
22 Look to me, and be saved, all ye ends of the earth!
For I am God, and there is none else.
23 By myself have I sworn,
The truth hath gone from my mouth,
The word, that shall not return,
That to me every knee shall bow,
That to me every tongue shall swear.
24 "Only in Jehovah," shall men say,
"Is salvation and strength;
To him shall come and be put to shame,
All that are incensed against him."
25 Through Jehovah shall all the race of Israel be delivered,
And in him shall they glory.

6.

Difference between the true God and idols, in regard to the aid which they can afford to their worshippers. — CH. XLVI.

1 BEL sinketh down; Nebo falleth;
Their images are laid upon beasts and cattle;
Those that ye once bore are packed upon them;
A burden to the weary beast!
2 They sink down; they fall together;
They cannot rescue the burden;
They themselves go into captivity.
3 Hearken to me, O house of Jacob,
And all the remnant of the house of Israel;
Ye that have been borne by me from your birth,
That have been carried by me from your earliest breath!
4 Even to your old age I am the same;
Even to hoar hairs I will carry you;

I have done it, and I will still bear you;
I will carry, and will deliver you.
5 To whom will ye liken me, and compare me?
Yea, to whom will ye compare me, that we may be like?
6 They lavish gold out of the bag,
And weigh silver in the balance;
They hire a goldsmith, and he maketh it a god;
They fall down, yea, they worship it.
7 They lift him upon the shoulder, and carry him;
They set him in his place, and there he standeth;
From his place he moveth not;
Yea, one may cry to him, yet doth he not answer,
Nor save him out of his distress.
8 Remember these things, and show yourselves men;
Lay them to heart, ye apostates!
9 Remember the former things in ancient times!
For I am God, and there is none else;
I am God, and there is none like me.
10 Declaring the end from the beginning;
From ancient times the things that were not yet done;
Saying, My purpose shall stand,
And I will do all my pleasure;
11 Calling from the East the eagle,
The man that executeth my purpose from a far country;
I have spoken it, I will also bring it to pass;
I have purposed it, I will also do it.
12 Hearken to me, ye stubborn-hearted,
That are far from deliverance!
13 I have brought near my deliverance; it is not far off;
My salvation shall not tarry;
I will give to Zion salvation,
To Israel, my glory.

7.

Fall of the Babylonian kingdom. — CH. XLVII.

1 COME down, and sit in the dust, O virgin, daughter of Babylon!
Sit on the ground without a throne, O daughter of the Chaldæans!
For thou shalt no longer be called the tender and delicate!

2 Take the mill-stones and grind meal;
Raise thy veil, lift up thy train;
Make bare the leg, wade through the streams!
3 Thy nakedness shall be uncovered,
And thy shame shall be seen.
I will take vengeance;
I will make peace with none.
4 Our Redeemer, Jehovah of hosts is his name,
The Holy One of Israel.
5 Sit thou in silence; go into darkness, O daughter of the Chaldæans!
For thou shalt no more be called the mistress of kingdoms.
6 I was angry with my people;
I profaned my inheritance,
And gave them into thy hand;
Thou didst show them no mercy;
Even upon the aged didst thou lay a very grievous yoke.
7 Thou saidst, "I shall be mistress forever";
So that thou didst not lay these things to thy heart,
Nor consider what would be the end of them.
8 But hear thou this, thou that art given to pleasure!
That sittest in security,
And sayest in thy heart, "I am, and there is none besides me;
I shall not be a widow,
Nor see myself childless!"
9 Behold, both these things shall come upon thee suddenly, in one day,
Loss of children, and widowhood;
In full measure shall they come upon thee,
In spite of thy many sorceries,
And the great abundance of thy enchantments.
10 Thou didst trust in thy wickedness, and saidst, "No one seeth me";
Thy wisdom and thy knowledge have led thee astray;
Thou saidst in thy heart, "I am, and there is none besides me";
11 Therefore shall evil come upon thee, of which thou shalt not know the dawn;
And mischief shall fall upon thee, which thou shalt not be able to expiate;

Suddenly shall desolation come upon thee, when thou thinkest not of it.
12 Persevere now in thy enchantments;
In the multitude of thy sorceries, in which thou hast labored from thy youth;
Perhaps thou mayst be profited by them!
Perhaps thou mayst make thyself feared!
13 Art thou wearied with thy many devices?
Let them stand up, then, and save thee,
The observers of the heavens, the star-gazers,
They that prognosticate at every new moon
The things that shall come upon thee!
14 Behold, they shall be like stubble; the fire shall burn them up;
They shall not deliver themselves from the power of the flame;
Not a coal shall be left of them to warm one,
Nor a spark of fire to sit by.
15 Thus shall it be with them with whom thou hast labored;
Thus with them with whom thou hast trafficked from thy youth;
They shall go every one his own way;
None shall help thee.

8.

Renewed assurances of restoration from Babylon. — CH. XLVIII.

1 HEAR this, O house of Jacob!
Ye that are called by the name of Israel;
Ye that have come forth from the fountain of Judah;
Ye that swear by the name of Jehovah,
And praise the God of Israel,
But not in truth and sincerity! —
2 For they call themselves of the holy city,
And stay themselves on the God of Israel,
Whose name is Jehovah of hosts: —
3 What hath happened I declared to you long ago;
From my mouth it proceeded, and I made it known;
On a sudden I effected it, and it came to pass.
4 Because I knew that thou art obstinate,
And that thy neck is a bar of iron,

And that thy brow is brass,
5 I declared it to thee long ago;
Before it came to pass, I made it known to thee;
Lest thou shouldst say, My idol effected it,
And my graven image, and my molten image ordained it.
6 Thou hast heard it; now see it all!
And will ye not confess it?
From this time I make you hear a new thing,
Even a hidden thing, which thou hast not known.
7 It is produced now, and not long ago;
Before this day thou hast not heard of it,
Lest thou shouldst say, Behold, I knew it.
8 Yea, thou heardest it not; yea, thou knewest it not;
Yea, it was not disclosed to thee long ago;
For I knew that thou wast wholly faithless,
And wast called rebellious from thy birth.
9 For the sake of my name I will defer my anger,
And for the sake of my praise I will restrain it from thee,
That I may not utterly cut thee off.
10 Behold, I have melted thee, and found no silver;
I have tried thee in the furnace of affliction.
11 For mine own sake will I do it;
For how would my name be blasphemed?
And my glory will I not give to another.
12 Hearken to me, O Jacob,
And Israel, whom I have called!
I am He, I am the first, and I the last.
13 Yea, my hand hath founded the earth,
And my right hand hath spread out the heavens;
I called them; they stood forth together.
14 Assemble yourselves, all of you, and hear!
Who among you hath declared these things?
He whom Jehovah loveth will execute his pleasure upon Babylon,
And his power upon the Chaldæans.
15 I, even I, have spoken; yea, I have called him;
I have brought him, and his way shall be prosperous.

16 Draw near to me, and hear ye this!
I spake not in secret from the beginning;
And since it began to be, I have been there;
And now hath the Lord Jehovah sent me with his spirit.

17 Thus saith Jehovah, thy Redeemer, the Holy One of Israel;
I am Jehovah, thy God, who teacheth thee what will profit thee;
Who leadeth thee in the way thou shouldst go.
18 O that thou wouldst hearken to my commandments!
Then shall thy peace be as a river,
And thy prosperity as the waves of the sea;
19 Then shall thy posterity be as the sand,
And the fruit of thy body as the offspring of the sea;
Thy name shall not be cut off, nor destroyed before me.

20 Come ye forth from Babylon, flee ye from the land of the Chaldæans with the voice of joy!
Publish ye this, and make it known;
Let it resound to the ends of the earth!
Say: "Jehovah hath redeemed his servant Jacob;
21 They thirst not in the deserts through which he leadeth them;
Waters from the rock he causeth to flow for them;
He cleaveth the rock, and the waters gush forth.
22 There is no peace, saith Jehovah, for the wicked."

9.

Glory of the Servant of God. Deliverance of the people. — CH. XLIX.

1 LISTEN to me, ye distant lands!
Attend, ye nations from afar!
Jehovah called me at my birth;
In my very childhood he called me by name.
2 He made my mouth like a sharp sword;
In the shadow of his hand did he hide me.
He made me a polished shaft;
In his quiver did he hide me.
3 He said to me, Thou art my servant;
Israel, in whom I will be glorified.
4 Then I said, I have labored in vain;
For naught, for vanity, have I spent my strength;
Yet my cause is with Jehovah,
And my reward with my God.
5 And now thus saith Jehovah,

Who formed me from my birth to be his servant
To bring Jacob to him again,
And that Israel might be gathered to him,—
For I am honored in the eyes of Jehovah,
And my God is my strength,—
6 He said, It is a small thing that thou shouldst be my servant,
To raise up the tribes of Jacob,
And to restore the preserved of Israel;
I will also make thee the light of the nations,
That my salvation may reach the ends of the earth.
7 Thus saith Jehovah, the Redeemer of Israel, his Holy One,
To him that is despised by men, abhorred by the people,
To the servant of tyrants;
Kings shall see, and stand up,
Princes, and they shall pay homage,
On account of Jehovah, who is faithful,
The Holy One of Israel, who hath chosen thee.
8 Thus saith Jehovah;
In the time of favor will I hear thee;
In the day of deliverance will I help thee;
I will preserve thee, and make thee a mediator for the people,
To restore the land, to distribute the desolated inheritances;
9 To say to the prisoners, Go forth!
To them that are in darkness, Come to the light!
They shall feed in the ways,
And on all high places shall be their pasture.
10 They shall not hunger, neither shall they thirst;
Neither shall the heat nor the sun smite them;
For he that hath compassion on them shall lead them;
To springs of water shall he guide them.
11 And I will make all my mountains a highway;
And my roads shall be prepared.
12 Behold! these shall come from far;
And behold! these from the North and from the West,
And these from the land of Sinim.

13 Sing, O ye heavens, and rejoice, O earth!
Break forth into singing, ye mountains!

For Jehovah comforteth his people,
And hath compassion on his afflicted ones.

14 Zion saith, "Jehovah hath forsaken me;
The Lord hath forgotten me."
15 Can a woman forget her sucking child,
So as not to have compassion on the son of her womb?
Yet, should they forget,
I will never forget thee!
16 Behold, I have graven thee on the palms of my hands;
Thy walls are ever before my eyes.
17 Thy children shall make haste;
They that destroyed and laid thee waste shall depart from thee.
18 Lift up thine eyes around, and see!
They all assemble themselves, and come to thee.
As I live, saith Jehovah,
Thou shalt surely clothe thee with them all, as with a rich dress;
Thou shalt bind them on thee, as a bride her jewels.
19 For thy waste and desolate places, and thy land laid in ruins,
Shall now be too narrow for the inhabitants;
And they that devoured thee shall be far away.
20 Thou, that hast been childless, shalt yet hear thy sons exclaim:
"The place is too narrow for me; make room for me that I may dwell."
21 And thou shalt say in thy heart,
Who hath begotten me these?
I surely was childless and unfruitful,
An exile, and an outcast; who then hath brought up these?
Behold, I was left alone; these, then, where were they?
22 Thus saith the Lord Jehovah:
I will lift up my hand to the nations,
And set up my standard to the kingdoms;
They shall bring thy sons in their arms,
And thy daughters upon their shoulders.
23 And kings shall be thy nursing fathers,
And queens thy nursing mothers;
Upon their faces shall they bow down before thee,

And lick the dust of thy feet.
Thus shalt thou know that I am Jehovah;
And they who trust in me shall not be put to shame.
24 Shall the prey be taken away from the mighty?
Or shall the spoil of the terrible be rescued?
25 Yea, thus saith Jehovah,
The prey shall be taken away from the mighty,
And the spoil of the terrible shall be rescued;
For with him that contendeth with thee will I contend,
26 And I will save thy children.
27 And I will cause thine oppressors to eat their own flesh;
With their own blood shall they be drunk, as with new wine;
And all flesh shall know that I Jehovah am thy saviour;
That thy redeemer is the Mighty One of Jacob.

10.

Remonstrance against unbelief and disobedience. — CH. L.

1 THUS saith Jehovah: Where is the bill of your mother's divorcement,
By which I dismissed her?
Or who is he among my creditors
To whom I have sold you?
Behold, for your iniquities are ye sold,
And for your transgressions was your mother dismissed.
2 Wherefore, when I came, was no man at hand?
When I called, was there none to answer?
Is my hand too short to redeem?
Or have I no power to deliver?
Behold, at my rebuke I dry up the sea,
And make the rivers a desert.
Their fish putrefy for want of water,
And die with thirst.
3 I clothe the heavens with blackness,
And make sackcloth their covering.

4 The Lord Jehovah hath given me the tongue of the learned,
That I might know how to strengthen with my words them that are weary;

He wakeneth me every morning,
He wakeneth mine ear,
That I may hear in the manner of the learned.
5 The Lord Jehovah opened mine ear,
And I was not disobedient,
Neither did I withdraw myself backward.
6 I gave my back to the smiters,
And my cheeks to them that pluck the beard;
I hid not my face from shame and spitting.
7 But the Lord Jehovah is my helper,
Therefore shall I not be confounded;
Therefore have I made my face like a flint,
For I know that I shall not be put to shame.
8 He that defendeth my cause is near;
Who will contend with me? Let us stand up together!
Who is my adversary? Let him come near to me!
9 Behold, the Lord Jehovah is my defender;
Who is he that shall condemn me?
Behold, they shall all waste away like a garment;
The moth shall consume them.

10 Who is there among you that feareth Jehovah,
That hearkeneth to the voice of his servant,
That walketh in darkness and hath no light?
Let him trust in the name of Jehovah,
And lean upon his God.
11 Behold, all ye who kindle a fire,
Who gird yourselves with burning arrows!
Walk ye in the light of your fire,
And in the burning arrows which ye have kindled.
This shall ye have from my hand;
Ye shall lie down in sorrow.

11.

The glorious deliverance of the people. — CH. LI. — LII. 12.

1 HEARKEN to me, ye that pursue righteousness,
Ye that seek Jehovah!
Look to the rock whence ye were hewn,
To the pit-quarry whence ye were digged!
2 Look to Abraham your father,

And to Sarah that bore you!
For I called him when only one,
And blessed him, and multiplied him.
3 Thus will Jehovah have pity upon Zion;
He will have pity upon all her desolations.
He will make her wilderness like Eden,
Her desert like the garden of Jehovah.
Joy and gladness shall be found therein;
Thanksgiving, and the voice of melody.

4 Hearken to me, O my people!
And give ear to me, O my nation!
For a law shall proceed from me,
And I will establish my statutes for the light of the nations.
5 My help is near; my salvation goeth forth;
My arm shall judge the nations;
Distant lands shall wait for me,
And in my arm shall they trust.
6 Lift up your eyes to the heavens,
And look down upon the earth beneath!
For the heavens shall vanish away like smoke,
And the earth shall decay like a garment,
And its inhabitants shall perish like flies.
But my salvation shall endure forever,
And my goodness shall not decay.

7 Hearken to me, ye that know righteousness,
The people in whose heart is my law!
Fear ye not the reproach of men,
Nor be disheartened by their revilings!
8 For the moth shall consume them like a garment,
And the worm shall eat them like wool.
But my goodness shall endure forever,
And my salvation from generation to generation.

9 Awake! awake! clothe thyself with strength, O arm of Jehovah!
Awake, as in the ancient days, in the generations of old!
10 Art thou not the same that smote Rahab,
And wounded the dragon?
Art thou not the same that dried up the sea,

The waters of the great deep, —
That made the depths of the sea a path for the redeemed to pass through?
11 Thus shall the ransomed of Jehovah return;
They shall come to Zion with singing;
Everlasting joy shall be upon their heads;
They shall obtain gladness and joy,
And sorrow and sighing shall flee away.

12 I, even I, am he that hath pity upon you;
Who art thou, that thou art afraid of man, that shall die,
Of the son of man, that shall perish like grass,
13 And forgettest Jehovah thy maker,
That stretched out the heavens,
And founded the earth,
And fearest continually every day,
On account of the fury of the oppressor,
As if he were taking aim to destroy thee?
Where now is the fury of the oppressor?
14 Soon shall the enchained be loosed;
He shall not die in the pit,
Nor shall his bread fail.
15 For I am Jehovah thy God,
That rebuketh the sea when his waves roar;
Jehovah of hosts is his name.
16 I have put my words into thy mouth,
And have covered thee with the shadow of my hand,
To establish the heavens, and to found the earth,
And to say to Zion, "Thou art my people!"
17 Awake, awake, stand up, O Jerusalem!
Thou that hast drunk from the hand of Jehovah the cup of his fury,
Thou that hast drunk to the dregs the cup of giddiness!
18 There is not one to lead her, of all the sons which she hath brought forth,
Nor is there one to take her by the hand, of all the sons which she hath nurtured.
19 These two things have come upon thee,
And who bemoaneth thee?
Desolation and destruction, and famine and the sword;
How shall I comfort thee?
20 Thy sons have fainted; they lie at the head of all the streets,

Like a deer in the net;
They are full of the wrath of Jehovah,
Of the rebuke of thy God.
21 Therefore, hear this, thou afflicted,
Thou drunken, and not with wine!
22 Thus saith thy Lord, Jehovah,
And thy God, that defendeth the cause of his people.
Behold, I will take from thy hand the cup of giddiness,
The cup of my wrath;
Thou shalt drink no more of it.
23 And I will put it into the hand of them that have afflicted thee;
That have said to thee, "Bow down, that we may pass over!"
And thou madest thy body as the ground,
And as the street, to them that passed over.

1 Awake, awake, put on thy majesty, O Zion!
Put on thy beautiful garments, O Jerusalem, the holy city!
For no more shall come into thee the uncircumcised and the unclean.
2 Shake thyself from the dust,
Arise and sit erect, O Jerusalem!
Loose thyself from the bands of thy neck,
O captive daughter of Zion!
3 For thus saith Jehovah:
For naught were ye sold,
And without money shall ye be ransomed.
4 For thus saith the Lord Jehovah:
My people went down to Egypt formerly to sojourn there,
And the Assyrian oppressed them without cause.
5 And now, what have I here to do, saith the Lord,
When my people is taken away for naught,
And their tyrants exult, saith Jehovah,
And all the day long my name is blasphemed.
6 Therefore shall my people know my name;
Therefore in that day shall they know
That I am he that said, Behold, here am I!

7 How beautiful upon the mountains are the feet of him that bringeth good tidings, of him that proclaimeth peace!

That bringeth good tidings, that proclaimeth salvation!
That saith to Zion, "Thy God is king!"
8 Hark! the voice of thy watchmen!
They lift up the voice together; yea, they shout!
For eye to eye shall they behold,
When Jehovah returneth to Zion.
9 Break forth into joy; shout together, ye ruins of Jerusalem!
For Jehovah hath pity on his people; he redeemeth Jerusalem.
10 Jehovah maketh bare his holy arm
In the sight of all the nations;
All the ends of the earth
Behold the salvation from our God.
11 Depart, depart ye; go ye out from thence;
Touch no unclean thing!
Go ye out from the midst of her;
Be ye clean, ye that bear the vessels of Jehovah!
12 For not in haste shall ye go forth,
Nor in flight shall ye pass along;
For Jehovah shall march in your front,
And the God of Israel bring up your rear.

12.

The Servant of Jehovah in his affliction, and his exaltation. — CH. LII. 13 — LIII.

Jehovah speaks.

13 BEHOLD, my servant shall prosper;
He shall be lifted up, and set on high, and greatly exalted.
14 As many were amazed at the sight of him, —
So disfigured and scarcely human was his visage,
And so unlike that of a man was his form, —
15 So shall he cause many nations to exult on account of him;
Kings shall shut their mouths before him.
For what had never been told them shall they see,
And what they never heard shall they perceive.

The Prophet for himself and fellow-prophets.

1 Who hath believed our report,
And to whom hath the arm of Jehovah been revealed?

The People speak.

2 For he grew up before him like a tender plant,
Like a sucker from a dry soil;
He had no form, nor comeliness, that we should look upon him,
Nor beauty, that we should take pleasure in him.
3 He was despised, and forsaken of men,
A man of sorrows, and acquainted with disease;
As one from whom men hide their faces,
He was despised, and we esteemed him not.
4 But he bore our diseases,
And carried our pains,
And we esteemed him stricken from above,
Smitten of God, and afflicted.
5 But he was wounded for our transgressions;
He was bruised for our iniquities;
For our peace was the chastisement upon him,
And by his stripes are we healed.
6 All we, like sheep, were going astray;
We turned every one to his own way,
And Jehovah laid upon him the iniquity of us all.

The Prophet speaks in his own name.

7 He was oppressed, that was already afflicted,
Yet he opened not his mouth;
As a lamb that is led to the slaughter,
And as a sheep before her shearers is dumb,
He opened not his mouth.
8 By oppression and punishment he was taken away,
And who in his generation would consider
That he was cut off from the land of the living,
That for the transgression of my people he was smitten?
9 His grave was appointed with the wicked,
And with the rich man was his sepulchre,
Although he had done no injustice,
And there was no deceit in his mouth.
10 It pleased Jehovah severely to bruise him;
But when he hath made his life a sacrifice for sin,
He shall see posterity; he shall prolong his days,
And the pleasure of Jehovah shali prosper in his hand.

Jehovah speaks.

11 Free from his sorrows, he shall see and be satisfied;
By his knowledge shall my righteous servant lead many to righteousness,
And he shall bear their iniquities.
12 Therefore will I give him his portion with the mighty,
And with heroes shall he divide the spoil,
Because he poured out his soul unto death,
And was numbered with transgressors;
Because he bore the sin of many,
And made intercession for transgressors.

13.

Promises of enlargement, moral renovation, and glory. — CH. LIV., LV.

1 SING, O thou barren, that didst not bear!
Break forth into singing, and shout for joy, thou that wast not in travail!
For more are the children of the desolate
Than of the married woman, saith Jehovah.
2 Enlarge the place of thy tent,
And let the canopy of thy habitation be extended!
Spare not; lengthen thy cords,
And make fast thy stakes!
3 For on the right hand and on the left shalt thou burst forth with increase;
And thy posterity shall inherit the nations,
And people the desolate cities.
4 Fear not, for thou shalt not be confounded;
Blush not, for thou shalt not be put to shame.
For thou shalt forget the shame of thy youth,
And the reproach of thy widowhood thou shalt remember no more.
5 For thy husband is thy Maker;
Jehovah of hosts is his name.
Thy redeemer is the Holy One of Israel;
The God of the whole earth shall he be called.
6 For as a woman forsaken, and deeply afflicted, hath Jehovah recalled thee,
And as a wife wedded in youth, that hath been rejected, saith thy God.

7 For a little moment I have forsaken thee,
But with great mercy will I gather thee.
8 In overflowing wrath I hid my face from thee for a moment.
But with everlasting kindness will I have mercy upon thee,
Saith thy redeemer, Jehovah.
9 As in the time of the waters of Noah, so shall it be now;
As I swore that the waters of Noah should no more go over the earth,
So do I swear that I will not be angry with thee, nor rebuke thee.
10 For the mountains shall depart,
And the hills be overthrown,
But my kindness shall not depart from thee,
Nor shall my covenant of peace be overthrown,
Saith Jehovah, that hath pity on thee.
11 O thou afflicted, beaten with the storm, destitute of consolation!
Behold, I lay thy stones in cement of vermilion,
And thy foundations with sapphires.
12 And I will make thy battlements of rubies,
And thy gates of carbuncles,
And all thy borders full of precious stones.
13 All thy children shall be taught by Jehovah,
And great shall be the prosperity of thy children.
14 By righteousness shalt thou be established;
Be thou far from anxiety, for thou shalt have nothing to fear,
And from terror, for it shall not come near thee.
15 If any be leagued against thee, it is not by my command;
Whoever shall be leagued against thee shall come over to thee.
16 Behold, I create the smith,
Who bloweth up the coals into a fire,
And produceth an instrument for his work;
I also create the destroyer to lay waste.
17 Whatever weapon is formed against thee, it shall not prosper;
And against every tongue that contendeth with thee, thou shalt obtain thy cause.
This is the inheritance of the servants of Jehovah,

And the blessing which they receive from me, saith Jehovah.

1 Ho, every one that thirsteth, come ye to the waters!
Even ye that have no money, come ye, buy and eat!
Yea, come, buy wine and milk,
Without money and without price.
2 Wherefore do ye spend your money for that which is not bread,
And your substance for that which doth not satisfy?
Listen attentively to me; so shall ye eat that which is good,
And your soul shall delight itself with delicacies.
3 Incline your ear, and come to me;
Hear, and your soul shall live!
And I will make with you an everlasting covenant;
I will give you the sure mercies of David.
4 Behold, I gave him for a commander to the nations;
For a prince, and a lawgiver to the nations.
5 Behold, the nation which thou knowest not thou shalt call;
And the nation which knew not thee shall run to thee,
For the sake of Jehovah, thy God,
And of the Holy One of Israel, for he hath glorified thee.

6 Seek ye Jehovah, while he may be found;
Call upon him while he is near;
7 Let the wicked forsake his way,
And the unrighteous man his thoughts;
Let him return to Jehovah, and he will have mercy upon him,
And to our God, for he will abundantly pardon.
8 For my thoughts are not your thoughts,
Neither are your ways my ways, saith Jehovah.
9 For as the heavens are higher than the earth,
So are my ways higher than your ways,
And my thoughts than your thoughts.
10 For as the rain and the snow descend from heaven,
And return not thither,
But water the earth, and make it bear and put forth its increase,
That it may give seed to the sower, and bread to the eater;

11 So shall my word be, that goeth forth from my mouth;
It shall not return to me void;
But it shall bring to pass that which is my pleasure,
And it shall accomplish that for which I send it.
12 For ye shall go out with joy
And be led forth with peace;
The mountains and the hills shall break forth before you into singing,
And all the trees of the field shall clap their hands.
13 Instead of the thorn shall grow up the cypress-tree,
And instead of the bramble shall grow up the myrtle-tree,
And it shall be to Jehovah for a name;
For an everlasting memorial, that shall not pass away.

14.

The heathen shall enjoy the privileges of the people of God, in the happy state of things which awaits them. — CH. LVI. 1-8.

1 THUS saith Jehovah:
Keep ye justice, and practise righteousness;
For the coming of my salvation is near,
And my deliverance is soon to be revealed.
2 Happy the man that doeth this,
And the son of man that holdeth it fast;
That keepeth the sabbath, and profaneth it not,
And restraineth his hand from doing evil.
3 And let not the stranger that joineth himself to Jehovah say,
Jehovah hath wholly separated me from his people.
And let not the eunuch say,
Behold, I am a dry tree!
4 For thus saith Jehovah concerning the eunuchs:
They that keep my sabbaths,
And take pleasure in doing my will,
And hold fast my covenant,
5 To them will I give in my house, and within my walls, a portion and a name,
Better than of sons and daughters;
An everlasting name will I give them,
That shall never fade away.
6 The strangers, also, that join themselves to Jehovah, to serve him,

To love the name of Jehovah, and to be his servants,
Every one that keepeth the sabbath, and profaneth it not,
And holdeth fast my covenant,
7 Them will I bring to my holy mountain,
And I will make them rejoice in my house of prayer;
Their burnt-offerings and sacrifices shall be accepted on mine altar;
For my house shall be called a house of prayer for all nations.
8 Thus saith the Lord Jehovah,
That gathereth the outcasts of Israel;
Yet will I gather others to him,
Besides those that are already gathered.

15.

Denunciations of punishment against idolatry and other sins. — CH. LVI. 9 — LVII.

9 COME, all ye beasts of the field,
Yea, all ye beasts of the forest, to devour!
10 His watchmen are all blind; they know nothing;
They are all dumb dogs, that cannot bark,
Dreaming, lying down, loving to slumber;
11 Yet are they greedy dogs that cannot be satisfied;
The shepherds themselves will not attend;
They all turn aside to their own way,
Every one of them to their own gain.
12 "Come on, let me bring wine,
And let us fill ourselves with strong drink,
And to-morrow shall be as to-day,
And even much more abundant."

1 The righteous man perisheth, and no one layeth it to heart;
And pious men are taken away, and none considereth
That because of the evil the righteous man is taken away.
2 He entereth into peace;
He resteth in his bed,
Every one that walketh in uprightness.
3 But draw near hither, ye sons of the sorceress,
Ye brood of the adulterer and the harlot!

4 Of whom do ye make your sport,
And at whom do ye make wide the mouth,
And draw out the tongue?
Are ye not rebellious children, a treacherous brood?
5 Burning with lust for idols
Under every green tree,
Slaying children in the valleys,
Under the clefts of the rocks?
6 With the smooth stones of the valley is thy portion;
These, these are thy lot;
Here thou pourest out thy drink-offering,
And presentest thy meat-offering;
Can I see such things, and be at rest?
7 Upon a high and lofty mountain settest thou thy bed;
Thither dost thou go up to offer sacrifice;
8 Behind the doors and the posts dost thou place thy memorial;
Thou departest from me, and uncoverest, and ascendest, and enlargest thy bed.
Thou makest an agreement with them;
Thou desirest their bed;
Thou choosest a place.
9 Thou goest to the king with oil,
And takest much precious perfume;
Thou sendest thine ambassadors afar,
Yea, down to the under-world.
10 In the length of thy journeys thou hast wearied thyself,
But thou sayest not, "I will desist";
Thou yet findest life in thy hand,
Therefore thou art not discouraged.
11 On account of whom art thou anxious, and of whom art thou afraid, that thou hast proved false,
And hast not remembered me, nor laid it to heart?
Behold, I have been silent a long time;
Therefore thou fearest me not.
12 But now I announce thy deliverance,
And thy works do not profit thee.
13 When thou criest, let thy host of idols deliver thee!
But the wind shall bear them all away;
A breath shall take them off;
But he that putteth his trust in me
Shall possess the land,

And shall inherit my holy mountain.
14 Men shall say, Cast up, cast up, prepare the road;
Remove every obstruction from the way of my people!
15 For thus saith the high and lofty One
That inhabiteth eternity, whose name is Holy:
I dwell in the high and holy place;
With him also that is of a contrite and humble spirit;
To revive the spirit of the humble,
And to revive the heart of the contrite ones.
16 For I will not contend forever,
Nor will I be always angry;
For life would fail before me,
And the souls which I created.
17 For the guilt of his covetousness I was angry;
I smote him, I hid myself, and was angry;
But yet he went on perversely in the way of his heart.
18 I have seen his ways, yet will I heal him;
I will guide him, and I will restore comfort
To him and to his mourners;
19 I create the fruit of the lips.
Peace, peace to him that is far off, and to him that is nigh,
Saith Jehovah; I will heal him.
20 But the wicked is like the troubled sea,
Which cannot rest,
Whose waters cast up mire and dirt.
21 There is no peace, saith my God, for the wicked.

16.

The worthlessness of festivals and fasts without rectitude and benevolence.
CH. LVIII.

1 Cry aloud, spare not,
Lift up thy voice like a trumpet,
And show my people their transgression,
And the house of Jacob their sins!
2 Yet they seek me daily,
And desire to know my ways,
As a nation that hath done righteousness,
And hath not forsaken the ordinances of their God;
They inquire of me concerning the judgments which bring salvation;

They long for the coming of God.
3 "Wherefore do we fast, and thou seest not?
Wherefore do we afflict our souls, and thou dost not regard it?"
Behold, in the day of your fasts ye pursue your pleasure,
And exact all your labors.
4 Behold, ye fast in strife and contention,
And smiting with the fist of wickedness.
Ye do not fast now
So that your voice shall be heard on high.
5 Is this the fast that I approve,
A day for a man to afflict his soul?
Is it that he should bow down his head like a bulrush,
And lie down in sackcloth and ashes?
Wilt thou call this a fast,
And a day acceptable to Jehovah?
6 Is not this the fast that I approve, —
To loose the bands of wickedness,
To undo the heavy burdens,
To let the oppressed go free,
And to break in pieces every yoke?
7 Is it not to break thy bread to the hungry,
And to bring the poor, that are cast out, to thy house?
When thou seest the naked, that thou clothe him,
And that thou hide not thyself from thine own flesh?
8 Then shall thy light break forth like the morning,
And thy health shall spring forth speedily;
Thy salvation shall go before thee,
And the glory of Jehovah shall bring up thy rear.
9 Then shalt thou call, and Jehovah will answer;
Thou shalt cry, and he shall say, Lo, here I am!
If thou remove from the midst of thee the yoke,
The pointing of the finger, and the injurious speech.
10 If thou bring forth thy bread to the hungry,
And satisfy the afflicted soul,
Then in obscurity shall light arise to thee;
Yea, thy darkness shall become as noonday;
11 Jehovah shall lead thee continually,
And satisfy thee in the time of drought,
And strengthen thy bones;
Thou shalt be like a watered garden, and a spring of water,

Whose waters never fail.
12 Thy people shall build the ancient desolations,
The ruins of many generations shall they restore;
Thou shalt be called the repairer of the breach,
The restorer of ways for inhabitants.
13 If thou restrain thy foot from the sabbath,
From doing thy pleasure on my holy day,
If thou shalt call the sabbath a delight,
The holy day of Jehovah honorable,
And shalt honor it by refraining from thy work,
From doing thy pleasure, and speaking vain words,
14 Then shalt thou delight thyself in Jehovah,
And I will cause thee to ride upon the high places of the earth,
And cause thee to enjoy the inheritance of Jacob, thy father;
For the mouth of Jehovah hath spoken it.

17.

The sins of the people delay their deliverance. — CH. LIX.

1 BEHOLD, Jehovah's hand is not shortened, that it cannot save,
Nor is his ear heavy, that it cannot hear;
2 But your iniquities have separated you from your God,
And your sins have hidden his face from you, that he doth not hear.
3 For your hands are polluted with blood,
And your fingers with iniquity;
Your lips speak falsehood,
And your tongue muttereth wickedness.
4 No one bringeth his suit with justice,
And no one pleadeth with truth;
They trust in vain words, and speak lies;
They conceive mischief, and bring forth destruction.
5 They hatch the eggs of the basilisk,
And weave the web of the spider;
He that eateth of their eggs dieth,
And when one of them is crushed, a viper breaketh forth.
6 Of their webs no garment is made,
Nor can one cover himself with their work;

Their works are works of iniquity,
And the deed of violence is in their hands.
7 Their feet run to evil;
They make haste to shed innocent blood.
Their thoughts are evil thoughts;
Oppression and destruction are in their paths.
8 The way of peace they know not,
Nor is there any justice in their steps;
They have made for themselves crooked paths;
Whoso goeth in them knoweth not peace.
9 Therefore is judgment far from us,
And deliverance doth not overtake us.
We look for light, and behold obscurity;
For brightness, and we walk in darkness.
10 We grope for the wall, like the blind;
We feel our way, like those that are deprived of sight;
We stumble at noonday as in the night;
In the midst of fertile fields we are like the dead.
11 We groan, all of us, like bears,
And like doves we make a continued moan;
We look for judgment, and it cometh not;
For salvation, and it is far from us.
12 For our transgressions are multiplied before thee,
And our sins testify against us!
For our transgressions are not hidden from us,
And our iniquities we know.
13 We have rebelled, and proved false to Jehovah;
We have departed from our God;
We have spoken violence and rebellion;
Our hearts have conceived and brought forth words of falsehood.
14 And justice is turned back,
And equity standeth afar off,
For truth falleth in the gate,
And rectitude cannot enter.
15 Truth is not to be found,
And he that departeth from evil is plundered;
And Jehovah saw it,
And it displeased him that there was no justice.
16 He saw that there was none to help,
And wondered that there was none to interpose;
Then his own arm wrought salvation for him,

And his righteousness it supported him.
17 He put on righteousness as a breastplate,
And the helmet of salvation upon his head;
He put on garments of vengeance for his clothing,
And clad himself with zeal, as with a mantle.
18 According to their deeds will he repay them, —
Wrath to his adversaries, recompense to his enemies;
To the distant coasts will he repay a recompense.
19 They in the west shall fear the name of Jehovah,
And they in the rising of the sun his glory,
When he cometh like a river straitened in its course,
Which a strong wind driveth along.
20 Yet shall a redeemer come to Zion,
For them that turn from their transgressions in Jacob, saith Jehovah.
21 And as for me, this is my covenant with them, saith Jehovah:
My spirit, which is upon thee,
And my words, which I have put in thy mouth,
They shall not depart from thy mouth,
Nor from the mouth of thy sons,
Nor from the mouth of thy sons' sons, saith Jehovah,
From this time forth forever.

18.

The glory of the new Jerusalem. — CH. LX.

1 ARISE, shine! for thy light is come,
And the glory of Jehovah is risen upon thee.
2 For, behold, darkness shall cover the earth,
And gross darkness the nations;
But upon thee shall Jehovah arise,
And his glory shall be seen upon thee.
3 Nations shall come to thy light,
And kings to the brightness that riseth upon thee.
4 Lift up thine eyes round about and see!
They all gather themselves together, and come to thee
Thy sons come from afar,
And thy daughters are carried at thy side.
5 Then shalt thou see, and be bright with joy;
Thy heart shall throb, and swell with delight,

When the riches of the sea shall be turned toward thee,
And the wealth of the nations shall come to thee.
6 A multitude of camels shall cover thee,
Dromedaries from Midian and Ephah;
From Sheba shall they all come.
Gold and frankincense shall they bring,
And proclaim the praises of Jehovah.
7 All the flocks of Kedar shall be gathered to thee,
And the rams of Nebaioth shall minister to thee;
They shall ascend mine altar, an acceptable offering,
And my glorious house I will adorn.
8 Who are these that fly like clouds,
And like doves to their habitations?
9 Behold, the distant coasts shall wait for me,
And the ships of Tarshish among the first,
To bring thy sons from afar,
And their silver and their gold with them,
Because of the name of Jehovah thy God,
Of the Holy One of Israel, for he glorifieth thee.
10 The sons of the stranger shall build up thy walls,
And their kings shall minister to thee;
For in my wrath I smote thee,
But in my mercy will I have pity upon thee.
11 Thy gates shall be open continually;
They shall not be shut by day or by night,
That the treasures of the nations may be brought to thee,
And that their kings may come with their retinues.
12 For that nation and that kingdom
Which will not serve thee shall perish;
Yea, those nations shall be utterly destroyed.
13 The glory of Lebanon shall come to thee,
The cypress, the plane-tree, and the larch together,
To adorn the place of my sanctuary,
That I may make the place where my feet rest glorious.
14 The sons of thine oppressors shall come bending before thee;
They that despised thee shall fall down at thy feet;
And they shall call thee the city of Jehovah,
The Zion of the Holy One of Israel.
15 Instead of being forsaken and hated,
So that no one passed through thee,
I will make thee an everlasting glory;

The joy of many generations.
16 Thou shalt also suck the milk of the nations,
And be nursed from the breast of kings;
And thou shalt know that I, Jehovah, am thy saviour,
That thy redeemer is the Mighty One of Jacob.
17 Instead of brass will I bring gold;
And instead of iron will I bring silver,
And instead of wood, brass,
And instead of stones, iron;
I will make thine officers peace,
And thy magistrates righteousness.
18 Violence shall no more be heard in thy land,
Wasting or destruction within thy borders;
Thou shalt call thy walls Salvation,
And thy gates Praise.
19 No more shall the sun be thy light by day,
Nor with her brightness shall the moon enlighten thee:
But Jehovah shall be to thee an everlasting light,
And thy God thy glory.
20 Thy sun shall no more go down,
Neither shall thy moon be hid;
For Jehovah shall be thine everlasting light,
And the days of thy mourning shall be ended.
21 Thy people shall be all righteous;
Forever shall they possess the land,
The scion of my planting,
The work of my hands, that I may be glorified.
22 The little one shall become a thousand,
And the small one a strong nation;
I, Jehovah, will hasten it in its time.

19.

Deliverance promised. — CH. LXI.

1 THE spirit of the Lord Jehovah is upon me,
For Jehovah hath anointed me;
He hath sent me to publish good tidings to the distressed,
To bind up the broken-hearted,
To proclaim liberty to the captives,
And the opening of the prison to them that are bound;
2 To proclaim the year of mercy from Jehovah,

And the day of vengeance from our God;
To comfort all that mourn;
3 To give gladness to the mourners in Zion;
To give them a beautiful crown instead of ashes,
The oil of joy for mourning,
The garment of praise for the spirit of heaviness,
So that they shall be called blessed terebinth-trees,
The plantation of Jehovah for his glory.
4 They shall build up the old ruins;
They shall raise up the ancient desolations;
They shall repair the cities laid waste,
The desolations of many generations.
5 Strangers shall stand up and feed your flocks,
And the sons of the alien shall be your ploughmen and vine-dressers;
6 But ye shall be named the priests of Jehovah,
Men shall call you the ministers of our God.
Ye shall eat the riches of the nations,
And in their glory shall ye make your boast.
7 For your shame shall ye have a double reward;
And for ignominy ye shall rejoice in your portion;
Therefore in your land ye shall possess double;
Everlasting joy shall be your portion.
8 For I, Jehovah, love justice,
I hate rapine and iniquity,
I will give them their reward with faithfulness,
And an everlasting covenant will I make with them.
9 Their race shall be illustrious among the nations,
And their offspring among the people;
All that see them shall acknowledge
That they are a race which Jehovah hath blessed.

10 "I will greatly rejoice in Jehovah;
My soul shall exult in my God;
For he hath clothed me with the garments of salvation;
He hath covered me with the mantle of deliverance.
As the bridegroom decketh himself with his turban,
And as the bride adorneth herself with her jewels."

11 For as the earth putteth forth her shoots,
And as a garden causeth its plants to spring forth,
So shall the Lord Jehovah cause salvation to spring forth,
And praise before all the nations.

20.

The restoration and glory of Israel. — CH. LXII.

1 FOR Zion's sake I will not keep silence,
And for Jerusalem's sake I will not rest,
Until her deliverance break forth like the shining light,
And her salvation like a blazing torch.
2 Then shall the nations see thy prosperity,
And all the kings thy glory;
Thou shalt be called by a new name,
Which the mouth of Jehovah shall give thee.
3 Thou shalt be a beautiful crown in the hand of Jehovah,
A royal diadem in the hand of thy God.
4 No more shalt thou be called the Desolate,
And thy land, the Forsaken.
But thou shalt be named My-delight-is-in-her,
And thy land the wedded Matron.
For Jehovah shall delight in thee,
And thy land shall be married.
5 For as a young man weddeth a virgin,
So shall thy children wed thee.
And as a bridegroom rejoiceth in his bride,
So shall thy God rejoice in thee.

6 Upon thy walls, O Jerusalem, have I set watchmen;
All the day, and all the night, shall they not keep silence;
O ye that praise Jehovah, keep not silence,
7 And give him no rest,
Until he establish Jerusalem, and make her a praise in the earth!
8 Jehovah hath sworn by his right hand, and his mighty arm:
No more will I give thy corn to be food for thine enemies,
Nor shall the sons of the stranger drink thy wine, for which thou hast labored.
9 But they that reap the harvest shall eat it,
And praise Jehovah;
And they that gather the vintage shall drink it,
In my holy courts.
10 Pass ye, pass ye through the gates;
Prepare the way for the people;

Cast ye up, cast ye up the highway,
Clear it from the stones;
Lift up on high a standard for the tribes!
11 Behold, Jehovah proclaimeth to the end of the earth:
"Say ye to the daughter of Zion, Behold, thy Deliverer cometh!
Behold, his reward is with him, and his recompense before him!"
12 They shall be called, The holy people, The redeemed of Jehovah.
And thou shalt be called, The Sought out,
The Not forsaken City.

21.

The destruction of Edom. — CH. LXIII. 1-6.

The People.

1 WHO is this that cometh from Edom?
In scarlet garments from Bozrah?
This that is glorious in his apparel,
Proud in the greatness of his strength?

Jehovah.

I that proclaim deliverance,
And am mighty to save.

The People.

2 Wherefore is thine apparel red,
And thy garments like those of one that treadeth the wine vat?

Jehovah.

3 I have trodden the wine-vat alone,
And of the nations there was none with me.
And I trod them in mine anger,
And I trampled them in my fury,
So that their life-blood was sprinkled upon my garments,
And I have stained all my apparel.
4 For the day of vengeance was in my heart,
And the year of my deliverance was come.

5 And I looked, and there was none to help,
And I wondered, that there was none to uphold;
Therefore my own arm wrought salvation for me,
And my fury, it sustained me.
6 I trod down the nations in my anger;
I crushed them in my fury,
And spilled their blood upon the ground.

22.

The prophet's hymn of thanksgiving and of prayer in view of the condition of Israel. — CH. LXIII. 7 — LXIV.

7 I WILL celebrate the mercy of Jehovah, the glory of Jehovah,
According to all that he hath done for us;
His great goodness to the house of Israel,
Which he hath bestowed on it in his tender mercy, and his great kindness.
8 He said, Truly they are my people;
Children that will not be false;
So he was their deliverer.
9 In all their straits they had no distress;
An angel of his presence saved them;
In his love and compassion he redeemed them,
He took them up and bore them all the days of old.
10 But they rebelled, and grieved his holy spirit;
Then did he change himself into their enemy;
He himself fought against them.
11 Then remembered his people the ancient days, the days of Moses, [saying,]
Where is he that brought them up from the sea with the shepherd of his flock?
Where is he that put his holy spirit within him?
12 That caused his glorious arm to accompany the right hand of Moses,
That divided the water before them,
To make to himself an everlasting name?
13 That led them through the deep,
As a horse through a desert, without stumbling?
14 As the herd descendeth into the valley,
The spirit of Jehovah led them to rest.

So didst thou lead thy people,
To make for thyself a glorious name.
15 Look down from heaven, and behold from thy holy and glorious habitation!
Where is thy zeal and thy might?
Thy pity and compassion for me, are they restrained?
16 Thou, surely, art our father;
Abraham is ignorant of us,
And Israel knoweth us not.
Thou, O Jehovah, art our father;
Our deliverer wast thou of old.
17 Why, O Jehovah, dost thou suffer us to wander from thy ways,
And harden our hearts against thy fear?
Return, for thy servants' sake,
The tribes of thine inheritance!
18 But a little while did thy holy people possess the land;
Then our enemies trampled upon thy sanctuary.
19 It has been with us as if thou hadst never ruled over us,
As if we had not been called by thy name.

1 O that thou wouldst rend the heavens, and come down;
That the mountains might tremble at thy presence,
2 As fire kindleth the dry stubble,
As fire causeth water to boil,
To make known thy name to thine adversaries,
That the nations might tremble at thy presence;
3 As thou once didst wonderful things, which we looked not for,
And camest down, so that the mountains trembled at thy presence.
4 For never have men heard, nor perceived by the ear,
Nor hath eye seen, a God beside thee,
Who doeth such things for those that trust in him.
5 Thou art the friend of those who joyfully do righteousness,
Those who remember thee in thy ways.
Behold, thou art angry, and we are punished;
Long doth the punishment endure, before we are delivered.
6 We are all of us an unclean thing;
Like a filthy garment is all our righteousness;
We are all withered like a leaf,

And our sins, like a storm, have blown us away.
7 There is none that calleth upon thy name,
That stirreth himself up to cleave to thee;
For thou hidest thy face from us,
And lettest us perish by our iniquities.
8 But now, O Jehovah, thou art our father;
We are the clay, and thou hast formed us;
We are all of us the work of thy hands.
9 Be not wroth, O Jehovah, to the uttermost,
Nor remember our iniquity forever!
Behold, look upon us, we beseech thee, we are all thy people!
10 Thy holy cities have become a wilderness;
Zion is become a wilderness, Jerusalem a desolation.
11 Our holy and glorious house,
Where our fathers praised thee,
Is burned with fire,
And all our precious things are laid waste.
12 Wilt thou contain thyself at these things, O Jehovah,
Wilt thou keep silence, and still grievously afflict us?

23.

The answer of Jehovah to the preceding prayer. The ungodly shall be punished, but the pious shall be gloriously delivered. — CH. LXV., LXVI.

1 I HAVE heard those that made no supplication;
I have been found by those who sought me not;
I said, Here I am, here I am,
To a people that called not upon my name.
2 I have spread out my hands all the day
To a rebellious people,
That walketh in an evil way,
According to their own devices;
3 To a people that provoke me to my face continually;
That sacrifice in gardens,
And burn incense on tiles;
4 That sit in sepulchres,
And lodge in caverns;
That eat swine's flesh,
And have broth of unclean things in their vessels;
5 Who yet say: Stand by thyself! come not near to me,

For I am holier than thou!
These are a smoke in my nose,
A fire that burneth continually.
6 Behold, it stands recorded before me;
I will not keep silence, but will requite;
I will requite it into their bosoms;
7 Your iniquities, and the iniquities of your fathers together, saith Jehovah,
Who burnt incense on the mountains,
And dishonored me on the hills,
I will pour the full recompense of their former deeds into their bosom.

8 Thus saith Jehovah:
As when juice is found in a cluster,
Men say, "Destroy it not, for a blessing is in it";
So will I do, for the sake of my servants, and will not destroy the whole;
9 I will cause a stem to spring forth from Jacob,
And from Judah a possessor of my mountains;
My chosen shall possess the land,
And my servants shall dwell there.
10 And Sharon shall be a fold for flocks,
And the valley of Achor a resting-place for herds,
For my people that have sought me.

11 But ye, who have forsaken Jehovah,
And have forgotten my holy mountain,
That prepare a table for Fortune,
And fill the cup for Destiny,
12 Yourselves do I destine to the sword,
And all of you shall bow down before the slaughter;
Because I called, and ye answered not,
I spake, and ye would not hear,
But did that which is evil in my sight,
And chose that in which I had no delight.
13 Therefore thus saith the Lord Jehovah:
Behold, my servants shall eat, and ye shall be hungry;
Behold, my servants shall drink, and ye shall be thirsty;
Behold, my servants shall rejoice, and ye shall be confounded;
14 Behold, my servants shall sing for gladness of heart,

But ye shall shriek for sorrow of heart,
And howl for anguish of spirit.
15 And ye shall leave your name for a curse to my chosen,
And the Lord Jehovah shall slay you;
But his servants will he call by another name.
16 Whoso blesseth himself in the land
Shall bless by the true God;
And he that sweareth in the land shall swear by the true God;
For the former troubles are forgotten,
And they are hid from mine eyes.
17 For behold! I create new heavens, and a new earth;
The former ones shall not be remembered,
Nor shall they be brought to mind any more.
18 But ye shall be glad and exult forever
In that which I create;
For behold! I create Jerusalem a rejoicing,
And her people a joy.
19 And I will exult in Jerusalem,
And rejoice in my people;
No more shall be heard therein
The voice of weeping and the cry of distress.
20 There shall not be there an infant child, nor an old man,
That hath not filled the measure of his years;
For he that dieth a hundred years old shall die a youth,
And the sinner dying a hundred years old shall be held accursed.
21 They shall build houses, and inhabit them;
They shall plant vineyards, and eat the fruit of them;
22 They shall not build, and another inhabit;
They shall not plant, and another eat;
For as the days of a tree shall be the days of my people,
Yea, long shall my chosen enjoy the work of their hands
23 They shall not labor in vain,
Nor bring forth children for early death;
For they are a race blessed by Jehovah,
And their offspring shall remain to them.
24 Before they call, I will answer;
And while they are yet speaking, I will hear
25 The wolf and the lamb shall feed together,
And the lion shall eat straw like the ox,
And dust shall be the food of the serpent

They shall not hurt, nor destroy, in all my holy mountain,
Saith Jehovah.

1 Thus saith Jehovah:
Heaven is my throne,
And the earth my footstool;
Where is the house that ye can build me,
And where is the place of my rest?
2 For all these things hath my hand made;
By it do all these things exist, saith Jehovah.
But to this man will I look,
Even to him who is humble and of a contrite spirit,
And who trembleth at my word.

3 He that slayeth an ox killeth a man;
He that sacrificeth a lamb beheadeth a dog;
He that maketh an oblation offereth swine's blood;
He that burneth incense blesseth an idol.

Yea, they have chosen their own ways,
And in their abominations their souls delight.
4 I also will choose their calamities;
What they dread I will bring upon them;
Because I called, and no one answered,
I spake, and they did not hear;
But they did what is evil in my sight,
And chose that in which I have no delight.

5 Hear the word of Jehovah,
Ye that tremble at his word!
Your brethren that hate you,
And thrust you out for my name's sake, have said,
"May Jehovah be glorified, that we may see your joy!"
But they shall be confounded.

6 A voice of tumult from the city!
A voice from the temple!
The voice of Jehovah, rendering recompense to his enemies!
7 Before she was in travail, she brought forth,
Before her pangs came, she was delivered of a son.
8 Who hath heard such a thing? Who hath seen such things?

Is a country brought forth in a day?
Is a nation born at once?
For as soon as Zion was in travail, she brought forth her children.
9 Shall I bring to the birth, and not cause to bring forth, saith Jehovah;
Shall I, who beget, restrain the birth? saith thy God.
10 Rejoice ye with Jerusalem,
And exult for her, all ye that love her!
Be very joyful with her, all ye that mourn for her!
11 That ye may suck, and be satisfied, from the breast of her consolations,
That ye may suck and be delighted with the fulness of her glory.

12 For thus saith Jehovah:
Behold, I will bring prosperity to her like a river,
And the wealth of the nations like an overflowing stream;
Ye shall suck at the breast,
Ye shall be carried on the arm,
And on the knees shall ye be dandled.
13 As one whom his mother comforteth,
So will I comfort you;
And in Jerusalem shall ye be comforted.
14 Ye shall see, and your heart shall rejoice,
And your bones shall flourish like a green plant,
And the hand of Jehovah shall be manifested to his servants,
And be moved with indignation against his enemies.
15 For behold, Jehovah cometh with fire,
Like a whirlwind are his chariots,
To breathe forth his anger in a glowing heat,
And his rebuke in flames of fire.
16 For with fire will Jehovah contend,
And with his sword, with all flesh,
And many shall be the slain of Jehovah.
17 They who sanctify and purify themselves in the groves,
Following one in the midst,
Who eat swine's flesh, and the abomination, and the mouse.
They shall all perish together, saith Jehovah.
18 For I know their works, and their thoughts;
The time cometh to gather all nations and tongues together;

They shall come, and behold my glory.
19 And I will give a sign among them,
And of those that escape I will send to the nations,
To Tarshish, Phul, and Lud, who draw the bow, to Tubal and Javan,
To the distant coasts, who never heard my name,
And who never saw my glory;
And they shall declare my glory among the nations.
20 And they shall bring all your brethren
From all the nations, an offering to Jehovah,
Upon horses, and in chariots, and in litters, and upon mules and dromedaries,
To my holy mountain, Jerusalem, saith Jehovah,
As the sons of Israel bring their gifts
In pure vessels to the house of Jehovah.
21 And of them will I also take
For priests and for Levites, saith Jehovah.
22 For as the new heavens,
And the new earth, which I make,
Endure before me, saith Jehovah,
So shall your race and your name endure.
23 And it shall be, from new moon to new moon,
And from sabbath to sabbath,
That all flesh shall come and worship before me, saith Jehovah.
24 Then shall they go forth and see
The dead bodies of the men that rebelled against me;
For their worm shall not die,
And their fire shall not be quenched,
And they shall be an abhorrence to all flesh.

MICAH.

INSCRIPTION.

1 The word of Jehovah, which came to Micah, the Morasthite, in the days of Jotham, Ahaz, and Hezekiah, kings of Judah; which was revealed to him concerning Judah and Jerusalem.

I.

Israel and Judah threatened with desolation and captivity on account of idolatry. — Ch. I. 2-16.

2 Hear, all ye nations,
Give ear, O earth, and all that is therein!
The Lord, Jehovah, appeareth as a witness against you,
The Lord from his holy palace.
3 Behold, Jehovah cometh forth from his dwelling-place;
He cometh down, and advanceth upon the high places of the earth.
4 The mountains melt under him,
And the valleys cleave asunder,
Like wax before the fire,
Like waters poured down a steep place.
5 For the transgression of Jacob is all this,
And for the sin of the house of Israel.
Where is the transgression of Jacob? Is it not at Samaria?
And where are the high places of Judah? Are they not at Jerusalem?
6 Therefore will I make Samaria a heap of stones in the field,
A place for the planting of a vineyard;

I will pour down her stones into the valley,
And lay bare her foundations.
7 All her graven images shall be beaten to pieces,
And all the hire of her harlotry shall be burned with fire,
And all her idols will I destroy.
For from the hire of a harlot did she gather her ornaments,
And to the hire of a harlot shall they return.
8 Therefore I will wail and howl;
I will go stripped and naked;
I will wail like the jackal,
And mourn like the ostrich.
9 For her wound is mortal;
It extendeth to Judah;
It reacheth to the gate of my people, even to Jerusalem.
10 Tell it not in Gath! weep not in Acco!
In Beth-Aprah roll yourselves in the dust!
11 Pass on, thou inhabitant of Saphir, naked and in shame!
The inhabitant of Zaanan no more goeth out;
The grief of Beth-Azel denieth you an abode.
12 The inhabitant of Maroth mourneth for his goods,
For evil came down from Jehovah to the gates of Jerusalem.
13 Bind the chariot to the courser, O inhabitant of Lachish!
Thou wast the beginning of sin to the daughter of Zion;
In thee were found the transgressions of Israel.
14 Therefore shalt thou resign the possession of Moresheth of Gath;
The houses of Achzib shall disappoint the kings of Israel.
15 A possessor will I bring to thee, O inhabitant of Mareshah;
The glory of Israel shall flee to Adullam.
16 Make thyself bald, cut off thy locks, for the children of thy love;
Enlarge thy baldness like the eagle;
For they have gone from thee into captivity.

II.

Punishment threatened on account of injustice and corruption. Promise of future prosperity. — CH. II.

1 WOE to them that devise iniquity,
And contrive evil upon their beds;
When the morning is light, they practise it,
Because it is in the power of their hand.
2 They covet fields, and take them by violence;
Houses, and take them from their owners.
They defraud a man of his house;
Yea, a man of his inheritance.
3 Therefore, thus saith Jehovah:
Behold, against this race do I meditate evil,
From which ye shall not remove your necks, nor lift up
your heads;
For it shall be a time of evil.
4 In that day shall this song be uttered concerning thee,
And this sad lamentation be made:
"We are utterly laid waste;
He hath changed the portion of my people;
How hath he torn it from me!
He hath taken away and distributed our fields."
5 Behold, thou shalt have no one henceforth
Who shall draw out a line for a portion,
In the congregation of Jehovah.

6 "Prophesy not," [say they,] "O ye that prophesy!"
If they prophesy not concerning these things,
The shame will not depart.
7 O ye that are called the house of Jacob,
Is the spirit of Jehovah impatient?
Are these his doings?
Are not my words kind to him that walketh uprightly?
8 But long since hath my people risen against me, as an
enemy;
Ye strip the mantle from the garment of those that pass
by securely, as men returning from war.
9 The women of my people ye cast out from their pleasant
abodes;

Ye deprive their children forever of the glory which I gave them.
10 Arise and depart
This land is not your rest!
On account of its pollution shall it be wasted,
And given to utter destruction.
11 If a man follow wind, and invent falsehood, and say,
"I will prophesy to thee of wine and strong drink!"
He will be the prophet for this people.

12 Yet will I fully gather thee, O Jacob,
I will surely assemble the residue of Israel!
I will put them together like sheep in a fold;
Like a flock in their fold shall they be in a tumult on account of the multitude of men.
13 He that forceth a way goeth before them;
They force their way, and pass through the gate,
And go forth by it;
And their king goeth before them,
Even Jehovah at the head of them.

III.

Against oppressive rulers and false prophets. Jerusalem threatened with destruction. — CH. III.

1 I ALSO said:
Hear, O ye heads of Jacob,
And ye leaders of the house of Israel!
Is it not for you to administer justice?
2 But ye hate what is good, and love what is evil;
Ye tear from men their skin,
Yea, their flesh from their bones;
3 Ye devour the flesh of my people,
And strip them of their skin,
And break their bones,
And cut them in pieces, as for the pot,
And as flesh for the caldron?
4 Then shall they cry to Jehovah,
But he will not hear them;

Yea, at that time will he hide his face from them,
Because they have done iniquity.

5 Thus saith Jehovah concerning the prophets, who deceive my people,
Who, while they bite with their teeth, proclaim peace,
But who, if one fill not their mouths, prepare war against him:
6 Therefore shall night come upon you, so that ye shall have no vision,
And darkness, so that ye shall not divine;
The sun shall go down upon the prophets,
And the day shall be dark to them.
7 Then shall the seers be ashamed, and the diviners confounded,
So that all of them shall hide their faces,
Because there is no answer from God.
8 But I am full of power, even of the spirit of Jehovah;
Full of uprightness and courage,
To declare to Jacob his transgression,
And to Israel his sin.
9 O hear this, ye heads of the house of Jacob,
And ye leaders of the house of Israel,
Who abhor justice,
And pervert all equity,
10 Who build up Zion with blood,
And Jerusalem with iniquity!
11 Her heads judge for reward,
And her priests teach for hire,
And her prophets divine for money,
And yet they lean upon Jehovah, saying,
"Is not Jehovah in the midst of us?
No evil can come upon us."
12 Therefore because of you shall Zion be ploughed as a field,
And Jerusalem become heaps of stones,
And the mountain of the temple like the heights of a forest.

IV.

A glorious future promised after the exile at Babylon. — CH. IV. — V. 1.

1 But it shall come to pass in the last days
That the mountain of the house of Jehovah shall be established at the head of the mountains,
And exalted above the hills;
And the nations shall flow to it.
2 And many nations shall go, saying,
"Come, let us go up to the mountain of Jehovah,
To the house of the God of Jacob,
That he may teach us his ways,
And that we may walk in his paths!"
For from Zion shall go forth a law,
And the word of Jehovah from Jerusalem.
3 He shall be a judge of many nations,
And an umpire of many kingdoms afar off.
They shall beat their swords into ploughshares,
And their spears into pruning-hooks;
Nation shall not lift up the sword against nation,
Neither shall they learn war any more.
4 But they shall sit every one under his vine,
And under his fig-tree,
And none shall make them afraid;
The mouth of Jehovah of hosts hath spoken it.
5 Though all the nations walk every one in the name of its God,
Yet will we walk in the name of Jehovah our God for ever and ever.
6 In that day, saith Jehovah, I will gather the halting,
And the far scattered I will assemble,
And those whom I have afflicted.
7 I will make the halting a remnant,
And the far scattered a strong nation;
And Jehovah shall reign over them in mount Zion,
Henceforth, even forever.
8 And thou, O tower of the flock,
O hill of the daughter of Zion, to thee it shall come,
To thee shall come the former dominion,
Even the kingdom of the daughter of Jerusalem.

9 And now why dost thou cry aloud?
Is there no king within thee?
Have thy counsellors perished,
That pangs have taken hold of thee, as of a woman in travail?
10 Yea, writhe, and be in anguish, O daughter of Zion, like a woman in travail!
For now shalt thou go forth from the city, and dwell in the field;
Thou shalt go even to Babylon;
Yet there shalt thou be delivered.
Jehovah will redeem thee from the hand of thine enemies.
11 Now many nations gather themselves against thee,
Who say, Let her be polluted,
And let our eyes gaze upon Zion!
12 But they know not the thoughts of Jehovah,
And understand not his purposes;
For he gathereth them as sheaves into the thrashing-floor.
13 Arise and thrash, O daughter of Zion!
For I will make thy horns iron,
And thy hoofs brass;
Thou shalt beat in pieces many nations,
And thou shalt devote their spoils to Jehovah,
Their substance to the Lord of the whole earth.

1 Yet now gather yourselves in troops, O people of troops!
They lay siege against us;
With a rod they smite the cheek of the judge of Israel.

V.

A mighty prince shall arise, and restore prosperity to Judah. — CH. V. 2–15.

2 BUT thou, Bethlehem Ephratah,
Who art small to be among the thousands of Judah,
Out of thee shall he come forth for me to be ruler in Israel,
Whose origin is from the ancient age, from the days of old!

3 But He [Jehovah] shall deliver them up,
Until she that bringeth forth hath brought forth;
Then shall the residue of his brethren return to the children of Israel.
4 He shall stand and rule in the strength of Jehovah,
In the majesty of Jehovah, his God;
And they shall dwell in security,
For he shall be great even to the ends of the earth.
5 And he shall be peace.
When the Assyrian shall come into our land,
To trample upon our palaces,
Then shall we raise against him seven shepherds,
And eight leaders of the people,
6 And they shall devour the land of Assyria with the sword,
The land of Nimrod within her gates.
Thus shall he deliver us from the Assyrian, when he cometh into our land,
And treadeth in our borders.
7 The residue of Jacob shall be in the midst of many nations
As the dew which cometh from Jehovah,
As drops of rain upon the grass,
Which tarrieth not for man,
Nor waiteth for the sons of men.
8 The residue of Jacob shall be among the nations,
In the midst of many kingdoms,
As a lion among the beasts of the forest,
As a young lion among flocks of sheep,
Who, when he assaulteth, treadeth down and teareth, and none can deliver.
9 Thy hand shall be lifted up over thine adversaries,
And all thine enemies shall be destroyed!

10 It shall come to pass in that day, saith Jehovah,
That I will destroy thy horses from the midst of thee,
And I will consume thy chariots;
11 I will destroy the fortified cities of thy land,
And throw down all thy strongholds;
12 I will destroy sorceries from thy borders,
And soothsayers shall not be with thee.
13 I will destroy thy graven images and thy statues from the midst of thee,

And thou shalt no more bow down to the work of thine
hands;
14 I will root out thy Astartes from the midst of thee,
And I will destroy thy fortified cities;
15 And I will execute vengeance in anger and in fury
Upon the nations which have not hearkened to me.

VI.

Controversy of Jehovah with his people. — CH. VI. 1-8.

1 HEAR ye what Jehovah saith!
Arise, contend thou before the mountains,
And let the hills hear thy voice!
2 Hear, O ye mountains, the controversy of Jehovah!
Hear, ye strong foundations of the earth!
For Jehovah hath a controversy with his people;
He contendeth with Israel.

3 "O my people, what have I done to thee,
And wherein have I offended thee?
Testify against me!
4 I brought thee up from the land of Egypt,
And from the house of bondage I redeemed thee;
I sent Moses, Aaron, and Miriam, to go before thee.
5 O my people, remember what Balak the king of Moab
devised,
And what Balaam, the son of Beor, answered him,
What happened from Shittim to Gilgal,
That ye may know the mercies of Jehovah."

6 Wherewith shall I come before Jehovah,
And bow myself before the most high God?
Shall I come before him with burnt-offerings,
With calves of a year old?
7 Will Jehovah be pleased with thousands of rams,
Or with ten thousands of rivers of oil?
Shall I give my first-born for the sin of my soul,
The fruit of my body for my transgression?

8 He hath showed thee, O man, what is good;
What doth Jehovah require of thee,
But to do justly, and to love mercy,
And to walk humbly before thy God?

VII.

Woe and destruction threatened on account of injustice and oppression. — CH. VI. 9–16.

9 THE voice of Jehovah crieth to the city,
And the man of wisdom will discern thee;
Hear ye the rod, and who hath threatened it!
10 Are there not yet in the houses of the unrighteous the treasures of iniquity,
And the scanty measure, which is abominable?
11 Shall I count her pure with the wicked balances,
And with the bag of deceitful weights?
12 For her rich men are full of violence,
And her inhabitants speak lies,
And their tongue is deceitful in their mouth.
13 Therefore will I sorely smite thee,
And make thee desolate on account of thy sins.
14 Thou shalt eat and not be satisfied,
And hunger shall be within thee.
Thou shalt remove, but shalt not save,
And what thou savest will I give up to the sword.
15 Thou shalt sow, but shalt not reap;
Thou shalt tread the olives, but shalt not anoint thee with oil,
And the grapes, but shalt not drink the wine.
16 For ye keep the statutes of Omri,
And all the works of the house of Ahab,
And walk in their devices;
Therefore will I make thee a desolation,
And thine inhabitants a derision;
And ye shall bear the reproach of my people.

VIII.

The small number of righteous men in the nation. — CH. VII. 1–6.

1 WOE is me! I live where the summer fruits are gathered,
And the vintage is gleaned;
There is no cluster to eat;
I long for the first-ripe fig.
2 The good man is perished from the land,
And there is none upright among men.
They all lie in wait for blood;
Every one hunteth his brother with a net.
3 Their hands are diligent for evil;
The prince asketh a bribe,
And the judge decideth for money!
The great man giveth judgment according to his desire;
They conspire to pervert justice.
4 The best of them is like a brier;
The most upright of them is sharper than a thorn-hedge.
The day of recompense, announced by thy watchmen, cometh;
Then shall come their perplexity.
5 Trust ye not in a friend!
Put no confidence in a guide!
From her that lieth in thy bosom
Keep the doors of thy mouth!
6 For the son dishonoreth his father,
The daughter riseth up against her mother,
And the daughter-in-law against her mother-in-law;
The inmates of a man's house are his foes.

IX.

Hope and promise of future deliverance and prosperity. — CH. VII. 7–20.

7 I WILL look to Jehovah;
I will hope in the God of my salvation;

My God will hear me.
8 Rejoice not over me, O my enemy!
Though I have fallen, I shall arise;
Though I sit in darkness,
Jehovah will be my light.
9 I will bear the indignation of Jehovah,
Because I have sinned against him,
Until he maintain my cause, and execute judgment for me,
Until he bring me to the light,
And I behold his mercy.
10 She that is my enemy shall see it, and shame shall cover her,
That said to me, Where is Jehovah thy God?
Mine eyes shall gaze upon her;
Soon shall she be trodden down, as the mire of the streets.

11 The day cometh when thy walls are to be built;
In that day shall the decree be far removed.
12 In that day shall they come to thee
From Assyria, and the cities of Egypt,
And from Egypt to the river,
From sea to sea, from mountain to mountain.
13 But first the land shall be desolate on account of its inhabitants,
For the fruit of their doings.

14 Feed thy people with thy crook,
The flock of thine inheritance,
That dwell solitarily in the forest in the midst of Carmel!
Let them feed in Bashan and Gilead, as in the days of old.

15 As in the day when thou camest from Egypt,
So will I show thee wonders.
16 The nations shall see, and be ashamed of all their might:
They shall lay their hands upon their mouths;
Their ears shall be deaf.
17 They shall lick the dust like the serpent;
Like the creeping things of the earth, they shall come trembling from their strongholds;
To Jehovah our God shall they come with awe,
And shall fear on account of thee.

18 Who is a God like thee, that pardoneth iniquity and
passeth by transgression,
In the remnant of his inheritance?
He retaineth not his anger forever,
For he delighteth in mercy.
19 He will again have compassion on us,
He will blot out our iniquities;
Yea, thou wilt cast all our sins into the depths of the sea
20 Thou wilt show faithfulness to Jacob,
And mercy to Abraham,
Which thou swarest to our fathers from the days of old.

NAHUM.

INSCRIPTION.

1 The prophecy concerning Nineveh. The book of the prophecy of Nahum, the Elkoshite.

The siege and destruction of Nineveh. — CH. I. — III.

1.

2 JEHOVAH is a jealous God, and an avenger;
Jehovah is an avenger, and full of wrath!
Jehovah taketh vengeance on his adversaries,
And keepeth indignation for his enemies!
3 Jehovah is slow to anger, but great in power;
He will by no means clear the guilty;
Jehovah cometh in the whirlwind and the storm,
And the clouds are the dust of his feet.
4 He rebuketh the sea, and maketh it dry,
And drieth up all the rivers.
Bashan languisheth, and Carmel,
And the flower of Lebanon languisheth.
5 The mountains tremble before him,
And the hills melt;
The earth is moved at his presence,
Yea, the world and all that dwell therein.
6 Who can stand before his indignation,
And who can abide before the fierceness of his anger?
His fury is poured out like fire,
And the rocks are cast down by him!
7 Jehovah is good,
A stronghold in the day of trouble;
He careth for them that trust in him;

8 But with an overwhelming flood will he make a full end of her place,
And darkness shall pursue his enemies.
9 What do ye meditate against Jehovah?
He will make a full end;
Not the second time shall the calamity come.
10 For while they are entangled like thorns,
And like those that are drunk with wine,
They shall be devoured as stubble fully dry.
11 From thee hath gone forth one that devised evil against Jehovah;
That meditated destruction.

12 Thus saith Jehovah:
Though they be flourishing, and likewise many,
Yet shall they be cut down, and pass away;
I have afflicted thee, but I will afflict thee no more.
13 For now will I break his yoke from off thee,
And will burst thy bonds in sunder.
14 And concerning thee hath Jehovah given command,
That thy name shall no more be sown.
From the house of thy god I will cut off the graven image and the molten image;
I will make thy grave; for thou hast become vile!

2.

15 BEHOLD upon the mountains the feet of him that bringeth good tidings,
That publisheth peace!
Keep, O Judah, thy feasts, perform thy vows!
For no more shall the destroyer pass through thee;
He is utterly consumed.
1 The ravager cometh up against thee, [O Nineveh!]
Guard the fortress; watch the way;
Gird up the loins; confirm the strength.
2 For Jehovah restoreth the glory of Jacob,
As the glory of Israel;
For the wasters have wasted them,
And destroyed their branches.
3 The shields of his mighty men are red;
His warriors are clothed in crimson;

His chariots glitter with the fire of steel in the day of his
preparation,
And the spears are brandished.
4 The chariots rave in the streets;
They run to and fro in the broad ways;
Their appearance is like torches;
They run like lightnings.

5 He calleth for his mighty men;
Thay stumble on their way;
They hasten to the wall;
But the mantelet is prepared,
6 The gates of rivers are opened,
And the palace melteth away.
7 Huzzab is uncovered; she is carried away captive,
Her maidservants sigh with the voice of doves,
And smite their breasts.
8 Nineveh was like a pool full of water of old;
Yet shall they flee away;
Stand! stand! shall they cry;
But none shall look back.
9 Seize the silver; seize the gold;
There is no end to the treasures;
There is abundance of all precious furniture.
10 She hath become void, and empty, and desolate;
The heart melteth, and the knees smite together;
Pangs are in all their loins,
And the faces of all gather blackness.

11 Where now is the dwelling of the lions,
And the feeding-place of the young lions,
Where the lion and the lioness walked,
And the lion's whelp, and none made them afraid?
12 The lion tore in pieces for his whelps,
And strangled for his lionesses,
And filled his dens with prey,
And his lairs with ravin.
13 Behold! I am against thee, saith Jehovah of hosts,
And I will burn thy chariots into smoke,
And the sword shall devour thy young lions.
And I will cut off thy prey from the earth,
And the voice of thy messengers shall no more be heard

3.

1 Woe to the city of blood!
She is all full of deceit and robbery;
She ceaseth not from plunder.

2 [Hark!] The noise of the whip!
The noise of the rattling of the wheels,
And of the prancing horses,
And of the bounding chariots!
3 The horseman lifteth up the flame of the sword,
And the lightning of the spear;
There is a multitude of the slain; heaps of dead bodies;
There is no end to the carcasses; they stumble over the carcasses.
4 It is because of the many whoredoms of the harlot,
The graceful beauty, the mistress of enchantments,
That sold nations by her whoredoms,
And kingdoms by her enchantments.
5 Behold, I am against thee, saith Jehovah of hosts
And I will lift up thy trail over thy face,
And I will show the nations thy nakedness,
And the kingdoms thy shame.
6 And I will cast abominable filth upon thee,
And I will dishonor thee, and make thee a gazing-stock
7 And all that see thee shall flee from thee,
And shall say, "Nineveh is laid waste;
Who will bemoan her?
Whence shall I seek comforters for thee?"

8 Art thou better than No-Ammon,
That dwelt by the rivers,
That had the waters round about her,
Whose fortress was the sea,
And whose wall was from the waters?
9 Ethiopia and Egypt were her strength, a countless multitude;
Phut and Lybia were thy helpers!
10 Yet was she carried away; she went into captivity;
Her children were dashed in pieces at the head of all the streets;
For her honorable men they cast lots,

And all her great men were bound in chains.
11 Thou also shalt drink to the full;
Thou, too, shalt be hidden;
Thou shalt seek a refuge from the enemy!
12 All thy strong-holds shall be like fig-trees with the first ripe figs;
If they be shaken, they fall into the mouth of the eater.
13 Behold, thy people shall be women in the midst of thee;
The gates of thy land shall be set wide open to thine enemies;
The fire shall devour thy bars.
14 Draw thee water for the siege,
Fortify thy strongholds.
Go into the clay, and tread the mortar;
Repair the brick-kiln!
15 Then shall the fire devour thee;
The sword shall cut thee off,
It shall devour thee like the locust;
Though thou art increased like the locusts,
Though thou art increased like the thick locusts.
16 Thy merchants have been more numerous than the stars of heaven;
The locusts spread themselves and fly away.
17 Thy princes are like locusts,
And thy captains like swarms of locusts,
Which encamp in the hedges in the time of cold;
But when the sun ariseth, they flee away,
And the place is not known where they are.
18 Thy shepherds slumber, O king of Assyria!
Thy nobles take their rest,
Thy people are scattered on the mountains, and none gathereth them.
19 Thy bruise is incurable;
Thy wound is mortal.
All that hear of thee shall clap their hands over thee;
For upon whom hath not thy wickedness passed continually?

ZEPHANIAH.

INSCRIPTION.

1 THE word of Jehovah, which came to Zephaniah, the son of Cushi, the son of Gedaliah, the son of Amariah, the son of Hizkiah, in the days of Josiah, the son of Amon, king of Judah.

I.

Destruction of Judah threatened. Exhortation to repentance. Punishment of the enemies of Judah. — CH. I., II.

2 I WILL utterly consume all things from the face of the land, saith Jehovah;
3 I will consume man and beast;
I will consume the birds of heaven, and the fishes of the sea,
And the stumbling-blocks with the wicked;
And I will cut off man from the face of the land, saith Jehovah.
4 I will stretch out my hand over Judah,
And over all the inhabitants of Jerusalem,
And I will cut off from this place the residue of Baal,
The name of the idol-sacrificers with the priests,
5 And those who bow themselves on the house-tops to the host of heaven,
And those who bow themselves and swear by Jehovah,
And also swear by their idol,
6 And those that turn back from Jehovah,
And those that seek not Jehovah, nor inquire for him.

7 Be silent before the Lord Jehovah!
For the day of Jehovah is near;

For Jehovah hath prepared a sacrifice;
He hath appointed his guests.
8 And in the day of the sacrifice of Jehovah it shall come to pass
That I will punish the princes and the sons of the king,
And all that are clothed with foreign apparel.
9 In that day also will I punish all that leap over the threshold,
That fill the houses of their master with violence and deceit.
10 And it shall come to pass in that day, saith Jehovah,
That there shall be the noise of a cry from the fish-gate,
And of a howling from the other part of the city,
And of great destruction from the hills.
11 Howl, ye inhabitants of Maktesh!
For all the trafficking people are cut down;
All they that bear silver are destroyed.
12 And it shall come to pass at that time,
That I will search Jerusalem with lamps,
And I will punish the men that are settled on their lees;
That say in their hearts,
"Jehovah doeth neither good nor evil."
13 Their substance shall become a spoil,
And their houses a desolation;
They shall also build houses, but not inhahit them;
And shall plant vineyards, but not drink the wine thereof.

14 The day of Jehovah is near, the great day;
It is near, and hasteth greatly;
The day of Jehovah shall resound;
Bitterly shall the mighty man cry for help.
15 That day is a day of wrath,
A day of distress and anguish,
A day of destruction and desolation,
A day of darkness and gloominess,
A day of clouds and thick darkness,
16 A day of the trumpet and the war-shout,
Against the fenced cities,
And against the high towers.
17 And I will distress the men, so that they shall walk like the blind,
Because they have sinned against Jehovah.

And their blood shall be poured out as dust,
And their flesh as dung.
18 Neither their silver nor their gold shall be able to deliver them in the day of the wrath of Jehovah,
But by the fire of his indignation shall the whole land be devoured;
For destruction, and that a speedy one, will he bring
Upon all that dwell in the land.

1 Search yourselves; yea, search,
O nation without shame!
2 Before the decree bring forth,
Before the day come upon you like chaff;
Before the fierce anger of Jehovah come upon you,
Before the day of the anger of Jehovah come upon you.
3 Seek ye Jehovah, all ye lowly of the land,
Ye, who obey his commands!
Seek righteousness; seek lowliness;
It may be that ye shall be hid in the day of the anger of Jehovah.

4 For Gaza shall be forsaken,
And Askelon a desolation;
Ashdod shall be driven out at noonday,
And Ekron shall be rooted up.
5 Woe to the inhabitants of the sea-coasts, the nation of the Cherethites!
This is the word of Jehovah against you, O Canaan, land of the Philistines:
"I will destroy thee, that there shall be no inhabitant."
6 And the sea-coast shall be pastures full of habitations for shepherds, and folds for flocks.
7 The coast shall be for the residue of the house of Judah;
Thereon shall they feed;
In the houses of Askelon shall they lie down in the evening;
For Jehovah their God will look upon them, and bring back their captives.

8 I have heard the reproach of Moab,
And the revilings of the sons of Ammon,
With which they have reproached my people,

And exalted themselves against their borders.
9 Therefore, as I live, saith Jehovah of hosts, the God of Israel,
Moab shall be as Sodom,
And the sons of Ammon as Gomorrah,
A possession for thorns, and a pit for salt, and a perpetual desolation.
The residue of my people shall spoil them,
And the remainder of my nation shall possess them.
10 This shall come upon them for their pride,
Because they have uttered reproaches, and exalted themselves against the people of Jehovah of hosts.
11 Jehovah will be terrible against them;
For he will destroy all the gods of the earth;
And before him shall worship, every one from his place,
All the islands of the nations.

12 Ye, also, O Ethiopians!
Ye shall be slain by my sword!
13 He will also stretch out his hand against the North,
And destroy Assyria,
And make Nineveh a desolation,
Even dry like a desert.
14 And flocks shall lie down in the midst of her,
Yea, all the tribes of wild beasts;
The pelican and the hedgehog shall lodge in the capitals of her pillars;
A cry shall resound in the window;
Desolation shall be upon the threshold;
For her cedar-work shall be laid bare.
15 This is the rejoicing city that dwelt in security,
That said in her heart, "I, and none besides me!"
Now is she become a desolation, a resting-place for wild beasts!
Every one that passeth by her shall hiss, and wag his hand.

II.

Jerusalem threatened for her sins. A happy future foretold. — CH. III.

1 Woe to her that is rebellious and polluted,
The oppressing city!
2 She listeneth to no voice,
She receiveth not admonition;
She trusteth not in Jehovah,
She draweth not near to her God.
3 Her princes within her are roaring lions;
Her judges are evening wolves;
They reserve nothing for the morning.
4 Her prophets are vainglorious,
Men of treachery;
Her priests pollute the sanctuary,
They violate the law.

5 But Jehovah is just in the midst of her;
He doeth no iniquity.
Every morning bringeth he his righteousness to light; he faileth not;
Yet the wicked knoweth not shame.
6 I have cut off nations; their towers are destroyed;
I have laid waste their streets so that none passeth through;
Their cities are made desolate, without a man, without an inhabitant.
7 Then I said, "Surely thou wilt fear me; thou wilt receive admonition,
That thy habitation may not be cut off,
As I have commanded concerning thee."
But they were diligent to commit iniquity
In all their doings.

8 Therefore wait for me, saith Jehovah,
Until the day when I rise up to the prey.
For my purpose is to gather the nations, to assemble the kingdoms,
To pour upon them my indignation,
Even all the heat of my wrath.

For with the fire of mine anger shall all the earth be devoured.

9 Then will I again bestow upon the nations pure lips,
So that they shall all of them call upon the name of Jehovah,
And serve him with one consent.
10 From beyond the rivers of Ethiopia
My suppliants, the sons of my dispersed ones, shall bring my offering.
11 In that day thou shalt not be ashamed
For all thy doings, wherein thou hast transgressed against me;
For I will take away from the midst of thee thy proud exulters,
And thou shalt no more exalt thyself upon my holy mountain.
12 I will leave in the midst of thee a humble and lowly people,
Who trust in the name of Jehovah.
13 The residue of Israel shall not do iniquity, nor speak falsehood;
Neither shall a deceitful tongue be found in their mouth;
Therefore shall they feed and lie down, and none shall make them afraid.

14 Sing, O daughter of Zion!
Shout, O Israel!
Rejoice and exult with all thy heart,
O daughter of Jerusalem!
15 Jehovah hath taken away thy punishments;
He hath removed thine enemies.
The king of Israel, Jehovah, is in the midst of thee;
Thou shalt see evil no more.
16 In that day shall it be said to Jerusalem, Fear not!
And to Zion, Let not thy hands hang down!
17 Jehovah thy God will be in the midst of thee;
The mighty one will save thee.
He will rejoice over thee with gladness;
He will pardon thee in his love;
He will exult over thee with singing.
18 I will gather them that mourn, far from the solemn assembly,

They were far from thee; the reproach was a burden upon thee.
19 Behold, at that time I will destroy all that afflict thee;
And I will save the halting, and gather the scattered,
And I will make them a praise and a name
In every land where they have been put to shame.
20 At that time I will bring you back,
And at that time I will gather you;
For I will make you a name and a praise among all the nations of the earth,
When I bring back your captives before your eyes, saith Jehovah.

HABAKKUK.

INSCRIPTION.

1 The prophecy which was revealed to the prophet Habakkuk.

The power, tyranny, and fall of the Chaldæans. The prophet's expostulation, prayer, and hopes in relation to the oppression of the Jews by them. God manifests himself for the deliverance of the Jews. — Ch. I. — III.

1.

2 How long, O Jehovah, do I cry, and thou dost not hear!
How long do I complain to thee of violence, and thou dost not save!
3 Why dost thou suffer me to see iniquity,
And why dost thou look upon wickedness?
For spoiling and violence are before me;
There is contention, and strife exalteth itself.
4 Therefore the law faileth,
And judgment is not pronounced according to truth;
For the wicked encompasseth the righteous,
Therefore wrong judgment is pronounced.

Jehovah.

5 Behold ye among the nations, and look!
Yea, wonder, and be astonished!
For I do a work in your days
Which ye will not believe though it be told you.
6 For behold, I raise up the Chaldæans,
A fierce and swift people,
Which go over the breadth of the earth,

To take possession of dwelling-places that are not their own.
7 They are terrible and dreadful;
From themselves go forth their law and their dignity.
8 Their horses are swifter than leopards,
And fiercer than evening wolves.
Their horsemen leap proudly;
Their horsemen come from far;
They fly like an eagle, hastening to devour.
9 All of them come for violence;
The multitude of their faces is directed forwards,
And they gather captives as sand.
10 They also scoff at kings,
And princes are to them a laughing-stock;
They deride every stronghold,
For they heap up earth and take it.
11 Then their spirit is uplifted, and they transgress, and become guilty;
This their strength is made their god.

The Prophet.

12 Art thou not from everlasting, O Jehovah, my God, my Holy One?
We shall not die!
Thou, O Jehovah, hast appointed them for judgment;
Thou, O Rock, hast ordained them for chastisement.
13 Thou art of purer eyes than to behold evil,
And canst not look on wickedness;
Why then dost thou look on transgressors,
And art silent, when the wicked swalloweth up the man that is more righteous than he?
14 And why makest thou men as the fishes of the sea,
As the reptiles that have no ruler?
15 They take up all of them with the hook,
They catch them in their net,
And gather them in their drag;
Therefore they rejoice and exult.
16 Therefore they sacrifice to their net,
And burn incense to their drag;
Because by them their portion is fat,
And their food plenteous.
17 Shall they therefore empty the net,
And slay the nations continually without mercy?

2.

1 I WILL stand on my watch-tower,
And set myself on the bulwark,
And watch to see what he will say to me,
And what I shall answer to my expostulation.

Jehovah.

2 And Jehovah answered me, and said,
Write the vision, and make it plain upon tablets,
That he may run that readeth it.
3 For the vision is yet for an appointed time,
But it hasteneth to the end; it shall not deceive;
If it tarry, wait for it;
For it shall surely come; it shall not long delay.
4 Behold, the soul of him that is puffed up shall not be at ease;
But the just shall live by his faithfulness.
5 Behold, the man of wine is outrageous;
The proud man remaineth not at rest;
He enlargeth his desire as the grave;
He is as death, and cannot be satisfied;
He gathereth to himself all the nations,
And collecteth to himself all the kingdoms.
6 Shall not all of them utter a song against him,
Yea, songs of reproach and derision concerning him?
And say, Woe to him that heapeth up that which belongeth not to him!
For how long a time?
That ladeth himself with goods taken in pledge!
7 Shall not they suddenly rise up that will oppress thee,
And awake, that will harass thee?
Yea, thou shalt be their booty.
8 Because thou hast plundered many kingdoms,
All the residue of the nations shall plunder thee:
For the blood of men, and for violence against the land,
Against the city and all its inhabitants.

9 Woe to him that procureth unjust gain for his house,
That he may set his nest on high,
That he may be delivered from the evil hand!
10 Thou hast devised shame for thine house;

By destroying many nations, thou hast brought ruin upon
thyself.
11 For the stone from the wall crieth out,
And the beam from the timber answereth it.

12 Woe to him that buildeth a town by blood,
And establisheth a city by iniquity!
13 Behold, it is determined by Jehovah of hosts,
That nations shall labor for the fire,
And kingdoms weary themselves for naught.
14 For the earth shall be filled with the knowledge of the
glory of Jehovah,
As the waters cover the sea.

15 Woe to him who giveth his neighbor drink;
Who poureth out the strong wine, and maketh him drunken,
That he may look upon his nakedness!
16 Thou shalt be filled with shame instead of glory;
Drink thou also, and show thy foreskin!
To thee shall come the cup in the right hand of Jehovah,
And foul shame shall be upon thy glory.
17 For the violence done to Lebanon shall cover thee,
And the destruction of the beasts which made them afraid,
On account of the blood of men, and violence against the
land,
Against the city and all its inhabitants.

18 What profiteth the graven image,
When the maker hath graven it?
Or the molten image, and the teacher of lies,
That the artificer trusteth in his work,
When he maketh dumb idols?
19 Woe to him who saith to the wood, Awake!
To the dumb stone, Arise!
Will it teach?
Behold, it is overlaid with gold and silver,
And there is no breath within it.
20 But Jehovah is in his holy temple;
Be silent before him, all the earth!

3.

1 The prayer of Habakkuk the prophet, in the form of an ode.

2 O Jehovah, I have heard thy words, and tremble.
O Jehovah, revive thy work in the midst of the years,
In the midst of the years make it known,
In wrath remember mercy!

3 God cometh from Teman,
And the Holy One from mount Paran;
His glory covereth the heavens,
And the earth is full of his praise.
4 His brightness is as the light;
Rays stream forth from his hand,
And there is the hiding-place of his power.
5 Before him goeth the pestilence,
And the plague followeth his steps.

6 He standeth, and measureth the earth;
He beholdeth, and maketh the nations tremble;
The everlasting mountains are broken asunder;
The eternal hills sink down;
The eternal paths are trodden by him.
7 I see the tents of Cushan in affliction,
And the canopies of the land of Midian tremble.
8 Is the anger of Jehovah kindled against the rivers,
Is thy wrath against the rivers,
Is thy indignation against the floods,
That thou ridest on with thy horses,
Upon thy chariots of victory?
9 Thy bow is made bare;
Curses are the arrows of thy word;
Thou causest rivers to break forth from the earth.
10 The mountains see thee and tremble;
The flood of waters overflows;
The deep uttereth his voice,
And lifteth up his hands on high.

11 The sun and the moon remain in their habitation,
At the light of thine arrows which fly,

At the brightness of the lightning of thy spear.
12 Thou marchest through the land in indignation;
Thou thrashest the nations in anger;
13 Thou goest forth for the deliverance of thy people,
For the deliverance of thine anointed.
Thou smitest the head of the house of the wicked;
Thou destroyest the foundation even to the neck.
14 Thou piercest with his own spears the chief of his captains,
Who rushed like a whirlwind to scatter us;
Who exulted, as if they should devour the distressed in a hiding-place.
15 Thou ridest through the sea with thy horses,
Through the raging of mighty waters.

16 I have heard, and my heart trembleth;
My lips quiver at the voice;
Rottenness entereth into my bones, and my knees tremble,
That I must wait in silence for the day of trouble,
When the invader shall come up against my people!
17 For the fig-tree shall not blossom,
And there shall be no fruit upon the vine;
The produce of the olive shall fail,
And the fields shall yield no food.
The flocks shall be cut off from the folds,
And there shall be no herd in the stalls.

18 Yet will I rejoice in Jehovah,
I will exult in God, my helper.
19 The Lord Jehovah is my strength;
He will make my feet like the hind's,
And cause me to walk upon my high places.

To the leader of the music on my stringed instruments.

OBADIAH.

1 The prophecy of Obadiah.

The destruction of Edom.

Thus saith the Lord Jehovah concerning Edom.
We have heard a message from Jehovah,
And an ambassador hath been sent among the nations
"Arise ye, and let us rise up against her to war."
2 Behold, I will make thee small among the nations;
Thou shalt be greatly despised.
3 The pride of thine heart hath deceived thee,
Thou that dwellest in the clefts of the rock,
Whose habitation is high,
Who sayest in thine heart,
"Who shall bring me down to the ground?"
4 Though thou lift thyself up as the eagle,
And though thou set thy nest among the stars,
Thence will I bring thee down, saith Jehovah.
5 If thieves had come upon thee,
Or robbers by night,
Would they not have ceased stealing when they had enough?
How art thou utterly destroyed!
If grape-gatherers had come upon thee,
Would they not have left gleanings of the grapes?
6 How is Esau searched through!
How are his hidden places explored!
7 All thine allies have brought thee to the border;
They that were at peace with thee have deceived thee, and prevailed against thee;
They that ate thy bread have spread a snare under thee;
There is no understanding in thee.

8 In that day, saith Jehovah,
I will destroy the wise men from Edom,
And understanding from the mount of Esau.
9 Thy mighty men, O Teman, shall be dismayed;
Every one shall be cut off from the mount of Esau.
10 For slaughter and for oppression of thy brother Jacob shall shame cover thee,
And thou shalt be destroyed forever.
11 In the day when thou stoodest over against him,
In the day when strangers carried away captive his forces,
And when foreigners entered his gates,
And when they cast lots upon Jerusalem,
Thou also wast as one of them.
12 But thou shouldst not have looked with delight on the day of thy brother in the day of his calamity;
Nor shouldst thou have rejoiced over the children of Judah in the day of their destruction,
Nor have spoken haughtily in the day of his distress.
13 Thou shouldst not have entered into the gate of my people in the day of their calamity,
Nor have looked with delight on their affliction in the day of their calamity,
Nor have laid hand on their substance in the day of their calamity,
14 Nor have stood in the cross-way to cut off their fugitives,
Nor have delivered up those that remained in the day of distress!
15 For the day of Jehovah is near upon all the nations:
As thou hast done, so shall it be done to thee;
Thy dealing shall return upon thine own head.
16 For as ye have drunk upon my holy mountain,
So shall all the nations drink perpetually,
Yea, they shall drink and swallow it down,
And they shall be as though they had not been.

17 But upon mount Zion shall be deliverance, and it shall be holy;
And the house of Jacob shall regain their possessions.
18 And the house of Jacob shall be a fire,
And the house of Joseph a flame,
And the house of Esau stubble,
And they shall kindle them and devour them.

And there shall be none remaining of the house of Esau;
For Jehovah hath spoken it.
19 And they of the south shall possess the mountain of Esau,
And they of the plain, the Philistines;
And they shall possess the fields of Ephraim,
And the fields of Samaria;
And Benjamin shall possess Gilead.
20 And the captives of this host of the sons of Israel shall possess the land of the Canaanites unto Sarepta,
And the captives of Jerusalem which are at Sepharad shall possess the cities of the south.
21 And saviors shall go up to mount Zion,
To rule the mount of Esau.
And the kingdom shall be Jehovah's.

NOTES.

NOTES.

NOTES ON JOEL.

All that we know of Joel by direct historical information is, that he was the son of a certain Pethuel. Some circumstances alluded to in his prophecy, however, have been supposed to indicate the time in which he lived. The prophecy relates to the kingdom of Judah. Hence it is probable that he was an inhabitant of that kingdom. It is also plain that the temple was standing when he wrote. See chap. i. 14; ii. 1, 14, 17. The enemies of the Jewish nation mentioned in this book are only the Egyptians, Idumæans, Philistines, and Phœnicians. Neither the Syrians nor Assyrians are alluded to, though he seems to have occasion to introduce all the enemies of his nation. Hence it has been inferred that he lived before the time of Isaiah, when the Syrians and Assyrians were the most formidable enemies of Judah. He alludes to the same enemies of his nation who are mentioned by Amos, and lays similar things to their charge; whence it has been inferred that he was a contemporary of that prophet. See iii. 2 – 7; comp. Amos i. 9 – 11. But as in the book of Amos the Syrians appear as the enemies of Judah, Joel is supposed to have written earlier; perhaps in the former part of the reign of Uzziah, or about eight hundred years before Christ. It is plain that the circumstances above enumerated are not in the highest degree conclusive; and in fact several different opinions have been maintained. But as it will be generally acknowledged that Joel is surpassed by none of the prophets in originality, or poetic excellence, it is well that he should stand at the head of the noble series.

Ch. I. 4. The Hebrew words, גָּזָם, אַרְבֶּה, יֶלֶק, and חָסִיל, translated in the common version *palmer-worm, locust, cankerworm,* and *caterpillar,* undoubtedly denote either four species of locusts, for which we have no names in our language; or, as some suppose, the locust in four stages of its growth. The epithets given in the translation are suggested by the etymology of the Hebrew proper names. On the supposition that all the names denote locusts, the subsequent description becomes more true and striking. In order to perceive the correct ness as well as the sublimity of Joel's description of the locusts, the reader should refer to some account of these insects in Dr. Harris's Natural History of the Bible, Calmet's Dictionary, or a similar work. The following account of them by Volney illustrates several particulars of the description. "Syria, as well as Egypt, Persia, and almost all the South of Asia, is subject to a calamity no less dreadful than that of the volcanoes and earthquakes I have mentioned, I mean those clouds of locusts so often mentioned by travellers. The quantity of these insects is incredible to all who have not themselves witnessed their astonishing numbers: the whole earth is covered with them for the space of several leagues. The noise they make in browsing on the trees and herbage may be heard at a great distance, and resembles that of an army in secret. The Tartars themselves are a less destructive enemy than these little animals. One would imagine that fire had followed their progress. Wherever their myriads spread, the verdure of the country disappears; trees and plants stripped of their leaves, and reduced to their naked boughs and stems, cause the dreary image of winter to succeed in an instant to the rich scenery of the spring. When these clouds of locusts take their flight, to surmount any obstacles, or to travel more rapidly a desert soil, the heavens may literally be said to be obscured with them. Happily this calamity is not frequently repeated, for it is the inevitable forerunner of famine, and the maladies it occasions." — *Travels*, Vol. I. *State of Syria*, Ch. I. § 5, p. 188.

6. — *a nation.* A poetical expression for a swarm of locusts, referring to their numbers, and their destructive power.

7. — *made white.* Either by being stripped of their bark by the locusts, or withered by their noxious touch.

15. — *as destruction from the Almighty.* Like that destruction which is suddenly inflicted by earthquakes, lightning, and tempests.

II. 2. — *the morning light.* This comparison may refer to the immense number of the locusts, and the suddenness with which they appear.

4. — *of horses.* The resemblance of the head of the locust to that of the horse has been mentioned by several travellers. From this circumstance they are called by the Italians *cavalette*, i. e. *littte horses.* — *horsemen.* Gesenius thinks the term will bear the meaning *steeds.* But the other is the usual meaning.

8. — *are not wounded.* Otherwise, *break not up*, i. e. their march. Less probable, especially as this idea is expressed in the last verse.

10. *The earth quaketh.* Such is the consternation caused by them, that all things seem to be going to destruction. The latter clause of the verse may refer to the obscuration of the sun by clouds of locusts. Beauplan compares "their flight to flakes of snow in cloudy weather; — when they fly, though the sun shines ever so bright, it is no lighter than when most clouded. The air was so full of them, that I could not eat in my chamber without a candle."

11. "God is sublimely introduced as animating his army by his voice."

14. —*flour-offering.* See Lev. ii. 1–11. As the word *meat* is now used, there is certainly an apparent incongruity in calling an offering in which there was no flesh, and of which the principal ingredient was flour, a meat-offering.

20. —*northern host.* The locusts are so called, because they entered from the north by the way of Syria. —*Eastern sea,* i. e. the Dead Sea. — *Western sea,* i. e. the Mediterranean. —*hath done great things.* Compare Herodotus. Ὁρᾷς τὰ ὑπερέχοντα ζῶα ὡς κεραυνοῖ ὁ θεὸς, οὐδὲ ἐᾷ φαντάζεσθαι· τὰ δὲ σμικρὰ οὐδέν μιν κνίζει; Οὐ γὰρ ἐᾷ φρονέειν ἄλλον μέγα ὁ θεὸς ἢ ἑαϋτόν. Herod. Polymn. § ι'.

28. —*prophesy*; i. e. speak under divine influence. There is no particular reference to prediction.

III. 12. —*will judge.* There is here an allusion to the meaning of the word *Jehosaphat,* which signifies *Jehovah judges.*

14. —*of judgment.* Called the valley of Jehosaphat in verse 12.

18. *Shittim.* A place on the confines of Israel and Moab on the southeast. See Josh. iii. 1. The meaning appears to be, that the great abundance described in the preceding verses shall be very extensive, supplying the remotest extremity of the land.

NOTES ON AMOS.

There appears no reason to question the correctness of the inscription or title prefixed to the book of Amos, which asserts that he flourished in the reign of Uzziah, king of Judah, and Jeroboam (i. e. the Second), king of Israel. His prophecies may have been delivered between 790 and 780 years A. C. Though born in Tekoa, a place about eleven miles south of Jerusalem, it seems to have been his chief employment as a religious teacher to admonish and warn the kingdom of Israel. From ch. vii. 14, we learn that he was not educated in the regular school of the prophets, but that, while engaged in a humble occupation, he heard a call from God that, he should assume the office of a prophet. Notwithstanding what has been said by some writers of the rusticity of Amos, it is not easy to perceive that he is inferior to the other prophets in method, perspicuity, or elegance. He, indeed, draws many images from pastoral life, and manifests a tender sympathy for the poor and the oppressed. But in these respects he is not, in a great degree, distinguished from other prophets. His prominent characteristic is what the poet Campbell calls the circumstantial distinct ness of his graphic touches. See iii. 12, v. 18, 19, 24, vi. He paints rather than describes. On the whole, it is not too high praise which Bishop Lowth bestows upon Amos, when he says that he is nearly equal to the very first prophets in elevation of sentiments and loftiness of spirit, and scarcely inferior to any in splendor of diction and beauty of composition.

Ch. I. 2. — *will roar;* i. e. God will soon spread terror like beasts of prey when they roar. — *top of Carmel.* Carmel, originally denoting *a garden*, is the name of a fertile promontory covered with groves, and proverbial for its fertility, jutting out into the Mediterranean on the southern borders of the tribe of Asher.

3. — *three, and for four;* i. e. repeated, numerous. — *thrashing-wains;* i. e. machines having iron serrated wheels, or perhaps cylinders with sharp pieces of iron in them. This machine being drawn by oxen over the bundles of grain, the grain was at once beat out from the ears, and the straw cut in pieces for the food of animals. See Jahn's Archæology, § 54. Comp. 2 Kings xiii. 7.

5. — *bar of Damascus;* i. e. the bar or bars of its principal gate or gates. In other words, I will destroy its principal defences, and give it a prey to enemies.

11. — *tore perpetually.* The metaphor is drawn from a wild beast tearing its prey in pieces.

II. 6. — *sell the righteous for silver;* i. e. betray his just cause for a bribe. — *for a pair of shoes;* i. e. for a very mean bribe.

7. — *pant for the dust,* &c. A hyperbolical expression denoting the avarice of the rich, who covet the very dust thrown by the poor upon their heads in grief. — *to dishonor my holy name;* i. e. by giving the heathen occasion to utter the reproach, What sort of God must that people have, which is guilty of such abominable practices? Ezek. xxxvi. 20.

8. — *lay themselves down;* i. e. they recline at idolatrous banquets, and that too on the garments of the poor, taken in pledge, which by law should be returned before sunset. Ex. xxii. 25, 26. — *procured by fines;* lit. *of the fined.*

III. 3. — *Can two,* &c.; i. e. Can I, on my part, continue to be with or to favor you, unless you on your part give a cordial obedience to my laws? Or the meaning may be, "As a journey, in which two engage, naturally supposes a settled meeting, so the announcing of God's designs by his prophets shows that he has made himself known to them."

4. — *roar.* Naturalists assert that, when the lion sees his prey, he roars before he rushes on it; and at this roaring many animals show great fear. See verse 8. He likewise roars over his prey. The sense seems to be, As the lion roars on account of his prey, so by my prophets I cry aloud against you, because ye are the objects of my vengeance. See verse 8.

5. — *spring up*, &c. The allusion is to a sort of trap-net, which springs, when touched in a certain part, and encloses the bird. So when calamity comes, none may flatter himself that he shall escape it. Comp. Is. xxviii. 15.

9. — *in the palaces*; i. e. the flat roofs of the palaces, the usual place of publishing events. Matt. x. 27.

12. — *corners of their sofas*. The corner of a sofa or divan was esteemed the most comfortable and honorable place. See Maundrell, p. 49, Amer. edit. — *damask*. This may refer to the city in which, or to the material of which, the couches were made.

15. — *summer-house*, &c. It appears that the wealthy had two houses, one for summer, the other for winter. See Jer. xxxvi. 22. — *houses of ivory*; i. e. ornamented with ivory. Sir John Chardin tells us, says Harmer, I. 126, that the late king of Persia caused a tent to be made which cost two millions. They called it the house of gold, because gold glittered everywhere about it.

IV. 1. — *kine of Bashan*. It seems to be doubtful whether the prophet intends dissipated women, or effeminate men. The vices charged upon them in this verse, and the apparent connection of the passage with verse 4, &c., are circumstances that favor the latter supposition. On the former supposition, *master* will denote a husband or keeper, and *castle*, verse 3, a *harem*. On the latter supposition, *master* will denote the king, and *castle*, an enemy's fortress; and the passage will be similar to iii. 12, and Hosea vii. 3 – 7.

5. — *extortions*. So the Chald.

6. — *cleanness of teeth*; i. e. famine, the teeth not being soiled by meat or bread.

V. 6. *Israel*. I adopt the reading supported by the Sept., the Arab., and the parallelism of the sense.

6. — *justice into wormwood*; i. e. who, instead of justice, which is sweet and pleasant, deal out injustice, which is bitter.

8. — *calleth up the waters*; i. e. to punish men by inundations.

12. — *in the gate*; i. e. defeat him unjustly in the court of justice.

16. — *skilful in lamentation*. A class of persons whose business it was to sing mournful songs at funerals existed not only in Judæa, but in other ancient countries. See Homer's Iliad, xxiv. 720, &c. Horace, Ars Poet. 431, &c.

18. — *ask for the day of Jehovah*: with hypocritical presumption, or impious derision. The day of Jehovah is used to denote any time in which Jehovah interposes to punish the wicked, or deliver the good, especially the former. Sometimes a time specially threatened or promised may be denoted.

20. — *darkness*. In the Scriptures *darkness* is often used to denote calamity, and *light* to denote prosperity.

25, 26. — *sacrifices*; i. e. I bore with you, led you, and fed you in the wilderness forty years without sacrifices; how then can ye imagine them to be substitutes for moral virtue? or how can ye suppose that I need or care for them? Especially since ye, like your ancestors, divide your outward homage between me and false gods. There is reference probably to the difficulty of procuring animals for sacrifice in the wilderness.

26.—*the shrine*, &c. The Hebrew word *idols*, or images, being in the plural, it is probable that כִּיּוּן, which occurs nowhere else, is not a proper name, but an appellative. For, if a proper name, it would not be likely to be in the construct state with *idols*, or to be in apposition with *idols*. From the etymology of the word (from כּוּן), and from the parallelism with *tabernacle*, I think the word denotes the board framework, or base, of a shrine or vehicle in which idols were carried. I find this idea suggested by Poole in his Annotations. It is adopted by Hitzig and De Wette. In this case there would be only one false deity mentioned, viz. that called *their king*, of which there might be several images or idols, and the star would refer to the deity called *their king* by way of sarcasm, because they had substituted him for Jehovah, their rightful King. The passage implies the addiction of the Hebrews in the wilderness to the Arabian star-worship. The planet Saturn was probably the star intended.

VI. 2.—*Calneh:* the name of a large city in Assyria, supposed by the ancients to be the same as Ctesiphon, situated on the eastern bank of the Tigris, opposite Seleucia. *Hamath:* a large and important city of Syria, situated on the Orontes, near the northern boundary of Palestine. *Gath:* one of the principal cities of the Philistines, the birthplace of Goliah. The reproof of the Israelites is implied rather than expressed. Why do ye forsake me, treat me with neglect and ingratitude, and worship other gods, although I have so highly exalted you among the nations?

3. Woe to those who suppose the day of Divine judgment to be distant, and constantly practise injustice and oppression in courts of justice.

6.—*the destruction of Joseph;* i. e. care not for the calamity of their country; Joseph being used for the whole nation of Israel.

8.—*pride of Jacob;* i. e. that in which Jacob prides himself, perhaps the holy land.

10.—*make mention of the name of Jehovah.* This phrase probably had by usage a conventional meaning, which is not apparent to us. As far as we can gather the general meaning from the connection, it is, that the distress was so extreme and hopeless that there was no heart, or no occasion, no motive, for saying, *Jehovah be praised*, or *Jehovah bless you and keep you!* *To make mention of the name of Jehovah* is, in the Scriptures, generally connected with praise rather than supplication.

12.—*upon rocks*, &c. The meaning seems to be, that it is as unreasonable and unnatural for them to pervert justice, as it would be to make horses run unshod upon flinty rocks, or to plough up rocks with oxen. In ancient times horses went unshod. —*with oxen.* I suppose the word *rocks* is to be supplied from the preceding line. But by a different pointing and division, namely, בַּבָּקָר יָם, we may translate, *will one plough the sea with oxen?*

13. — *in a thing of naught;* i. e. in their possessions, which were liable to be taken from them at any moment.

14. — *brook of the desert;* i. e. the Kedron.

VII. 1. — *king's mowing;* i. e. what was cut for the use of the horses of the king.

2. — *is small;* i. e. brought low by former judgments.

4. — *great deep.* In vision the fire seemed to devour water and land.

8. — *set a plumb-line;* i. e. I will execute full punishment.

9. — *high-places,* — *sanctuaries;* i. e. for calf-worship and other forms of idolatry.

13. — *sanctuary;* i. e. for calf-worship.

14. — *no prophet, nor the son,* &c.; i. e. I was not educated to be a prophet; I was not trained up in the school of the prophets, nor was I the disciple of any prophet. Or, perhaps, the expression may be simply a strong negation. I was no prophet; nay, not so much as a prophet's son.

17. — *divided by the line;* i. e. by means of a measuring-line your lands shall be portioned out among your enemies. — *polluted land;* i. e. foreign land, which, on account of idolatry, was regarded by the Jews as impure in comparison with their own. See Ezek. iv. 13.

VIII. 3. — *in silence;* i. e. not in the usual way, with loud wailing and lamentation, so great was the number of the dead.

5. — *new moon be gone.* The day of the new moon, on the first day of the month, was observed as a festival among the Jews, Numb. x 10, xxviii. 11, on which it was unlawful to buy and sell. Nehem. x. 31.

9. — *go down at noon.* It is customary for the Hebrew and other Oriental poets, and indeed all poets, to represent calamity by darkness, midnight darkness, the setting of the sun, an eclipse, &c. Hence *the going down* of the sun at noon represents sudden, unexpected, awful calamity; a fall from the height of prosperity to the lowest depths of misery. Comp. Mic. iii. 7, Jer. xv. 9. An Arabic poet, quoted by Schultens, expresses his feelings on the loss of his friend in the language, "His death darkened my day, when I had just reached noon."

11. — *the word of Jehovah.* This refers not so much to instruction in duty as to counsel, which might extricate them from their miserable situation, and which they now disregarded when their prophets gave it.

14. — *sin of Samaria;* i. e. the calf-idol set up in Bethel, and perhaps other idols.

IX. 1. — *standing by the altar.* In mental vision the prophet sees some emblem of Jehovah's presence, whether a fiery appearance or a human form is uncertain, standing by the altar of burnt-offering of the temple at Jerusalem. By his having left the mercy-seat, and taken his stand by the altar, it may be denoted that he designed that multitudes of men should be destroyed, as it were victims on the altar. Comp. Is. xxxiv. 6. —*capital.* The Hebrew is in the singular, but may denote each of the capitals of the columns at the side of the principal entrance to the temple. Perhaps it should be rendered in the singular, denoting an ornament in the form of a chaplet of flowers, or a pomegranate, over the lintel of the door. Some suppose the symbolical action here commanded to indicate the destruction of the temple, which would occasion, or be followed by, the destruction of the nation. Others suppose the destruction of the king, princes, &c. to be pointed out, whose ruin would involve the rest of the people in destruction.

3. —*serpent.* It is uncertain what particular sea-monster is intended.

7. *Ethiopians;* i. e. I hold you in no higher regard than the distant barbarous Ethiopians.

12. —*which shall be called by my name;* i. e. be conquered by me, and so become my property, my possession. Comp. 2 Sam. xii. 28; Is. iv. 1; Deut. xxviii. 10.

13. —*draw near,* &c.; i, e. The harvest shall be so abundant that it shall scarcely be gathered in before it is again time to plough.

NOTES ON HOSEA.

The only knowledge which we have of the life of Hosea is that which is contained in the doubtful title of his book, viz. that he was the son of a certain Beeri, and coeval with Uzziah, Jotham, Ahaz, and Hezekiah, kings of Judah, and with Jeroboam II., king of Israel. From the contents of the book it is probable that he did not exercise his office until after the death of Jeroboam, when the kingdom of Israel was in a state of great distraction and anarchy; i. e. from about 783 to 740 years before Christ.

So far as language is concerned, Hosea is by far the most difficult of the prophets. He is sententious, concise, and abrupt. He often omits the connective particles, and it is sometimes impossible to discover the connection of his thoughts. He is more remarkable for the copiousness of his figures, than for his skilful use of them. In the general character of his imagery he is at greater variance with the taste of the Western world than any other of the prophets. There are not wanting in his poetry, however, passages of great tenderness, beauty, and even sublimity.

Ch. I. 2. —*wife of lewdness.* It is evident that, according to a mode of representation not uncommon with the Hebrew prophets, the idolatry of the Israelites, and their sin in forsaking Jehovah, are set forth under the symbol of the conduct of an adulterous woman to a kind husband; and the treatment of Israel by Jehovah is represented by the conduct of the prophet toward the adulteress. But there have been different opinions in regard to the question whether the actions and events here represented actually took place, or whether they are simply parabolical or symbolical.

It cannot be doubted that the prophets sometimes used as symbols, in the instruction of the people, real actions addressed to their eyes. But against the supposition that the actions here ascribed to the prophet are historical, it may be objected that they are not consistent with a pure morality or with the common feelings of a respectable man. It is very difficult to suppose that Hosea could have supposed the voice of God commanded him to take a notorious strumpet, or a woman who was sure to be one, and to retain her as his wife after repeated adulteries, and the birth of one, two, and three adulterous children, and all this for the purpose of giving a vivid impression of an idea. The actions ascribed to the prophet, and their fruits, would also require too much time to be useful for the purpose of impression. Comp. Ezek. ch. iv.; Jer. xxv. 15, &c. — *children of lewdness;* i. e. children of a lewd mother, who were symbols of what the children of Israel should suffer for the idolatry of the nation.

4. — *Jezreel.* This word denotes, according to the connection, *God will scatter*, or, *God will plant.* It seems to be used in the former sense in this verse, and in the latter in ch. ii. 22. As it is an historical, as well as a symbolical name, I could not translate it, as I have the other names in this chapter. — *blood of Jezreel;* i. e. shed in Jezreel by the kings of Israel, who had a palace in that city. See 1 Kings xxi. 13; 2 Kings ix. 15, 24; x. 7; xvii. 3.

II. 8. — Lit. *which they made into Baal;* otherwise, *which they wrought for Baal;* i. e. for ornaments of images of Baal, or furniture or dress for his worship.

13. — *Baals;* i. e. images of Baal.

14. — *Therefore,* &c. At first view some other transition particle, such as *nevertheless,* would seem to be more suited to the connection. But it is not necessary to depart from the usual meaning of לָכֵן and which it has in verses sixth and ninth (8 and 11 Heb.). In Is. xl. 2, we read, "Speak ye encouragement to Jerusalem, ... for she hath received from the hand of Jehovah double for all her sins." So here God is represented as saying, ver. 9 – 13, that he would severely punish his people, and *therefore* would allure her, &c. *to the desert;* i. e. From the distant countries to which she is led captive, I will safely conduct her home through the desert. The language seems to be borrowed from the former deliverance of the Jews from Egyptian slavery, when Moses and Aaron persuaded the Israelites to go into the desert, &c.

15. — *valley of Achor;* i. e. *of trouble*, or *confusion*. The valley of Achor, though a scene of confusion and trouble, was yet the door, or beginning, of hope to the Israelites under Joshua, and thence they were soon led to the possession of the promised land. See Josh. vii. 24, 25, 26; viii. 1, &c. So, after exile and suffering, the Jews should unexpectedly be delivered from their distresses, finding, as it were, another valley of Achor.

16. *Baal.* This term in its common use denoted nothing more than *lord* or *master*, and therefore was usually applied to the husband by the wife. But it should not be used any more, because it had been applied to a false god. Such should be the detestation of idolatry.

18. — *covenant with the beasts,* &c.; i. e. that they shall do no harm to my people.

20. — *know Jehovah.* There may be an allusion here to the etymological signification of the term Jehovah, viz. immutable, eternally the same. I will betroth thee to me in faithfulness, and thou shalt know by experience that I am unchangeably the same. Comp. xii. 5. Or, in reference to verse 8, the meaning may be that they should perceive and mark the goodness of Jehovah. Or the phrase may denote simply an increased knowledge of God.

21. — *I will hear the heavens;* i. e. when they ask, as it were, that they may send their rain on the earth. — *the earth;* i. e. when it supplicates, as it were, for rain.

22. — *the corn,* &c.; i. e. when they wish, as it were, to supply the wants of man. — *Jezreel;* i. e. all nature shall hear and minister to the people whom *God shall plant* (this is here the meaning of the term *Jezreel*); i. e. cause to increase and flourish in their own land.

23. — *I will plant.* The original word has an allusion to the name *Jezreel;* i. e. *God will plant.*

III. 1. — *love a woman;* i. e. the wife, who had forsaken the prophet, and become an adulteress. It is immaterial whether we understand Gomer of the preceding chapter to be intended or not. I disregard the Hebrew points. — *raisin cakes;* i. e. such as were used in the worship of idols.

2. — *bought.* "The price which he is here said to buy her with, seems not as a dowry, whereby he should first purchase her for a wife, but such a portion as though, through the power he had over her, he might for her ill deserts have quite put her away forever, or (if he had been so minded) have by rigor taken her and shut her close up, and used all severity and hardship toward her, he did notwithstanding allow her, to maintain her not in luxury, but in a competent manner, so as she could not but be sensible at once both of his displeasure in cutting her so short, and of his great kindness in allowing her so much, who deserved nothing, till upon her bethinking herself, for which he allowed her a good time, he should again receive her to the privileges of a wife; which reception might be well looked on as a new marriage, and his allowance to her as a buying of her; though not so much a

purchasing to himself a right in her, as a buying or hiring her to be honest and fit to be received again by him." — *Pococke.*

3. — *wait for me:* wait my pleasure, be devoted to me. See Jer. iii. 2. — *so will I also wait for thee;* i. e. I will not marry another, and finally separate myself from thee, but will wait the issue of thy probation, and be prepared to receive thee to all the privileges of a wife.

"The prophet's being bid yet to love that woman, and his dealing with her, so as not quite to reject her, but yet to restrain her to a shorter allowance, and requiring her to abide for him many days, without enjoyment of such favors from him as formerly she had enjoyed, but as one sequestered from her former courses, and from the company both of himself and any other, till he should see fit again to receive her nto greater favor, is plainly answered by God's not clean neglecting Israel, but still sustaining her, yet so as that she should be brought to a lower condition than formerly, and not live in that height of dignity and jollity as formerly she had done, but be deprived of all those glories and pomps, in respect both to her civil and ecclesiastical state, wherein she formerly prided herself, and as she had not those visible tokens of his presence among them, nor a public profession of his service, so neither the use of such idol services and feasts, wherein she formerly delighted and revelled." — *Pococke.*

4. — *ephod:* a part of the high-priest's ornaments. See Ex. xxviii. 4; Lev. vii. 7. Some suppose that *ephod* in this place denotes an image. — *teraphim:* a sort of household gods from which the superstitious sought answers respecting doubtful affairs. It may be, however, that the teraphim, or teraphs, in this verse denote the Urim and Thummim, belonging to the breastplate of the high-priest. According to Philo, the Urim and Thummim were two small images inserted between the double folds of the breastplate, one of which symbolically represented *Revelation,* the other, *Truth.* Among the Egyptians the supreme judge used to wear suspended from his neck a small image of sapphire, as the symbol of truth. See Diod. Sic. I. 48. 75; Æl. VII. 14. 34. See also Spencer, Lib. III. Dis. VII. cap. 1.

IV. 2. — *blood reacheth,* &c.; i. e. incessant murders are committed; one overtakes another.

4. — *let no man;* i. e. reproof and rebuke will be words thrown away. Comp. Is. i. 5; Ezek. iii. 26. — *contend with the priest:* which was regarded as proof of great obstinacy and incorrigibleness. See Deut. xvii. 12.

5. — *thy mother;* i. e. the whole nation of Israel. See ch. ii. 4, 5.

6. — *no more be my priest;* i. e. the people shall no more have the sacerdotal office among them.

7. — *their glory;* i. e. their greatness, according to the parallel expression, *become great.*

8. — *the sins of my people;* i. e. they do not rebuke sinners with fidelity, lest the number of sacrifices, of which they received a portion, should be diminished.

12. — *stocks;* i. e. idols of wood. — *staff revealeth:* they resort to their staff for a revelation of the future. A species of divination.

13. — *terebinth:* a tree common in Palestine, which grows to a large size, and is of a great age.

14. — *I will not punish,* &c.; i. e. I will not endeavor to correct the daughters, while the fathers and husbands set them such an example of licentiousness.

15. — *Bethaven.* There was a place of that name in the neighborhood of Bethel. See Josh. vii. 2. But in this passage the prophet, who is fond of symbolical names, intends Bethel itself, calling that city, in derision, Bethaven, i. e. *house of vanity* or *sin,* in reference to the worship of the golden calves which prevailed there. See also ch. v. 8.

16. — *like a lamb, &c.;* i. e. "Under the sad condition of a solitary, disconsolate lamb, left alone to live as it can in a desert, wide place, is expressed the sad condition that Israel for their refractoriness shall be brought to."

18. — *love shame;* i. e. sin, which brings shame; shameful deeds.

19. — *bound them up with its wings;* i. e. so that they shall be borne away by their enemies irresistibly and in various directions, like clouds driven by the wind.

V. 1. — *snare at Mizpah,* — *net upon Tabor,* &c. The meaning may be, that the priests had ensnared the people into sin by offering idol sacrifices upon Mizpah and Tabor, as being high places, or that they had ensnared the people into idolatry, as huntsmen spread their nets upon Mizpah and Tabor.

5. — *The pride of Israel,* &c. This line is repeated in vii. 10. On account of the different senses in which the words עָנָה and גָּאוֹן are used in the Old Testament, it is quite ambiguous, so that Jerome, in the Vulgate, renders in this verse as in our text, but in vii. 10 he renders, *and the pride of Israel shall be brought low in his presence,* or *before him.* At first view this last rendering seems to be best supported by the connection, so that in the last edition I adopted it, with the Sept., Michaelis, Newcome, De Wette, and others. But as the meaning which I now adopt is not at variance with the connection, and has better support from the *usus loquendi,* it seems to deserve the preference. Thus Job xvi. 8 בְּפָנַי יַעֲנֶה, *beareth witness to my face.* Were it not for the בְּפָנַי in connection with עָנָה I should prefer the other rendering.

There is also room for doubt as to the meaning of the line as now translated. More commonly the term גָּאוֹן denotes *glory, excellency,* that in which one takes pride; but sometimes *haughtiness.* Hence the meaning may be, that the proud and haughty spirit of self-confidence in Israel testified to their rebellion against God, and their desert of punishment, without any other evidence. Or, the meaning may be, that God himself, in whom the Israelites prided themselves as their God, testified against them by the calamities which he brought upon them. Comp. Amos viii. 7; iv. 7. Or, that the idols, in which they prided themselves, being found unable to help them, bore open witness against their wickedness and folly, and would not let them go unpunished. I rather prefer the sense of *haughtiness.*

6. *With their flocks,* &c.; i. e. they will offer large sacrifices in vain.

7. — *strange;* i. e. spurious. The meaning is, that they have educated their children in idolatry. — *new moon consume;* i. e. they shall be consumed within a month, or a short time.

8. *Look behind thee;* i. e. the enemy is at thy heels.

11. — *crushed with punishment;* i. e. broken or brought low by judgments from God. — *the decree;* i. e. of Jeroboam or some other king in favor of calf-worship, or some other kind of false worship.

VI. 1. *Come,* &c. *Saying* is to be supplied, as often elsewhere.

2. *After two days,* &c.; i. e. within a few days, shortly. See 1 Kings xvii. 12; Is. vii. 21. The language of the verse seems to be borrowed from the situation of a person restored from hopeless sickness or a grievous wound in a short time.

3. — *sure as the morning.* Comp. Jer. xxxiii. 20.

5. — *I have hewn;* i. e. I have threatened them with severe calamity and destruction. — *judgments;* i. e. The punishment, threatened by the prophets, has been sent in such a manner that all should perceive that it came from God.

9. — *Shechem.* It appears from Josh. xxi. 21 that Shechem was a city of refuge, a place appointed for the residence of the Levites. Thus it happened that many murders were committed in the way to it, and many priests engaged in them.

11. — *a harvest;* i. e. *of punishment.* See viii. 7, x. 13; Joel iii. 13.

VII. 2. — *their doings;* i. e. the evil consequences of their doings. — *encompass.* See Ps. xvii. 11, xviii. 5. — *before my face;* i. e. they do not escape my notice.

4. *He ceaseth to stir;* i. e. the fire. The design of this clause seems to be, to show that the oven is completely heated, or very hot; the point of comparison being merely the heat of the oven. — The people, burning with lust, are compared to a hot oven at its highest degree of heat, when no more fuel can be added to it by the baker.

5. — *stretcheth out his hand;* i. e. to pass and take the cup.

6. "Their heart is compared to an oven into which the baker having put sufficient fuel and fire, leaving them together, though he do no more at present but lay him down to sleep all the night, yet in the morning finds it burning all in a flame. So they, while they lie in wait, or secretely intend or plot mischief, having their hearts filled with the fuel of evil concupiscence, and fraught with wicked thoughts, desires, and designs, though they suppress them for a while, and seem to be at rest, yet have them still working and kindling in them, so that, as soon as opportunity shall offer, these their hidden designs break forth like a flame of fire into open act." — *Pococke.*

8. — *a cake not turned.* This comparison has by some been under-

stood to describe the character, by others the condition, of Ephraim. According to the former, the meaning will be that Ephraim, by joining in the heathen worship while he professed to worship Jehovah, had become neither bread nor dough, but something worthless. According to others, Ephraim is pressed upon by the nations like a cake, which is eagerly devoured by a hungry man before it is half baked. According to others, Ephraim is like a cake spoiled in the baking by negligence; burnt up, because it is not turned; i. e. Ephraim is ruined by neglecting his privileges; by disregard to the laws of God. I prefer the last.

9. — *Strangers*, &c.; i. e. foreign nations which destroyed the strength of Ephraim, either by invasion or by extorting tribute for assistance rendered. — *knoweth it not:* i. e. though his resources have been consumed by foreign nations, and like a gray-haired man he is near death, yet he is so proud, secure, and stupid as not to give heed to his low condition, and endeavor to recover from it by a return to God and to duty.

12. — *proclaimed in their congregation;* i. e. by the prophets.

13. — *would redeem*, &c. Comp. xiii. 14.

14. — *howl upon their beds;* i. e. on account of their sufferings.

15. i. e. "Whether I inflicted punishment on them, or showed them favor, they neglected me for their idols."

16. *They return not*, &c. Perhaps the meaning rather is, *They return to — not the Most High*, i. e. to idols. — *reproach;* i. e. matter of reproach. — *deceitful bow;* i. e. one which sends the arrows wide of the mark.

Ch. VIII. 1. — *the trumpet*, &c. This is the language of Jehovah to the prophet, commanding him to proclaim what follows. Comp. Is. lviii. 1.

2. — *we know thee, we, thine Israel.* In a season of danger they plead for the favor of God, on account of their past relation to him and their outward privileges, as descendants of Jacob, called Israel, because he prevailed with God, although they neglected the worship of Jehovah.

4. — *not by me:* — *I knew it not;* i. e. without inquiring of me by means of the priests and the prophets.

5. *An abomination*, &c.; otherwise, *He hath cast off thy calf*, &c.; otherwise, *Thy calf cast them off;* i. e. thy calf, which thou worshippest, has caused thy inhabitants to be rejected by me, and involved in misery.

6. — *from Israel it came;* i. e. the calf was set up for worship by Israel without any authority from me.

7. — *sown the wind*, &c.; i. e. by setting up and worshipping idols they have been engaged in a business as vain and foolish as that of sowing the wind; nay, more, they have labored to their own injury: since men usually reap a harvest of what they sow, bearing a great increase compared with the seed. Hence, by sowing the dangerous element of wind, they might expect to reap a whirlwind.

8. —*a vessel*, &c.; i. e. held in great contempt, like a cracked earthen vessel which no one wants. Ps. xxxi. 12.

9. —*wild ass*. As the wild ass was not a formidable animal, but only refractory, loving to have his own way, it was probably intended to describe Israel rather than Assyria. — *hireth lovers*; i. e. sends gifts to foreign nations in order to obtain their alliance and friendship.

10. —*from the burden of their king, and their princes*; i. e. They shall be relieved from the burdens of their own kings and princes, of which they complain so much, by being made to bear heavier burdens in captivity. The line is ironical. So Jerome, Grotius, and others.

11. —*shall he have altars*; i. e. he shall have them erected by others in those idolatrous countries to which he is led away captive. See Deut. iv. 28; Jer. xiv. 13.

12. — *Though I write*, &c.; i. e. by my prophets give precept upon precept.

13. —*they slay flesh*, &c.; i. e. for the purpose of gratifying their own appetites, rather than of pleasing me.

14. —*palaces:* probably fortified palaces similar to castles; in which they trusted for protection, rather than in the favor of Jehovah, sought by reformation and obedience.

IX. 1. — *lovest hire*; i. e. like a harlot.

2. —*new wine shall deceive*; i. e. disappoint their expectations in regard to its quantity. So *fundus mendax, spem mentita seges*, in Horace. Perhaps the meaning may be, however, that they shall be disappointed in the enjoyment of what they raise, being carried into captivity.

4. —*polluted*. See Numb. xix. 14.

6. —*gather them*, i. e. for burial; i. e. they shall die in Egypt. See Jer. viii. 2; Ezek. xxix. 5.

7. — *man of the spirit*; i. e. who professed to be inspired with the spirit of God, synonymous with *prophet* in the preceding line. —*hatred*; i. e. against God.

8. *If Ephraim seek an answer from my God*; i. e. If any one among the generally corrupt Ephraimites seeks Divine direction. I am not satisfied with any exposition of this obscure line which I have seen. That which I have given is essentially the same as that of Drusius in Poole's Synopsis. The literal rendering I suppose to be, *If Ephraim is watching*, or *looking out, with my God*, i. e. *near*, or *in the presence of, my God*. See Hab. ii. 1. Hitzig and De Wette translate the line affirmatively, *Ephraim watches with my God*. They suppose the meaning to be that Ephraim resorts to the false prophets, who prophesy smooth things, and places their utterances on a par with those of God's genuine prophets. But to suppose that the phrase *with my God* means *with the prophets of my God*, is to adopt a very harsh ellipsis. Ewald renders the line *Ephraim is a watchman*, or *spy, against my God*, which, though grammatically allowable, yields no sense appropriate to the connection.

9. — *of Gibeah.* See Judges xix. 22.

10. — *as grapes,* &c.; i. e. they were as acceptable to me as grapes to a traveller in the wilderness. See xi. 1. — *to shame:* to idols, which disappoint and bring shame to their worshippers.

13. — *rich pasture;* i. e. probably in a beautiful place.

14. *Gilgal:* a place situated between Jericho and the Jordan, where idols were worshipped. See xii. 11; Amos iv. 4.

15. *All their wickedness;* i. e. the height of it, the most flagrant instances of it. — *my house;* i. e. my family.

16. — *root is dried up.* The punishment here threatened was probably suggested by the idea of *fruitfulness* implied in the etymology of the name Ephraim. See Gen. xli. 52.

X. 2. — *divided;* i. e. between the true God and false ones; or, separated from God, and joined to idols.

3. *We have no king;* i. e. they shall be overcome by enemies, and be forced to say that they had no king that could help them or do them any good.

4. — *making covenants;* i. e. with foreign nations, contrary to the Divine law. — *judgment springeth up,* &c. This may be understood to mean, that what is dealt out for justice proves to be as noxious as hemlock. Comp. Amos vi. 12. Or *judgment* may denote punishment, which speedily and in full measure followed their crimes, like the rapid and luxuriant growth of hemlock in the fields. The expression *springeth up* favors the last meaning.

5. — *calf.* The feminine plural in the Hebrew seems to be used to denote one calf by way of eminence. Comp. Ps. lxxiii. 22; Prov. ix. 1.

8. *Aven:* probably used for *Bethaven;* i. e. Bethel. See note on iv. 15. — *the sin:* the place or occasion of sin.

9. *More than:* see Judges xix., xx. — *they stood,* viz. the Israelites; i. e. in great measure uninjured. — *not overtake them;* i. e. the battle was fought about Gibeah, and the tribes of Israel were not much afflicted by it.

10. — *bind them;* i. e. make them captives. — *two iniquities;* i. e. the calves in Dan and Bethel.

11. — *to tread out the corn;* i. e. to perform the lightest and most agreeable of the works of husbandry, by which the oxen or heifers were not worn out, but rather grew fat and frolicsome, since by the Divine law they were indulged with the liberty of feeding during their labor. — *lay the yoke,* &c. Literally, *I will come over upon,* or *assail.*

12. — *rain righteousness upon you;* otherwise, *teach you righteousness.*

13. — *ye shall reap injustice;* i. e ye shall suffer injustice or wrong-doing from others. — *the fruit of falsehood;* i. e. such fruit as is worthy of a hypocritical affectation of piety. Possibly the phrase, *ye shall reap injustice,* may mean, by a Hebrew usage, *the consequence* of injustice, i. e. *wretchedness. The fruit of falsehood* may also mean *false fruit,* that which *disappoints,* or is unlooked for. But the analogous cases do not quite support such a view of the meaning of this pas-

sage. — *thy way.* In this connection *way* seems to denote the perverse ways in general which were devised by the people in order to obtain relief from their calamities, instead of resorting to God. Otherwise *way* may denote *idolatry*, especially *calf-worship.*

14. *Shalman, &c.* The prophet seems to allude to a fact not recorded by any of the sacred historians.

15. *Bethel;* i. e. the idolatrous worship of Bethel. —*In the morning;* i. e. suddenly. Otherwise, *like the morning dawn.*

XI. 2. —*those that called them;* i. e. the prophets.

4. —*human cords;* i. ė. not as beasts are made to go, but by gentle, persuasive methods. The Chaldee paraphrase is beautiful: "As beloved children are drawn, I drew them with the strength of love." —*lift up the yoke.* There may be an allusion to the custom of raising the yoke when it pressed the cheeks of the laboring beast, so as to allow it to eat.

5. —*to Egypt;* i. e. they shall not have an opportunity to resort to Egypt for aid. Or, they shall not go into Egyptian servitude, but to a worse, in a more distant country, Assyria.

8. *Admah.* See Gen. xiv. 8.

XII. 1.—*feedeth on wind;* i. e. adopts and is delighted with vain windy plans; indulges the vain hope of safety and prosperity by forming alliances with the great powers, Assyria and Egypt. —*east wind;* which was not merely unprofitable, but noxious and destructive. —*oil is carried, &c.;* i. e. as a present, to obtain the aid and alliance of the Egyptians.

3. — *took his brother, &c.* It seems to be mentioned in praise of the zeal of their ancestor Jacob in obtaining the blessing of God, that in the womb he performed an action which was an omen of his superiority over his brother, and of his obtaining the blessing of the first-born. — *in his strength, &c.;* i. e. in his adult vigor. —*with God;* i. e. with the angel, in whom dwelt his spirit, *numen*, and who was the representative of God.

4. —*he found, &c.;* i. e. God found Jacob, and spake with us, his posterity, in connection with him.

5. *Jehovah, &c.* There is here an allusion to the etymological meaning of the name Jehovah, the *eternal* or *unchangeable*, he who always will be that which he is. As he manifested himself to your ancestor Jacob, so he will manifest himself to you, his descendants, if you seek his favor with the same earnestness and perseverance which he exhibited.

7. —*a Canaanite;* i. e. not a true Israelite, not a true son of Jacob is Ephraim, but an odious Canaanite, whose chief business was traffic, and who was notorious for dishonesty. Otherwise, *a trafficker.* But this is not so emphatic. Comp. Lev. xviii. 3; Ezek. xvi. 3.

9. —*cause thee to dwell in tents.* It has been a matter of great doubt among expositors, whether these words are to be regarded as a promise

or a threat. As the words of the preceding line *I, Jehovah, have been thy God*, i. e. thy protector, seem naturally to introduce a promise of good, and as it is the manner of the Hebrew prophets, especially of Hosea, to introduce promises of future blessings very abruptly in the midst of threatenings, I incline to the opinion that the meaning is, that, on condition of repentance and trust in the God of their fathers, he would again cause them to dwell securely in tents, however troubled and calamitous was their present condition. The other view of the meaning is, that God would remove them from their land, and cause them to dwell in tents away from their homes, as on the annual festivals they could only be accommodated in tents without the city.

12, 13. *Jacob fled*, &c. The object of these obscure verses may be to show from what a small beginning, and from what a low condition, God raised the Hebrew nation to prosperity, and thus to make their ingratitude appear more criminal.

XIII. 2. — *kiss the calves.* A mode of worship. See 1 Kings xix. 18.

3. — *chimney.* More strictly *hole* or *window* for the smoke.

7. — *Therefore have I become*, &c. There is some doubt in regard to the tense in which the verbs in this and the following verses should be rendered. The rendering which I have adopted seems to me best supported by Hebrew grammatical usage, and as consistent as any with the connection. The prophet so identifies himself and his contemporaries with the people of Israel in their whole past history up to their progenitor Jacob, comp. xii. 2, that it is sometimes difficult to determine whether he refers to the past, the present, or the future

9. — *It hath been thy destruction.* Valuable as is the sentiment in the common version, the original will scarcely authorize it. The rendering which I adopt requires only the supply of the finite verb. The literal translation being, "It hath destroyed thee, O Israel, that [thou hast been] against me, against thy help." See vii. 13.

12. — *is treasured up ;* i. e. is not forgotten by the Deity, but will receive punishment. See the note to my version of Job xiv. 17.

13. — *tarry long*, &c. ; i. e. he would extricate himself from his straits and calamities by repentance.

14. — *the grave.* Literally, *the under-world, Sheol.* The terms "death" and "Sheol" are evidently used in a figurative sense here to denote the lowest, most hopeless state of national depression. For the sake of rhetoric I retain the term *grave* here rather than "Sheol" or "under-world." — *thy destruction ;* i. e. thy destructive power, or, the destruction inflicted by thee. In this verse, as in the tenth, it is better to read אַיֵּה, *where*, instead of אֱהִי, *I will be.* This completes the figure begun in verse thirteenth in a manner more agreeable to Hebrew ideas than the other mode of rendering. This was the reading of the Sept., Arab., Syr., Aquila. It was adopted by many of the older critics (see Poole's Synopsis), and by most of the moderns, such as Newcome, Gesenius, Hitzig, De Wette, and others. I was formerly unwilling to adopt this reading and rendering, on account of the connection

verses 13 and 14 with the sentiment in verse 15. But the transitions from threatening to promise are, in the prophetic writings, often very abrupt. Comp. Amos ix. 11; Mic. ix. 1, 10; Is. xliii. 28; xix. 17, 18, &c.; xlix. 11; xlii. 25; xliii. 1, &c.; xxx. 17, 18. It was a settled thing in the minds of the prophets that Israel was one day to be in a state of glory. Hence it is not unnatural that, in their severest threatenings of national degradation and ruin, the prophets should remember the promise of God to the fathers of the nation, and predict a restoration to national prosperity and glory. It is as if they said, when describing the national ruin, the punishment of sin, To such a state of degradation shall the nation be reduced by sin, before the glorious future shall come. —*hidden from mine eyes;* i. e. my purpose is unchangeable. This purpose relates to the promise of the preceding verse, which is not inconsistent with previous destruction to be brought on those who refused to repent and obey God's laws, as set forth in the fifteenth and following verses. For a very illustrative passage, see Is. iv. 4, 5.

XIV. 2. —*sacrifices of our lips.* Literally, calves or bullocks of our lips.

3. —*on horses.* Comp. Deut. xvii. 16; Ps. xxxiii. 17; Is. xxxi. 1.

7. —*his shadow;* i. e. of Israel.

NOTES ON ISAIAH.

According to the Hebrew inscription of the book ascribed to Isaiah, and to other indications contained in it, this prophet lived in the reigns of Uzziah, Jotham, Ahaz, and Hezekiah, kings of Judah; i. e. from about 758 to 710 years before the Christian era. From chapter sixth, which is with reason supposed to indicate his call to the prophetic office, it is plain that he began to exercise it in the last year of Uzziah. As there are no prophecies in the book which seem to belong to the reign of Jotham, it has been conjectured that in the first verse of the sixth chapter we should read, "In the year in which King *Jotham* died." But this is unnecessary. Since, if Isaiah delivered prophecies during that reign, they may not have been committed to writing, or they may have been lost. From the thirty-ninth chapter it appears that he flourished until the fourteenth year of Hezekiah. After this time we find no notice of him, except in an improbable Jewish tradition.

Isaiah is said, in the inscription, to have been the son of a certain Amoz, or Amots. Many of the fathers of the Church supposed this Amoz to be the same with the prophet Amos. This error arose from the circumstance that the Septuagint version uses the same Greek word to denote both; whereas the Hebrew word for Amos is different from that for Amoz. There is a Rabbinical tradition, that Amoz was the brother of King Amaziah; but it rests on no proper historical grounds, and is improbable. From facts recorded in the seventh chapter, &c., and from the thirty-sixth to the thirty-ninth, as well as from the general tenor of his writings, we gather reason to ascribe to him unbounded moral courage and fervent patriotism, united with an earnest and rational piety.

Isaiah has usually been regarded, by English critics, as the very first among the Hebrew poets. No one can fail to admire the strength and majesty of language, the richness of thought and imagery, the vividness of representation, and the easy, earnest flow of expression, which distinguish various portions of the collection of prophecies ascribed to Isaiah. But to me it seems that in no one of the highest characteristics of poetry is that wonderful production, the book of Job, inferior to any of the pieces ascribed to Isaiah; while it surpasses them all in variety and comprehensiveness of thought, and in depth and tenderness of feeling.

Since the time of the German critic Doederlein, who first expressed doubts of the genuineness of Is. xl. – lxvi., it has been questioned, on internal grounds, whether various portions of the book of Isaiah were written by that prophet. Gesenius, the celebrated commentator upon Isaiah, allows to him the authorship of only about one third part of the book ascribed to him. Of the remaining portion he supposes by far the greater part to have been written by an unknown prophet just before the return of the Jews from the exile at Babylon. The portions which Gesenius regards as not written by Isaiah are chapters xiii., xiv. 1 – 27, xv., xvi. 1 – 12, xxi. 1 – 10, xxiv., xxv., xxvi., xxvii., and from xxxiv. to the end of the book. The prophet, or prophets, whose writings are contained in the collection ascribed to him, are however regarded as genuine prophets as Isaiah himself, and in spirituality and comprehensiveness of religious views perhaps his superiors. When they are called, as they sometimes are, the ungenuine Isaiah, it is only meant that the writings of some great unknown prophet or prophets have been ascribed to the wrong author. As it is universally acknowledged that some Psalms have been ascribed to David and some Proverbs to Solomon, of which they were not the authors, so it is supposed that the collectors of the Hebrew prophetic literature ascribed the admirable productions of some unknown authors to so eminent a prophet as Isaiah. The views of Gesenius have been adopted by nearly all the distinguished commentators on Isaiah in Germany; such as Maurer, Hitzig, Ewald, Umbreit, and De Wette.

Ch. I. 1. *The visions.* With Gesenius I take the original word to be a collective term, used as in 1 Sam. iii. 1, Prov. xxix. 18, to signify *the prophesying*, or the *prophecies*, of Isaiah. It appears probable that this inscription was at first prefixed to the first twelve chapters, forming a collection of prophecies relating to Judah and Jerusalem. That it was not originally prefixed to the whole book is probable from his mentioning Judah and Jerusalem without reference to the foreign nations against which many prophecies are directed. Vitringa, who is followed by Lowth and other learned critics, supposes that the former part of the title was originally prefixed to the single prophecy, or discourse, contained in the first chapter, and that when the collection of all Isaiah's prophecies was made, the enumeration of the kings of Judah was added to make it at the same time a proper title for the whole book.

This chapter with the rest is termed *a vision.* But the reader will observe that it contains nothing properly prophetic, but only a picture of the depravity of the times, probably the times of Ahaz, with general promises and threatenings according to the principles of the Jewish religion. The prediction of future events is not to be regarded as the sole, or even as the principal, business of the prophet. He was a preacher of religion, whose principal business it was to exert an influence upon his contemporaries.

2. — *Hear, O ye heavens.* "God is introduced as entering upon a solemn and public action, or pleading before the whole world against his disobedient people. The prophet, as herald, or officer to proclaim the summons to the court, calls upon all created beings, celestial and terrestrial, to attend, and bear witness to the truth of his plea and the justice of his cause." — *Lowth.*

5. — *Where,* &c.; i. e. *On what part.* The meaning is, that already they had been so severely bruised, or punished, that there was scarcely a whole limb left, on which they could be smitten. This interpretation is favored by what follows: *From the sole of the foot,* &c.; otherwise, Why will ye be smitten more? Why will ye renew your rebellion?

6. — *pressed;* i. e. The blood and matter have not been excluded by gentle pressure. "The art of medicine in the East consists chiefly in external applications; accordingly, the prophet's images in this place are all taken from surgery. Sir John Chardin, in his note on Prov. iii. 8, 'It shall be health to thy navel and marrow to thy bones,' observes, that 'the comparison is taken from the plasters, ointments, oils, and frictions, which are made use of in the East upon the belly and stomach in most maladies. Being ignorant, in the villages, of the art of making decoctions and potions, and of the proper doses of such things, they generally make use of external medicines.' — HARMER's *Observations on Scripture,* Vol. II. p. 488. And in surgery their materia medica is extremely simple; oil making the principal part of it. 'In India,' says Tavernier, 'they have a certain preparation of oil and melted grease, which they commonly use for the healing of wounds.' *Voyage Ind.* So the good Samaritan poured oil and wine on the wounds of the distressed Jew; wine, cleansing and somewhat astringent, proper for a fresh wound; oil, mollifying and healing. Luke x. 34" — *Lowth.*

8. — *daughter of Zion;* i. e. Zion itself. For a learned and satisfac-

tory account of the expression, see Gesenius's Lex. on the word בַּת. — *as a shed in a vineyard:* "A little temporary hut covered with boughs, straw, turf, or the like materials, for a shelter from the heat by day, and the cold and dews by night, for the watchman that kept the garden, or vineyard, during the short season while the fruit was ripening (see Job xxvii. 18), and presently removed, when it had served that purpose. See Harmer's *Observ.* I. 454. They were probably obliged to have such a constant watch, to defend the fruit from the jackals." The meaning is, that all things around the city lay desolate, like the withered vines of a cucumber-garden around the watchman's hut; in other words, that the city alone stood safe, amid the ruins caused by the enemy, like the hut in a gathered garden of cucumbers. It now appears to me that the rendering "*delivered*" city is untenable. The rendering "*watch-tower,*" "*castle for watching,*" recently proposed by Gesenius and Hitzig, seems also by no means sufficiently supported by Hebrew usage, when we consider how often the term occurs in another sense. I therefore adopt the plain meaning of the terms, though it may seem unpoetical and incongruous to compare a city with a city.

9. *Jehovah of hosts.* "This," says Gesenius, "is the most common name of God in the genuine Isaiah, and in Jeremiah, Zachariah, and Malachi. It represents him as the ruler of the hosts of heaven, i. e. the angels and the stars. Sometimes, but less frequently, we meet with the appellation, Jehovah, *God* of hosts. Hence some suppose the expression *Jehovah of hosts* to be elliptical. But it is not a correct assertion that Jehovah, as a proper name, admits of no genitive. For such relations and adjuncts as are expressed by the genitive often depend upon proper names. So in Arabic poetry one is called *Rebiah of the poor*, in reference to his liberality. So in Scottish poetry we have the expressions *Cuchullin of shields, Diaran of the forest.* In explaining the expression we need only supply the idea of God, included in the name Jehovah."

10. *Ye princes of Sodom.* "The incidental mention of Sodom and Gomorrah, in the preceding verse, suggested to the prophet this spirited address to the rulers and inhabitants of Jerusalem, under the character of princes of Sodom and people of Gomorrah." — *Lowth.* In imputing to the inhabitants of Jerusalem the character of the people of Sodom and Gomorrah, the prophet refers without doubt to their general depravity, and not to any particular vice or vices.

11. — *the fat, the blood.* The fat and the blood are particularly mentioned, because these were in all sacrifices set apart to God. The fat was always burnt upon the altar, and the blood was partly sprinkled, differently on different occasions, and partly poured out at the bottom of the altar. See Lev. iv. Oblations and sacrifices were acceptable to God, so far only as they were expressions of right feeling toward God in him that offered them. They were therefore vain, and odious in the sight of God, when brought by those who were destitute of such feelings. Comp. Amos v. 21 – 24.

12. — *to appear before me;* i. e. to visit the sanctuary. — *to tread*

my courts; i. e. to profane them. This interpretation seems to me preferable to the common one, which regards the expressions *to appear before me*, and *to tread my courts*, as synonymous. See xxviii. 3. So, in Rev. xi. 2, the heathen are said to tread under foot (πατεῖν) the holy city. See also 1 Mac. iii. 45. 51; iv. 60.

13. *The new moon also, and the sabbath, and the calling of the assembly;* supply "*are an abomination to me,*" from the preceding line. Or the construction may be, *As to the new moon, and the sabbath, and the calling of the assembly, — Iniquity and festivals I cannot endure.* For an account of the manner in which the new moon was celebrated, see Numb. xxviii. 11, &c. — *the calling of the assembly.* For an account of the festivals in which the solemn assembly was *proclaimed*, or called together by proclamation of a herald, see Lev. xxiii. 2 – 8; Numb. xxviii. 18 – 25. The Mahometans still call the followers of the prophet to prayer by a similar method. — *Iniquity and festivals;* i. e. religious festivals celebrated by the unrighteous, or followed by the commission of all manner of wickedness by those who celebrate them. Lowth's translation of this line is founded on a conjectural reading, which appears to be wholly unnecessary.

15. Lifting up of the hand is the well-known token of supplication, not only among the Jews, but various ancient and modern nations. To hide, or turn away, the face, is an equally intelligible token of disregard and neglect. — *Your hands are full of blood.* It has been remarked by several critics, that this line is probably to be understood figuratively, as referring to the oppression of the weak and helpless, of widows and orphans. It is not impossible, however, that it may refer to a state of society when homicides were frequent, and when the perpetrators were suffered to escape with impunity.

18. — *argue together;* i. e. as before a court of justice. The common interpretation of this verse, which makes it express solely the extent of the Divine mercy, has with some reason been called in question. The connection seems to favor the supposition that the meaning is, that the Jewish nation should be purified by the reformation, or by the destruction, of the wicked. Comp. ver. 25 – 28; iv. 4.

21. — *a harlot;* a well-known image for *an idolatress.*

22. *Thy silver*, &c.; i. e. thy most distinguished men have become corrupt; as the image is illustrated in the next verse. — *adulterated with water.* According to Gesenius the original expression is, Thy wine is *circumcised, mangled*, or, as we should say, *murdered*, with water. So Martial, Ep. i. 18, *Scelus et jugulare Falerum.* It should be remembered that what is called *mixed* wine in other parts of Scripture is a very different thing from watered wine. The former is wine made stronger by a mixture of powerful and intoxicating ingredients.

24. — *ease me.* "Anger arising from a sense of injury and affront, especially from those who from every consideration of duty and gratitude ought to have behaved far otherwise, is an uneasy and painful sensation; and revenge, executed to the full on the offenders, removes that uneasiness, and consequently is pleasing and quieting, at least

for the present." — *Lowth.* That the prophet should have ascribed such a sentiment to the Deity, is to be explained by referring to the age and people for which he wrote. See my Introduction to Psalms, p. vii., &c.

29. — *terebinths, gardens.* "Sacred groves were a very ancient and favorite appendage of idolatry. They were furnished with the temple of the god to whom they were dedicated, with altars, images, and with everything necessary for performing the various rites of worship offered there; and were the scenes of many impure ceremonies, and of much abominable superstition." — *Lowth.*

30. — *a garden in which is no water.* "In the hotter parts of the Eastern countries, a constant supply of water is so absolutely necessary for the cultivation, and even for the preservation and existence of a garden, that, should it want water but for a few days, everything in it would be burnt up with the heat, and totally destroyed. There is therefore no garden whatever in those countries, but what has such a certain supply, either from some neighboring river, or from a reservoir of water collected from springs, or filled with rain-water in the proper season in sufficient quantity to afford ample provision for the rest of the year. Moses, having described the habitation of man newly created as a garden, planted with every tree pleasant to the sight and good for food, adds, as a circumstance necessary to complete the idea of a garden, that it was well supplied with water: 'And a river went out of Eden to water the garden.' Gen. ii. 10." — *Lowth.* See also Gen. xiii. 10; Jer. xvii. 8; Ecclus. xxiv. 40, 41; Prov. xxi. 1; Eccles. ii. 5, 6.

Chapters II., III., and IV. undoubtedly form one continued discourse. Though it contains no allusion to a personal Messiah, it describes a state of things which, in other passages, Isaiah represents as being introduced by a wise, righteous, and mighty King, raised up by Jehovah. It was probably written about the end of the reign of Jotham, or the beginning of that of Ahaz.

II. 2. — *at the head of.* This is strictly literal. Comp. Amos vi. 7; Mic. ii. 13. — *shall flow;* shall come in great numbers and with great eagerness, like a mighty river.

4. *He shall be,* &c. The connection with the preceding verses requires the pronoun to be referred to Jehovah.

5. — *in the light of Jehovah;* i. e. in the path illuminated by him; i. e. follow his instructions and obey his laws. See li. 4; Prov. vi. 23; Ps. cxix. 105.

6. — *of the East;* i. e. Eastern manners, corruptions. Lit. *filled from the East.*

7. — *of horses.* In violation of the law. Deut. xvii. 16.

13 – 16. By the accumulation of images in these verses the prophet probably means to describe particularly the powerful and wealthy inhabitants of Jerusalem. Ships of Tarshish are mentioned, because they contributed to the wealth of Jerusalem. Ships sailing to Tar-

shish denoted probably the largest kind of ships; Tarshish being the most distant celebrated mart to the inhabitants of Palestine in those times. — *beautiful flags.* So Gesenius, who observes that the Phœnician and Egyptian vessels had their flags and sails of purple and other splendid colors. See Ezek. xxvii. 7. Comp. also the parallelism in verses 13 – 16.

20. — *the moles and the bats;* i. e. they shall thrust them into dark corners, holes, &c., the usual residence of moles and bats.

III. 3. — *skilful in charms;* i. e. he would take away everything in which they trusted, both bad and good, the charmers as well as the prophets. See Hosea iii. 4.

4, 5. A description of the anarchy which would follow the loss of the eminent men of the state.

6. — *in his father's house;* i. e. a man of family and opulence, who has kept himself aloof from the dissensions of the times, confining himself, as it were, to his father's house. — *this ruin;* i. e. the ruined state.

7. — *bread nor raiment.* "'It is customary through all the East,' says Sir John Chardin, 'to gather together an immense quantity of furniture and clothes; for their fashions never alter.' Princes and great men are obliged to have a great stock of such things in readiness for presents on all occasions. 'The kings of Persia,' says the same author, 'have great wardrobes, where there are always many hundreds of habits ready, designed for presents, and sorted.' This explains the meaning of the excuse made by him that is desired to undertake the government; he alleges that he has not wherewithal to support the dignity of the station by such acts of liberality and hospitality as the law of custom required of persons of superior rank." — *Lowth.*

12. — *destroy the way,* &c.; i. e. lead thee to destruction.

16. — *foot-clasps,* &c.: making a tinkling, in order to attract notice, with the foot-clasps, or bracelets, which the Eastern women were accustomed to wear round their ankles.

18. — *net-works.* Probably net-work caps, ornamental coverings for the head. — *crescents;* i. e. small ornaments, in the shape of a half-moon, worn on the neck. Judges viii. 21 – 28.

19. — *ear-rings;* or, more literally, *ear-drops* or *pendants.* — *veils.* The Hebrew term is borrowed from their waving motion.

20. — *ankle-chains;* i. e. chains connecting the foot-clasps, and thus regulating the gait. — *belts,* or girdles: a very expensive part of an Eastern lady's dress. — *perfume-boxes:* answering the purpose of what are now called *smelling-bottles.* — *amulets;* i. e. gems, or plates of gold or silver, having magical formulas inscribed on them, and worn round the neck, or in the ears, as charms against danger and misfortune.

22. — *purses,* containing their money, and probably attached to the belt. — *mirrors:* small, or, as we should say, pocket mirrors, of polished metal.

23. — *large veils:* probably a thin gauze covering worn by females over their other garments when they went out, sometimes thrown over their heads, and sometimes over their shoulders.

26. Sitting on the ground was a posture that denoted deep mourning and distress. Comp. Lam. ii. 10, and note. Zion is here spoken of in the third person. In the preceding verse she is addressed in the second.

IV. 1. — *seven women.* "The number of men slain in battle shall be so great, that seven women shall be left to one man. They will take hold of them, and use the most pressing importunity to be married; in spite of the natural suggestions of jealousy, they will be content with a share only of the rights of marriage in common with several others, and that on hard conditions, renouncing the legal demands of the wife on the husband (see Ex. xxi. 10), and begging only the name and credit of wedlock, and to be freed from the reproach of celibacy." See ch. liv. 1, 4.

2. — *increase of Jehovah.* The Hebrew term is often used in this sense. See Gen. xix. 25; Hosea viii. 7; Ezek. xvi. 7; Ps. lxv. 11 (10). Taken in this collective sense, which is confirmed by the parallel phrase *fruit of the land,* the *increase, produce,* or *growth* of Jehovah will denote the productions of the land sacred to Jehovah, or under his peculiar care. See Maurer *ad loc.* Calvin understands it of a spiritual growth, or such a growth or harvest of men as Jehovah produces; but this does not correspond so well with the parallelism and the connection. Otherwise, *branch of Jehovah,* denoting that, though the tree, which represents the nation, would be in a great measure destroyed, a branch or sprout would remain, from which the nation would revive and have new growth. See vi. 13.

3. — *written down for life;* i. e. predestined to live; have their names written in God's book of life.

4. — *the spirit of judgment,* &c.; i. e. by putting forth his spirit, or power, in punishing and exterminating.

V. This chapter is supposed by the most eminent critics to have been written a short time after the preceding passage, in the early part of the reign of Ahaz.

2. — *sour grapes.* This rendering of the original term is ably supported by Gesenius *ad loc.* The word probably denotes small unripe grapes, offensive to the smell as well as to the taste.

7. This verse in the original affords an instance of the paronomasia, or play upon words, which was considered a great ornament of style with the Hebrews:

> He looked for *mispat*, and behold, *mispach!*
> For *zedakah*, and behold, *zeakah!*

Many examples of it occur in Isaiah. I have not been able to imitate it in English consistently with the dignity of style which belongs to the subject.

14. —*greedy throat;* lit. *greediness,* which, from the verb connected with it, and the parallelism, appears to be used for *greedy throat.*

17. —*lambs feed;* i. e. on the land of the proud and wealthy, who have gone down to Hades, as mentioned in v. 14.

18. —*draw calamity with cords,* &c.; i. e. who sin with a high hand, with exertion and industry, as it were, and thus draw punishment upon themselves. The Hebrew terms translated *calamity* and *punishment* literally denote *iniquity* and *sin.* But by usage they sometimes denote the consequences of sin. So the common version in Zech. xiv. 19; Lam. iii. 39. Thus in this passage the strange idea of drawing sin by sin is avoided.

27. —*girdle,* &c. See note on Job xii. 21.

30. —*its clouds;* i. e. the dark clouds which have overshadowed the land of Judah.

VI. 6. —*glowing stone.* The use of the original word in other passages seems to require this rendering. Heated stones were used by the Orientals to heat milk, to cook meat, bread, &c. It seems probable that stones were heated on the altar to cook the meat of the sacrifices, or to consume the sooner that which was to be consumed See Bochart. Hieroz. P. I. Lib. II. cap. xxxiv.

9. *Hear ye, indeed.* Though the verbs are in the imperative form, the language is evidently that of strong emotion, expressing what would be the result of the prophet's preaching, through the wickedness of the Jews.

10. —*Make gross.* In the language of prophecy, this means merely, Declare that they will be gross. See Jer. i. 10; Ezek. xliii. 3; Hos. vi. 5. —*their hearts.* The heart was regarded as the seat of the understanding by the Hebrews.

VII. 3. *Shear-Jashub.* This symbolical name signifies, *A remnant shall return.*

8. *But the head of Syria,* &c.; i. e. Syria shall not enlarge its dominions by the conquest of Jerusalem. —*And within threescore,* &c. Gesenius gives some good reasons for the supposition that the words included in brackets are spurious. It is at least extremely probable that they are out of place.

12. *I will not tempt Jehovah.* Ahaz seems to answer the prophet with an ironical sneer, expressing his unbelief and his contempt of the prophet in the language of religious reverence.

14. —*the damsel;* i. e. *my* damsel, the damsel betrothed to me. I see not what other force the article can have in this connection. So in Prov. vii. 19, "*The* goodman" means "*my* husband." So in our idiom, *the* governor, *the* schoolmaster, is *our* governor, &c. The term translated *damsel* means a young woman of marriageable age, without reference to virginity. To express that idea Isaiah would have used a different word, viz. בְּתוּלָה. —*shall conceive.* The rendering *hath conceived* is equally allowable; in which case the damsel must be

regarded not only as the betrothed, but as the wife of the prophet. As "the son" was to be a sign to Ahaz, "the damsel," who was to be his mother, must have been then living. — *Immanuel;* i. e. *God-is-with-us*, a symbolical name, — such as was very common with the Hebrews, — to signify that God would be on the side of Judah (Ps. xlvi. 1, 7, 11; Is. xliii. 2; Gen. xxi. 20), and protect and save them from the combined armies of Rezin, king of Syria, and Pekah, king of Israel. As to the *sign*, it seems to have consisted in the symbolical name to be given to the child by his mother. Thus in viii. 18, "Behold, I, and the children which Jehovah hath given me, are signs and tokens in Israel," &c.; i. e. by the names of good omen which through the influence of the Divine spirit have been given us; the word *Isaiah* meaning *Jehovah-is-salvation; Immanuel, God-is-with-us;* and *Shear-Jashub, a remnant shall return.* Such appears to be the obvious meaning of this much disputed passage, on which I merely give my judgment, as in duty bound, without discussing different opinions, or giving all the reasons which might be adduced for my own.

15. *Milk and honey shall he eat,* &c. By comparing this with verse 22, the meaning may appear to be that the land would remain wasted for some time, so that the child Immanuel, in common with the people to which he was a sign, and which he, as it were, represents, should have nothing but milk and honey to eat. This wasting of the land would continue till Immanuel should be able to refuse the evil and choose the good; i. e. attain to some intelligence, so as to make moral distinctions. How many years are denoted, seems not absolutely certain from any passage. But in ch. viii. 3, 4, two or three years, and perhaps more, were to elapse before the promised deliverance should come to Judah through the instrumentality of the Assyrians.

17. *Even the king of Assyria.* These words are regarded as a marginal gloss, that has been introduced into the text by mistake, by Houbigant, Secker, Lowth, Eichhorn, Gesenius, and others.

18. —*fly, bee:* images to denote numerous and vexatious enemies.

20. —*shave,* &c., an image denoting the entire and ignominious desolation of a country. —*with the king of Assyria.* Gesenius suspects these words to be a gloss. It certainly is not the manner of Isaiah to explain a metaphor, which is not doubtful, in this way. If it be a gloss, it is no doubt a correct one.

21, 22. These verses are intended as circumstances indicative of desolation, and not of a mitigation of the calamity. The meaning is, that, on account of the reduced population, pastures should be abundant, and the few inhabitants that were left should abound with milk, &c., being destitute of corn, wine, &c.

VIII. 1. *Hasteth-the-prey, Speedeth-the-spoil.* So Hitzig, Maurer, Fürst. Otherwise, He-hasteth-to-the-prey, He-speedeth-to-the-spoil. In either case, it is a symbolic name, denoting that Damascus and Syria would soon become the spoil of the king of Assyria. In verses 6 and 7, the same thing is threatened against Judah.

7. *The king of Assyria and all his glory.* This also is supposed by Gesenius to be a marginal gloss, though a correct one.

8. —*thy land;* i. e. thy native land.

10. *For God is with us.* The prophet evidently refers to the symbolical name of the child. Ch. vii. 14.

11. —*a strong hand;* i. e. *a powerful inspiration.*

12. —*a confederacy*; i. e. a dangerous confederacy, one threatening destruction to Judah.

14. —*sanctuary;* i. e. refuge, asylum.

16. —*revelation, word;* i. e. which were given to the prophet and by him communicated. Ch. viii. 1–16. —*with my disciples,* &c.; i. e. with their aid and inspection. See verse 2.

20. *To the word,* &c. See verse 16. —*bright morning,* &c.; i. e. a night of affliction shall come upon them, from which no morning of deliverance should come.

IX. 1.—*circle of the gentiles.* This circular district, of which the Hebrew appellation afterwards passed into the proper name *Galilee,* seems at first to have included only a small portion of the tribe of Naphtali, bordering on Phœnicia. See Josh. xx. 7; 2 Kings xv. 29. In subsequent times it included more territory.

5. —*greave;* i. e. the soldier's shoe, high and hollow, bound on with thongs and strongly shod with nails.

6. —*a child, a son;* i. e. a royal child, a king's son. —*upon his shoulder:* referring to an emblem of royalty usually worn on the shoulder, whether a sceptre or a robe; or perhaps merely to the circumstance that a burden is usually borne upon the shoulder. —*mighty potentate,* or *hero.* There is much room for doubt whether the rendering *mighty potentate* or *hero,* or *mighty God,* should be preferred. The general meaning of both renderings is the same. If the rendering "mighty God" be preferred, the meaning will be, that the promised king will be powerful and invincible like God. See Ezek. xxxi. 11; xxxii. 21; Job xli. 25. The note of the well known German commentator, Maurer, is a good one: "That these words, i. e. *mighty potentate,* or *mighty God,* are not to be separated, is evident from ch. x. 21, where they are joined. But it is a question whether *mighty hero,* Ges., or *mighty God,* Ros., is the true rendering. For in ch. x. 21, where the words are applied to the Deity, the rendering *mighty hero* is suitable, since Jehovah is often called a hero, [mighty in battle,] as in Ps. xxiv. 8. So in this passage, i. e Is. ix. 6, where it is applied to the Messiah, it may be rendered *mighty God,* as well as *mighty hero;* for kings are often called gods, as in Ps. lxxxii. 6, (comp. Zech. xii. 8,) and the Messiah is the most noble of kings. It is hard to say, therefore, which of these renderings is to be preferred. My mind, however, inclines to adopt *mighty hero* as the correct version, on account of a similar passage in Ezek. xxxii. 21; xxxi. 11." —*everlasting father;* i. e. perpetual guardian and friend of his people. Another version, adopted by some respectable scholars, is *father of spoil* or *booty,* i. e. divider of spoil. —*prince of peace;* i. e. prince

who brings peace to his people. It appears from the connection that the Messianic prince was to establish peace by utterly prostrating the enemies of his people.

Ch. IX. 8 – X. 4. "This whole passage," says Lowth with great justice, "reduced to its proper and entire form, and healed of the dislocation which it suffers by the absurd division of the chapters, makes a distinct prophecy, and a just poem, remarkable for the regularity of its disposition, and the elegance of its plan." It was probably written soon after the events described in 2 Kings xv. 29, xvi. 7, &c.

15. This explanation is rather too flat to have proceeded from the prophet. It looks like a gloss, and is supposed to be such by several eminent critics.

20. —*flesh of his arm;* i. e. of him that should be his help and strength The image denotes the inveterate hostility between the tribes.

X. 3. —*your glory;* i. e. your precious things, wealth in which you glory.

12. —*fruit,* &c.; i. e. his boasting, which follows.

15. —*not wood;* i. e. very different from wood, — the maker of the staff.

16. —*fat ones;* i. e. his stout, strong warriors.

17. —*his thorns and briers;* i. e. the army of the Assyrians, which is no more able to resist God, than thorns and briers to resist a fire.

18. —*forest, field,* &c.; i. e. his warriors. —*spirit even to the flesh;* i. e. entirely, altogether. The following line seems also to make it probable that the proverbial expression above intimates the faintness of spirit, as well as weakness of body, which would precede their destruction.

22. — *overflow with righteousness;* i. e. bring in righteousness like a flood.

27. —*fat steer;* lit. *Thy yoke shall break on account of fatness.* It seems to be a metaphor, imperfectly expressed, drawn from a steer, who, in the fulness of strength and spirits, breaks the yoke.

28. *He is come,* &c. A description of the Assyrian army approaching Jerusalem.

34. *Lebanon:* an image denoting the proud Assyrian host.

XI. 10. —*gentiles;* i. e. foreign nations.

13. —*enmity in Judah;* lit. enemies of Judah; i. e. enemies of Ephraim within Judah.

14. —*fly upon the shoulders:* an image drawn from birds of prey, which pounce on the backs of those animals which they mean to seize. It seems to represent the Israelites as invading the Philistines, who shall turn their backs on them, or flee before them.

15. *Egyptian sea;* i. e. *the Red sea.* But as *the river* in the next line undoubtedly denotes the Euphrates, which now separated the captives in Assyria from their native land, the Egyptian sea may be used in a figurative sense to denote as great an obstacle as that which was in the way of the Hebrews when pursued by Pharaoh. It may, however, be understood literally. See verse 11.

XIII. 2. *Cry aloud to them;* i. e. to the Medes. See verse 17.

3. — *consecrated ones;* i. e. chosen, prepared, and set apart for war, as if for a sacred office, or for the accomplishment of the purposes of God against Babylon. — *proud exulters;* i. e. the Persians, who are called by Herodotus, I. 89, "very proud by nature."

4. *The noise,* &c. Here the prophet seems to listen, and to hear at a distance the sound of the approaching army.

6. — *Like a destruction:* a destructive storm, &c.

10. — *the stars of heaven,* &c. "The Hebrew poets, to express happiness, prosperity, the instauration and advancement of states, kingdoms, and potentates, make use of images taken from the most striking parts of nature, from the heavenly bodies, from the sun, moon, and stars, which they describe as shining with increased splendor, and never setting; the moon becomes like the meridian sun, and the sun's light is augmented sevenfold; see Is. xxx. 26. New heavens and a new earth are created, and a brighter age commences. On the contrary, the overthrow and destruction of kingdoms is represented by opposite images; the stars are obscured, the moon withdraws her light, and the sun shines no more; the earth quakes, and the heavens tremble, and all things seem tending to their original chaos. See Joel ii. 10; iii. 15, 16; Amos viii. 9; Matt. xxiv. 29." The foundation of these images, which is not mentioned by Lowth, may be the circumstance that the Deity is commonly represented as interposing for judgment in dark clouds, tempests, &c., *which hide the sun,* &c. Some refer the foundation of these images to the emotions of the mind produced by calamity and danger, or the reverse; and suppose the passages in which they occur to mean, that in calamity everything looks dark and gloomy, the sun seems to shine less brightly, &c., and that in prosperity all nature seems to acquire new beauty and splendor.

22. *Wolves, jackals.* Gesenius gives the rendering *jackals* for both the Hebrew terms here rendered *jackals* and *wolves.* Perhaps the latter term, תַּן, included several howling animals, *the jackal, wolf, wild dog,* &c.

XIV. 12. *Lucifer,* i. e. morning-star. This traditional rendering of the Sept., Vulg., Targ., Rabbin., is best suited to the connection, and has some support from etymology. Otherwise, taking the word as a verb, "Howl, son of the morning," as in xiv. 31.

13. — *the mount of assembly,* &c. A high mountain where the gods were supposed to hold their assemblies, and which seems to have occupied the same place in the Babylonian mythology as Olympus in the Grecian. Compare what is said of mount Meru, in the Hindoo theology. See Southey's Curse of Kehama, Book X. and the notes.

31. — *a smoke;* i. e. clouds of dust caused by an invading army.

XV. 1. *Ar of Moab.* Ar was the metropolis of Moab, situated on the southern bank of the Arnon, now called Rabba. — *Kir of Moab* Kir was a fortified city in Moab now called Kerrek, or Karrak.

2. — *the temple;* i. e. of their gods.

5. *Eglath-shelishijah.* This phrase occurs elsewhere only in Jer. xlviii. 34. Taking both passages into view, it seems most probable that it is a proper name.

9. — *a lion;* i. e. an enemy; perhaps Judah. Comp. Gen. xlix. 9.

XVI. 1. — *the lambs.* These were probably due as tribute from Moab. See 2 Sam. viii. 2; 2 Kings iii. 4.

2. — *nest;* i. e. the young in the nest, nestlings.

3–5. These verses seem to be the language of the Moabitish fugitives to the Jews. Verse sixth contains the answer of the Jews. No idiom is more common in the Old Testament than the omission of the words *saying, saith he, say they,* &c. — *Offer counsel; give decision.* The Jews seem to be exhorted to intervene, and arbitrate between the Moabites and their enemies.

4. — *my outcasts;* lit. my outcasts of Moab; i. e. of me, Moab.

8. *They reached,* &c. A hyperbolical description of the shoots of the vine. — *the sea;* i. e. the Dead Sea.

14. — *like the years of a hireling;* i. e. it will happen at this exact time, as the hireling leaves off work at the appointed hour.

XVII. 10. — *foreign soil;* i. e. far-fetched, valuable shoots.

11. — *day of possession;* i. e. the time when you expect to take possession of the harvest.

XVIII. 1. — *rustling wings;* i. e. of armies; referring, at the same time, to the noise of the wings of armies and that of the wings of birds. The country intended was probably Ethiopia, and a portion of Egypt, probably Upper Egypt, formerly united with it under a powerful monarch, Tirhakah, hostile to the Assyrians. The prophet seems to intend to give this nation, regarded as the ally or friend of Israel, an intimation of the designs of God with respect to the destruction of the Assyrians.

2. — *tall and fair.* More literally, *drawn out,* and *polished* or *made smooth;* hence *shining, brilliant,* and hence *fair, beautiful.* In xlv. 14 the Ethiopians are said to be *men of stature.* As they were not remarkable for extent of territory, it seems best to understand the terms of personal tallness and a smooth, glossy, fair skin. Herodotus, III. 20, calls the Ethiopians "the largest and fairest of all men." Some have, from the idea of a *polished* or *sharpened* sword, supposed *fierce* to be the meaning of the epithet under consideration. But this seems forced. I should have preferred the more literal rendering, *polished, shining,* or *brilliant;* but according to English usage these terms cannot be well applied here.

4, 5. *I will sit still,* &c. I will be quiet and suffer the enemy to proceed to a certain extent without interruption; *but before the vintage,* or before they have accomplished their plans, I will interpose, and bring sudden destruction upon them.

6. — *upon it;* i. e. upon the vineyard. But by the shoots and branches

are to be understood, not the productions of the earth, but the dead bodies of enemies.

XIX. 10. — *pillars;* the pillars of the state; the principal men.

14. — *mingled;* a metaphor drawn from the practice of mingling spices, &c. with wine, thus making it more intoxicating.

17. — *to whom,* &c.; lit. *to whom one mentions it.*

18. *City of the Sun.* There seems to be little doubt that Heliopolis, elsewhere called On and Bethshemesh, is the city intended. See note on Jer. xliii. 13. But on account of the various readings, and other circumstances, it is doubtful what name is here given to it. The rendering *City of the Sun* is according to the established meaning of the Hebrew word. See Job ix. 7; Judg. viii. 13, xiv. 18. In the former edition I rendered the phrase *City of Deliverance,* as Rosenmueller rendered the word on one account, and Gesenius on another. I still think my former rendering preferable, if it could be supported on philological grounds. For it is the custom of the prophets in such cases to give, not mere proper names, but symbolical names, — names significant of some trait of character, or of some action or event, as in Jer. xxxiii. 16, xlviii. 19. But for the rendering *Deliverance* there is no support in Hebrew usage, and only a doubtful analogy in the Syriac, according to Ros., and in the Arabic, according to Ges. If the writer had meant to express the idea of *deliverance* in the name, why did he not make use of a Hebrew word for the purpose? Besides, the name *City of the Sun* may be emphatic, as the name of the place where was a temple for the worship of the sun. It may be mentioned as remarkable that the city should swear by Jehovah of hosts, which was called the City of the Sun from the circumstance that it was a place celebrated for sun-worship.

23. — *shall worship;* i. e. Jehovah.

XXI. 1. — *it cometh;* i. e. the army of the Medes and Persians.

2. *Go up,* &c. These are the words of Jehovah, which the prophet hears in his vision. For the sake of dramatic vivacity the words *saying, saith he, saith the Lord,* are often omitted. So verse 5. — *All sighing;* i. e. caused by the tyranny and oppression of Babylon.

5. *Arise,* &c.; i. e. There is a cry, To arms! in consequence of information from the watch.

9. — *cast broken,* &c.; i. e. by Cyrus with the Medes and Persians.

10. *O my threshing;* i. e. O my oppressed, trampled-upon people of Israel.

11, 12. The meaning of this short and enigmatical prophecy cannot be given with confidence. The people of Dumah, a Gentile city on the confines of Syria and Arabia, and beyond Seir, seem to have been alarmed by some impending calamity, perhaps the probable approach of an Assyrian army, and to have sent to the great prophet of Israel to inquire what hope he could give them in view of their threatened *night* of calamity. The answer seems to be one of discouragement

The prophet seems to say that, after the morning of undisturbed peace which they had enjoyed, they must expect a night of calamity; as in the natural world night follows morning. The prophet seems also to say, that, though they belonged to the Gentile world, they might inquire of a prophet of the true God, and to encourage them to come again. Possibly the word *return*, in the last line, may mean *repent*, or *turn to God*, as a condition of receiving a favorable answer. But in this connection, and in reply to Gentiles, an exhortation to repentance could hardly have been expressed in this single word.

XXII. 1. — *valley of vision;* i. e. Jerusalem, so called on account of the prophets, that published their messages in it.

8. *The veil*, &c.; i. e. She is reduced to the last degree of disgrace and wretchedness; the image being drawn from a matron, who is insulted and abused. — *in such a day*, &c. They are represented as looking round for merely human resources, instead of looking to God for help.

15. It has been supposed that Shebna was a foreigner; at least, that he was a man of mean birth. The prophet may be supposed to address him while standing near the superb monument the erection of which he was superintending, which he may have placed near the sepulchres of the kings.

16. — *a habitation;* i. e. a sepulchre.

22. — *key*, &c. An image denoting the highest office which a king could give to a subject.

23. — *as a peg*. A large spike, or peg, was usually inserted into the strong walls of Oriental houses when they were constructed, upon which were hung various articles of furniture. It denotes figuratively the security of Eliakim, and the extent of his ability to give wealth and honor to all his family. — *a glorious seat;* i. e. his father's house, and all his own family, shall be gloriously seated, shall flourish in honor and prosperity, and shall depend upon him, and be supported by him.

24. — *all the glory;* i. e. all that shall be made honorable through his influence. — *Every small vessel*, &c.; i. e. all his family and dependants, from the lowest to the highest, will be supported by his authority and power.

25. This verse seems from the connection to refer to Shebna, not to Eliakim.

XXIII. 1. — *ships of Tarshish;* i. e. Tyrian ships, which were sent to Tarshish, a colony of Tyre in Spain.

2. — *did crowd;* i. e. either with merchandise, or, hyperbolically, with their own persons.

4. *I have not travailed;* i. e. I am as if I had not travailed, &c., I am now childless; i. e. My citizens have been destroyed by war, famine, &c.

10. — *daughter of Tarshish;* i. e. Tarshish itself, or its inhabitants, which formerly suffered from the oppressions and exactions of Tyre, but is now the free possessor of her own territory. See note on ch. i. 8.

11. *Canaan ;* i. e. Phœnicia.

12. — *daughter of Sidon;* i. e. Sidon itself, the Sidonians.

17. — *hire, harlot,* &c. These words are here used figuratively to denote the revenue which was gained by the Syrians from commerce with various foreign nations.

XXIV. 1. That Chapters XXIV. – XXVII. form one connected prophecy, is the nearly unanimous opinion of the best commentators. Modern critics, such as Gesenius, Ewald, Maurer, and others, are of opinion, on historical and æsthetical grounds, that it could not have been written by Isaiah, but by some prophet near the close of the exile at Babylon, or soon after the return from it.

4. *The world;* i. e. the kingdom, as in xiii. 11. So in the New Testament, Luke ii. 1; Acts xi. 28.

16. *The plunderers.* In the original we have an instance of the paronomasia, the same root being five times repeated, thus: *The plunderers plunder, yea, the plunder the plunderers plunder.*

20. — *a hammock:* suspended upon a tree, in which the watchman of the fruit in the Eastern gardens used to sit, to guard himself from surprise from some wild beast. See Niebuhr's *Description of Arabia,* p. 128.

22. — *be visited;* i. e. in mercy, for deliverance. See xxiii. 17; Jer. xxvii. 22; xxxii. 5.

23. *The moon shall be confounded,* &c.; i. e. Jehovah shall reign in Jerusalem with a splendor surpassing that of the sun and moon. — *his ancients;* i. e. the principal men of the Jewish nation, represented as courtiers around a prince.

XXV. 6. — *kept on the lees;* i. e. of wines kept long on the lees. The word used to express the lees in the original signifies the *preservers;* because they preserve the strength and flavor of the wine. "All recent wines, after the fermentation has ceased, ought to be kept on their lees a certain time; which greatly contribute to increase their strength and flavor. Whenever this first fermentation has been deficient, they will retain a more rich and sweet taste than is natural to them in a recent true vinous state; and unless further fermentation is promoted by their lying longer on their own lees, they will never retain their genuine strength and flavor." Sir Edward Barry, Observations on the Wines of the Ancients. *Lowth.*

7. — *covering, veil,* &c.; i. e. He will take away every occasion of grief; everything inconsistent with uninterrupted enjoyment. The head used to be covered with a veil, as an emblem of grief, among the Hebrews. See 2 Sam. xv. 30; Esth. vi. 12.

10. — *dung-pool;* i. e. a place where manure was prepared by casting straw into it.

XXVI. 7. *smooth way;* i. e. in which he is not likely to stumble.

10. — *in the land of uprightness;* i. e. the general prevalence of virtue will exert no influence upon him.

13. We have been under the dominion of foreign kings, and it is only by thine aid that we have been rescued from them, and can again honor thee as our Lord and King.

19. — *thy dead;* i. e. the dead of thy people, O Jehovah. This may be understood literally, like Daniel xii. 2. But it seems more agreeable to the context to understand it figuratively. In the preceding verse the desired restoration of the Jews from extreme national depression is represented by an image drawn from natural birth. In this verse the same thing is promised under the image of a resurrection from death to life. — *of my people;* lit. *my dead bodies.* This may be understood of a literal resurrection, as Gesenius, Umbreit, and others suppose. Comp. Dan. xii. 2. It may, however, be understood figuratively of the regeneration of the state after the captivity. So Henderson, Maurer, and Lowth. Comp. Ezek. xxxvii. 1-14. — *For thy dew:* the dew of God; i. e. the divine power exerted in favor of the Jews, raising them, as it were, from the dead. — *the dew upon plants;* i. e. causing them to revive and flourish. Such is the rapidity with which grass grows in the East, that several travellers describe its appearance, when rain has followed a drought, as a resurrection of vegetable nature. See Calmet's Dictionary, Art. *Grass.* Dr. Russel, in his Natural History of Aleppo, says: "In those hot climates the spring is of short duration. All summer the earth is without rain. Everything is burnt up, and the fields are turned into a desert. But when the autumnal rains fall, a few plentiful showers produce a sudden resurrection of vegetable nature; the pastures are clothed again with grass, the trees are covered with green leaves, and all things assume a fresh and delightful aspect." Another writer says: "And here a strong argument, that may further and most infallibly show the goodness of their soil, shall not escape my pen; most apparent in this, that when the ground there hath been destitute of rain nine months together, and looks all of it like the barren sands in the deserts of Arabia, where there is not one spire of green grass to be found, within a few days after those fat and enriching showers begin to fall, the face of the earth there (as it were by a new resurrection) is so revived, and throughout so renewed, as that it is presently covered all over with a pure green mantle." — Sir T. Roe's Voyage to India, quoted in Calmet's Dict.

XXVII. 1. — *leviathan;* i. e. Babylon. — *fleet;* i. e. to escape, inclined to flee from men.

4. — *thorns and thistles;* i. e. the enemies of the Jews.

5. *Unless they take hold;* i. e. unless the enemies of the Jews submit, and turn to Jehovah. The collocation of the words in the next two lines is in imitation of the Hebrew. It was no doubt designed to give emphasis to the sentiment. It reminds one of the reciprocal Mussulman salutation, "Peace be on you, on you be peace!"

7. — *those that slew him.* I here disregard the Masoretic points.

8. — *by sending her away;* the sending of the Jews into captivity is

represented under the image of the divorce of a wife from her husband. —*punish her;* i. e. the Jewish nation.

9. —*the altar;* i. e. the altar near the temple in Jerusalem, or, as a collective noun, *altars* dedicated to idolatry; or Jehovah's altars, as included in the ruin of Jerusalem.

10. —*fortified city;* i. e. Jerusalem.

11. —*burn them;* i. e. gather them for fuel.

XXVIII. 2. — *a mighty one;* i. e. the king of Assyria.

7. —*even these;* i. e. the inhabitants of Judah, in distinction from Ephraim.

9. —*weaned,* &c. "The scoffers mentioned below, v. 14, are here introduced as uttering their sententious speeches; they treat God's method of dealing with them, and warning them by his prophets, with contempt and derision. 'What,' say they, 'doth he treat us as mere infants, just weaned? Doth he teach us like little children, perpetually inculcating the same elementary lessons, the mere rudiments of knowledge, precept after precept, line after line, here and there, by little and little?'—imitating at the same time, and ridiculing, in v. 10, the concise prophetical manner. God, by his prophet, retorts upon them with great severity their own contemptuous mockery; turning it to a sense quite different from what they intended. 'Yes,' saith he, 'it shall be in fact as you say; ye shall be taught by a strange tongue, and a stammering lip, in a strange country; ye shall be carried into captivity by a people whose language is unintelligible to you, and which ye shall be forced to learn like children: and my dealing with you shall be according to your own words; it shall be command upon command for your punishment.'" — *Lowth.*

15. —*covenant with death,* &c. The meaning of the irreligious Jews seems to be, that by means of their strongholds and their military preparations, perhaps also by promised aid from Egypt (comp. ch. xxx.), they were in no danger from enemies who might invade or pass through their country. —*overflowing scourge.* This is what is called a mixed metaphor, probably referring to the Assyrian army invading and passing through Judæa on its way toward Egypt. —*falsehood, deceit;* i. e. the merely human defences and alliances, which the prophet regards as false and deceitful, and puts his own view of such defences and alliances into the mouth of the mockers. It is as if the mockers had said, We put our trust in means of defence which you the prophets regard as deceitful and false.

16. — *laid in Zion as a foundation a stone.* There are three opinions in regard to the application of this verse. The most recent is that of Hitzig, Ewald, and Knobel, that the stone is mount Zion itself, or the temple on it, considered as the dwelling-place of Jehovah and the seat of his worship and of the theocratic government of his people. The prophet, according to this view, represents that safety is to be found, not in foreign alliances, but in trust in Jehovah and in his worship and service. The second opinion is that the great future deliverer, the

Messiah, is denoted. The third opinion is that of Grotius, Gesenius, and others, that Hezekiah, the reigning king at the time, is referred to. Against the second opinion it may be urged that the stone appears to be represented as already laid in Zion, and recommended as the object of trust and confidence to the contemporaries of the prophet in view of the dangers by which they were then surrounded, especially the prospect of an Assyrian invasion. Against the third opinion it seems to be a well-founded objection, that King Hezekiah, or any actual reigning king, could hardly have been represented as in so high a degree the object of confidence and the source of protection. The epithets applied to the stone are too grand to admit of this theory. Besides, we should have expected a more explicit indication of the reigning king, if he had been intended. Perhaps this last remark may also apply to the second theory. The use made of passages of the Old Testament by writers of the New has often no reference to the primary meaning, or that which was in the mind of the writer, but only to an allegorical sense. The first opinion respecting this highly figurative passage may seem liable to the fewest objections, and to deserve the preference. Comp. Zech. xii. 3; Is. x. 32, xiv. 32, xxix. 2, 7, xxx. 29, xxxi. 4; Ps. lxxxvii. 1, 2. — *He that trusteth*, &c.; i. e. He that trusteth in Jehovah, who will defend Jerusalem, will not betake himself to flight, but seek safety in mount Zion and in the city of God's peculiar love and care.

19. — *every morning*, &c. Not repeated invasions are denoted, but the successive evils of one threatened invasion.

21. *Perazim*, &c. See 2 Sam. v. 20. — *strange act*, &c.; i. e. not only to inflict punishment in general, but to inflict it upon his own peculiar people, the descendants of Abraham, Isaac, and Jacob. — *strange work*; i. e. to deal with the people of Israel in a very different manner from that in which he had dealt with them; i. e. to punish them severely, instead of bestowing peculiar favor upon them.

23 – 29. Comp. ch. xxvii. 7 – 9.

XXIX. 2. — *as Ariel.* Here is an allusion to the etymological signification of the name which is given to Jerusalem, *the lion of God;* i. e. she shall be an invincible city. See verse 7.

9. *Be in amazement*, &c. More strictly, perhaps, *Amaze yourselves, and be amazed! Blind yourselves, and be blind!* I have little doubt that in each clause we have only different forms of the same Hebrew verb, used in substantially the same sense. It is an instance of the paronomasia, which was regarded as a great elegance in Hebrew composition. Similar instances of strengthening the language by repetition are found in Hab. i. 5; Is. xxiv. 19, xxvii. 5; Zeph. ii. 1. The explanation of this verse is that of Vitringa in his very satisfactory note, Ewald, Hitzig, and Gesenius in his Commentary. As to its general import, it seems to be to set forth the stupidity and blindness of the Jewish rulers, who disregarded the utterances of the prophets. Comp. vi. 10. The German imitates the Hebrew paronomasia better than

the English. Thus Ewald: "Erstaunt und staunt! Erblindet und blindet!"

10. — *the prophets, the seers.* Koppe, Eichhorn, and Gesenius regard these words as explanatory glosses; a very plausible conjecture.

21. — *to fail;* i. e. in his suit or cause.

XXX. 6. *The loaded beasts;* i. e. carrying presents for Egypt. If this line be genuine, it must be rendered as in the text; or, more literally, *The burden of the beasts southward.* If the meaning be, *The burden,* i. e. *The prophecy, concerning the beasts of the south,* I think it must be an ungenuine title placed there by a later hand; otherwise it would interrupt the connection, and make two pieces out of what the author evidently intended for one.

7. *The Blusterer,* &c.; i. e. making great parade, and affording little help, through cowardice, inactivity, or selfishness. There is a play upon the word *Rahab,* a poetical name for Egypt, which denotes *arrogant, proud.*

13. — *breach;* i. e. rent, or crack.

18. *And yet.* See Ges. Lex. on the word לָכֵן.

26. — *the wound,* &c.; i. e. from the Assyrians.

28. — *the winnowing-fan,* &c. This was a sort of shovel with which the grain, mixed with cut-up straw and stubble, was tossed into the air, so that the wind might separate them. Hence the meaning that God would scatter the nations as the husbandman scatters the mixed straw and grain, and scatter them, not for the purpose of purification, but with the fan of destruction.

XXXI. 7. — *for sin;* i. e. instruments of sin. See Am. viii. 14.

9. — *fire,* &c.; i. e. upon the altar.

XXXII. 13. — *upon all the houses,* &c.; i. e. upon their ruins.

15. *And the wilderness,* &c. Comp. xxix. 17, &c. This seems to be the language of poetry, denoting in general that there shall be a great change in the state of things; that the high shall be abased, and the lowly exalted.

16. — *wilderness, fruitful field;* i. e. in every part of the land.

19. — *the forest;* i. e. the army of the enemy. — *the city,* &c. From the connection, especially ver. 13, it would seem that Jerusalem is intended. It would *be brought very low* before the great deliverance should come. Others suppose Nineveh, or Babylon, the principal city of the enemies of the Jews, to be intended.

XXXIII. 4. — *as the locust gathereth.* As locusts in vast numbers cover a field and devour its fruits irresistibly and with impunity, so shall the Israelites take possession of the spoils of the vanquished enemies. They shall gather spoils at pleasure, without resistance and with impunity.

7. — *the mighty men;* i. e. the Jewish leaders, who had been sent as ambassadors to the king of Assyria.

9. The utter desolation of the land by enemies, is described in highly poetical language.

14. — *devouring fire*, &c. When the wicked and idolatrous Israelites saw the nations, or the Assyrian army, destroyed, ver. 12, by the interposition of God, as by devouring fire, they were alarmed, being conscious that they had by their own idolatry offended God, who had inflicted such destruction upon the Assyrians. They are therefore represented as exclaiming, Who among us can dwell in devouring fire, before which so vast an army is as dry thorns? Who can dwell in everlasting burnings, which have burned up the Assyrians like lime?

17. — *a wide-extended land;* i. e. thou shalt not be hemmed in by a siege, but shalt go freely and safely about the country.

"Juvat ire, et Dorica castra,
Desertosque videre locos, litusque relictum."
Virg. Æn. II. 28.

18. — *past terror:* "haec olim meminisse juvabit," Virg. — *scribe;* i. e. the secretary who prescribed the tribute to be collected from the inhabitants. — *numbered the towers;* i. e. the commander of the enemy's forces, who took a survey of the fortifications of the city for the purpose of finding the best place for making an assault upon it.

20. — *cords;* which bound the tent to stakes or pins, driven into the ground.

21. — *broad streams*, &c.; Jerusalem shall not need to be defended by broad streams, like Babylon. God would be a defence, which no ship could pass through.

23. *Thy ropes*, &c. This is addressed to Assyria. The mention of ships in ver. 21 leads the prophet to compare the enemy to a ship wrecked in a storm. Comp. Horace, Od. 14, Lib. 1.

XXXIV., XXXV. The great majority of German critics, such as Eichhorn, Gesenius, Rosenmueller, De Wette, Maurer, Hitzig, Ewald, Umbreit, and Knobel, suppose this discourse to have been written not by Isaiah, but by some unknown poet, who lived at the time of the Jewish exile in Babylon. Some of them suppose that he lived about the close of it. I have no doubt of the correctness of this opinion.

XXXIV. 3. — *mountains flow down*, &c.; i. e. as it were be dissolved in it.

4. *And all the hosts*, &c. The political revolution by which mighty kingdoms are destroyed is represented poetically and hyperbolically as a revolution of the whole natural world. See note on xiii. 10. — *melt away;* viz. like lamps, or wax candles. "The metaphor," says Vitringa, "is borrowed from the prevailing notion, that the heaven was a solid spherical expanse, in which the stars were set as gems, and that this by heat, &c. might be melted and dissolved." The representation that the stars are fixed in the sky like lamps, or candles, occurs also in Hor. Epod. XVII 5, "Defixa sidera cœlo"; also in Pliny, Nat. Hist.,

Cap. VIII. § 6, "sidera, quæ affixa diximus mundo." Comp. Matt. xxiv. 9; Apoc. vi. 13. — *like a scroll;* somewhat like an ancient volume, or book-roll, which used to be wound round a stick, as a map in modern times.

5. — *my sword,* &c.; i. e. the sword of God shall be, as it were, drunk with wrath.

9. — *into pitch,* &c. This language is to be regarded as metaphorical, denoting entire and awful destruction. It may be borrowed from the history of Sodom and Gomorrah.

10. *None shall pass through it.* This is to be understood figuratively, as expressive of great desolation. There is no more reason to understand it in a literal and exact sense, than the expressions in the preceding verse.

11. — *measuring-line,* &c.; i. e. it shall be completely destroyed, as it were by rule and system.

12. — *a kingdom;* perhaps by choosing a king, and preventing the kingdom from being dissolved.

14. — *night-spectre.* Here the poet alludes to a popular superstition of the Jews respecting the existence of a night-spectre. According to the Rabbins, it bore the form of a female elegantly dressed, and lay in wait for children by night. Similar are the Greek and Roman fables respecting the female Empousa, the Onokentauroi, the Lamiæ, Striges; and the Arabian Ghûles, i. e. female monsters, dwelling in deserts, and tearing men in pieces.

16. — *book of Jehovah.* The prophet seems to contemplate the insertion of his prophecy in the sacred books of the Jews, from which those that followed him might judge of the correctness of his prophecy.

XXXV. 1. — *the rose.* I have retained this rendering on account of the poetical associations connected with it. But it seems most probable that a crocus is referred to, *Colchicum autumnale.*

7. — *the glowing sand,* &c. This is commonly supposed to refer to the phenomenon frequent in the deserts of Arabia and Egypt, and occasionally seen in the southern parts of Russia and France, called *the mirage.* It consists in this, that the desert, either wholly or in parts, presents the appearance of the sea, or of a lake, so that the most experienced travellers are sometimes deceived. Accordingly the meaning of the line will be, that the parched desert, which has the appearance of a lake, shall be changed into a real lake. Almost all Eastern travellers have noticed the phenomenon. It is not certain, however, that there is a reference to it in this passage, as the sense is perfect if we understand the term as denoting burning sand, without any false appearance.

Chapters XXXVI., XXXVII., XXXVIII., and XXXIX. consist chiefly of an account of the invasion of Sennacherib in the latter part of the reign of Hezekiah. It is quite evident, on a careful comparison, that this account is borrowed, with alterations, from 2 Kings xviii., xix., and 2 Chron. xxxii. Or possibly this passage and that in Kings may both have been derived from an older document. For this and other reasons, it could not have been written by Isaiah. For the Second Book of Kings closes with the reign of Zedekiah, long after Isaiah's death.

XXXVI. 8. *Engage*, &c. There is the same ambiguity in the original as in the English word *engage*. It may mean *enter into conflict*, or *enter into an agreement*. —*riders*. Rabshakeh here alludes to the ignorance of horsemanship among the Jews. There was no scarcity of warriors among the Jews, but they were unable to ride.

12. —*to eat*, &c.; i. e. unless the people hear me, they will be reduced to the same extreme misery which is coming upon you, their leaders.

22. —*scribe*; i. e. the king's. —*annalist*: whose duty it was to record the deeds of the king and the events of his reign.

XXXVII. 3. —*the children*; i. e. we are in as miserable, helpless a condition as a woman in travail, who is so far exhausted as not to be able to bring her infant into the world.

7. —*a spirit*, &c.; i. e. I will, by a divine influence, induce him to return.

25. —*with the sole of my feet*; i. e. advancing with my immense army, which requires rivers to quench its thirst.

29. —*ring into thy nose*: a metaphor drawn from the practice of putting a ring into the nostrils of wild beasts, such as the bear, the buffalo, the lion, in order to lead them, and manage them at pleasure.

XXXVIII. 11. —*stillness*; i. e. *the realm of stillness*, viz. Sheol.

12. —*rolled up*, &c.; i. e. like the piece of cloth which the weaver rolls together when finished. —*the thrum*: which tied the web to the weaver's beam. An image of death drawn from the weaver, who, when his work is finished, cuts it out of the loom.

XL. 2. —*expiated*: more literally, *paid off*, *discharged*; i. e. by the punishment which she has endured in the captivity at Babylon.

3. *A voice crieth*, &c.; i. e. the voice of God, which the prophet seems to hear. Comp. ver. 6; Hab. ii. 1. "The idea is taken from the practice of Eastern monarchs, who, whenever they entered upon an expedition or took a journey, especially through deserts and unpractised countries, sent harbingers before them to prepare all things for their passage, and pioneers to open the passes, to level the ways, and to remove all impediments."

6. *All flesh*, &c. The principal idea is, the stability of the promises of God, which is more conspicuous when contrasted with the frailty of man.

7. —*breath of Jehovah*: referring to a hot east wind, which destroyed every green thing where it prevailed. See Exod. xv. 8; Job xv. 30;

Ps. ciii. 16. — *Truly the people*, &c. This line is not found in the Septuagint version; it seems to interrupt the sense and the parallelism, and may be a gloss accidentally introduced from the margin into the text since the Septuagint version was made.

11. — *nursing ewes.* See Gen. xxxiii. 13. "Their flocks," says Sir J. Chardin, speaking of those who live in the East after the patriarchal manner, "feed down the places of their encampment so quick, by the great numbers that they have, that they are obliged to move them too often, which is very destructive to their flocks on account of their young ones, who have not strength enough to follow." Harmer, p. 126.

13. — *searched out ;* lit. *weighed.*

15. — *very little thing ;* lit. *an atom.*

19. — *silver chains ;* i. e. for the purpose of supporting it, or fastening it to the wall.

22. — *above the circle of the earth ;* i. e. surveying from the height of heaven the round flat surface of the earth, surrounded by water. — *as a canopy* or *awning.* "It is usual," says the Oriental traveller, Dr. Shaw, "in the summer season, and upon all occasions when a large company is to be received, to have the court sheltered from heat, or inclemency of the weather, by a velum, umbrella, or veil, as I shall call it; which, being expanded on ropes from one side of the parapet wall to the other, may be folded or unfolded at pleasure."

26. — *faileth to appear.* The heavenly bodies are represented as a vast army, assembled as for a military review.

27. *My way ;* i. e. my condition. — *passeth by ;* i. e. he neglects it; suffers it to pass by, without attending to it.

XLI. 1. — *strength ;* i. e. in order to answer me.

7. — *fastened it ;* i. e. the image, the idol.

9. — *led by the hand ;* lit. taken hold of. See v. 13.

15. — *thrashing-wain.* See Calmet's Dictionary upon the word *Thrash.*

27. — *behold them !* i. e. the returning exiles from Babylon.

28. — *no man ;* i. e. who could predict the future. — *counsel ;* i. e. respecting the future.

XLII. 1. — *my servant ;* i. e. the Jewish church ; the pious Israelites collectively ; the better part of the people with the prophets at their head, as distinguished from the whole nation. Comp. ver. 18 – 22, xliii. 8, 10, xlix. 1 – 9, l. 4 – 10, lii. 13, liv. 17, xliii. 10 ; also the Introduction, pp. xlix. – lvi. — *law.* This term, in ver. 1, 2, 3, seems to denote the law included in the religion of Jehovah.

6. — *a covenant ;* i. e. a mediator. By a mediator is meant one who, like Moses, should be the medium of God's communications to his people, a restorer of the theocracy.

19. — *blind, if not my servant,* &c. Compare with verses 1 – 4. There is the same variation of language respecting *the servant of God* in these chapters, as there is in the New Testament respecting the Christian Church. Sometimes she is the pillar and ground of the

truth, and sometimes she has defiled her garments. So Israel, the servant of God, is sometimes described as he was meant to be, and as he should have been, as in xlii. 1–4, lii. 13–liii. 12; sometimes as he actually was. The name is sometimes given to the whole race, and sometimes to the faithful portion of it; sometimes to the real, sometimes to the nominal Israel. Comp. Rom. ix. 6.

21. — *his goodness' sake:* otherwise, *for the sake of his salvation.*

XLIII. 1. — *called thee,* &c.; i. e. specially chosen thee. See Exod. xxxi. 2.

3. *Egypt for thy ransom,* &c.; i. e. I will give such rich and powerful nations as Egypt, Ethiopia, and Sheba a prey to a conqueror instead of thee; as it were, for thy ransom. Rosenmueller, however, adduces several curious quotations from Arabic writers to show that the meaning is simply, that the Jewish nation was *dearer to God* than the above-mentioned nations.

10. *And my servant,* &c.; i. e. and ye are my servant, whom I have chosen for the express purpose of making known my laws and religion. Here the parallelism of the plural term *witnesses* with the singular *servant* is a strong confirmation of the opinion that the *servant of God* denotes a body of men, the Jewish church, the Israel of God. — *I am He;* i. e. the Being described in the preceding verses, the only Being acquainted with future events, and possessing other attributes of Deity.

14. — *to the ships,* &c.; i. e. in order to escape from the invading enemy.

20. — *shall honor me;* i. e. on account of the unexpected fruitfulness of the wilderness, and the abundant supply of water.

27. — *forefathers:* otherwise, *first father,* referring to Jacob, or Adam.

XLIV. 5. The first clause may be rendered, *Another shall write upon his hands, To Jehovah;* i. e. I belong to Jehovah. See xlix. 16. — *call upon the name,* &c.; i. e. look to the nation of Israel for help, as possessing the true religion, and being under the protection of Jehovah, &c. — *praise the name;* lit. *address flatteringly the name,* &c.

10. *Who hath formed,* &c. A question addressed to idolaters.

11. — *all his fellows;* i. e. all who assisted him to make the idol.

20. — *toileth for ashes;* lit. feedeth upon, &c.; i. e. pursues with delight that which will prove vain and unprofitable, like ashes instead of food.

XLV. 3. — *treasures of darkness;* i. e. long hidden in dark vaults. "Sardis and Babylon, when taken by Cyrus, were the wealthiest cities in the world. Crœsus, celebrated beyond all the kings of that age for his riches, gave them up to Cyrus, with an exact account in writing of the whole, containing the particulars with which each wagon was loaded, when they were carried away; and they were delivered to Cyrus at the palace at Babylon." Xenoph. Cyrop. Lib. VIII.

4. *I have called thee*, &c. I have called thee to thine honorable office, and that expressly by name. — *spoken to thee as a friend:* more literally, I have addressed thee in a kind or friendly manner.

7. *I form the light, and create darkness.* It appears to me probable, notwithstanding the doubts of some eminent critics, that the prophet here alludes to the Persian doctrine of two independent principles, a good and an evil. "With reference to this absurd opinion, held by the person to whom this prophecy is addressed, God, by his prophet, in the most significant terms, asserts his omnipotence and absolute supremacy (in this verse); declaring that those powers whom the Persians held to be the original authors of good and evil to mankind, representing them by light and darkness as their proper emblems, are no other than the creatures of God, the instruments which he employs in the government of the world, ordained or permitted by him in order to execute his wise and just decrees; and that there is no power, either of good or evil, independent of the one Supreme God, infinite in power and in goodness." — *Lowth.*

11. *Ask of me*, &c. Ye can ask me with success; with a prospect of having your wishes fulfilled. For I know and control the future. Ye may therefore commit your future destination with confidence to my care.

15. — *hidest thyself;* i. e. thy purposes.

19. — *in secret*, &c.; i. e. I have by my prophets spoken publicly, freely, and plainly. It is not necessary to suppose that the prophet alludes to heathen oracles, or even to Jewish necromancers.

XLVI. 1. *Bel.* A Babylonian deity, the same as Baal of the Phœnicians and Syrians. Some suppose that, according to the astrological mythology of the East, the sun, others that the planet Jupiter, is denoted. It was called by the Romans Jupiter Belus. — *Nebo*, another Babylonian god, probably represents the planet Mercury, regarded as the scribe of the heavens. It was customary in ancient times, especially in the East, to carry the gods of vanquished nations into the country of the conquerors, not merely for the sake of their valuable ornaments, but from the belief that the destruction of the vanquished country was thereby rendered more complete. — *ye once bore:* in solemn procession.

2. *They cannot rescue the burden;* i. e. the idols, considered as gods, cannot deliver their images.

13. — *my glory;* i. e. the glory which it is in my power alone to bestow.

XLVII. 2. Grinding with the hand-mill was the work of female slaves. See Ex. xi. 5. "It is extremely laborious," says Sir John Chardin, "and esteemed the lowest work in the house." — *the streams:* in flight from the enemy, or in going into captivity.

10. *Thy wisdom,* &c.; i. e. thy state policy, of which thou art so vain.

11. — *the dawn;* i. e. the succeeding dawn, or remedy, or the preceding dawn, or origin. See viii. 20. — *to expiate;* i. e. to avert or to escape by a sin-offering.

15. The first clause of this verse may refer to sorcerers, &c., and the last to nations which had been connected in friendship and commerce with Babylon.

XLVIII. 14. *Who among you;* i. e. Who among the Chaldæan astrologers and wise men.

16. The first three lines of this verse seem to be the language of the Deity, the last that of the prophet. The words *I have been there* seem to imply that the event to which he refers, i. e. the expedition of Cyrus against Babylon, was to take place through the agency of the speaker, i. e. God, who was thus able to inform and commission the prophet. "A quo tempore illud fuit, i. e. existere cœpit, i. e. primi motus Cyri, qui jam cœperunt, et aliquamdiu durârunt." — *Vitringa.*

XLIX. 3. *Israel;* i. e. Thou art the true, the genuine Israel, worthy of that honorable name. The faithful and pious Israelites, at the head of whom were the prophets with the writer, in distinction from the whole nation, ver. 5, are thus named. Comp. li. 7.

19. — *my hands,* &c.; i. e. for the sake of continual remembrance I have delineated, as with paint, the city of Jerusalem upon the palms of my hands. Bishop Lowth remarks: "This is certainly an allusion to some practice, common among the Jews at that time, of making marks on their hands or arms by punctures on the skin, with some sort of sign or representation of the city or temple, to show their affection and zeal for it. They had a method of making such punctures indelible by fire, or by staining. It is well known that the pilgrims at the holy sepulchre get themselves marked in this manner with what are called the ensigns of Jerusalem." Maundrell, p. 126, Amer. edit.

23. — *lick the dust,* &c.: a hyperbolical expression for *prostrate themselves before thee, as thy suppliants.* "It is well known," says Bishop Lowth, "that expressions of submission, homage, and reverence always have been, and are still, carried to a great degree of extravagance in the Eastern countries. When Joseph's brethren were introduced to him, 'they bowed down themselves before him with their faces to the earth.' Gen. xlii. 6. The kings of Persia never admitted any one to their presence without exacting this act of adoration; for that was the proper term for it."

L. 1. This verse intimates that it was not from levity, caprice, passion, or necessity, that he had sent the Jews into captivity; that his conduct was wholly unlike that of a Jewish husband when he gave his wife a bill of divorcement, or a Jewish father when he sold his children to a creditor.

2. — *no man at hand;* i. e. to attend to my admonitions. Jehovah came and called, when he sent his prophets.

4. — *in the manner of the learned.* As the same Hebrew term, למּוּדים is used in both parts of this verse, it is not probable that, in so close a connection, they have a different meaning, otherwise the term might be rendered *learners* or *disciples*, as in ch. xiii. 16; a rendering which at first view seems better suited to the connection. But the meaning may be, *that I*, without a regular education, *may hear in the manner of the learned* prophets. Comp. Amos vii. 14, 15; Is. liv. 13.

11. In reference to *the walking in darkness*, i. e. in calamity, in the preceding verse, the prophet denounces those who try to escape from the darkness by kindling lights of their own, by trusting to their own devices and resources, and rejecting the light from heaven, i. e. the counsels of the prophets.

LI. 1. — *the rock;* i. e. to Abraham and Sarah.

10. *Rahab:* a sort of poetical nickname for Egypt, *rahab* signifying *arrogant.* — *the dragon;* i. e. the crocodile, a common emblem of the same country.

17. — *cup of giddiness;* i. e. the cup of the Divine anger, which causes to reel, makes giddy.

21. — *drunken, and not with wine;* i. e. reduced to a helpless condition by the cup of God's anger.

LII. 3. *For naught;* i. e. the nations gave no price for you, and have no right to retain you. Ye were delivered by me into their hands on account of your sins.

6. — *that said, Behold, here am I!* i. e. that I it was, the true God, Jehovah, who promised my presence and aid, because I keep my promise.

7. *How beautiful*, &c. "The watchmen discern afar off, on the mountains, the messenger bringing the expected and much wished for news of the deliverance from the Babylonish captivity. They immediately spread the joyful tidings, ver. 8, and with a loud voice proclaim that Jehovah is returning to Zion to resume his residence on his holy mountain, which for some time he seemed to have deserted. This is the literal sense of the place.

"'How beautiful upon the mountains are the feet of him that bringeth glad tidings,' is an expression highly poetical for 'How welcome is his arrival! how agreeable are the tidings which he brings!'" — *Lowth.*

It is not necessary to inquire who is denoted by the messenger, and who by the watchmen. The principal thought in the passage is, that glad tidings were brought of the deliverance of the Jews, and it is a part of the poetical embellishment of the scene, that a messenger should be represented as seen running over the mountains to bring them, and that watchmen, stationed upon towers for the purpose of discerning whatever approached the city, should perceive his approach and exultingly pass to each other the news of his arrival.

8. — *eye to eye;* i. e. very near and plainly. See Numb. xiv. 14 — *returneth to Zion.* Comp. Zech. viii. 3; Joel iii. 21.

13. — *my servant*, &c. In the Introduction, pp. xlix. - lvi., I have shown that this term has a collective sense, denoting the people of God, the true Israel, in contradistinction not only from Gentiles, but from Israelites by birth who were unworthy of the name. Some highly respectable interpreters suppose the whole Jewish nation to be denoted, in contradistinction from other nations, or Gentiles. In this latter case the Gentiles would be represented as speaking in liii. 2 – 6.

LIII. 3. — *hide their faces;* i. e. cannot bear to look at. Otherwise, *As one that hideth his face from us;* i. e. as one who, from any cause, leprosy, for instance, is induced to cover his face.

4. — *from above.* This appears to me plainly implied in its connection with the parallel line.

8. — *he was smitten;* lit. *they* were smitten, the blow was upon *them.* The use of the plural pronoun in this place is considered by those who understand the term *servant of Jehovah* in a collective sense as denoting the Jewish nation, or the better part of it, as favorable to that explanation. See xliv. 26.

9. — *the rich man.* The parallelism, the connection of the line with the following, and Scripture usage favor the supposition that *rich* is intended to be synonymous with *wicked* in the preceding line. The idea of pride, oppression, and impiety is often associated with that of wealth in the Scriptures, and supposed to be implied in the term, so that woes are denounced against *the rich* without any express reference to their wickedness. See Job xxvii. 19; Micah vi. 12; Ps. xlix. 6; Luke vi. 24, xvi. 19, &c., xviii. 24, 25; James i. 11, v. 1. See Lachemacher's Observ. on Is. liii. 9. — *his sepulchre.* It is doubtful whether this rendering, or that of the common version, *in his death,* is to be preferred. The former has the parallelism decidedly in its favor. The phrase *in his death* seems also a superfluous appendage. בָּמָה, from which the Greek *βωμός* was probably derived, probably denotes *sepulchre* in Ezek. xliii. 7. It is true that this is a less usual signification of the term; but the writer, having used the common word for sepulchre, קֶבֶר, in the former half of the parallelism, was obliged to employ a less usual term, or a generic term meaning *high place,* in the latter half. Thus in ch. xxii. 16,

> That thou hewest out thy *sepulchre* on high,
> And gravest out *a habitation* for thyself in the rock.

I admit, however, that it is a matter of great doubt which rendering is to be preferred. The Hebrew term is plural in either case: *his sepulchres,* or *his deaths.* Some make this an argument for the collective meaning of the phrase *servant of God.*

10. — *when he hath made:* or, *when thou hast,* &c. — *see posterity;* i. e. have posterity of his own.

11. — *see;* i. e. what is mentioned in the preceding verse.

LIV. 1. *Sing, O thou barren.* The Jewish commonwealth is represented as barren during the exile at Babylon, when, being divorced from Jehovah, their husband, ver. 5, they were not multiplied.

4. — *shame of thy youth;* i. e. the slavery in Egypt. — ***widowhood:*** the captivity of Babylon.

LV. 3. — *sure mercies of David;* i. e. such mercies as were more than once emphatically promised to David. See 2 Sam. vii. 12 – 17, &c.; Ps. lxxxix. 20 – 37.

4. — *him for a commander,* &c.; i. e. the ancient King David, mentioned in the preceding verse. The extent of the dominion promised to David is referred to for the purpose of illustrating the power and glory which shall be given to the Jewish people, when they shall hear the voice of God and obey it. It is only in a typical or allegorical sense that this verse can be applied to the Messiah.

5. — *thou knowest not:* the Jewish people is addressed.

11. — *the word;* i. e. the promise.

LVI. 9. The beasts of the forest are the enemies of the Jews; the flock, the Jews; the watchmen, the prophets, priests, and rulers.

LVII. 1. — *because of the evil.* This may mean, that good men are removed, as a punishment to the people for their wickedness; or, that good men are removed, that they may escape impending calamities.

10. — *life in thy hand;* i. e. vitality, vigor, strength.

19. *I create the fruit;* i. e. by the blessings which I confer, I give cause for thanksgiving.

LVIII. 2. — *judgments which bring salvation:* comp. lix. 9; i. e. punishment of their enemies, with which the salvation of the Jews was supposed to be connected.

8. — *health;* i. e. deliverance, restoration to prosperity.

LIX. 9. — *judgment.* See note on lviii. 2.

14. — *the gate;* i. e. the place where courts were held.

LX. 1. — *shine.* Jerusalem, having long been sitting in darkness, i. e. in affliction, is now invited to enjoy the light of prosperity. See ver. 19, 20. *To shine* is to be bright, to be covered with light.

8. *Who are these?* In his mind's eye the prophet beholds immense hosts hastening toward Jerusalem, and inquires with wonder, Who are these?

13. — *feet rest;* i. e. the temple.

16. *Thou shalt also suck;* i. e. kings shall bring their treasures and resources to enrich thee.

18. *Thou shalt call thy walls, Salvation;* i. e. because they shall be secure against every assault. — *And thy gates, Praise;* i. e. they shall never be entered by an enemy, and thus give thee occasion to praise God.

19. *Light* is often used for prosperity. The meaning, therefore, is, that the light of the sun shall be nothing in comparison with the glorious state of felicity which Jehovah will cause Jerusalem to enjoy.

LXI. 3.—*beautiful crown;* i. e. head-dress, turban, instead of ashes on their heads, the emblem of sorrow.

LXIII. 9. *In all their straits,* &c. A sort of enigmatical expression, meaning that in the most threatening circumstances the protection of God saved them from serious injury.

19.—*called by thy name;* i. e. called the people of Jehovah.

LXIV. 5. *Long,* &c. I am not satisfied with this or any other translation of this line which I have seen. Lowth alters the text by conjecture. The common version has it, *In those,* i. e. in thy ways, *is continuance, and we shall be saved.* De Wette, *In them,* i. e. in our sins, *has been continuance, and shall we be saved?*

8.—*our father;* i. e. our Creator, Author.

LXV. 3.—*on tiles.* The prophet probably alludes to some idolatrous practice prevalent at Babylon. Rosenmueller remarks, that the bricks found in the supposed seat of Babylon in modern times, inscribed with certain characters, may be the relics of the superstition alluded to.

4.—*in sepulchres, in caverns;* i. e. to practise necromancy or divination.

11. *Fortune, Destiny;* or *Gad* and *Meni,* worshipped by Babylonians as gods of fortune, of which the former is supposed to have represented the planet Jupiter, and the latter Venus.

20.—*infant child, old man;* i. e. young and old; i. e. the whole nation shall reach the full measure of human life. Otherwise: There shall not be there an infant of days, (i. e. which lives only a few days,) nor an old man, &c. —*For he that dieth,* &c. And such shall be the length of their lives, that to die a hundred years old will be considered as being cut down in youth; a premature death inflicted as a punishment upon the wicked.

LXVI. 3. *He that slayeth an ox,* &c.; i. e. The disobedient, wicked man who offers sacrifices is as offensive as a murderer in the sight of God. Allowance is to be made for the strong language of poetry. The naked idea is, that sacrifices unaccompanied by piety were very offensive to God.

17. *Following,* &c.; i. e. following a priest, or leader of a procession, who directed the ceremonies in the midst of the groves.

24.—*their worm;* i. e. the worm that consumes them.

NOTES ON MICAH.

In the title of the book, Micah is said to have been a Morasthite, that is, an inhabitant of Mareshah,* a city belonging to the tribe of Judah, and to have prophesied in the reign of Jotham, Ahaz, and Hezekiah; i. e. from about 759 to 710 A. C. We have also the testimony of Jeremiah, † that he flourished under Hezekiah. The prophecies which remain to us seem to belong to the reign of the last-mentioned king. Micah was, therefore, a contemporary of Isaiah, though he may not have borne the prophetic office quite so soon. Beauty, sublimity, tenderness, clearness of expression, and justness of views in regard to human duty, have with reason been ascribed to Micah by various critics. There is considerable resemblance between him and his contemporary, Isaiah.

I. 3. — *cometh forth;* i. e. will soon come forth.

6. — *vineyard.* "Samaria was situated on a hill, the right soil for a vineyard."

7. *And to the hire of a harlot shall they return.* The meaning seems to be, As the idols and their ornaments were made of the presents which the idolatrous Israelites contributed, so they shall be carried away by foreign idolaters, and adorn idols and temples in a foreign land. Or, as Calvin supposes, the meaning may be more general. All their wealth, which they acquired by their idolatrous worship, and looked on as rewards from their idols, with which they committed spiritual fornication, as it was like the hire of a harlot, so it should come to the same pass, as usually the hires of harlots do, which by the curse of God on them come to naught, and do them no good."

8. — *naked;* i. e. without an upper garment. His dress would be neglected like that of Eastern mourners. — *ostrich.* See my note on Job xxx. 29.

10. — *in the dust.* This expression, in the original, is an instance of the paronomasia, or play upon words, which the Hebrews seem to have regarded as a great ornament of style, and to have admitted into the most serious composition. *Beth-Aphrah,* according to its etymological signification, means *house of dust.* In allusion to this signification he says, Roll yourselves in the dust. As if we should say, O Brookfield, thy brooks are dried up! There is a similar play upon the meaning of the names of the cities, mentioned in the following lines, *Saphir* signifying *fair* or *elegant; Zaanan* resembling the verb signifying *to go out; Maroth* denoting *bitterness; Beth-Azel, house of firmness* or *abiding; Achzib* being derived from a verb, signifying *to deceive,* and *Mareshah* from one signifying *to inherit,* or *possess.*

16. — *like the eagle;* i. e. when he sheds his plumage.

* Jos. xv. 44; 2 Chron. xi. 8.

† Jer. xxvi 18, 19.

II. 5. — *draw out a line*, &c.; i. e. shall not *measure a portion;* i. e. the land shall be wholly taken from them and be possessed by foreigners.

9. — *glory*, &c.; i. e. good apparel, or glorious land.

IV. 8. — *tower of the flock*, &c. The parallelism seems to show that the expression denotes a tower on Zion, or Zion itself. *The flock* is the people of God. See Jer. xiii. 17.

13. — *hoofs brass*, &c. Here is an allusion to the mode of thrashing described in the note on Amos i. 3.

V. 1. *Yet now gather*, &c.; i. e. O Jerusalem, to defend thyself against a siege. — *O people of troops*, &c.; lit. *daughter of troops.* So *daughter of Zion* denotes *inhabitants of Zion*, referring to the predatory bands which frequently issued from Jerusalem.

2. — *small to be among the thousands;* i. e. to be one of those bodies, or divisions, over which chiliarchs, or captains of thousands, presided. — *origin.* The noun thus translated is derived from the verb rendered "kings *shall come out* of thee." Gen. xvii. 6. — *ancient age.* In Is. xxiii. 7, the original phrase is used to denote the antiquity of the city of Tyre. It is the same which is translated *of old* in ch. vii. 20, referring to the promises of God to the ancestors of the Jews. — *days of old.* This is the literal meaning of the Hebrew. The original expression is precisely the same as that which is thus translated in ch. vii. 14 and Is. lxiii. 9, 11; Mal. iii. 4; Deut. xxxii. 7. Nor is the expression ever used in the Old Testament to denote absolute eternity.

4. — *Astartes;* i. e. images of Astarte.

5. — *seven, eight;* i. e. an abundance of defenders. See Eccl. xi. 2.

7. — *dew*, &c.; i. e. they shall be multiplied and shall flourish under the care of God, without aid from man.

9. *Thy hand.* Supply *O Israel!*

VI. 2. — *contendeth;* i. e. as a party before a court of justice.

6. *Wherewith*, &c. The prophet represents the people as replying to the expostulation of Jehovah.

14. — *remove;* i. e. thy children, goods, &c.

16. — *the reproach of my people;* i. e. the same injurious treatment of which ye were once guilty to my people, ye shall yourselves receive from the heathen.

VII. 1. — *first-ripe fig;* i. e. fruit of the best kind, and the object of strongest desire. The meaning seems to be, "I long to see a good man as ardently as, before the time of figs, one desires those which may here and there be found ripe."

7. *I will look*, &c. The prophet seems to speak here in the person of the people.

11. — *the decree;* i. e. the oppressive tribute, decreed by their enemies; or, it may be, all the tyrannical decrees of their oppressors. Oth-

erwise, *In that day shall the limits be extended;* i. e. of the walls of the city, so as to make room for the vast numbers which should come to Jerusalem.

NOTES ON NAHUM.

Of the circumstances of Nahum's life nothing is known, except that he was a native of Elkosh (ch. i. 1), a village of Galilee, the ruins of which were shown to Jerome, as he informs us, *Procem. in Com. in Nah.* A much less probable opinion is that Elkosh was a village in Assyria, situated not far from Nineveh. As to the time in which this prophet flourished, the most common and most probable opinion, gathered from the contents of the admirable little poem, the only production of his which has come down to us, seems to me to be, that he lived during the reign of Manasseh, whilst the tribe of Judah was yet in their own country, and after the captivity of the ten tribes. See i. 12 – 15; ii. 1, 2. The majority of recent critics, however, agree with Jerome in referring Nahum's ministry to the latter part of the reign of Hezekiah. The point of time when the prophecy was written is supposed by some to be immediately after the destruction of Sennacherib's host near Jerusalem. (2 Kings xix. 35.) As the prophet makes no allusion to this event, Maurer places it a little earlier, viz. when Sennacherib sent his threatening message to Hezekiah. (2 Kings xviii. 9; xix. 10, &c.) But this is conjecture. He predicts the deliverance of his country from the Assyrians, and the destruction of Nineveh, the capital city of their enemies. This destruction he sets forth as determined against them by God, in the language of poetry, not of history. He does not indicate the manner in which, or the nation by which, the destruction of Nineveh was to be effected.

Nahum stands in the very first rank of the Hebrew poets. What he has left constitutes a complete and regular poem, distinguished by a certain classic elegance, which shows that care and study were united with genius in its production. His description is extremely vivid, and his language rich and forcible, and abounding in beautiful images.

I. 2. — *keepeth indignation:* i. e. remembers and punishes their offences. See Ps. ciii. 9; Jer. iii. 12.

4. — *flower of Lebanon;* i. e. the growth or cedars of Lebanon.

8. — *her place;* i. e. of Nineveh. — *darkness:* a common metaphor, denoting destruction. See Job xv. 22, &c.

9. — *against Jehovah;* i. e. by warring against his people and his holy city, Jerusalem. — *Not the second time;* i. e. her destruction shall be completed by the first blow. See 1 Sam. xxvi. 8.

10. — *entangled*, &c.; i. e. in inextricable difficulty, staggering in their purposes.

11. — *one*. Some suppose a particular Assyrian king to be denoted, as Tiglathpileser, &c.; others, the Assyrian kings successively.

12. — *thee;* i. e. Judah.

14. — *concerning thee;* i. e. the king of Assyria. — *be sown;* i. e. thy race shall become extinct.

II. 1. *Guard the fortress*, &c. The Ninevites are ironically exhorted to prepare for defence.

3. — *his mighty men:* the army which should come against Nineveh.

5. — *He calleth*, &c.; i. e. the Assyrian king calls for his warriors to defend the wall, who through haste and trepidation stumble on their way. — *mantelet:* a machine, similar to the *vineæ*, or *testudines*, of the Romans, i. e. movable sheds, under cover of which the besiegers made their assaults. See Ivanhoe, Ch. XXVII. note.

6. — *The gates of rivers:* a metaphor denoting the great number of the inhabitants of Nineveh which passed through, or the great number of enemies which now *streamed* or *flowed* into them. Comp. Is. ii. 2. Some understand rivers as denoting canals running from the Tigris through the city, the gates of which canals being removed, the city would be inundated and the palace destroyed.

7. *Huzzab is uncovered;* i. e. insulted, treated like a prostitute. See Is. xlvii. 2, 3. It seems probable that Huzzab is a proper name, that of the queen of Nineveh. Gesenius understands the term הֻצַּב as a participle from צָבַב, and translates it *and is made to flow down*, referring to Nineveh. Others derive the word from נָצַב, translating it, *It is decreed; she is uncovered*, &c. The whole will thus refer to Nineveh. In favor of the rendering which I have adopted, making the term the proper name of the *queen* of Nineveh, is the consideration that maid-servants, that is female slaves, are mentioned in connection with her. If Nineveh itself were denoted, why are female slaves specially introduced?

8. — *a pool*, &c.; i. e. very populous.

10. — *void*, &c. The original is strongly emphatic. The words are of the same sound, forming what is called a paronomasia. They increase in length, as they point out great, greater, and greatest desolation. *Bukah, u-mebukah, u-mebullakah.*

11. — *lions*, &c; i. e. Where is Nineveh, whose inhabitants were as bold and rapacious as lions, and which was as full of plunder as a lion's den of ravin?

III. 3. — *lightning of the spear.* Comp. Hom. Il. X. 154, XI. 65.

4. — *sold nations by her whoredoms;* i. e. by her intercourse or alliances with foreign nations, she brought them into subjection to her.

5. — *over thy face.* The metaphor is borrowed from the mode of punishing prostitutes in ancient times, viz. to strip them naked, or

throw their clothes over their heads, and thus expose them to public execration.

8. — *No-Ammon.* By this name is undoubtedly denoted ancient Thebes, the splendid metropolis of ancient Egypt, called by the Greeks Diospolis, and celebrated by Homer (Il. IX. 383) as the city of a hundred gates, ἑκατόμπυλοι· The name No-Ammon was given to it from the circumstance that it was the chief seat of the worship of Jupiter Ammon; No-Ammon denoting the *portion* or *possession* of Ammon. The grandeur of its temples, obelisks, statues, &c. is apparent from its ruins, which are still the wonder of the world. When and by whom the destruction of Thebes here alluded to took place, is uncertain. Gesenius supposes that it was effected by Tartan, the general of Sargon, king of Assyria, about seven hundred and sixteen years before Christ. See Is. xx. The Nile is called *the sea.*

11. — *drink,* &c.; i. e. of the cup of misery or punishment. — *hidden;* i. e. unknown, as if thou hadst never existed.

18. — *shepherds;* i. e. rulers, prefects.

NOTES ON ZEPHANIAH.

The first verse in the prophecy of Zephaniah gives us all the knowledge we have of him, viz. that he lived in the reign of Josiah, 642–611 A. C., and that he was descended from ancestors whose names are there mentioned. The particular enumeration of his ancestors may have been owing to their eminence, or may have been introduced to distinguish him from the other Zephaniah. That he was a descendant of King Hezekiah is not probable. Of his life and character we have no information.

The book of Zephaniah consists of two pieces, one included in ch. i., ii., and the other in ch. iii. Both however relate to the same subject, and contain threatenings against the corrupt and idolatrous Jews, and exhortations to amendment, followed by predictions of the destruction of the principal enemies of the Jewish nation and of its restoration to a state of peace and prosperity.

I. 4. — *priests;* i. e. those who were of the race of Aaron, and professed to be priests of Jehovah.

5. — *their idol;* lit. *their king,* i. e. Moloch. Comp. Amos v. 26.

7. — *his guests.* This may be understood of birds and beasts of prey, which should feast themselves upon the dead bodies of the slain; or, less probably, of the enemies of the Jews, the Babylonians.

8.—*foreign apparel.* There is no need of supposing an idolatrous practice to be denoted. The prophet refers to the dissipated and proud, who adopted the dress of foreign nations.

9.—*over the threshold.* The connection seems to show that this expression denotes breaking into houses by violence. It is said that the Arabs used actually to ride into houses for plunder. Others explain it as denoting the Philistines, in reference to a custom mentioned in 1 Sam. v. 5.

12.—*on their lees.* The thoughtless tranquillity of the rich is compared to the fixed, unbroken surface of fermented liquors.

II. 2.—*like chaff;* i. e. swiftly as chaff driven by the wind; otherwise, *The day,* i. e. time, *passeth away like chaff.*

5.—*nation of the Cherethites;* probably in the southern part of Philistia. See Ges. Lex. ad verb., and Ros. on Ezek. xxv. 16.

14.—*A cry,* &c.; i. e. of some hideous bird.

III. 8. *Therefore wait for me,* &c. This is an ironical threat that punishment should surely come.

11.—*not be ashamed;* i. e. thy guilt and thy punishment shall cease. —*exalt thyself;* i. e. against me; thou shalt no more be proud, contemning my laws.

NOTES ON HABAKKUK.

Respecting the life of Habakkuk, and the time in which he lived, we have no historical record. The story, in the apocryphal part of Daniel, that he brought food to Daniel in the lion's den, is sufficiently refuted by its fabulous aspect, and especially by its inconsistency with the contents of this poem. From these we may infer, with considerable probability, that he lived not far from the beginning of the Chaldæan period, when the poet saw the growing power of the Chaldæans, and in his mind's eye discerned the calamities which his country was to receive from them. Ch. i. 6. The actual destruction of the Jewish nation is not referred to or implied in any part of the poem. The most common and by far the most probable opinion in regard to the date of the prophecy is, that it was delivered in the reign of Jehoiakim, A. C. 606–604. The prophet was therefore a contemporary of Jeremiah. Jahn argues from ch. i. 2–4, which he considers as a description of Jewish immorality, that he must have lived in the early part of the reign of Manasseh. I think he is mistaken in the application of those verses; and that they are descriptive of the evils inflicted by the Chaldæans. At first view, indeed, it would seem that the Chaldæans, vs. 5–11, are introduced as agents to chastise the Jews for the iniquities mentioned in vs. 2–4. But from a survey of the whole poem, or from ch. ii. in particular, it appears that the Chaldæans are introduced as enemies that were to be punished.

The production of Habakkuk is to be regarded as a whole; as constituting one poem or prophecy, in its form somewhat dramatic. The subject is the calamities which had been brought, or which were threatened to be brought, upon his country by the Chaldæans. The prophet boldly expostulates with the Deity on account of these calamities, ch. i. 2–17, and his expostulation seems to be followed by the revelation to him of the future punishment of the Chaldæans. Ch. iii. seems to set forth a manifestation of the Deity, as actually interposing, in answer to the prayer of the prophet for the destruction of the enemies of the Jews, which was threatened in ch. ii.

In general poetic effect, in strength and beauty of thought, in the union of the loftiest conceptions of lyric poetry with a considerable degree of clearness, and in elegance and purity of diction, Habakkuk is hardly surpassed by any of the Jewish poets. As a specimen of lyric poetry, ch. iii. is probably unequalled.

I. 4.—*law faileth*, &c. The oppression of the Chaldæans would interrupt the regular administration of justice. This must always be the case when a country is invaded. It appears to me inconsistent with the whole tenor of the poem to understand ver. 2–4 as a description of the wickedness of the Jews. According to the representation of the poet throughout, the Jews are the righteous, the Chaldæans the wicked.

7.—*their law and their dignity;* i. e. they acknowledge no law and no dignity but their own.

9.—*multitude*, &c. Otherwise, *direction*, &c. See Fürst's Lexicon on מְגַמָּה.

11.—*their god;* i. e. they trust to their strength, and to their weapons of war, rather than to God, according to the character ascribed to Mezentius, Virg. Æn. X. 773:

> "Dextra, mihi Deus, et telum, quod missile libro,
> Nunc adsint!"
>
> "My strong right-hand and sword assist my stroke!
> Those only gods Mezentius will invoke."—*Dryden.*

17.—*empty the net;* i. e. dispose of the captives already taken.

II. 1.—*what I shall answer to my expostulation*, or *upon my expostulation.* This rendering, though obscure at first view, on account of the conciseness of the original and the peculiarity of the sentiment, is, I think, the true one, and is that of the ancient versions. I judged it best not to paraphrase the line. The meaning of the prophet is, that he would wait to see what by divine inspiration he should be enabled to answer himself and others, in regard to his own expostulation with God, or his complaints respecting the Divine government, in ch. i., and thus quiet his mind.

2. — *may run;* i. e. let the characters be very large and legible, so that one may read them running, — may not need to stop, but hold on his course. In this case, as in others, I have preferred a strictly literal *translation* to one which might express my *interpretation* of it more clearly. Others may interpret it differently. Thus Houbigant supposes the word *run* to be used in a figurative sense, so as to make the line mean, "That he may *read it quickly* who reads it." Thus we speak of *running over* a book. Others, that he who reads it may run and proclaim the tidings.

4. — *Behold, the,* &c. This has special reference to the Chaldæans, in comparison with whom the Jews are called "just" in the antithetic line. — *shall live;* i. e. be safe, prosperous, happy. — *faithfulness;* i. e. his truth and integrity.

9. — *evil hand;* i. e. from the assaults of his enemies.

11. — *the stone,* &c.; i. e. the very stones of the cities overthrown by the Chaldæans proclaim their violence and cruelty.

13. — *for the fire;* i. e. for that which is soon to be burned up, viz. Babylon, their capital city. — *for naught;* i. e. for that which shall be brought to nothing. Comp. Jer. li. 58.

14. — *knowledge of the glory,* &c.; i. e. the perfections of God will be widely displayed in the destruction of Babylon, and the deliverance of his people.

15. — *giveth his neighbor drink.* Under this image the meaning is conveyed, that Babylon, in various ways, by arts and arms, had subjected nations to her, and treated them with the utmost scorn.

17. — *Lebanon* in this verse probably represents Judæa. — *shall cover thee;* i. e. fall, as a just retribution upon thine own head. — *destruction of the beasts;* i. e. the desolation and slaughter of the inhabitants of the land, with which they were terrified, as wild beasts by hunters. For as Lebanon in this verse denotes the land of Israel, so the beasts of Lebanon denote the people of Israel.

20. *Be silent.* "When an Asiatic sovereign goes to the mosque on any of their great festivals, such as the Bairam, the deepest *silence* reigns among all his retinue, viziers, foreign ambassadors, &c. They all bow respectfully before him, but no word is spoken, no sound uttered. It is to this species of reverence that the prophet alludes." — *Adam Clarke.*

III. 1. *The prayer,* &c. It appears to me probable that this title was inserted by some transcriber. This chapter appears not to be an independent production, but to be connected with what precedes, as a part of a whole poem. — *an ode;* probably of a particular kind, unknown to us. Otherwise, *in the manner of an elegy.*

2. — *revive thy work;* i. e. again manifest that power for the deliver-

ance of thy people which was manifested in times past. —*the years;* i. e. the years of calamity through which we have been passing.

3. *God cometh from Teman.* It seems to me that it is much more appropriate to the connection, to understand the poet as representing, in lofty poetic language, borrowed in some measure from scenes in the Jewish history, a present or future interposition of the Deity, than to suppose that he is merely mentioning historical facts for their encouragement, according to the translation of the common version. The objections of Schnurrer, who is followed by Rosenmueller, to this view, do not make sufficient allowance for the bold and lyrical character of the representation.

3. —*Selah.* The most probable supposition in regard to this term is, that it was a direction to the singers *to be silent;* i. e. *to pause a little,* while the instruments played an interlude or symphony. See Ges. ad verb. As it is not a part of Scripture, and is of no use, I omit it in the text.

4. *His brightness;* otherwise, *the* brightness or splendor; i. e. which issued from the dark clouds with which the Deity was enveloped. —*Rays,* &c. May not this denote that lightnings were in his hands? See Job xxxvi. 32, *He covereth his hands with lightning.* Also xxxvii. 3, 11, 15.

6. —*measureth,* &c. If we might disregard Hebrew usage and trust to an Arabic root, the rendering might be *shaketh,* &c.

7. — *Cushan:* a poetical word for *Cush.* Professor Robinson, in his edition of Calmet, supposes Cush to denote, — 1. a country in Africa, viz. Ethiopia, south of Egypt; 2. in Southern Arabia; and 3. the regions of Persis, Chusistan, and Susiana. See Ges. Lex. ad verb., and Robinson's Calmet, Art. *Cush* and *Ethiopia.*

9. —*made bare;* i. e. taken from its case. Harmer informs us, from Sir John Chardin, that the Oriental bows were wont to be carried in a case hung to the girdle. The *arrows* of the Almighty are thunderbolts. As to the translation of the line, I have but little confidence in it, but give what seems least objectionable. The idea is, that the weapons which God commands to execute judgment have curses and destruction as their consequences.

11. —*remain,* &c. The representation seems to be, that there was darkness, and storm with lightning, &c., as instruments of Divine punishment. The sun and moon remained obscured by clouds in their habitation, when the lightnings, the arrows and spears of the Almighty, flew. Comp. Joel ii. 10; Zeph. i. 15. Some understand *the arrows* and *spear* as denoting weapons employed by Hebrew warriors, which weapons by their brightness and thickness obscured the light of the sun, &c. This does not seem so agreeable to the connection, or to similar passages in the Old Testament.

13. —*to the neck.* This is probably a phrase which had a determined signification when employed by the author, but is now ambiguous. I should understand it of the depth to which they razed the foundations, as it were *man-deep,* so that, if a man stood in them, his head only would be above them.

17.—*blossom;* i. e. *put forth its fruit.* For the fig-tree does not strictly put forth blossoms, but shoots out the figs, like so many little buttons, with their flowers, small and imperfect as they are, within them.

NOTES ON OBADIAH.

There is no information in the sacred records respecting the life of Obadiah, and the time in which he lived, nor any tradition worthy of the least regard.

It is probable that he was a contemporary of Jeremiah, as it appears from ver. 11 that he wrote after the destruction of Jerusalem, and denounced punishments against the Edomites similar to those which are contained in Jeremiah. Comp. Jer. xlix. There is an agreement not only in the sentiments, but also in words, and even in whole verses, between Obadiah and Jer. xlix. I should think the latter borrowed from the former.

The book of Obadiah was probably placed by the collector of the prophets next to Amos, and before several more ancient prophets, for no other reason than that in Amos ix. 12 mention is made of the conquest of Edom by the Jews.

3.—*clefts of the rock;* better, perhaps, *recesses, refuges, asylums of the rock.* The agreement of the expressions used by the prophets in regard to ancient Edom with what we know of that country is very striking. It will be interesting to the reader to compare some description of the celebrated city of Petra with this passage. An account of the wonderful ruins of this city, with a wood-cut representing the entrance to it, may be found in the History of Arabia, No. LXVIII. of the Family Library, pp. 142–151. The reader needs not to be reminded that many of these ruins are of more modern date than the period of the prophecy. There is probably an allusion to it in Jer. xlix. 16:—

"Thy terribleness hath deceived thee,
The pride of thy heart,
Because thou dwellest in the recesses of the rock,
And holdest the height of the hill.
Though thou set thy nest on high, like the eagle,
From thence will I bring thee down, saith Jehovah."

5.—*have ceased stealing,* &c.; lit. *Would they not have stolen their sufficiency.* But the parallelism shows that I have given the sense. The idea is, that it was to be more thoroughly wasted than common robbers usually perform their work, who through hurry or satiety leave some property to its possessor.

7. — *to the border.* The meaning seems to be, that the allies of the Edomites had brought them to the borders of their country, and there abandoned or delivered them to their enemies. The phrase may have had an emphatic or proverbial meaning, which is lost to us.

16. *For as ye have drunk;* i. e. as ye Jews have partaken of the cup of Divine punishment, so shall all the nations partake of it. Comp. Jer. xxv. 27, 28.

END OF VOL. I.

Cambridge: Stereotyped and Printed by Welch, Bigelow, & Co.

www.ingramcontent.com/pod-product-compliance
Lightning Source LLC
LaVergne TN
LVHW010145110826
845151LV00002B/429
9781425537890